HANDBOOKS

D0063212

BALTIMORE

GEOFF BROWN

Contents

▶ **Discover Baltimore**.........**18**
Planning Your Trip 20
Explore Baltimore 22
• The Two-Day Best of Baltimore..22
• Local Favorites 23
• Top 10 for Kids 24

▶ **Sights**........................**25**
Downtown and Inner Harbor.....27
Fell's Point 35
Little Italy 37
Canton........................40
Federal Hill 41
Mount Vernon 44
Hampden and Homewood.......50
Greater Baltimore..............53

▶ **Restaurants** **58**
Downtown and Inner Harbor.....60
Fell's Point 64
Little Italy 71
Canton........................74
Federal Hill 78
Mount Vernon 84
Hampden and Homewood.......90
Greater Baltimore..............95

▶ **Nightlife** **96**
Live Music.....................98
Dance Clubs 100
Bars 100
Wine Bars 107
Lounges 108
After Hours....................109
Gay and Lesbian 110

▶ **Arts and Leisure** **112**
The Arts 114
Festivals and Events 124
Recreation 131

▶ **Shops**........................**150**
Architectural Salvage...........154
Arts and Crafts 155
Books and Music 156
Clothing and Accessories
    for Men 159
Clothing and Accessories
    for Women 160
Furniture and Home Decor 164
Gifts 165
Health and Beauty 166
Kids' Stores....................168
Pet Supplies and Grooming......168
Shoes.........................169
Shopping Centers 171
Vintage and Antiques...........172

▶ **Hotels**........................**175**
Downtown and Inner Harbor.....178
Fell's Point 181
Little Italy 184
Canton........................184
Federal Hill 185
Mount Vernon 186
Hampden and Homewood.......186
Greater Baltimore..............187

▶ **Excursions from Baltimore** .**188**
Annapolis 191
Frederick......................198
Easton and St. Michaels........204

▶ **Background**..................**211**

▶ **Essentials** **227**

▶ **Resources** **239**

▶ **Index**.........................**242**

Maps

▶ Map 1: Downtown
   and Inner Harbor 4-5

▶ Map 2: Fell's Point
   and Little Italy 6-7

▶ Map 3: Canton............. 8-9

▶ Map 4: Federal Hill....... 10-11

▶ Map 5: Mount Vernon 12-13

▶ Map 6: Hampden
   and Homewood 14-15

▶ Map 7:
   Greater Baltimore......... 16-17

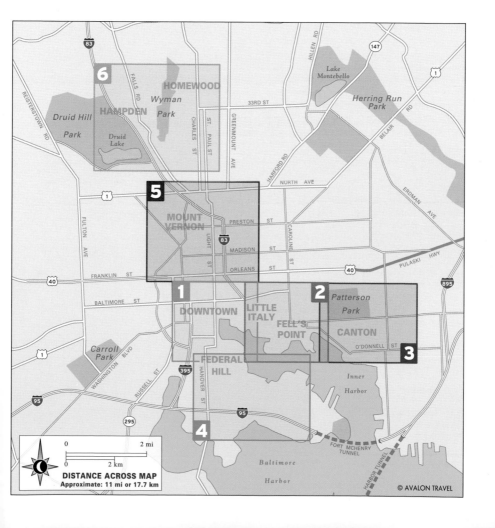

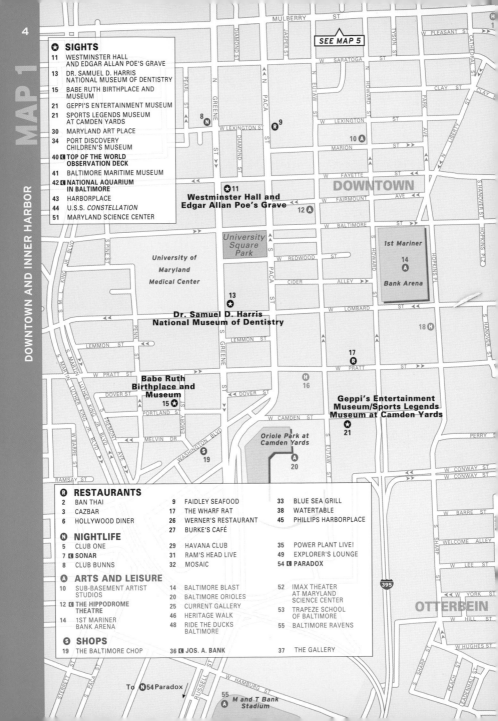

SEE MAP 5

⊙ SIGHTS

11	WESTMINSTER HALL AND EDGAR ALLAN POE'S GRAVE
13	DR. SAMUEL D. HARRIS NATIONAL MUSEUM OF DENTISTRY
15	BABE RUTH BIRTHPLACE AND MUSEUM
21	GEPPI'S ENTERTAINMENT MUSEUM
21	SPORTS LEGENDS MUSEUM AT CAMDEN YARDS
30	MARYLAND ART PLACE
34	PORT DISCOVERY CHILDREN'S MUSEUM
40 C	TOP OF THE WORLD OBSERVATION DECK
41	BALTIMORE MARITIME MUSEUM
42 C	NATIONAL AQUARIUM IN BALTIMORE
43	HARBORPLACE
44	U.S.S. CONSTELLATION
51	MARYLAND SCIENCE CENTER

DOWNTOWN

OTTERBEIN

University Square Park

University of Maryland Medical Center

Westminster Hall and Edgar Allan Poe's Grave

Dr. Samuel D. Harris National Museum of Dentistry

1st Mariner Bank Arena

Babe Ruth Birthplace and Museum

Geppi's Entertainment Museum/Sports Legends Museum at Camden Yards

Oriole Park at Camden Yards

M and T Bank Stadium

® RESTAURANTS

2	BAN THAI	9	FAIDLEY SEAFOOD	33	BLUE SEA GRILL
3	CAZBAR	17	THE WHARF RAT	38	WATERTABLE
6	HOLLYWOOD DINER	26	WERNER'S RESTAURANT	45	PHILLIPS HARBORPLACE
		27	BURKE'S CAFÉ		

Ⓝ NIGHTLIFE

5	CLUB ONE	29	HAVANA CLUB	35	POWER PLANT LIVE!
7 C	SONAR	31	RAM'S HEAD LIVE	49	EXPLORER'S LOUNGE
8	CLUB BUNNS	32	MOSAIC	54 C	PARADOX

Ⓐ ARTS AND LEISURE

10	SUB-BASEMENT ARTIST STUDIOS	14	BALTIMORE BLAST	52	IMAX THEATER AT MARYLAND SCIENCE CENTER
12 C	THE HIPPODROME THEATRE	20	BALTIMORE ORIOLES	53	TRAPEZE SCHOOL OF BALTIMORE
14	1ST MARINER BANK ARENA	25	CURRENT GALLERY	55	BALTIMORE RAVENS
		46	HERITAGE WALK		
		48	RIDE THE DUCKS BALTIMORE		

Ⓢ SHOPS

19	THE BALTIMORE CHOP	36 C	JOS. A. BANK	37	THE GALLERY

To Ⓝ 54 Paradox

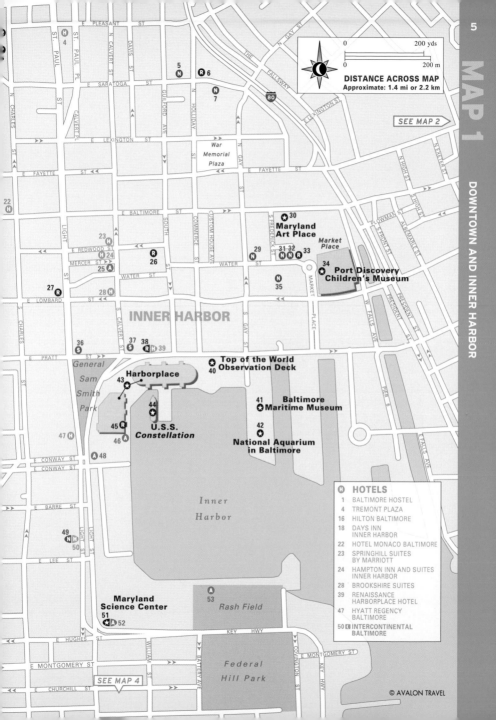

DISTANCE ACROSS MAP
Approximate: 1.4 mi or 2.2 km

0   200 yds
0   200 m

SEE MAP 2

War Memorial Plaza

30 Maryland Art Place

Market Place

34 Port Discovery Children's Museum

INNER HARBOR

Top of the World Observation Deck 40

Harborplace 43

41 Baltimore Maritime Museum

44

45
46

U.S.S. Constellation

42 National Aquarium in Baltimore

General Sam Smith Park

47

48

Inner Harbor

49
50

Maryland Science Center

51
52

53 Rash Field

KEY HWY

SEE MAP 4

Federal Hill Park

© AVALON TRAVEL

HOTELS

1   BALTIMORE HOSTEL
4   TREMONT PLAZA
16 HILTON BALTIMORE
18 DAYS INN INNER HARBOR
22 HOTEL MONACO BALTIMORE
23 SPRINGHILL SUITES BY MARRIOTT
24 HAMPTON INN AND SUITES INNER HARBOR
28 BROOKSHIRE SUITES
39 RENAISSANCE HARBORPLACE HOTEL
47 HYATT REGENCY BALTIMORE
50 INTERCONTINENTAL BALTIMORE

SEE MAP 5

★ **SIGHTS**

1 PHOENIX (OLD BALTIMORE) SHOT TOWER
2 JEWISH MUSEUM OF MARYLAND
6 REGINALD F. LEWIS MUSEUM OF MARYLAND AFRICAN AMERICAN HISTORY & CULTURE
7 STAR-SPANGLED BANNER FLAG HOUSE
22 BALTIMORE PUBLIC WORKS MUSEUM
66 FREDERICK DOUGLASS-ISAAC MYERS MARITIME PARK
84 FELL'S POINT VISITOR CENTER
85 ROBERT LONG HOUSE

WASHINGTON HILL

Phoenix (Old Baltimore) Shot Tower

Jewish Museum of Maryland

LITTLE ITALY

Star-Spangled Banner Flag House

Reginald F. Lewis Museum of Maryland African American History & Culture

SEE MAP 1

Baltimore Public Works Museum

Pier 6 Concert Pavilion

Inner Harbor

0   200 yds
0   200 m

DISTANCE ACROSS MAP
Approximate: 1.4 mi or 2.3 km

SEE MAP 4

Frederick Douglass-Isaac Myers Maritime Park

© AVALON TRAVEL

RESTAURANTS

3	ATTMAN'S	43	LA CAZUELA
9	DA MIMMO	44	PETER'S INN
10	CAESAR'S DEN	47	ZE MEAN BEAN CAFÉ
11	VACCARO'S	49	CAPTAIN JAMES LANDING
12	AMICCI'S	50	SIP & BITE RESTAURANT
13	LA TAVOLA	51	PAZO
14	GERMANO'S TRATTORIA	54	BLUE MOON CAFÉ
15	ALDO'S	55	DING HOW
16	SABATINO'S	56	LOUISIANA
17	INDIA RASOI	60	PIERPOINT
18	LA SCALA	62	BERTHA'S
19	MCCORMICK & SCHMICK'S	63	BRICK OVEN PIZZA
23	DELLA NOTTE	65	THE BLACK OLIVE
36	LEBANESE TAVERNA	68	DU CLAW BREWING CO.
37	CINGHIALE	71	KALI'S COURT
38	CHARLESTON	73	SHUCKER'S
40	OBRYCKI'S CRAB HOUSE	79	JIMMY'S RESTAURANT
41	SALT		
42	HENNINGER'S TAVERN		

NIGHTLIFE

8	CLUB ORPHEUS	83	THE CAT'S EYE PUB
52	ONE EYED MIKE'S	86	THE WHARF RAT
53	FRIENDS	87	JOHN STEVEN
70	DUDA'S TAVERN	89	V-NO
78	MAX'S ON BROADWAY		

ARTS AND LEISURE

21	PIER 6 CONCERT PAVILION	76	FREDERICK DOUGLASS "PATH TO FREEDOM" WALKING TOUR
24	MAC HARBOR EAST		
26	LANDMARK THEATRES	77	SECRETS OF A SEAPORT WALKING TOUR
45	PATTERSON BOWLING CENTER		
48	SEGS IN THE CITY	88	CHARM CITY YOGA
64	VAGABOND THEATER	90	CAPT. DON'S FISHING CHARTER

SHOPS

28	KASHMIR IMPORTS	57	EL SUPRIMO
29	HANDBAGS IN THE CITY	58	A GOOD YARN
30	GLARUS CHOCOLATIER	59	MAJA
31	BENJAMIN LOVELL	61	POPPY AND STELLA
33	SASSANOVA	67	PAD
34	URBAN CHIC	69	SU CASA
35	SOUTH MOON UNDER	72	THE SOUND GARDEN
46	ANOTHER PERIOD IN TIME	74	CORDUROY BUTTON
		80	CUPCAKE
		81	TRIXIE'S PALACE

HOTELS

4	1840S CARROLLTON INN	32	COURTYARD BY MARRIOTT
5	FAIRFIELD INN & SUITES	39	BLUE DOOR ON BALTIMORE
20	PIER 5 HOTEL	75	THE ADMIRAL FELL INN
25	HOMEWOOD SUITES BY HILTON BALTIMORE	82	CELIE'S WATERFRONT INN
27	BALTIMORE MARRIOTT WATERFRONT	91	THE INN AT HENDERSON'S WHARF

Patterson

2 Patterson Park

3 A

Park

CANTON

Northwest

Harbor

© AVALON TRAVEL

SEE MAP 2

NOBLE ST
BALTIMORE ST
LEVERTON AVE
LEVERTON AVE
E LOMBARD ST
MT PLEASANT AVE
E PRATT ST
CLAREMONT AVE
GOUGH ST
CHESTLE PL
BANK ST
BENEFIT ST

HIGHLANDTOWN

EASTERN AVE

FLEET ST

SCHUCK ST
FOSTER AVE
MUELLER ST
FAIT AVE
CLYDE ST
HUDSON ST
HARMONY CT
DILLON ST

BREWER'S HILL

O'DONNELL ST
ELLIOTT ST
TOONE ST
BOSTON ST

To ✪ 24 **SS John Brown**
and 🅢 25 About Faces

🅐 26

🅐 28

🅐 7
🅡 8
🅡 9
🅢 27

✪ SIGHTS
2 🄲 PATTERSON PARK   24   S.S. *JOHN BROWN*

🅡 RESTAURANTS
1	THREE	13	CAKELOVE
4	GECKO'S	16	HELEN'S GARDEN
6	BIRCHES	17	CLADDAGH PUB
8	MATTHEW'S PIZZERIA	18 🄲	MAMA'S ON THE HALF SHELL
9	ANNABEL LEE TAVERN	19	NACHO MAMA'S
10	TUTTI GUSTI	20	PY
		23 🄲	BO BROOKS

🅝 NIGHTLIFE
5	BARTENDER'S	14	MAHAFFEY'S
11	THE CHESAPEAKE WINE COMPANY		

🅐 ARTS AND LEISURE
3	DOMINIC "MIMI" DIPIETRO FAMILY ICE SKATING CENTER	22	WEST MARINE
		26	MERRITT ATHLETIC CLUBS CANTON
7	CREATIVE ALLIANCE AT THE PATTERSON	28	CHARM CITY SKATE PARK

🅢 SHOPS
12	CLOUD 9	25	ABOUT FACES
15	2910 ON THE SQUARE	27 🄲	DOGMA

🅗 HOTELS
21 🄲 INN AT 2920

0	200 yds
0	200 m

DISTANCE ACROSS MAP
Approximate: 1.55 mi or 2.5 km

SEE MAP 1

E MONTGOMERY ST

E CHURCHILL ST

E HENRIETTA ST

WARREN AVE

FEDERAL HILL

FEDERAL HILL Park

E WHEELING ST

E HAMBURG ST

POULTNEY ST

GRINDALL ST

E CROSS ST

CROSS ST

Cross Street Market

E WEBER ST

E WEST ST

W ROPEWALK LN

E ROPEWALK LN

E OSTEND ST

W OSTEND ST

E GITTINGS ST

E CLEMENT ST

BIRCKHEAD ST

RIVERSIDE

Riverside Park

E HEATH ST

E BARNEY ST

E WELLS ST

E MCCOMAS ST

Swann Park

PORT COVINGTON

✪ SIGHTS

| 27 | FEDERAL HILL PARK | 33 | BALTIMORE MUSEUM OF INDUSTRY |
| 28 | THE AMERICAN VISIONARY ART MUSEUM | 35 | THE DOMINO SUGARS SIGN |

ⓡ RESTAURANTS

5	CORKS	24	THE BICYCLE
6	SOBO CAFÉ	26	RUSTY SCUPPER
9	MATSURI	37	THE WINE MARKET
11	NICK'S OYSTER BAR	40	L. P. STEAMER'S
13	JUNIOR'S WINE BAR	41	PAZZA LUNA
16	RYLEIGH'S OYSTER	42	HARVEST TABLE
20	REGI'S	43	HULL STREET BLUES
21	TEN-O-SIX	44	BALTIMORE CUPCAKE COMPANY
22	BLUE AGAVE		

ⓝ NIGHTLIFE

8	MUM'S	31	LITTLE HAVANA
10	8X10	32	CAPTAIN LARRY'S
15	PUB DOG	45	J. PATRICK'S IRISH PUB
17	ZEEBA LOUNGE		

ⓐ ARTS AND LEISURE

19	LIGHT STREET CYCLES	34	DOWNTOWN SAILING CENTER
23	SCHOOL 33 ART CENTER	36	MERRITT FORT AVENUE
25	RIVERSIDE PARK	38	GALLERY IMPERATO

ⓢ SHOPS

2	BABE	18	PATRICK SUTTON HOME
3	SHOFER'S	29	AMERICAN VISIONARY ART MUSEUM EYE SHOP
4	HOLLY G.		
7	LE PETIT COCHON	30	ANTIQUE CENTER AT FEDERAL HILL
12	SOBOTANICAL		
14	M SALON	39	STUDIO 921 SALON & DAY SPA

ⓗ HOTELS

| 1 | SCARBOROUGH FAIR B&B |

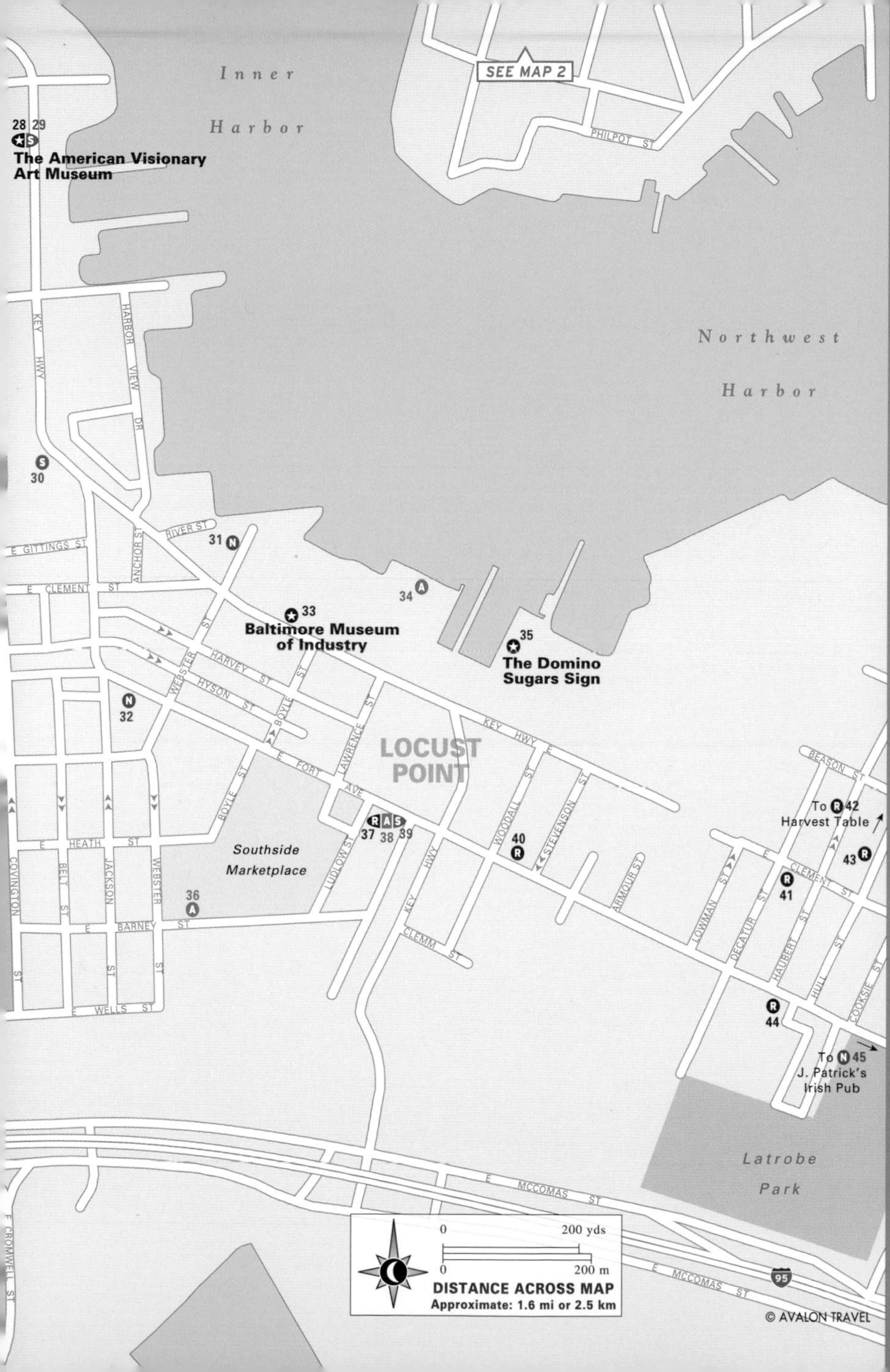

Inner

Harbor

SEE MAP 2

PHILPOT ST

Northwest

Harbor

28 29
The American Visionary
Art Museum

KEY HWY

HARBOR VIEW DR

S
30

RIVER ST

E GITTINGS ST

31 N

34 A

E CLEMENT ST

S RICHARDSON ST

33
Baltimore Museum
of Industry

HARVEY ST

HYSON ST

WEBSTER

35
The Domino
Sugars Sign

KEY HWY

LAWRENCE ST

N
32

FORT AVE

BOYLE ST

LOCUST
POINT

WOODALL ST

STEVENSON ST

BEASON ST

To N 42
Harvest Table

ARMOUR ST

Southside
Marketplace

37 38 39

KEY HWY

WOODALL ST

DECATUR ST

CLEMENT ST

43 R

E HEATH ST

COVINGTON ST

BELT ST

JACKSON ST

WEBSTER

40
R

R
41

36
A

E BARNEY ST

CLEMM ST

HAUBERT ST

HULL ST

COOKSIE ST

E WELLS ST

R
44

To N 45
J. Patrick's
Irish Pub

Latrobe
Park

E MCCOMAS ST

E CROMWELL ST

0   200 yds
0   200 m

N

DISTANCE ACROSS MAP
Approximate: 1.6 mi or 2.5 km

E MCCOMAS ST

95

© AVALON TRAVEL

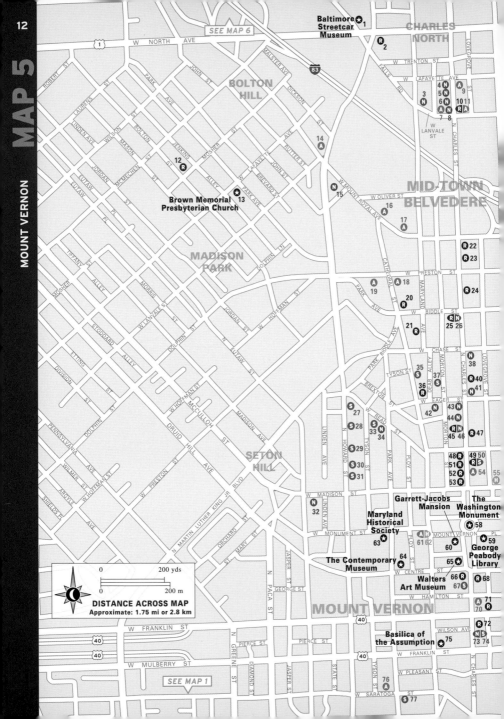

E NORTH AVE

GREENMOUNT WEST

Green Mount Cemetery

OLIVER

E MT ROYAL AVE

Madison

Square

★ SIGHTS

1	BALTIMORE STREETCAR MUSEUM	59	GEORGE PEABODY LIBRARY	64	THE CONTEMPORARY MUSEUM
13	BROWN MEMORIAL PRESBYTERIAN CHURCH	60	GARRETT-JACOBS MANSION	65	WALTERS ART MUSEUM
58	THE WASHINGTON MONUMENT	63	MARYLAND HISTORICAL SOCIETY	75	BASILICA OF THE ASSUMPTION

● RESTAURANTS

2	JOE SQUARED	25	THE BREWER'S ART	51	THAIRISH
10	TAPAS TEATRO	36	CITY CAFÉ	52	INDIGMA
12	B	39	THE PRIME RIB	53	DONNA'S
20	ABACROMBIE	40	MINATO	56	IGGIE'S
21	DUKEM	45	BRASS ELEPHANT	66	IXIA
22	NEO VICCINO	47	KUMARI	68	SASCHA'S 527 CAFÉ
23	XS	48	THE HELMAND	71	TIO PEPE
24	THAI LANDING	49	AKBAR	72	SOTTO SOPRA

● NIGHTLIFE

3	CHARM CITY ART SPACE	15	MOUNT ROYAL TAVERN	42	EDEN'S LOUNGE
4	THE DEPOT	26	THE BREWER'S ART	43	THE HIPPO
5	CLUB CHARLES	32	COCONUTS CAFE	44	RED MAPLE
6	CLUB 1722	34	THE DRINKERY	46	THE TUSK LOUNGE
8	METRO GALLERY	38	THE 13TH FLOOR	73	AN DIE MUSIK LIVE
		41	GRAND CENTRAL		

● ARTS AND LEISURE

7	VELOCIPEDE BIKE PROJECT	17	THE LYRIC OPERA HOUSE	61	MOUNT VERNON WALKING TOURS
9	EVERYMAN THEATRE	18	THEATRE PROJECT	69	MERRITT'S DOWNTOWN ATHLETIC CLUB
11	THE CHARLES THEATRE	19	THE JOSEPH MEYERHOFF SYMPHONY HALL		
14	MICA BROWN CENTER	54	MEREDITH GALLERY	70	C. GRIMALDIS GALLERY
16	ARTSCAPE	57	CENTER STAGE	76	THE 14KARAT CABARET

● SHOPS

27	THE IMPERIAL HALF BUSHEL	30	DUBEY'S ART AND ANTIQUES	37	SHOP GENTEI
28	DRUSILLA'S BOOKS	31	CROSSKEYS ANTIQUES	50	BLU VINTAGE
29	ANTIQUE ROW STALLS	33	READ STREET BOOKS	67	A PEOPLE UNITED
		35	PRETENTIOUS POOCH	74	AN DIE MUSIK
				77	DIMENSIONS IN MUSIC

● HOTELS

55	4 EAST MADISON INN	62	PEABODY COURT BY CLARION

SEE MAP 2

© AVALON TRAVEL

● SIGHTS

1	AMARANTHINE MUSEUM	
33	MARYLAND ZOO IN BALTIMORE	
34	HOWARD P. RAWLINGS CONSERVATORY AND BOTANIC GARDENS OF BALTIMORE	
37	LACROSSE MUSEUM & NATIONAL HALL OF FAME	
38	HOMEWOOD HOUSE	
41	BALTIMORE MUSEUM OF ART	

● RESTAURANTS

2	WOODBERRY KITCHEN	
10	GOLDEN WEST CAFÉ	
12	CAFÉ HON	
13	SUZIE'S SOBA	
19	DOGWOOD	
24	A COMMON GROUND	
27	ANGELO'S PIZZA	
29	ROCKET TO VENUS	
35	THE AMBASSADOR DINING ROOM	
42	GERTRUDE'S	
43	DONNA'S	
44	PAPERMOON DINER	
48	THE YABBA POT	

● NIGHTLIFE

45 THE OTTOBAR

● ARTS AND LEISURE

4	THE ROTUNDA CINEMATHEQUE	
8	THE ANTREASIAN GALLERY	
20	BIKRAM YOGA	
30	GOYA CONTEMPORARY	
31	THE G SPOT	
32	DRUID HILL PARK	
39	THEATRE HOPKINS	

To A4 The Rotunda Cinematheque

HAMPDEN

Amaranthine Museum

Roosevelt Park

Druid Hill Park

Maryland Zoo in Baltimore

Howard P. Rawlings Conservatory and Botanic Gardens of Baltimore

Druid Lake

Jones Falls

W 39TH ST

W 38TH ST

ST. MARTINS RD

CRAYCOMBE AVE

KESWICK RD

TUDOR ARMS AVE

BEECH AVE

BERRY ST

BISHOPS RD

Ⓡ 35

Ⓗ 36

37

**Lacrosse Museum &
National Hall of Fame**

CANTERBURY RD

W UNIVERSITY PKWY

ST. PAUL

COTGROVE ST

GREENWAY

**TUSCANY-
CANTERBURY**

BERRY ST

BERRY ST

27 Ⓡ

Ⓢ 26

Ⓢ 28

W 36TH ST

HUBNER ST

CRISP ST

SAN MARTIN DR

HOMEWOOD

Wyman

Park

N CHARLES ST

ST PAUL ST

E UNIVERSITY PKWY

40 Ⓗ

CHESTNUT AVE

HARDING PL

GILMAN TER

**Homewood
House ★ 38**

Ⓐ 39

Johns Hopkins

University

E 33RD ST

GUILFORD AVE

**CHARLES
VILLAGE**

W 33RD ST

E 32ND ST

SINGER AVE

ELDER LN

WYMAN PARK DR

REMINGTON RD

WYMAN PKWY

**Baltimore
Museum
of Art 42**

★ Ⓡ

41

ART MUSEUM DR

**43
Ⓡ**

E 31ST ST

COTGROVE

ST PAUL

HARGROVE

N CALVERT ST

HUNTER ST

FIELD ST

BAY ST

TROJAN ST

PACIFIC ST

KIMSWY

W 31ST ST

FOX ST

W 30TH ST

HOWARD ST

E 30TH ST

HARGROVE ALLEY

**Ⓡ
44**

REMINGTON

FALLS RD

SISSON ST

W 28TH ST

ATKINSON ST

HAMPDEN AVE

MILES AVE

HUNTINGDON AVE

W 29TH ST

W LORRAINE AVE

W 25TH ST

N CHARLES ST

MARYLAND AVE

MORTON ST

ST PAUL

CALVERT ST

E 26TH ST

Ⓝ 45

Ⓢ 46

**47
Ⓢ**

W 25TH ST

E 25TH ST

MACE AVE

Ⓡ 48

SEE MAP 5

Ⓢ **SHOPS**	
3 CORADETTI GLASSWORKS	17 SPROUT
5 Ⓒ ATOMIC BOOKS	18 RED TREE
6 DOUBLEDUTCH BOUTIQUE	21 AVENUE ANTIQUES
7 CRAIG FLINNER GALLERY	22 LOVELYARNS
9 FORM	23 KISS N MAKE UP
11 THE TRUE VINE	25 MA PETITE SHOE
14 SHINE COLLECTIVE	26 IN WATERMELON SUGAR
15 Ⓒ MILAGRO	28 HOWL
16 SEEDS	46 REPTILIAN RECORDS
	47 THE KELMSCOTT BOOKSHOP
Ⓗ **HOTELS**	
36 INN AT THE COLONNADE	40 HOPKINS INN

0   200 yds

0   200 m

DISTANCE ACROSS MAP
Approximate: 1.75 mi or 2.8 km

© AVALON TRAVEL

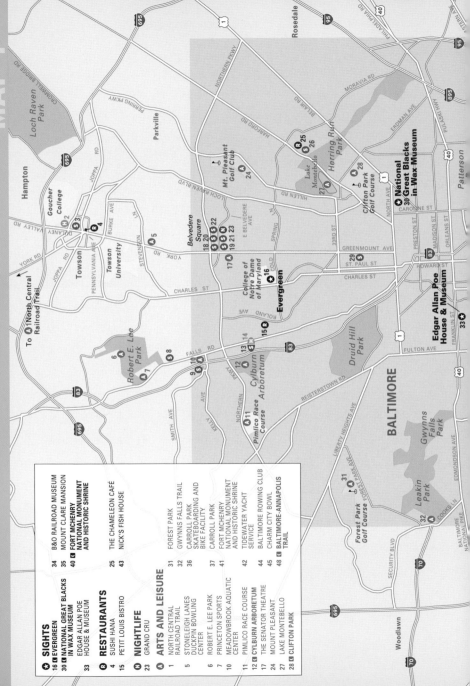

SIGHTS
16 EVERGREEN
30 NATIONAL GREAT BLACKS IN WAX MUSEUM
33 EDGAR ALLAN POE HOUSE & MUSEUM

34 B&O RAILROAD MUSEUM
35 MOUNT CLARE MANSION
40 FORT MCHENRY NATIONAL MONUMENT AND HISTORIC SHRINE

RESTAURANTS
4 SUSHI HANA
15 PETIT LOUIS BISTRO

25 THE CHAMELEON CAFÉ
43 NICK'S FISH HOUSE

NIGHTLIFE
23 GRAND CRU

ARTS AND LEISURE
1 NORTH CENTRAL RAILROAD TRAIL
5 STONELEIGH LANES DUCKPIN BOWLING CENTER
6 ROBERT E. LEE PARK
7 PRINCETON SPORTS
10 MEADOWBROOK AQUATIC CENTER
11 PIMLICO RACE COURSE
12 CYLBURN ARBORETUM
17 THE SENATOR THEATRE
24 MOUNT PLEASANT
27 LAKE MONTEBELLO
28 CLIFTON PARK

31 FOREST PARK
32 GWYNNS FALLS TRAIL
36 CARROLL PARK SKATEBOARDING AND BIKE FACILITY
37 CARROLL PARK
41 FORT MCHENRY NATIONAL MONUMENT AND HISTORIC SHRINE
42 TIDEWATER YACHT SERVICE
44 BALTIMORE ROWING CLUB
45 CHARM CITY BOWL
48 BALTIMORE-ANNAPOLIS TRAIL

DISTANCE ACROSS MAP
Approximate: 11 mi or 17.7 km

2 mi

2 km

©AVALON TRAVEL

SHOPS

3	TOWSON TOWN CENTER	19	DAEDALUS BOOKS AND MUSIC
8	SAMUEL PARKER CLOTHIER	20	BRATT DECOR
9	BALTIMORE CLAYWORKS	21	MATAVA TOO
13	JOANNA GRAY OF LONDON	22	NOUVEAU
13	VILLAGE OF CROSS KEYS	26	BEDIBOO
18	BELVEDERE SQUARE	29	NORMAL'S BOOKS AND RECORDS
		38	HOUSEWERKS
		39	SECOND CHANCE
		47	ARUNDEL MILLS MALL

HOTELS

2	SHERATON BALTIMORE NORTH	46	FOUR POINTS BY SHERATON BWI AIRPORT
14	RADISSON HOTEL AT CROSS KEYS		

Fort McHenry National Monument and Historic Shrine

B&O Railroad Museum

Mount Clare Mansion

Patapsco River

Baltimore Harbor

Inner Harbor

HARBOR TUNNEL

FORT MCHENRY TUNNEL

FRANCIS SCOTT KEY BRIDGE

FORT SMALLWOOD RD

PENNINGTON AVE

PATAPSCO AVE

Brooklyn Park

Glen Burnie

ARUNDEL EXPWY

RITCHIE HWY

Cherry Hill Park

HANOVER ST

BALTIMORE ANNAPOLIS BLVD

Linthicum Heights

CAMP MEADE RD

GLEN BURNIE BYPASS

DORSEY RD

Baltimore-Washington Thurgood Marshall International Airport

AVIATION BLVD

HARBOR TUNNEL THROUGHWAY

Patapsco Valley State Park

BALTIMORE WASHINGTON PKWY

SOUTHWESTERN BLVD

University of Maryland- Baltimore County

Arbutus

WILKENS AVE

CATON AVE

WASHINGTON BLVD

Carroll Park Golf Course

Carroll Park

RUSSELL ST

HANOVER ST

FREDERICK AVE

ROLLING RD

Patapsco Valley State Park

Catonsville

Hanover

Harmans

Arundel Mills Mall

Dundalk

DUNDALK AVE

O'DONNELL ST

O'DONNELL ST

Discover Baltimore

Stand on the sleek, brick promenade of Baltimore's Inner Harbor and look out over the calm water. Seagulls hover and float above, an air horn bleats from a docking sightseeing boat, kids plead with their parents to go back to the aquarium. There are gleaming office buildings and condo towers and luxury yachts, but also historic sailing ships and redbrick row houses tucked into the landscape, up near the green oasis of Federal Hill. From this vantage point, it might seem that Baltimore is an easy place to figure out. But Baltimore is a wise survivor; it withstood challenges and took risks, and that's why it has managed to not only keep its footing but to reinvent itself.

This city is a far more complex place than this picture-postcard image reveals. You'll need to wander along Fell's Point's bumpy, ballast-stone streets (the stones arrived as ballast in the holds of sailing cargo ships), through Hampden's independent shops, and among the magnificent architecture of Mount Vernon to start to understand it.

A southern city in character, but a northern one in geography, Baltimore is a small metropolis; the Greater Baltimore area is home to some 2.2 million people, but Baltimore City has only about 650,000 residents. It's a town of society teas and horse races, raucous street festivals and experimental music, and oddball characters and living legends.

Started as a former colonial trading outpost that grew into a boomtown, Baltimore was one of the biggest cities in early America. A British invasion fleet was repelled at Fort McHenry in 1814, and the U.S. national anthem was born here. Built up by immigration and industry during World War II, the city fell on hard times in the 1970s that are still evident in many places. Yet Baltimore set the standard for successful urban renewal in the early 1980s, with Harborplace and the Inner Harbor. A new phase of development in the early 21st century led to further growth all around the waterfront.

Baltimore has been showing up on a lot of national lists that use words like "underrated" and "hidden treasure." Why is that? Ask one of the many people who call Baltimore home. They'll tell you that they wouldn't dream of living anywhere else to pursue their lives, their art, and their dreams. They chose to be themselves, beholden to no one, here in the town by the water that they call home.

Planning Your Trip

▶ WHERE TO GO

Downtown and Inner Harbor

Baltimore was built around the Inner Harbor, its waterfronts once teeming with steamships. As the economy changed, the wharves began to rot—and so did downtown Baltimore. An innovative redevelopment plan called Harborplace became a model for urban renewal, and today the Inner Harbor is home to museums, restaurants, the National Aquarium in Baltimore, and waterfront promenades. The surrounding downtown area is a mix of offices, museums, and historic buildings. Camden Yards is home to grand stadiums for the Orioles and Ravens.

Fell's Point

One of Baltimore's oldest neighborhoods, Fell's Point is a place where tug boats still operate from the old City Recreation Pier, and it's the site of historic buildings and unique characters. Bars and restaurants line the ballast-stone streets, as do small shops; take a walk down Thames Street, then follow the boardwalk around Henderson's Wharf and wind your way back to the brick row houses and hidden courtyards. Fell's Point was its own settlement until it was absorbed by

Baltimore Town in 1773, and still retains an independent character.

Little Italy

As Italian immigrants settled here in the mid-1800s, they began to open businesses and restaurants and made a new community for themselves. The surrounding area has changed a great deal in the past decade, with fancy townhomes and condos now rising to the north and south. There are three important museums here: the Star-Spangled Banner Flag House, the Reginald F. Lewis Museum of Maryland African American History & Culture, and the Jewish Museum of Maryland.

Canton

East of Fell's Point is another historic waterfront community, but one that's undergone a transformation. Condos and new construction line the waterfront, while just a street away, century-old brick row houses and narrow streets provide a glimpse of old Canton. O'Donnell Square is the hub of Canton's busy nightlife, where bars and restaurants host the young, party-minded people who live in the area (and beyond). One of the city's most-used public spaces, Patterson Park, marks the northern border of Canton.

Oriole Park at Camden Yards

outdoor movies during the summer in Little Italy

Federal Hill

Named for the large hill that provides one of the best vantage points of downtown Baltimore and the Inner Harbor, Federal Hill is a thriving residential, shopping, and entertainment district, with activity often centered around the refurbished Cross Street Market, one of the many city-owned markets in Baltimore. Bars, clubs, and restaurants along Charles Street and Light Street make the heart of Federal Hill a boisterous place on warm weekend nights.

Mount Vernon

Home to the finest 19th-century architecture in Baltimore, Mount Vernon was founded as the site of the nation's first monument to its first president. As the city's fortunes rose, many of the new captains of industry and Baltimore's landed bluebloods built grand marble homes in the blocks that radiate out from The Washington Monument on Mount Vernon Place. Today, Mount Vernon is the cultural hub of the city, home to the Walters Art Museum and The Joseph Meyerhoff Symphony Hall, where the Baltimore Symphony Orchestra performs.

Hampden and Homewood

An old 1800s mill settlement, Hampden is now a home to young, hip residents as well as established working families. "The Avenue"

The Washington Monument, on Mount Vernon Place

(36th St.) offers expensive home furnishings and apparel as well as thrift-store scores, plus bars and restaurants. Quirky and un-sanitized, Hampden is one of the city's hidden charms. Just east of Hampden is Homewood, a neighborhood that surrounds Johns Hopkins University. It's an area of broad avenues and small parks, as well as cultural icons like the Baltimore Museum of Art and Homewood House.

▶ WHEN TO GO

The best seasons to visit Baltimore are spring and fall. May and June bring warm, bright skies and gardens in bloom, and there's lots to do, from street festivals to baseball games to biking. September and October's cooler weather brings relief after a long, hot summer; fall is a great time to take advantage of the city's walkable terrain or go leaf-peeping out in the country.

Summer is very hot and humid and can make being outside (during the worst days) unbearable. The heat doesn't last all summer, though, and beautiful, merely "warm" days are common. Winter usually begins mildly here, though cold spells in January and February are common (but brief), as is the odd February snowstorm.

Explore Baltimore

▶ THE TWO-DAY BEST OF BALTIMORE

Day 1

▶ From your downtown or Federal Hill hotel, begin your day by heading east to Locust Point, and get a hearty breakfast at Harvest Table. Then, walk a few steps north, to the waterfront promenade of the Tide Point complex, for a great view of Fell's Point and the city.

▶ Head back to Fort Avenue, and then due east by car (or on foot, if you're feeling energetic) for about a mile to the Fort McHenry National Monument, where Baltimore's stout defense turned back a British invasion fleet during the War of 1812—and led Francis Scott Key to pen "The Star-Spangled Banner."

▶ You can see where the flag that loaned its name to the song was created at Little Italy's Star-Spangled Banner Flag House. Nearby are two attractions that showcase the roles played by African Americans in Baltimore's early history: Right next door is the Reginald F. Lewis Museum of Maryland African American History & Culture, and in Fell's Point, the Frederick Douglass-Isaac Myers Maritime Park. And the Phoenix Shot Tower is where molten lead was dripped into perfect spheres, creating "shot" for U.S. troops in the 19th century.

▶ Stop at Mount Vernon's Sascha's 527 Café for a light lunch, then head to The Washington Monument—the nation's first—and climb up to the top for another great view of Baltimore. Stroll through the amazing collections of the Walters Art Museum. Enter the renowned Peabody Institute of Music, but lower your voice to admire the immense George Peabody Library.

▶ Continue your tour of Baltimore history and culture at the Baltimore Museum of Art in Homewood, then sample some regional cuisine on the wonderful patio at the BMA's restaurant Gertrude's.

▶ After dinner, head to Mount Vernon for a performance (symphony, opera, play, or musical). Grab post-show dessert at the

Fort McHenry National Monument

George Peabody Library

Sure, the Inner Harbor is great — but where do Baltimoreans go to get away from the throngs of tourists? If you're looking to see more than the obvious choices and experience Baltimore like a local, here's a quick guide to some of the local favorites beloved by Charm City's residents.

Sunday mornings May to December bring farmers and vendors under the I-83 overpasses downtown (near the Shot Tower) to the **Baltimore Farmers Market,** where you can have fresh bacon and eggs, and grab some fruit for the road.

For entertainment, locals love movies, and not at the megaplex. The **MICA Brown Center,** an angular glass marvel at the Maryland Institute College of Art, is a hit with the art crowd, so expect to see experimental, challenging films, along with the occasional mainstream offering. Sunday mornings at the **Charles Theatre** mean Cinema Sundays, which feature new releases and classic films, along with bagels, coffee, and guest speakers. And **free outdoor movie series** like the Little Italy Open Air Film Festival have become a Baltimore summer tradition.

Outdoor activities for Baltimoreans mean one of the many neighborhood festivals that run almost all year long, like Little Italy's **St. Anthony Festival** in early June, Fell's Point's **LatinoFest** in mid-June, Mount Vernon's **Artscape** in mid-July, and the semi-counterculture **Hampden-Fest** in mid-September. Spring is **steeplechase**

season; if the infield at Preakness is too crass for you, pack a picnic and catch one of several races held Saturdays each season among the rolling hills of northern Baltimore County.

the Charles Theatre

Brass Elephant restaurant's opulent upstairs bar, The Tusk Lounge, or take the elevator up to The 13th Floor in the grand old Belvedere building nearby for a commanding view of the city at night.

Day 2

▶ Start your day like a local at Jimmy's Restaurant in Fell's Point. The legendary diner is a favorite of neighborhood lifers, politicians, businessmen, media people, and tourists alike.

▶ Then head west (it's a two-mile trip that's

very walkable) to the Inner Harbor. You'll see the giant neon Domino Sugars sign looming across the harbor; it's in Federal Hill, but the best view is from Fell's Point (it's even more impressive at night). This is still a working harbor, so you'll see cargo ships and tugboats churning past sailboats and yachts as you walk. Head for the National Aquarium in Baltimore, where you can wander through the Australia exhibit and take in the dolphin show (and morning animal feedings). Grab a crustacean-rich lunch at Phillips Harborplace.

► The Inner Harbor isn't all about the thrill of the new: There are several great historic attractions here as well. Climb aboard the U.S.S. *Constellation*, a Civil War–era warship. The Baltimore Maritime Museum isn't an actual museum; it's a quartet of historic vessels (including a WWII-era submarine) and a lighthouse around the Inner Harbor.

► Then walk back east along the marinas and the waterfront to Harbor East, the city's newest neighborhood. Go shopping at an upscale boutique like South Moon Under. Treat yourself to an opulent, truly Italian dinner at Cinghiale.

► Spend the evening shopping for souvenirs and gifts (and maybe even something for yourself) along Pratt Street, at the Gallery, the Power Plant, and Harborplace. Upgrade your outfit a little and head to

U.S.S. *Constellation*

the warm, stylish Pazo in Harbor East for some wine and tapas. Or head to Little Italy for drinks and dessert, choosing from a wide variety of classic Italian restaurants, from casual (like Sabatino's) to more special-occasion (like Aldo's).

TOP 10 FOR KIDS

- At the **Baltimore Museum of Industry,** kids can learn how the city's fortunes (and the city itself) rose and fell during the past 200 years.

- At the **B&O Railroad Museum,** little ones can play on huge iron locomotives, and even board a train for a three-mile trip.

- Check out **Fort McHenry National Monument,** where, in 1814, U.S. troops held off a British invasion – and a flag above the fort inspired "The Star-Spangled Banner."

- The **Maryland Science Center** has plenty of experiments, dinosaurs, and gizmos for kids to energetically embrace.

- Head to the **Maryland Zoo in Baltimore** early to watch the animals wake up and eat their breakfast (families can also breakfast at the zoo on warm weekends).

- Dive in to the **National Aquarium in Baltimore,** where options range from breakfast with the dolphins to overnight sleepovers.

- Have a fun, crab-smashing dinner at **Obrycki's Crab House** in Fell's Point.

- Unleash your kids into a world of exhibits about everything from nature to robots at **Port Discovery Children's Museum.**

- Take a land and water tour of town with **Ride the Ducks,** featuring DUKWs – big, lumbering amphibious vehicles.

- On weekends, kids can sign up as "powder monkeys" on the **U.S.S. Constellation,** to learn what life was like for children working on a Civil War-era warship.

SIGHTS

Here's the first thing you should know about the aquatic part of Baltimore's most famous geographical feature, the Inner Harbor: The shimmering water you walk past, boat upon, and dine near is not part of the Chesapeake Bay. It's actually the Patapsco River, which eventually flows into the bay some 10 miles eastward. Still, Baltimore was founded as a New World port back in the late 1600s because of the Patapsco: The bounty of the bay and the fertile lands around that body of water led colonial European settlers to set up shop and shipbuilding operations along the banks of the river. That commerce led to the founding of many fortunes and the growth of Baltimore into one of early America's largest, most prosperous cities. Those early urban commerce and transport barons and civic leaders spread their wealth gradually away from the waterfront, and built themselves businesses, homes, parks, houses of worship, and eventually universities and schools that helped Baltimore continue to grow for the next 300 years.

Around the waterfront, Baltimore is a very walkable city, though the distances between some destinations can be a bit daunting. The land rises gently—and constantly—from the Inner Harbor to the northern neighborhoods, but is basically flat in every other direction. As you walk through the city, you'll pass through different types of neighborhoods—historic, modern, working-class, upscale, and underprivileged—that sometimes share

HIGHLIGHTS

LOOK FOR ◖ TO FIND RECOMMENDED SIGHTS.

◖ **Best Rooftop Rainforest:** Sure, the **National Aquarium in Baltimore** has huge tanks filled with sharks and dolphins, but take the escalator up to the wonderful rain forest early in the morning to see and hear birds, primates, lizards, and other denizens of this hot, humid, lush aerie greet the day (page 31).

◖ **Best Aerial View:** There's no finer way to get a completely 360° view of the city of Baltimore than from the huge glass windows around the **Top of the World Observation Deck,** located on the 27th floor of the World Trade Center at the Inner Harbor; go around sunset for the most dramatic photo opportunities (page 34).

◖ **Best Park:** You can judge the success of a city park by the diversity of the residents who use it; that makes Canton's **Patterson Park** the finest in Baltimore, with 155 acres of rolling hills and trees; don't miss out on climbing the pagoda for a great view of the city's waterfront neighborhoods (page 40).

◖ **Best Neon Sign:** No amount of flashy new waterfront condos or upscale residences can dim the warm red industrial glow of the enormous **Domino Sugars sign** in Federal Hill that watches over the Inner Harbor and Fell's Point (page 43).

◖ **Best Place for a Picnic:** Grab a freshly made crab-cake sandwich from nearby Cross Street Market and walk a few blocks up to the top of **Federal Hill Park** for a regal view of the boats and bustle of the Inner Harbor (page 43).

◖ **Best Cathedral:** America's first cathedral has just undergone a stunning renovation and restoration that makes the **Basilica of the Assumption** shine even more brightly than the day it was opened in 1821 (page 44).

◖ **Best Museum:** It's hard to understand the breadth and quality of the collections at the **Walters Art Museum** in Mount Vernon until you see them yourself; from Old Masters to Asian artifacts and ancient empires, there's something astounding and unexpected in every gallery and around every corner (page 48).

◖ **Best Historic Mansion That's Not Downtown:** Head north up Charles Street, past the grand homes and universities of northern Baltimore, to the soaring columns, amazing art collections, and lush landscapes of the house known simply as **Evergreen** (page 55).

◖ **Best Place to Rekindle Your Patriotism:** From a squat, star-shaped fortress perched on a spit of land southeast of downtown, some 60 brave soldiers held off an invading British fleet in 1814 and spared the city of Baltimore; thus was born the U.S. national anthem, "The Star-Spangled Banner," and the legend of the **Fort McHenry National Monument and Historic Shrine** (page 55).

◖ **Best Museum the Likes of Which You've Never Seen Before:** Built by the vision and will of one determined couple, the **National Great Blacks in Wax Museum** will change the way you view the history of race relations in America, and inform you about how African Americans have made their place in an often hostile society (page 57).

© GEOFF BROWN

Patterson Park's pagoda

common boundaries, leading to striking contrasts. Still, walking through the streets offers the best view into the daily lives of Baltimoreans.

There are several don't-miss attractions in Baltimore, places where the history of the region and America was altered forever. Fort McHenry National Monument is one of those places; on a smaller scale, so is the gravesite of Edgar Allan Poe, and even Fell's Point, where the legendary Baltimore clipper ship was built during the late 1700s. The city is also home to several magnificent art collections, such as the Walters Art Museum and the Baltimore Museum of Art, and unique attractions that have to be seen firsthand to really understand (like the National Great Blacks in Wax Museum). That's part of the charm and mystery of Baltimore: Be prepared to be surprised by what you'll find here.

Downtown and Inner Harbor   Map 1

BABE RUTH BIRTHPLACE AND MUSEUM
216 Emory St., 410/727-1539,
www.baberuthmuseum.com
HOURS: Apr.-Oct. daily 10 A.M.-6 P.M. (7 P.M. during Oriole game days), Nov.-Mar. daily 10 A.M.-5 P.M.
COST: $6 adult, $3 child, $4 senior

Though he may have "built" Yankee Stadium with his Herculean baseball exploits, George Herman "Babe" Ruth was born in 1865 in a humble redbrick row house on tiny Emory Street, about 10 blocks west of what would one day become Baltimore's Inner Harbor. Ruth would go on to be the first major sports megacelebrity in modern American history, setting home run records and setting tongues wagging with his larger-than-life persona and talents. The Ruth home (along with much of downtown Baltimore) fell into disrepair in the late 1960s, but was saved, protected, and restored; it opened (along with an adjacent row house) as a museum in 1974. In 1992, Oriole Park at Camden Yards ushered in the new era of throwback baseball stadiums just a few blocks to the east, making a stop at Ruth's birthplace an easy pilgrimage for baseball purists. Today, the home contains a cozy collection of Ruthian ephemera, exhibits, and authentic jerseys and gear worn or owned by the Babe that will thrill baseball history buffs. This site is also part of the Sports Legends at Camden Yards museum, which has a vast collection of Baltimore and Maryland sports memorabilia and exhibits.

BALTIMORE MARITIME MUSEUM
Inner Harbor piers, 410/396-5528,
www.baltomaritimemuseum.org
HOURS: Mar.-Oct. daily 10 A.M.-5:30 P.M., Nov.-Feb. daily 10 A.M.-4:30 P.M.
COST: $10-16 adult, $5-7 child, $8-13 senior, free for kids 5 and under

This isn't a museum of dusty bells, sails, and sextants. In fact, there's no building at all: The museum consists of three historic ocean-going vessels and a fascinating "screwpile" lighthouse. (A fourth vessel, the U.S.S. *Constellation,* is an affiliated attraction that operates independently.) The oldest ship is the Lightship 116 *Chesapeake,* parked next to the National Aquarium's entrance; it served as a floating, illuminated beacon to shipping around the Chesapeake Bay and Atlantic Ocean, twice surviving hurricanes so powerful they snapped the ship's anchor chain. Just behind the Chesapeake is the USS *Torsk,* a 1944 U.S. Navy submarine that sank the last two Japanese warships lost before Japan's surrender. Visitors can climb through the claustrophobic cabins and passageways of the sub, which was decommissioned in 1968. Head next to the USCGC *Taney* (located behind the ESPN Zone and Power Plant Live! complex), which has its own connection to World War II: It's the last surviving ship to have been at Pearl Harbor during the Japanese attack in 1941 that led to America's entrance into the war. Last

THE INNER HARBOR THAT SAVED BALTIMORE

Bustling brick-lined walkways, pavilions filled with eateries and shops, and historic vessels in the middle of a major American port city are common enough these days; but back in 1980, Baltimore's Harborplace was really the only place in the nation to experience such sights. Designed by the same team that created Boston's Faneuil Hall – another example of a re-purposed urban space – Harborplace was a multimillion-dollar gamble taken by city leaders to stave off the urban blight of the 1960s and 1970s that threatened to destroy Baltimore.

The project was a big success for several reasons, some of which were not initially clear when construction began. One obvious force behind the Inner Harbor's popularity was James Rouse, a developer with a sense of purpose and history (he created the town of Columbia, south of Baltimore, which was America's first completely planned community). Working with dedicated city and community leaders, business tycoons, and architects from other cities, the team charged with turning an unpleasant industrial waterfront into a destination began

with just a few buildings and features: the National Aquarium, the World Trade Center, and the pavilions of Harborplace. Much of the waterfront was wide open and undeveloped when Harborplace opened, only filling in gradually as people realized it was not only going to work, it was going to be a huge success. National and international media attention focused on Baltimore's revolutionary new waterfront project, and cities from across the globe sent representatives here to learn how this gritty, industrial town managed to lure millions of visitors to its downtown each year with the creation of the Inner Harbor. It was dubbed "the Baltimore renaissance," and while much of the city continued to spiral into decay, the salvation of the downtown area helped keep the city afloat long enough to reap the benefits of the booming economic growth of the late 1990s. Those gains can be seen in the new construction that's rising on property that was once littered with decaying warehouses, piers, and rubble: Today, luxe new residences built by developers like Ritz-Carlton and the Four Seasons rise along the waters of the Inner Harbor.

© GEOFF BROWN

Renovated office buildings and new corporate towers line the Inner Harbor's revitalized waterfront.

is the Seven Foot Knoll Lighthouse, which might seem a little short for a lighthouse. Not so for Maryland's coastal geography: The region around the Chesapeake Bay and Patapsco River's confluence is so flat that lighthouses didn't need to be particularly tall to be seen by ships in the late 1800s, so this design was used because it could be erected in the soft mud and sands of the bay. The Baltimore Maritime Museum's ships and lighthouse can be visited individually, or as a group for a reduced rate.

DR. SAMUEL D. HARRIS NATIONAL MUSEUM OF DENTISTRY

31 S. Greene St., 410/706-0600,
www.dentalmuseum.umaryland.edu
HOURS: Wed.-Sat. 10 A.M.-4 P.M., Sun. 1-4 P.M.
COST: $6 adult, $3 child, $3 senior

It's difficult enough to get a person to go to the dentist regularly, so why would anyone want to go to an entire museum dedicated to the least favorite medical profession? But this museum—which became a Smithsonian affiliate in 2001—has plenty of exhibits worth, um, chewing over. Most prominent in their extensive collection is one of George Washington's lower dentures (made of ivory, not wood), as well as four prints of Andy Warhol's portrait of St. Apollonia, the patron saint of dentistry (there's also a nearly 900-year-old stained glass tribute to this plier-wielding saint). Rotating exhibits have names like "Saliva: A Remarkable Fluid" and "Marvelous Mouth," and there's a goofy jukebox that plays hokey vintage commercials for dental hygiene products dating as far back as the 1950s. Sure, it's not as easy a sell to the kids as the National Aquarium, but where else are you going to see Queen Victoria's gilded dental instruments?

GEPPI'S ENTERTAINMENT MUSEUM

301 W. Camden St., 410/625-7060,
www.geppismuseum.com
HOURS: Tues.-Sun. 10 A.M.-6 P.M.
COST: $10 adult, $7 child, $9 senior

A more apt name for this amazing collection might be "The American Pop Culture Museum," because the items found here represent some of the finest examples of U.S. cartooning, comic books, and mass-market memorabilia in the nation. From Colonial-era political cartoons to the golden age of comics and beyond, as well as grand movie posters from the 20th century, to rare collectibles and toys, this relatively new museum (located upstairs from the Sports Legends Museum at Camden Yards) is a treasure trove of American culture. Founded by (and named after) Steve Geppi, a native Baltimorean who has made a fortune in the comic book distribution, collectible, and licensing business, the museum is a reflection of his love of comics and pop culture, and will make giddy little kids out of visitors who find a favorite treasured comic book, doll, or decoder ring. The collections cover all the major and minor studios and publishers, from Disney to EC to Marvel, and they trace the development of simple line drawings in newspapers into huge international marketing icons that permeate every aspect of our culture.

HARBORPLACE

203 E. Pratt St., 410/332-4191, www.harborplace.com
HOURS: Mon.-Thurs. 10 A.M.-9 P.M., Fri.-Sat. 10 A.M.-10 P.M., Sun. 11 A.M.-7 P.M.
COST: Free

It's difficult to imagine now, but the land occupied by Harborplace was, in the early 1960s, covered with huge, semi-rotting piers and abandoned industrial and warehouse space. No one came down to the harbor; in fact, people avoided it like the plague, because it was ugly and occupied by a variety of unsavory characters, many of whom, in fact, might have carried the plague. The real estate around the harbor was similarly undesirable, and in the 1970s, the city actually sold dilapidated houses in the Otterbein neighborhood (in between Oriole Park and Federal Hill) for $1 if people promised to fix them up; houses in Otterbein now regularly sell for $450,000. Short version: Things looked bad.

But city political and business leaders took a chance, and it paid off. Beginning with the nearby Charles Center project, and then moving to the waterfront, the city gambled millions of dollars—and hired some of the nation's most

© GEOFF BROWN

The heart of Baltimore's urban renewal, Harborplace helps draw millions of visitors to the city each year.

visionary urban planners—to give Baltimore an anchor on which it could try to avoid complete collapse.

The pavilions of Harborplace, along with the National Aquarium and the World Trade Center (that pentagonal building), were the original occupants of the Inner Harbor, and they had the waterfront to themselves for a while. Interestingly, Harborplace was originally built to give the citizens of Baltimore a new, modern, picturesque location to meet, hang out, and enjoy the city's waterfront. Perhaps ironically, the area instead became a tourist draw, and is now the city's most popular destination, drawing millions of visitors a year to the wide variety of attractions along the reclaimed waterfront.

MARYLAND ART PLACE
8 Market Pl., Power Plant Live!, 410/962-8565, www.mdartplace.org
HOURS: Tues.-Sat. 11 A.M.-5 P.M.
COST: Free
Established back in 1981, Maryland Art Place

(MAP) is an interesting creature: It's a nonprofit gallery and exhibition space for artists from Baltimore and the surrounding area to both show their work and have a direct conduit to the public. Sculpture, painting, drawing, and more technological media, many by new and up-and-coming artists, are on display here. Two well-regarded programs (Critics' Residency and Curators' Incubator) produce large shows of art and writing each year. MAP is located at the edge of the bar/restaurant complex called Power Plant Live!, though it has usually closed its doors for the night by the time the thirsty young crowds arrive.

MARYLAND SCIENCE CENTER
601 Light St., 410/685-2370, www.mdsci.org
HOURS: Tues.-Thurs. 10 A.M.-5 P.M., Fri. 10 A.M.-8 P.M., Sat. 10 A.M.-6 P.M., Sun. 11 A.M.-5 P.M.; longer summer hours, including Mon.
COST: $14.50 adult, $10 child, $13.50 senior
At the beginning of the 21st century, the Maryland Science Center underwent a welcome increase both in size and scope, and the

© GEOFF BROWN

The Maryland Science Center is home to an IMAX theater, planetarium, observatory, and dinosaur exhibit.

additions make this once somewhat dry attraction now a must-see, especially if you're traveling with kids. A new Dinosaur Mysteries exhibit showcases huge re-creations of the prehistoric beasts, but also lets kids dig through sand for fossils as the simulated roar of *Tyrannosaurus rex* reverberates through the room. Newton's Alley features lots of hands-on (and feet-on) exhibits that kids can touch, punch, and climb, from a laser harp to climbing and balance rigs. There's a planetarium that shows off the mysteries of the universe. On clear Friday nights, head for the observatory, which opens free of charge and also sets up smaller telescopes for peeks up at the heavens. Older kids with a taste for experiments should head to Wetlab, where they'll pull on some goggles and lab coats and perform science projects involving glop, goop, and gunk. And of course there's the requisite IMAX theater, showing both nature- and science-themed films, as well as Hollywood fare at night. The entire center is awash in hands-on computer stations and touchable, squeezable exploration stations for visitors to sample and learn about biology, chemistry, and space science (and even try on a mini-NASA flight suit). There's a popular demonstration stage where experts explain everything from nanotechnology to black holes.

The Science Center is one of those attractions that kids go bonkers over, running from exhibit to exhibit, playing and touching everything they can, while adults spend their time gently wrangling the kids through the hallways. All the popular national touring exhibits about science (the kind that feature human bodies or artifacts from shipwrecks) will stop here, usually requiring an additional fee. And once you're done, at the museum's entrance, you can rent a Segway for a quick, refreshing zip around the Inner Harbor.

NATIONAL AQUARIUM IN BALTIMORE
501 E. Pratt St., 410/576-3800, www.aqua.org
HOURS: Mon.-Thurs. 9 A.M.-5 P.M., Fri. 9 A.M.-8 P.M., Sat. 9 A.M.-6 P.M., Sun. 9 A.M.-5 P.M.; longer summer hours
COST: $21.95 adult, $12.95 child, $20.95 senior

When the National Aquarium in Baltimore

STROLLING AND SLEEPING WITH SHARKS: THE NATIONAL AQUARIUM'S IMMERSION TOURS

If you've got some extra time in your trip and want a really (pardon the pun) deep experience at the National Aquarium, sign up in advance for one of the many immersion and extended tours. During the day (and early in the morning), there are a series of behind-the-scenes tours that show off the labs where new residents are studied or acclimated, take you into the cafeterias where the food for the fussy eaters of the animal kingdom is prepared, and let you walk above the enormous shark tank on a thin wooden walkway, beneath which the sleek hunters glide by just inches from your feet. If that's too wild for you, breakfast with the dolphins is a less-toothy option. At night, there are three exciting aquarium sleepovers available for kids: just outside the shark tanks, up in the rain forest, and in the Australia: Wild Extremes wing (note that any children must be accompanied by an adult for each sleepover).

opened in 1981, it was one of the nation's first mega-aquariums, built after then–Baltimore Mayor William Donald Schaefer visited the New England Aquarium in Boston. Baltimore's National Aquarium was the cornerstone of the Inner Harbor's redevelopment plan, meant to lure both residents and, hopefully, tourists to the waterfront. In the decades since that opening, the aquarium has expanded to keep up with crowds both increasingly large and increasingly difficult to impress.

Start your visit at the main aquarium building, which is home to a vast collection of exotic fish and environments, from Amazon river forest to a North Atlantic seacoast (home to some terribly cute puffins). There's an impressive, if slightly fearsome, collection of sharks, which glide around their own massive 225,000-gallon circular tank. And there's an even larger tropical reef tank with dozens of brightly colored and oddly shaped residents. If the sharks are too creepy for you, check out the much more cuddly frogs exhibit, or sit down and hang on at the new 4-D Immersion

© GEOFF BROWN

Fish, birds, reptiles, and marine mammals all call the National Aquarium home.

Theater, where high-definition, 3-D nature films are paired with "you-are-there" effects like sounds, smells, sea spray, and vibrations. Atop the main building is a living, walk-through tropical rainforest—if you've arrived early, head here first, as the birds and reptiles that scurry and flitter all around you are most active in the morning.

The marine mammal pavilion is home to Play! The Dolphin Show, where you can watch the aquarium's Atlantic bottlenose dolphins perform impressive leaps and show off their balance skills. You'll also learn about these intelligent, curious animals, and maybe even get the chance to give them some hand signals to spur their performances.

The newest major permanent attraction is Animal Planet Australia: Wild Extremes, a glass-enclosed mini-Australia, complete with a 35-foot waterfall and a variety of habitats found along a river gorge. As you wander through the gorge, you'll see all sorts of fish, birds, and reptiles, ranging from the laughing kookaburra bird to the not-half-as-funny snake known as the death adder.

If you're in town for a while, check out some of the Aquarium's immersive tours, which include behind-the-scenes exploration of the inner workings of the facility. You can walk the narrow, wooden walkway above the huge shark tank, feed the dolphins breakfast, or (for kids) spend the night in the rainforest, the Australia exhibit, or outside the shark tank.

PORT DISCOVERY CHILDREN'S MUSEUM

35 Market Pl., 410/727-8120, www.portdiscovery.org
HOURS: Daily 10 A.M.-4 P.M.
COST: $11.75 for all ages

Just north of the Inner Harbor, this award-winning attraction is an immense hit with children because it seems like it was designed by kids. Adults might not understand why their kids are so ga-ga about this place, but watch the way children run and explore the various halls and exhibits and it's clear they're delighted. There are wacky rooms with mis-proportioned objects, lots of construction goodies and smart, creative

playthings, and plenty of noisy, tactile toys for toddlers. There's KidWorks, a huge, three-story climbing structure (and a big, dark, black slide through which kids can descend) for bigger kids; smaller fry can wander through Egyptian-tomb-themed mazes and play (and, amazingly, learn) in the Wonders of Water room, which lets kids make their own fountains and manipulate a river system, complete with dams and boat lock. (It's so hands-on that raincoats and rubber shoes are provided—but be aware it's closed on many summer Mondays.) There's even The Oasis, where you and your kids can chill out between exhibits. Summertime afternoons can get a bit crowded, so plan on visiting early or late in the day.

SPORTS LEGENDS MUSEUM AT CAMDEN YARDS

301 W. Camden St., 410/727-1539, www.baberuthmuseum.com
HOURS: Apr.-Oct. 10 A.M.-6 P.M. (7 P.M. on Oriole game days), Nov.-Mar. 10 A.M.-5 P.M.
COST: $10 adult, $6.50 child, $8 senior

Maryland has produced and worshipped an astonishing array of professional athletes, from George Herman "Babe" Ruth to Johnny Unitas to Cal Ripken, Jr. The now-destroyed Memorial Stadium, which hosted both football's Baltimore Colts and baseball's Baltimore Orioles, was occupied by fans so devoted and passionate that one national sportswriter dubbed it the "world's largest outdoor insane asylum." This obsession with sports is lovingly celebrated at the Sports Legends Museum, from the major league stars and teams to smaller sports and lesser lights who played just as hard. Besides the big sports exhibits on the Orioles (including the team's Hall of Fame, and the numbers 2,131 that hung on the Camden Yards warehouse when Cal Ripken, Jr. broke the consecutive-games-played streak) and the now-residing-in-Indianapolis Colts (and a smaller Ravens exhibit), there's plenty of other sports history in Baltimore as well. The museum showcases artifacts from the city's two Negro League Baseball Teams and highlights local legends of basketball, football, and the less-well-known sport of lacrosse (there's even a lacrosse goalie simulation to test if you flinch under the onslaught of a virtual shot, which in real life can hit nearly 100 mph). The museum is also home to the Maryland State Athletic Hall of Fame.

Camden Station, the grand brick building that houses both the Sports Legends Museum and Geppi's Entertainment Museum, is an 1856 Baltimore & Ohio Railroad station with its own storied history; a brief exhibit about the structure is on the first floor.

(TOP OF THE WORLD OBSERVATION DECK

401 E. Pratt St., 410/837-4516
HOURS: Wed.-Sun. 10 A.M.-9 P.M.
COST: $5 adult, $3 child, $4 senior

Baltimore's World Trade Center, designed by architects at I. M. Pei's firm and completed in 1977, was one of the first new buildings to rise at the then-underdeveloped Inner Harbor. Today, it's merely one of many skyscrapers along the water, though it still claims one distinction: At a not-terribly-impressive 32 stories, it remains the world's tallest equilaterally sided pentagonal building. On the 27th floor is the Top of the World Observation Deck, which is without a doubt the best vantage point for a 360-degree view of Baltimore. Wander around the room to get a sense of how Baltimore spreads out from the bustle, tourism, and commerce of the Inner Harbor to the far-ranging blocks of two-story row houses that make up so much of the city. There are mounted binoculars and maps to help orient visitors, and an elevator ride to this deck around sunset is a great way to see Charm City in a whole new light.

U.S.S. CONSTELLATION

Pier 1, 301 E. Pratt St., 410/539-1797,
www.constellation.org
HOURS: Daily 10 A.M.-5:30 P.M.
COST: $10 adult, $5 child, $8 senior

The ornate, sleek, and imposing three-masted warship that welcomes visitors to Baltimore's Inner Harbor holds nearly 150 years of history in her hull. Perhaps the last all-sail warship built by the U.S. Navy, this magnificent vessel—the second to carry the *Constellation*

name—was built back in 1853 in Virginia atop the keel of the first U.S.S. *Constellation,* which was built in Baltimore in 1797. (A long-simmering controversy as to this vessel's lineage and actual age was basically settled in 2002.) The *Constellation* frequently sailed across the Atlantic, serving as a U.S. Navy ship that would hunt down slave ships leaving Africa, and served admirably against the Confederacy during the U.S. Civil War.

Years of neglect led to major internal damage and decay; in 1994, the *Constellation* was declared unsafe and slowly towed to a repair facility for five years of repairs, using traditional methods and more advanced techniques to return the vessel to its original 1855-era appearance and preserve the ship. (You might notice the ship's orientation is not always the same: Sometimes she's bow out, sometime she's bow in. This rotation, which takes place about once a year, allows the hull to be exposed evenly to the elements.) Today, the ship is the last surviving Civil War–era Navy vessel, and despite more than a century of repairs both sound and ill-considered, the *Constellation* is an amazing piece of living history that even features daily cannon firings.

Climb aboard for a self-guided tour of the ship, but if you have the time, wait for the guided tour, which will help explain the myriad of strange ropes, pulleys, doors, hatches, and other sailing ship details. You can tour almost every square inch of the *Constellation* from stem to stern; on weekends, twice a day, kids can sign up as Powder Monkeys, and learn what life was like for the young children (some as young as 11) who worked on 19th-century ships, doing a variety of grueling, dangerous jobs that would make today's Federal regulatory officials collapse in horror.

WESTMINSTER HALL AND EDGAR ALLAN POE'S GRAVE

519 W. Fayette St., 410/706-2072,
www.westminsterhall.org
HOURS: Mon.-Fri. 8:30 A.M.-5 P.M.
COST: Free

The main thing you should know about this eerie, historic church and graveyard is this:

© GEOFF BROWN

The U.S.S. *Constellation* is the last surviving Civil War-era Navy vessel.

The dead came first. Generally, the establishment of a church leads to the founding of an attendant graveyard, but that's not the case with Westminster Hall and Burying Ground, located just west of downtown Baltimore. Built as a Presbyterian cemetery in 1786, the large, Gothic church didn't rise among the tombstones (and above several of them, resulting in crude catacombs that riddle the church's foundation) until 1852. The graveyard's most prominent occupant is the American master of the macabre, Edgar Allan Poe, who in fact was buried in this same cemetery not once, but twice. (His wife and... cousin, Virginia, is interred with him.) Francis Scott Key's son Philip Barton Key is also buried here, as are several other prominent Baltimoreans of the 18th and 19th centuries. The current Poe family monument is right inside the graveyard's fence, at the corner of Fayette and Greens Streets, and is the scene each January 19 (Poe's birthday) of a visit from the Poe Toaster, a mysterious figure who leaves three red roses and a bottle of cognac on Poe's gravestone.

The entire property is owned by the neighboring University of Maryland School of Law, and run by a non-profit; the church itself is no longer an active church but an event space and hall available for rental.

Fell's Point   Map 2

BALTIMORE PUBLIC WORKS MUSEUM

751 Eastern Ave., 410/396-5565,
www.baltimorepublicworksmuseum.org
HOURS: Tues.-Sun. 10 A.M.-4 P.M.
COST: $3 adult, $3 child, $2.50 senior

It's a little hard to believe, but this grand, looming Second Empire edifice at the corner of President Street and Eastern Avenue is...a sewage pumping station, completed back in 1912 as the city played catch-up with modern sewer systems. Even today, it still pumps one-third of Baltimore City's waste off to a sewage treatment plant far from downtown (and yes, the building's business is what you smell as you approach). A small museum on the station's ground floor explores a bit of Baltimore's public works and plumbing history (including some wooden pipes from the city's early years). There's a good, if small, display about public health engineer and Baltimore legend Abel "Reds" Wolman, the man who gave the city purified drinking water. Behind the building is an outdoor re-creation of a Baltimore intersection and the myriad of pipes that lurk beneath the streets and sidewalks, if you were wondering what was going on beneath those manhole covers.

FELL'S POINT VISITOR CENTER

1732 Thames St., 410/675-6751,
www.preservationsociety.com
HOURS: Sun.-Thurs. 10 A.M.-5 P.M., Fri.-Sat. 10 A.M.-8 P.M.
COST: Free

Tucked between the popular bars and boutiques on Thames Street (pronounced by lifelong Fell's Point residents not like the famous London river for which it's named, but with a soft "th" as in "thumb"), this onetime barn for horse-drawn trolleys now houses a well-stocked visitors center, where you can pick up abundant information about the historic waterfront

community. There's also an exhibit that explains the importance of the Baltimore clipper privateer ships during the War of 1812 (and the anger they incurred from the British Navy for their tactics and speed), as well as a collection of nautical artifacts and Baltimore-related souvenirs and gifts.

FREDERICK DOUGLASS-ISAAC MYERS MARITIME PARK

1417 Thames St., 410/685-0295,
www.douglassmyers.org
HOURS: Mon.-Fri. 10 A.M.-5 P.M., Sat.-Sun. 11 A.M.-6 P.M.
COST: $8 adult, $7 child, $7.50 senior

This mixture of old and new buildings was once home to the Chesapeake Marine Railway and Dry Dock Company, a business founded in 1868 by African Americans to provide shipwright services to the bustling port city of Baltimore. Frederick Douglass lived as a slave here in Fell's Point, right near where Isaac Myers helped start the company. Douglass learned about shipwright work, which he said helped him fake his way to escape and freedom in 1838, and he was an inspiration to Myers.

© GEOFF BROWN

The Frederick Douglass-Isaac Myers Maritime Park honors the early African American leader and businessman.

Today, this building houses a variety of small exhibits about life for African Americans in Fell's Point and the business Myers ran. Kids can try their hand at some of the jobs the workers here would have performed, including "caulking," in which (now simulated) tar-soaked rope was pounded into the slots between boat hull planks to make it watertight. The park is part of the Living Classrooms Foundation, which works with at-risk city youth to provide positive learning environments that include maritime activities and history.

ROBERT LONG HOUSE
812 S. Ann St., 410/675-6750,
www.preservationsociety.org
HOURS: Tours daily at 1:30 P.M.
COST: $1
The Robert Long House is the city's second oldest surviving home, a good-sized brick abode dating from 1765 (not that the house has

made it easy on those who tried to preserve it). Robert Long was a quartermaster for the fledging Colonial Navy, and he built this building to serve as both his office and his house. For the next two centuries, it managed to stand, if in serious disrepair, until 1969, when it was slated for demolition as part of a project to level much of Fell's Point for a highway. The Fell's Point Preservation Society saved the home in 1975, and began a lengthy restoration of the building and its outdoor spaces. The repairs and rebuilding was then destroyed in a serious fire in 1999, but a second restoration has once again re-created Long's colonial home. The well-lit rooms (the windows in this home are quite large) are filled with period furniture and tools of the quartermaster's trade; the gardens at the side of and behind the house are small but splendid, and many of the herbs grown there today are the same kinds Long and his family would have cultivated.

Little Italy   Map 2

JEWISH MUSEUM OF MARYLAND
15 Lloyd St., 410/732-6400, www.jhsm.org
HOURS: Tues.-Fri. and Sun. noon-4 P.M.
COST: $8 adult, $3 child, $4 student
The location of the Jewish Museum of Maryland—just north of Fell's Point—was set by the path taken by Jewish immigrants to Baltimore, and the path they took when they arrived here, in what was the nation's second-busiest immigration port (behind only Ellis Island). Most Jewish immigrants to Baltimore during the 19th century arrived at the docks of Fell's Point and Locust Point (near Fort McHenry), and headed north to the area of east Baltimore between Baltimore and Lombard Streets and east of Central Avenue. The third-oldest synagogue in the nation, on Lloyd Street, was built in 1845 (and is currently undergoing renovations). There were so many delicatessens that this part of town was known as "Corned Beef Row," though only a few delis now remain.

The main exhibit hall of the Jewish Museum

re-creates the thriving Jewish community that made its home in this part of the city—showing the inside of houses (and an outhouse), as well as shops, businesses, and even busy street vendors and grocers. There's a small deli exhibit as well, and the audio played in the ersatz eatery uses snippets of real dialogue from typical deli patron conversations. A second display space hosts temporary exhibits that cover a wide variety of scenes from the Jewish experience, from the great Jewish-owned department stores of the 20th century to displays of art examining feminist Judaism.

PHOENIX (OLD BALTIMORE) SHOT TOWER
801 E. Fayette St., 410/605-2964,
www.carrollmuseums.org
HOURS: Sat.-Sun. mornings, by appt. only
COST: $5 adult, $4 child
The tall, unusual brick spire that reaches more than 234 feet into the air at the intersection of

President and Fayette Streets, and dates from 1828, was an ingenious structure that was crucial to the U.S. military. It took more than one million bricks to build this tower, which is one of only a few left standing in America. So: What's a shot tower, you ask? Old rifles (and modern shotguns) fired not bullets but round, spherical projectiles called shot: To create shot, bright armorers realized they could drop hot lead from a great height through a special sieve and into cool water, creating nearly perfectly spherical shot. This tower produced shot for the U.S. military through the Civil War and into the late 1800s, and was declared a National Historic Landmark in 1972. Though the interior remains as it was back in the 19th century, the public is no longer allowed inside the tower, so it's more of a landmark worth recognizing during your travels than a destination.

© GEOFF BROWN

the stark design of the Reginald F. Lewis Museum of Maryland African American History & Culture

REGINALD F. LEWIS MUSEUM OF MARYLAND AFRICAN AMERICAN HISTORY & CULTURE

830 E. Pratt St., 443/263-1800, www.africanamericanculture.org
HOURS: Tues.-Sat. 10 A.M.-5 P.M., Sun. noon-5 P.M.
COST: $8 adult, $6 senior, free for children under age 6

Clad in deep black granite, and rising at one of the city's most historic intersections at a place where old Baltimore and new mingle together, this bold, monolithic museum examines the lives and history of the Maryland's African American population. It examines the separate and very unequal societies that segregation created, and it also shows how African Americans made their own thriving and vibrant communities and culture, and created their own joys and futures when equality was an impossible dream. The three permanent exhibits here—"Building Maryland, Building America," "Things Hold, Lines Connect," and "The Strength of the Mind"—reveal the lives of African Americans, from the days of slavery through the gradual gains made during the Civil Rights era.

There are great images and artifacts from the parallel communities and cultures that existed across Maryland, from waterfront resorts to radio stations to neighborhoods, all built

because of segregation, both legalized and cultural. Videos of Maryland African Americans play throughout the exhibits, and the commentaries and histories told by those people help bring much of the museum's written displays to life.

A broad, crimson steel wall arcs through the center of the entire building and even extends outside. This Red Wall of Freedom serves to show the interruptions to the continuity of the culture of African Americans, and the tension that still surrounds race relations in America. The museum is named for, and was created, thanks to the estate of the late Reginald Lewis, a Baltimore native and prominent lawyer and venture capitalist who built Beatrice PLC into a multibillion-dollar company.

STAR-SPANGLED BANNER FLAG HOUSE

844 E. Pratt St., 410/837-1793, www.flaghouse.org
HOURS: Tues.-Sat. 10 A.M.-4 P.M.
COST: $7 adult, $5 child, $6 senior

This national historic site is based around the

FOLLOW "THE STAR-SPANGLED BANNER"

Trace the path of the creation of our national anthem through the streets of Baltimore. The enormous 42-foot-long flag that inspired Francis Scott Key to write "The Star-Spangled Banner" was created in a small house at the corner of Pratt and Albemarle Streets in the Jonestown neighborhood of downtown Baltimore, just north of what is now Little Italy. Begin your tour here, and stroll through the rooms the flag occupied as Mary Pickersgill and three family members proudly stitched the 15-star flag from heavy wool and cotton. In 1813, it was delivered to the garrison at Fort McHenry, where it was flown daily – and during the entire 25-hour bombardment the invading

British fleet hurled at the undermanned fortress. It was this flag that Francis Scott Key saw fluttering high over the fort as the British fleet withdrew. The piece of paper Key used to write his poem "The Star-Spangled Banner" now resides at the Maryland Historical Society, though it's not on public display; a reproduction is on the first floor of the Society's museum.

The flag itself underwent a massive reconstruction starting in 1999; it's on display at the Smithsonian's National Museum of American History in Washington, D.C. – though pieces of the original flag are at the Flag House museum, located next to Mary Pickersgill's house.

small, tidy brick home on the corner of Pratt and Albemarle Streets that was the residence of Mary Pickersgill, a flag maker and seamstress of some renown. From a receipt found in the 1930s, we know that she was paid $574.44

when she delivered two flags for Baltimore's Fort McHenry in 1813. The larger flag was huge indeed, measuring 30 feet by 42 feet—the same size as the large, glass flag wall that lines one side of the museum—and it was this

© GEOFF BROWN

Mary Pickersgill sewed the flag that became the Star-Spangled Banner in this modest home.

banner, fluttering slowly above Fort McHenry during the 1814 British bombardment, that inspired Francis Scott Key to pen the song "The Star-Spangled Banner." The museum has some relics from the actual battle, including a fragment of the original flag (which now resides at the Smithsonian's National Museum of American History in Washington, D.C), and historic exhibits including an interactive kids' gallery, with 19th-century kid-sized costumes to wear. In the Pickersgill house, actors in period costumes portray family members and residents of the home, welcoming guests and answering questions. The best days to visit include Flag Day (June 14) and Defender's Day (Sept. 12), a Baltimore-specific holiday that celebrates the defeat of the land and sea British invasion in 1814.

Canton   Map 3

◖ PATTERSON PARK
Patterson Park and Eastern Aves., 410/276-3676,
www.pattersonpark.com
HOURS: Daily dawn-dusk
COST: Free

One of the city's oldest parks, the land now known as Patterson Park used to be a 200-acre estate (owned by William Patterson) that marked the far eastern edge of what was called Baltimore Town. During the War of 1812, while soldiers at nearby Fort McHenry were holding off a British invasion fleet, a second Redcoat force moved on land toward Baltimore from the east. When they reached Patterson Park, they found some 100 cannon and 20,000 soldiers waiting for them; at the sight of such a massive defense, the British withdrew. Today, the 155-acre park (which includes land east of Linwood Ave.) is a thriving center of activity for the surrounding residents, from life-long Baltimoreans who grew up around the park to newcomers like young professionals and Latino immigrants. There are walking and jogging paths throughout the hills, fields, and wooded areas of the park, a recently rebuilt boat lake (which isn't as big as that name implies), and plenty of great views of the city from the high ground at the north end of the park. There's also a public swimming pool, tennis courts, soccer fields, and a covered ice-skating rink. Patterson Park is host to variety of festivals, events, and sports leagues throughout the year.

The park's most notable feature is the pagoda, which is actually a Victorian design, not an Asian one. Completed in 1892, the 60-foot-tall observation tower (only open on Sundays noon–6 P.M. May–October) was completely restored in 2002 and offers spectacular panoramic views of Baltimore. It's also a popular meeting place and gathering spot for the park's many visitors.

S.S. *JOHN BROWN*
Pier 1, 2000 S. Clinton St., 410/558-0646,
www.liberty-ship.com
HOURS: Wed. and Sat. 9 A.M.-2 P.M.
COST: Free, donation appreciated

Baltimore played a pivotal role in the national war effort during World War II because of the mighty industrial production its factories and citizens could bring to bear for the United States. One of the city's greatest contributions were medium-sized cargo ships, built at the Bethlehem-Fairfield Shipyards, known as Liberty ships. These mass-produced ships (some 2,750 were built) ferried huge amounts of cargo across the Atlantic to England to help it hold out against Nazi Germany.

The S.S. *John Brown* is one of only two surviving examples of this type of ship; built in Baltimore, the *John Brown* is now preserved as a piece of living history by a group of former sailors and history buffs. Climb aboard to explore the huge grey vessel, starting with a small history exhibit that explains the war and the role of the Liberty ships. Then head deep into the heart of the ship, where you can see (and hear) the massive machinery that moved the *John Brown* across the Atlantic. The ship makes occasional Living History cruises around the Baltimore waterfront, and even makes the trip up the Patapsco from its home pier in Canton to the Inner Harbor for special events.

Federal Hill   Map 4

THE AMERICAN VISIONARY
ART MUSEUM

800 Key Hwy., 410/244-1900, www.avam.org
HOURS: Tues.-Sun. 10 A.M.-6 P.M.
COST: $12 adult, $8 child, $8 senior

Drive past the large, old brick buildings that rise on the south side of the Inner Harbor, where Key Highway makes a hard right turn, and you'll see, in bright neon colors, the words "O Say Can You See." Or maybe you'll notice the enormous, 60-foot-high patchwork whirligig twirling overhead. Or maybe you'll spy the tree hung with hundreds of glittering ornaments, or the glass mosaic egg, or…well, there are plenty of ways to be entranced by the amazing, extraordinary, and unpredictable American Visionary Art Museum. The brainchild of local arts and social activist Rebecca Hoffberger, AVAM opened in 1995, and celebrates astounding works of art made by people who are not traditionally trained artists. Inside, you'll find a rotating series of exhibits (found by ascending a long winding walkway) showcasing painting, sculpture, and other types of art, all made with intense passion and incredible dedication. The newer barn building, to the south, contains larger works, including a great tribute to John Waters film regular Divine. The gift shop, run by famed Chicago retailer Ted "Uncle Fun" Frankel, is also an unexpected treat: you'll find the store shelves and alcoves packed with weird souvenirs and original artwork.

© GEOFF BROWN

The American Visionary Art Museum celebrates the works of people who are not traditionally trained artists.

SIGHTS

BALTIMORE MUSEUM OF INDUSTRY

1415 Key Hwy., 410/727-4808, www.thebmi.org
HOURS: Tues.-Sat. 10 A.M.-4 P.M., Sun. 11 A.M.-4 P.M.
COST: $10 adult, $6 child, $6 senior

Baltimore is a city that was largely built on the strengths of its industrial base—and the backs and sweat of the citizens who worked in the shipyards, steel mills, factories, shops, and industrial plants that used to pack the city and its waterfront. Those industries have, more often than not, fallen silent or been rendered obsolete, but the Baltimore Museum of Industry preserves the power of that history. Some of America's greatest products—from Noxzema and Bromo Seltzer to gas lighting and aircraft innovations—were created, built, or perfected around Baltimore, and their stories are told here. Look for the enormous red crane out front as you head down Key Highway; it's a great place to stop, not just geographically, but culturally and historically, between a visit to Fort McHenry and the American Visionary Art Museum.

The first exhibits tell the story of Baltimore of the late 19th and early 20th centuries, with a re-created pharmacy, print shop, garment factory, and an original oyster cannery building. The large, waterfront Decker Gallery (named for one of the men who founded Black & Decker, the tool manufacturing giant based just north of the city) houses the

Baltimore's industrial heritage is on display at the Baltimore Museum of Industry.

COURTESY HARRY BLUM AND THE BALTIMORE MUSEUM OF INDUSTRY

museum's biggest items; just outside the window is the steam-powered tugboat *Baltimore,* built in 1906 and a stalwart of the once-thriving port that used to sprawl across this waterfront. Visual relics are a big part of the fun of this museum, from old painted metal signs to

A HIGHWAY DOESN'T RUN THROUGH IT: HOW FELL'S POINT AND FEDERAL HILL ESCAPED DESTRUCTION

As you stroll through the historic cobblestone streets and centuries-old row houses of Fell's Point and Federal Hill – two of Baltimore's greatest historic neighborhoods – imagine what would have happened if a plan to build a huge elevated highway right through the heart of downtown Baltimore had come to fruition. It was the mid-1960s, and ideas about progress and development didn't include urban renewal or historic neighborhoods – they were all about highways and suburbs, and a plan to run eight lanes of I-95 right through the middle of town seemed like a good idea, considering the state of downtown. Local residents of both Fell's Point and Federal Hill who didn't want to see the heart of Baltimore plowed under with concrete banded together to fight the federal and state highway planners. They eventually won and Fell's Point's and Federal Hill's historic row houses were spared – creating the thriving neighborhoods so many people now call home and allowing Harborplace to rise on the same ground once slated for highway pilings.

great glowing neon beacons for cars, insurance, and seafood.

◖ THE DOMINO SUGARS SIGN

1100 Key Hwy., 410/752-6150
HOURS: Call to schedule tour
COST: Free

The glowing red neon of this sugar processing plant's 120-foot-tall "Domino Sugars" sign has kept watch over Baltimore's harbor for more than 50 years. The plant offers a short tour, by appointment only, that demonstrates how the raw sugar that comes into the plant via barge and tanker is processed and leaves via Key Highway in the iconic five-pound bags of Domino Sugar. But to really get a great view of this Baltimore waterfront icon, take a nighttime stroll east along the Inner Harbor and into Fell's Point.

◖ FEDERAL HILL PARK

Battery Ave. and Key Hwy., 410/396-7900
HOURS: Daily dawn-dusk
COST: Free

There's no better place to get a great view of Baltimore's Inner Harbor—and the city itself—than from the top of Federal Hill. Rising up dramatically from the waterfront along the south side of the Inner Harbor, this grassy mound was originally mined for paint pigment in Colonial times, and still has some old tunnels within it that occasionally give way, leading to saggy hillsides and sunken footpaths. The hill has been a public park since the late 1700s, and was originally known as Signal Park, as observers could spot merchant and passenger ships on the Patapsco River as they approached the harbor. The park was renamed Federal Hill in 1789, after the news and celebration following the ratification of the U.S. Constitution (creating a "federal" government). Today, it's home to a park and a playground, and it's a great place for a scenic picnic that includes fresh food from nearby Cross Street Market. At the park's northern edge, several Civil War–era cannon are aimed right at downtown, symbolizing the weapons placed in a similar location by Union troops in 1861 to send a stern message to the Confederate-sympathizing residents of the city.

© GEOFF BROWN

The iconic Domino Sugars sign, near Federal Hill, is visible from everywhere in the Inner Harbor.

SIGHTS

Mount Vernon
Map 5

BALTIMORE STREETCAR MUSEUM

1901 Falls Rd., 410/547-0264,
www.baltimorestreetcar.org
HOURS: Sat.-Sun. noon-5 P.M.
COST: $7 adult, $5 child, $5 senior

The location of this great little museum—tucked on a small, winding back section of Falls Road, at the base of a cliff and next to I-83—speaks volumes about the current standing of streetcars in civic importance. But from the late 1800s to the 1940s, more than a thousand streetcars crisscrossed Baltimore, carrying people to work, play, shop, and see the city. This museum, entirely volunteer-operated, has several good displays of the evolution of the railcar from glorified horse-drawn carriage to fully electrified modern conveyance, and working models and dioramas of streetcars. The best part (particularly for kids), though, is the salvaged, repaired, and working streetcars that leave about every 30 minutes for a clackety trip down the tracks. The train conductors (and the rest of the staff) obviously love their hobby, and are thrilled to talk streetcars and Baltimore history with visitors. There's even a car barn down the tracks a bit that, if you ask nicely, they'll open up to reveal some of their works in progress (no kids allowed in there, alas—too unsafe).

(BASILICA OF THE ASSUMPTION

409 Cathedral St., 410/727-3565,
www.baltimorebasilica.org
HOURS: Mon.-Fri. 7 A.M.-4:30 P.M., Sat.-Sun.
7 A.M.-conclusion of 5:30 P.M. mass
COST: $2 donation requested for tour

Maryland was founded by Lord Baltimore as a place of religious tolerance, at least in terms of the 17th century; this meant that Catholics (like

The oldest Catholic cathedral in America is Baltimore's Basilica of the Assumption.

© GEOFF BROWN

HOLY BALTIMORE

Because Baltimore was founded by the Catholic Lord Baltimore (whose religion made him an unpopular person in his native Protestant England), the city has always been slightly more tolerant of different religions than other old East Coast metropolises. Fittingly, there are plenty of historically important houses of worship and sites with religious significance in the city.

In addition to the oldest cathedral in the nation, the **Basilica of the Assumption,** there's the **St. Jude Shrine** (512 W. Saratoga St., 410/685-6026), which is the nationwide center for devotions to St. Jude, the patron for "cases despaired of"; petitioners seeking solace from across the nation and globe travel to this building for prayers. The first Roman Catholic sisterhood of women of African decent in the world, the **Oblate Sisters of Providence,** was founded in Baltimore thanks to the work of Mother Mary Lange; they still operate from Baltimore today, though there is no formal museum to visit. Another site of interest to Catholics is the **Mother Seton House and Old St. Mary's Seminary** (600 N. Paca St., 410/523-3443), where Saint Elizabeth Ann Seton (the first U.S.-born saint) led her young charges and founded what became the American parochial school system.

Protestants have played a major role in the city's history as well, and four historic churches tell the tale of early Baltimore's rise in fortunes. Just east of Oriole Park at Camden Yards rises the **Old Otterbein United Methodist Church** (112 W. Conway St., 410/685-4703), completed in 1786 and the oldest extant church in Baltimore. The historic **Lovely Lane Museum and United Methodist Church** (2200 St. Paul St., 410/889-4458) is considered to be the mother church of American Methodism. In Mount Vernon, the grand, ancient-looking **Mount Vernon Place United Methodist Church** (10 E. Mount Vernon Pl., 410/685-5290) dates from only 1872, but appears to be centuries old. Nearby **Brown Memorial Presbyterian Church** (1316 Park Ave., 410/523-1542) in Bolton Hill boasts fantastic Gothic architecture and 11 stunning Louis Tiffany stained-glass windows.

Baltimore's Jewish population was once one of the largest on the East Coast, though many Jews moved out of the city during the prolonged turmoil and decay that marked the late 20th century. The third-oldest synagogue in America, the 1845 **Lloyd Street Synagogue** in East Baltimore, is currently undergoing a lengthy renovation that should return it to health, much like the surrounding neighborhood's recent renewal.

Lord Baltimore) were more welcome here than in other English colonies. Fittingly, Baltimore is the nation's oldest Catholic diocese, and the first Catholic cathedral in America was the Basilica of the Assumption, completed in 1821. (The official name of the cathedral is the Basilica of the National Shrine of the Assumption of the Blessed Virgin Mary.)

The imposing building was designed and brought to life by two men: John Carroll, the first American Catholic bishop (and a member of the storied Carroll family); and Benjamin Henry Latrobe, the architect of the Capitol in Washington, D.C. The two men wanted to create a uniquely American cathedral, one that spoke of a new American architecture combined with Rome's building codes—but a building that did not merely echo European designs. Latrobe's work on the Capitol gave him the experience and ideas that led to the Basilica's massive dome. The dome can be seen more clearly today than in recent decades, due to a massive, multimillion-dollar restoration, completed in 2006, that gave the building new life and vitality.

The sweeping skylights, domes, rosettes, and curves of the interior of the Basilica have a delicacy and stately nature that echoes that of the Capitol, but the architecture has a more sacred style—though it doesn't invoke the often ominous feel of European cathedrals. Tours include the main chapel and church, as well as the undercroft and crypt, where almost all of Baltimore's archbishops are laid to rest.

BROWN MEMORIAL PRESBYTERIAN CHURCH

1316 Park Ave., 410/523-1542,
www.browndowntown.org

HOURS: Daily 9 A.M.–6 P.M.

COST: Free

As the Basilica is the spiritual capital for Baltimore's Catholics, Brown Memorial is the pinnacle of hallowed ground for the city's Presbyterians. Built in 1870, and dedicated to George Brown, a founder of the Baltimore and Ohio Railroad, this Gothic Revival church rises about the stately row houses of Bolton Hill, long one of the city's most exclusive neighborhoods (though today, art students from the nearby Maryland Institute College of Art occupy many of the houses). The Gothic architecture gives the church a spectacular vaulted ceiling, painted a dark, royal purple; there's also a great 1930 pipe organ.

But the real reason to visit the church are the 11 recently restored Louis Tiffany stained-glass windows, some of which are nearly three stories tall and among the largest he ever created. Installed in 1905, each depicts a tale or re-creates a scene from the Bible; the craftsmanship and scale of the works still inspire and astound visitors and worshippers alike.

THE CONTEMPORARY MUSEUM

100 W. Centre St., 410/783-5720,
www.contemporary.org

HOURS: Wed.–Sun. noon–5 P.M.

COST: Suggested donation: $5 adult, $3 student

This is a museum where the unexpected is the norm—whether it's an exhibit about cell phones, an audio tour of the neighborhood that takes you out of the museum and onto the streets, or a series of Post-It notes. Video and audio art are often on display here, as are photographs and other types of re-purposed commercial media. There are three or four exhibitions each year, presented one at a time (this isn't the biggest space in town, though it's not small), and if you're interested in being challenged, this is one of the best places in Baltimore to experience the new.

The city's most elaborate and ornate downtown residence is the Garrett-Jacobs Mansion.

GARRETT-JACOBS MANSION

11 W. Mount Vernon Pl., 410/539-6914,
www.garrettjacobsmansion.org

HOURS: Tours Tues.–Sat. 1–4 P.M.

COST: $3

John Work Garrett was president of the mighty Baltimore and Ohio Railroad during the growth of the nation during the mid- and late 19th century; the echoes of his fortune and fancies are still visible throughout the city of Baltimore. And there's no relic grander then the stately Mount Vernon home he bought for his son Robert. Admittedly, it was only somewhat grand when it was bought, but by the time Robert's wife and widow Mary Garrett (who would remarry Dr. Henry Jacobs) was through acquiring three other adjoining homes, hiring John Edward Pope to rework the architecture, installing a massive Louis Tiffany stained-glass dome and windows, and turning most of the block into a sprawling 40-room mansion…well, by then, it was the finest home in all of Baltimore.

Today, this enormous residence is home to the Engineer's Club, a private members-only society. Guided tours are available, and they begin among the massive, elaborately carved pillars and sheets of dark mahogany in the home's entrance hall. Other cost-is-no-object details include gold bathroom fixtures, a feature of another Garrett residence, Evergreen, located just north of Loyola College in north Baltimore.

GEORGE PEABODY LIBRARY

21 E. Mount Vernon Pl., 410/659-8179, www.library.jhu
.edu/collections/specialcollections/rarebooks/peabody
HOURS: For viewing only, Tues.-Fri. 10-10:15 A.M. and
3-3:15 P.M., Sat. 10-10:15 A.M.
COST: Free

The towering stacks room of the George Peabody Library is one of Baltimore's most recognizable and treasured spaces. Five stories tall, and topped with a magnificent skylight, the library is home to 300,000 volumes covering history, architecture, and art, all tucked within soaring columns and ornate cast-iron balconies and a dramatic marble floor. The library's collection is part of Johns Hopkins University's special collections, and is located at the world-renowned Peabody Institute of Music, which means that the space hosts a variety of events, including lectures, concerts, and private affairs throughout the year. Note that this is a real, live working library, so there is limited time to view the room, and please be considerate of those doing research.

MARYLAND HISTORICAL SOCIETY

201 W. Monument St., 410/685-3750, www.mdhs.org
HOURS: Wed.-Sun. 10 A.M.-5 P.M.
COST: $4 adult, $3 child, $3 senior

Sprawling over two buildings (one new, one old), and home to a massive, seven-million-piece library that contains some amazing pieces of history (including "The Star-Spangled Banner" manuscript, as written by Francis Scott Key), the Maryland Historical Society is one of the city's hidden jewels. Start your tour with a look at the exhibit explaining the European settling of the Baltimore region, and explore the maritime history of Fell's Point and Baltimore (home to daring privateers the British regarded as little more than pirate scum).

Then head to the new building (it's the one topped by the statue of the dog Nipper, listening intently to a Victrola—a relic from a now-demolished RCA building) and its three stories of history; start on the first floor, which recounts the legacy of the region from Native American times to the present day. The exhibits don't flinch from the state's less admirable moments, including slavery and bigotry (even though the society's third president was Jewish).

There are some great items on display that cover the state's history, including an amazing shadowbox made using items from the horrific Civil War battle of Antietam, the 1763 contract that hired Mason and Dixon to survey the countryside, and a typewriter used by H. L. Mencken. Baltimore was once a renowned silverware city, and examples of intricate silversmith work occupy a landing between the two buildings.

The second floor houses an impressive portrait gallery, with much of it painted by a member of the vast Peale family of artists. The society's final gallery, on the third floor, is an amazing collection of Baltimore furniture from the past two centuries, including an assortment of Baltimore Painted Furniture from the 1800s.

© GEOFF BROWN

Follow Nipper to the Maryland Historical Society.

There's a semi-hidden wonder on this floor: By the elevators lurks an enormous, one-eighth-scale diorama of a fictitious 1930s-era circus called Bozo Brothers. There are more than 9,000 miniature people and animals in the work; its display here, among the fine oak and mahogany pianos, armchairs, and armoires, is a much-appreciated peculiarity that suits the character of Baltimore well.

◖ WALTERS ART MUSEUM

600 N. Charles St., 410/547-9000, www.thewalters.org
HOURS: Wed.-Sun. 10 A.M.-5 P.M.
COST: Free

Think what you will about the ruthless American industrialists of the 19th century: They certainly knew how to leave a legacy. William Thompson Walters, a native of Pennsylvania who moved to Baltimore and made a fortune in wholesale liquor before the Civil War (and, post-war, another fortune in banking and railroads), moved to a grand home in exclusive Mount Vernon Place in 1858 and set about collecting paintings, sculptures, and antiquities. By the mid-1870s, Walters was allowing the public into his home to see his collection (for a fee—donated to charity, of course), which was an impressive trove of European and Asian artworks. His son, Henry Walters, helped in the acquisition of items, and expanded the breadth of the collection into new areas. His biggest score was the 1902 purchase (for $1 million) of the entire contents of a palazzo in Rome, including works by greats like El Greco, and seven astounding sarcophagi that are some of the museum's most amazing pieces.

Henry Walters left his incomparable collection to the city of Baltimore, and new construction and the donation of an adjoining mansion (Hackerman House) have made the Walters Art Museum one of the nation's finest small museums. It's rare to find such a incredibly deep and impressive collection from so many different cultures, epochs, and media in one place. The Walters amazes with every exhibit, and never lets up throughout the various buildings' multiple levels and passageways. Egyptian mummies and burial items are just down the hall from medieval European reliquaries; rows of Asian jade sculptures line the walls of Hackerman House, while the Chamber of Wonders in the

the Chamber of Wonders at the Walters Art Museum

BARGAIN BALTIMORE: SIGHTSEEING

The two biggest and best museums of art in Baltimore – the **Baltimore Museum of Art** and the **Walters Art Museum** – waived their entrance fees in 2007. That's an entire day's worth of world-class antiquities and art, for nada.

You can stroll along the city's **waterfront promenade,** taking in the views of a historic waterfront city during the seven-mile walk. Take Baltimore's 3.2-mile **Heritage Walk** by yourself all around downtown, stopping at 20 sights (some of which are far from the rejuvenated Inner Harbor), or just do half of it with a free guide, starting at the Inner Harbor. Stroll the paths and grounds around **Fort McHenry National Monument** for free, and imagine the sight of an invading British fleet coming straight at the fort.

For really great vistas (and photo opportunities), buy an all-day pass ($9) for the **Water Taxi.** It runs all across the Inner Harbor and out to Fort McHenry, and 15 other stops all across the harbor.

The **National Aquarium in Baltimore** offers $8 adult admission on Fridays after 5 P.M. during the fall and winter. Fans of flora can visit the **Howard P. Rawlings Conservatory** in Druid Hill

Park for a mere $2 suggested donation. On Friday nights, you can view the heavens through the telescopes at the Crosby Ramsey Observatory at the **Maryland Science Center** for free.

COURTESY BALTIMORE AREA CONVENTION AND VISITORS ASSOCIATION

at the National Aquarium in Baltimore

original building re-creates a 17th-century nobleman's room of exotic animals, natural wonders, and heavenly observations. Tourists may often skip the Walters in favor of the bigger Baltimore Museum of Art, but the museums' collections complement one another, and the Walters should be considered a mandatory destination. Best of all, admission is free.

THE WASHINGTON MONUMENT

600 N. Charles St., 410/396-0929
HOURS: Tues.-Fri. 10 A.M.-5 P.M., Sat.-Sun. noon-4 P.M.
COST: $1

The first city to begin construction of a monument honoring the father of the United States was Baltimore; the 178-foot-high column and statue of a mounted George Washington now watches over Mount Vernon Place. Completed in 1829, this was the first real tribute to

Washington that was built in the country, and it was designed by Robert Mills, the same man who would construct the enormous 555-foot-high obelisk dedicated to Washington in the capital city that bears his name. In the base of the monument is a small museum chronicling Washington's achievements, but the real thrill comes during the climb to the summit. There are 228 narrow stone stairs that wind up a cramped passageway to almost the top of the column, and vantage point at the top offers great views of historic Mount Vernon and the rest of central Baltimore. In a typically wonderful and quirky Baltimore tradition that began around 1971, colored holiday lights are strung from the monument in early December, and there's a well-attended lighting ceremony (complete with fireworks) to help mark the beginning of the winter holiday season.

AMARANTHINE MUSEUM

2010 Clipper Park Rd., 410/523-2574,
www.amaranthinemuseum.com
HOURS: Sat.-Sun. 3-5 P.M., weekdays by appt.
COST: $5

This is a museum in the way the encyclopedia is a book; the answer to "What's it about?" is "everything." A series of rooms, passages, and chambers, the Labyrinth at the Amaranthine (the word means eternally beautiful), created by the late Les Harris, charts "the history of art and the creative process in civilization, interpreted in inspired form by one of the foremost artists of our day," as the museum's website puts it. The best way to enter this museum is with no preconceptions; just go inside and begin the experience. This is a great companion visit to the American Visionary Art Museum because it encompasses Harris's vast vision, though he was a traditionally trained artist.

BALTIMORE MUSEUM OF ART

10 Art Museum Dr., 443/573-1700, www.artbma.org
HOURS: Wed.-Fri. 11 A.M.-5 P.M.,
Sat.-Sun. 11 A.M.-6 P.M.
COST: Free

One of the city's two great museums (along with Mount Vernon's Walters Art Museum), the Baltimore Museum of Art (BMA) has a world-class holding of works from across the globe and the centuries. Founded in 1914, the museum's grand, classical main building (designed by John Russell Pope) was opened in 1929, though entry today is gained through a modern, modest building to the right of this structure.

The BMA's treasures include masterpieces from a wide variety of eras and cultures, but its greatest asset is the legendary **Cone Collection,** donated by Baltimore sisters Claribel and Etta Cone upon Etta's death in 1949 (Claribel had passed away in 1929). Fueled by the profitable

© GEOFF BROWN

See the fantastic Cone Collection and modern masterpieces for free at the Baltimore Museum of Art.

TWO TO CHEW ON: OFF-THE-BEATEN-PATH MUSEUMS

In addition to the heavies of the Baltimore museum world – grand institutions like the Baltimore Museum of Art, the Walters Art Museum, and the American Visionary Art Museum – there are a good variety of quality smaller museums that focus on everything from bold new modern art to streetcars to dentistry. If your schedule permits it, it's well worth the time to seek out some of these sights, as their size and the lack of crowds means you'll get a much more personal experience, whether it's on a guided tour or by speaking with a docent or staffer.

There are a couple of smaller museums that stand out as being particularly visit-worthy. First is the late artist/thinker/genius Les Harris's **Amaranthine Museum,** which is about as fascinating a look at mankind's voyages and thoughts about art through the ages as you'll find. And the **Dr. Samuel D. Harris National Museum of Dentistry** is a surprisingly intriguing (no, really) look at how people have viewed their teeth and the practice of maintaining them.

Cone textile business, the sisters personally amassed an astonishing body of works from renowned artists (and, more often than not, close friends of the Cones) including Cézanne, Gauguin, Matisse, Picasso, and van Gogh. The sisters collected some 3,000 works of art in their lives, including more than 500 works by Matisse alone; the collection is regarded as one of the most comprehensive samplings of post-Impressionism in existence. Visitors can even take a virtual tour of the Cone sisters' massive, adjoining apartments and see how the artworks were displayed in their homes.

The BMA added a contemporary art wing in 1994, and it houses an impressive array of works from artists like Andy Warhol, Jasper Johns, Jackson Pollock, and Baltimore native

Grace Hartigan. European, African, Pacific, and American artists are also well represented in the museum's halls. Outside the museum are the Sculpture Gardens, which include works from Auguste Rodin and Alexander Calder (the view of the gardens from the patio of the BMA's restaurant, Gertrude's, is a local favorite). The museum also boasts the Antioch Mosaics, a large collection of early A.D. tile works from what is today Turkey.

The BMA and the Walters Art Museum share another distinction: Both institutions have waived their entry fees (though special shows may still require a ticket purchase).

HOMEWOOD HOUSE
3400 N. Charles St., 410/516-5589, www.museums.jhu.edu/homewood
HOURS: Tues.-Fri. 11 A.M.-4 P.M., Sat.-Sun. noon-4 P.M.
COST: $6 adult, $3 child, $5 senior

Homewood House is one of the rare surviving examples of what were once country homes for Baltimore's wealthy Colonial-era residents. Charles Carroll, who had signed the Declaration of Independence, gave $10,000 to his son Charles Jr. in 1801 for the construction of a summer home on 130 acres north of Baltimore City. That home—called Homewood House, and finished at a final cost of more than $40,000—sits today on the eastern edge of the campus of Johns Hopkins University. It's a magnificent example of Federal architecture that inspired copies and reproductions across the nation; the details of construction are revealed in the angry letters Charles Sr. wrote his son as the costs spiraled with every material and design upgrade Charles Jr. insisted upon. Homewood House today is no drab historical drag; it's a riot of well-researched and proper colors, patterns, and furniture that makes the home feel lived-in and accessible. The floor is covered with varnished, painted sailcloth designed to resemble a marble floor (the sailcloth was made in Hampden's Clipper Mill, which supplied sails to many of fledgling America's sailing vessels). Some of Charles Jr.'s personal effects are still here, as is much of the home's original furniture.

SIGHTS

HOWARD P. RAWLINGS CONSERVATORY AND BOTANIC GARDENS OF BALTIMORE

3100 Swan Dr., Druid Hill Park, 410/396-0180

HOURS: Tues.-Sun. 10 A.M.-4 P.M.

COST: Free

Located in Druid Hill Park, this is the last remaining example of Baltimore's public conservatories, which once adorned many of the city's parks. The historic, Victorian-era complex includes two buildings from 1888 (the Palm House and the Orchid Room), as well as three newer buildings from the 20th century. Each of the five buildings is home to a distinct type of flora, representing five different climate types (Mediterranean, tropical, and desert join the palms and orchids of the original structures). There are also abundant outdoor gardens perfect for spring strolls, and several flower shows are held throughout the year. The five-story Palm House is the centerpiece of the conservatory; huge palm trees fill the grand and graceful glass dome, designed by the same architect who designed City Hall.

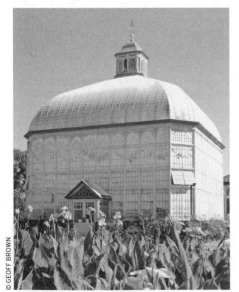

© GEOFF BROWN

the Palm House at the Rawlings Conservatory in Druid Hill Park

LACROSSE MUSEUM & NATIONAL HALL OF FAME

113 W. University Pkwy., 410/235-6882, www.uslacrosse.org/museum

HOURS: June-Jan. Mon.-Fri. 10 A.M.-3 P.M.; Feb.-May Tues.-Sat. 10 A.M.-3 P.M.

COST: $3 adult, $2 child, free for children under age 5

Invented by Native North Americans as a combination sport/festival/warrior basic training regime (and called "baggataway" by the Iroquois, one of the dozens of tribes that played the sport), the modern game of lacrosse is Maryland's official team sport—and Baltimore has produced some of lacrosse's greatest players and teams. Popular throughout the Northeast for more than a century (official rules were adopted right after the end of the Civil War), the sport has grown across the country in the past decades, and is a staple of prep school and Eastern college athletics. The museum traces the game from its role in Native American society (including the Ottawa/Ojibwe tribe's use of a game of lacrosse to distract British soldiers during a 1763 assault on Fort Michilimackinac, in what is now Michigan) to its popularity today. Photos, videos, and the evolution of the lacrosse stick from a well-bent branch into a specialized, carbon-fiber, goal-scoring tool help document the game's growth. The sport's national hall of fame is also here, showcasing the greatest men and women to ever play what is known as "the fastest game on two feet."

MARYLAND ZOO IN BALTIMORE

Druid Hill Park, 410/366-5466, www.marylandzoo.org

HOURS: Daily 10 A.M.-4 P.M.

COST: $11 adult, $9 child, $10 senior

Located within one of the city's largest parks (Druid Hill Park, to the west of Hampden), the Maryland Zoo in Baltimore was created by the state legislature back in 1876, and is America's third-oldest zoo. The facility is in the middle of a major renovation, which means that some animals (like the reptiles) had to be given to other zoos; the newly refurbished sections that have re-opened have been a hit with visitors. Recently, most of the attention has gone to the African Journey exhibit, which welcomed a new member to its herd in 2008: Samson, an African elephant, and the zoo's first elephant birth (weighing in at a svelte 285 pounds).

A list of the most popular attractions and habitats should start with the Polar Bear Watch, where visitors take in the watery residence of bears Magnet and Alaska from an arctic-style buggy. Guests can also take a camel ride, tote their little ones to the Maryland Wilderness and Children's Zoo (where they can pet African pygmy and Nubian goats), or listen to a zookeeper discuss the details of one of the zoo's more than 1,500 inhabitants. There's even an overnight family campout in the spring, complete with campfire and nighttime exploration of the park.

Some insider tips: As the zoo covers more than 160 acres of "natural" environments, full of water and animals, it's a good idea to wear bug repellent if you're visiting during Baltimore's warmer, more humid months (May–Sept.). And the African black-footed penguin exhibit (at Rock Island) is best seen in the early morning, when the animals awake for breakfast.

Greater Baltimore   Map 7

B&O RAILROAD MUSEUM

901 W. Pratt St., 410/752-2490, www.borail.org
HOURS: Mon.-Sat. 10 A.M.-4 P.M., Sun. 11 A.M.-4 P.M.
COST: $14 adult, $8 child, $12 senior

Historians make a pretty good case that railroads helped build America—and the birthplace of American railroading was in 1828, on Baltimore's Pratt Street, with the creation of the Baltimore & Ohio Railroad. This facility was first known as the Mt. Clare Shops, and was a huge repair and maintenance center too, taking up some 100 acres. Now, though many of the original buildings remain, the museum is surrounded by row houses, but they're still in the shadow of the 123-foot-high roundhouse that is the centerpiece of the museum. Originally

heavy metal on the rails at the B&O Railroad Museum

SIGHTS

BALTIMORE LEADS THE WAY

Many cities can lay claim to notable innovations and inventions, but Baltimore's residents have been providing North America with a long and impressive list of firsts since before the formation of the United States. The Ouija board was created here in 1892, as was saccharine, the American Humane Society, and the world's first telegraph line, which ran from Baltimore to Washington, D.C. Many of the medical procedures used around the world today were developed by pioneering surgeons and physicians at Johns Hopkins Hospital. Here are just a few of the other pioneering people, moments, and ideas from Baltimore's history:

FIRST STAGECOACH ROUTE – 1773
This horse-drawn carriage service connected Baltimore to Philadelphia (some 90 miles north) across a series of rough, dangerous, unimproved roads.

FIRST CITY TO USE HYDROGEN GAS FOR STREETLIGHTS – 1816
Sure, hydrogen is kind of dangerous, but it beat the old oil-filled lamps and helped Baltimore maintain its role as a sophisticated, advanced city.

FIRST AMERICAN UMBRELLA FACTORY – 1828
Though the first person to come into Baltimore carrying an open umbrella was attacked for being strange, the rain- and sun-deflecting device was soon embraced by Americans.

FIRST COMMERCIAL AND PASSENGER RAILROAD – 1828
The debut of the Baltimore and Ohio (B&O) Railroad was the critical step in the growth of a still-young America; the quick, reliable routes to and from points west led to a huge growth in industry and commerce.

FIRST ICE-CREAM FREEZER – 1848
Ice cream had been around for centuries, but it had to be eaten almost immediately after its creation or stored near blocks of ice; a Baltimore man patented a powerful electrically powered cooling device and compartment that could keep ice cream frozen indefinitely.

FIRST AFRICAN AMERICAN ON THE SUPREME COURT – 1967
Supreme Court Justice (and native Baltimorean) Thurgood Marshall's landmark decision and opinion in the 1954 *Brown v. Board of Education* case led to the gradual dismantling of legal segregation in the United States.

built in 1872, the structure served as an enormous turn-around point (a gigantic turntable was used) for steam locomotives and other rail cars. Partially destroyed in 2003 by a huge blizzard, the now-restored roundhouse holds many of the historic train cars in the museum's collection, covering the growth of railroads from a small transportation option into a continental industrial behemoth. There's a short, 20-minute train ride on the same rail line first laid down nearly 200 years ago; the ride takes visitors past some of the outlying buildings still used to repair cars, as well as some of the decaying structures used in the past (and some of

Baltimore's less-than-thriving neighborhoods). There are some impressive model train set-ups outside the roundhouse, and plenty of rolling stock everywhere on the grounds—even in the parking lot—to impress kids of all ages.

EDGAR ALLAN POE HOUSE & MUSEUM
203 N. Amity St., 410/396-7932,
www.ci.baltimore.md.us/government/historic/
poehouse.php
HOURS: Wed.-Sun. 9 A.M.-5 P.M.
COST: $3 adults, children free
The neighborhood around the modest brick home here on Amity Street hasn't seen a lot of

amity lately, but inside the house—in which Poe lived from 1833 to 1835—visitors can learn about Edgar Allan Poe's brief life in Baltimore (he died here long after he had lived here, perishing in 1849 while passing through the city, and is buried at downtown's Westminster Hall). He lived here with his grandmother, his aunt, and his cousin Virginia (who, somewhat ickily, would go on to become Mrs. Poe), and it was while living here that Poe began to enjoy some success from the stories he wrote. The home is decorated and furnished as it would have been during the time Poe lived here, and a few of Poe's belongings, like a travel desk and telescope, are here, as are images of Poe and some of the 1884 illustrations for "The Raven." The house today shares the block (which is little more than an alley street) with a large public housing development named for Poe; the immediate area is not recommended for sightseeing, but visitors to the site should have no problems.

EVERGREEN

4545 N. Charles St., 410/516-0341, www.museums.jhu.edu/evergreen
HOURS: Tues.-Fri. 11 A.M.-4 P.M., Sat.-Sun. noon-4 P.M.
COST: $6 adult, $3 child, $5 senior

Unlike Homewood House and Mount Clare Mansion, two surviving examples of early Baltimore summer estates, the vast, stunning home called Evergreen wasn't a warm-weather escape; it was a full-time residence. Bought by Baltimore & Ohio Railroad tycoon John W. Garrett (whose father had bought him the Garrett-Jacobs Mansion in Mount Vernon) in 1878 for his son T. Harrison Garrett, Evergreen was once a meager 12-room home; by the time it was given to Johns Hopkins University in 1942, it tallied some 48 rooms. It's a Gilded Age residence, built in 1857 and today perhaps the finest free-standing historic home in Baltimore City. Upon Robert's death, the house transferred to Robert's son John Work Garrett and his wife Alice, who were patrons of the arts and letters, and the home grew to house their collections and reflect their areas of interest. Paintings by Modigliani,

Picasso, and Degas hang in the long living room; Louis Tiffany lamps and chandeliers abound; and one of the home's five libraries has murals that were painted on-site by Jose Miguel Covarrubias at the Garrett's request. The Victorian-era custom of displaying one's wealth is well represented here, most notably in the bathroom with the 24K gold-leafed toilet. But the Garretts were far more interested in knowledge, learning, and appreciating works of art; a gymnasium was converted into a small theater by Leon Bakst. Leave plenty of time to explore and learn about this amazing house, located just north of the Loyola University campus in North Baltimore—it's another hidden treasure that rewards visitors with its unexpected splendor.

FORT McHENRY NATIONAL MONUMENT AND HISTORIC SHRINE

2400 E. Fort Ave., 410/962-4290, www.nps.gov/fomc
HOURS: Daily 8 A.M.-5 P.M.
COST: $7 adult, children free

In 1814, star-shaped Fort McHenry was the lynchpin in the defense of the city of Baltimore during the War of 1812. The fort was squarely in the sights of the invading British army that had just burned Washington, D.C. to the ground; a fleet of warships was bound and determined to pass the fort and attack Baltimore, while a second prong of attack—an army of British soldiers—marched into the city from the east. The British bombardment was massive, yet the defenders—numbering only 60 men—managed to hold off the Brits after an evening of relentless fire. When the smoke cleared and the dawn came, the enormous American flag sewn by Baltimorean Mary Pickersgill languidly flapped above the fort, letting a prisoner in one of the British vessels—Francis Scott Key—know that Fort McHenry remained in American hands. The invasion failed; Key was released; and the verses he had written after realizing the battle's outcome would (eventually) become "The Star-Spangled Banner," the national anthem.

Start the tour with the obligatory, aged informational film (starring an actor in period

© GEOFF BROWN

o'er the ramparts at Fort McHenry, due east of Federal Hill

attire playing a barely important character from the War of 1812) in the fort's visitors center: the only reason to endure the film is for what happens at the end, which is a manipulative but effective theatrical tool that cannot be revealed. Suffice to say, it will stir whatever patriotism lives within you.

Then head down the walkway to the fort itself, which is the only site in the United States designated as both a National Monument and a Historic Shrine. You can tour the bastions and barracks, which remain mostly as they were back in 1814, and see the powder magazine that was struck by a British shell during the bombardment—but did not explode, which would have probably turned the tide of the battle against the American defenders. The surrounding waterfront park and trail is popular with locals for running and picnicking, and a stroll around the grounds gives a great view of Canton's working waterfront and the Francis Scott Key Bridge in the distance.

MOUNT CLARE MANSION

1500 Washington Blvd., 410/837-3262,
www.mountclare.org

HOURS: Tours Tues.-Sat. 10 A.M.-4 P.M.

COST: $6 adult, $4 child, $5 senior

It's hard to envision, but in the mid-18th century, much of Baltimore was still rolling countryside and woods. Many wealthy European settlers built grand summer homes far from the small downtown (which could get oppressively hot and smelly during summers). Charles Carroll, a prominent lawyer (but not the Charles Carroll who signed the Declaration of Independence), built Mount Clare at the center of Georgia, his 800-acre plantation west of the growing city of Baltimore. Completed in 1760, this grand Colonial house would be home to Carroll and his wife, Margaret Tilghman Carroll; they hosted Martha Washington and the Marquis de Lafayette.

Today, Mount Clare is the city's oldest surviving house from this time period. Though much of it has been lost to the centuries, the central part of the home remains in amazingly undamaged condition. Paintings of Charles and Margaret by the famed painter Charles Wilson Peale hang in the vast living room, and the period furniture on display shows off some amazing craftsmanship. The Carrolls were one of early Maryland's most successful and prolific families, and about half of the period furniture in the house belonged either to Charles Carroll or a relative. The mansion occupies just over two acres in Carroll Park, which is now one of Baltimore's grittier neighborhoods, but don't let that keep you from visiting a truly remarkable piece of Colonial Baltimore history.

◖ NATIONAL GREAT BLACKS IN WAX MUSEUM

1601-03 E. North Ave., 410/563-3404, www.ngbiwm.com

HOURS: Tues.-Sat. 9 A.M.-6 P.M., Sun. noon-6 P.M.

COST: $12 adult, $10 child, $11 senior

Opened in 1983, this amazing, unique, and powerful museum—built and guided by the vision of the late Dr. Elmer Martin and his wife, Dr. Joanne Martin—chronicles the indignities, tragedies, successes, and triumphs of Africans in America. It's also a very disturbing place if you're not ready for the incredibly graphic scenes of the slave trade (the Middle Passage) and violence against African Americans depicted in certain parts of the museum: Be warned, these are not for young children or those with delicate sensibilities. The majority of the museum charts the course of African Americans in the United States from their African heritage to the present day, using wax figures and mannequins to depict leaders, innovators, and common Americans throughout the centuries. The museum covers major events and movements in African American culture and history, as well as showing scenes from the lives of regular African Americans, from sharecroppers to a grim urban scene of crime and violence. One of the museum's most-cited exhibits explains the story of Henry "Box" Brown, who mailed himself to freedom in a packing crate sent from the slave state of Virginia to free Pennsylvania in 1848; his escape is re-created here.

This museum is a labor of love and duty to history, and is not the beneficiary of a huge endowment; the wax figures, displays, and scholarship are not slick nor seamless. But there's no other museum in America like this astonishing tribute and memorial to the struggles and achievements of African Americans, and though it's located far from the gleaming Inner Harbor, it's worth a visit for those who want to see how many African Americans view their role in American history.

RESTAURANTS

Baltimore's culinary scene has really flourished in the past decade, and while the city may still reside in the not-quite-top tier of great American dining cities, it now stands much higher on that list than in years past. There are a handful of smart, talented, and canny chefs doing great work in Baltimore, experimenting and reaching for new heights—while listening to the city's admittedly fickle dining public.

For too long, Baltimore's restaurants reflected the city's staid, traditional character a bit too well. Yet the city's dedication to the tried-and-true did have one delicious result: There are a plethora of diners and old-fashioned restaurants in Baltimore where you can sample some menu items that haven't changed in more than five decades. This is the city

made famous by a movie called *Diner,* after all—there are a lot of great, unique, family-run places to grab a club sandwich or tuna melt (and you should always order fries, and get gravy on them if possible).

Alongside these beloved 24-hour joints and diners, gourmets today have a veritable cornucopia of new, intriguing restaurants from which to chose. Some are sleek new cathedrals to the modern art of food preparation and dining habits, while others are rehabbed row houses and old industrial buildings that re-examine classic meals. Several Baltimore restaurateurs and chefs have really hit their stride, and the hungry diners of Charm City have responded enthusiastically by embracing a lot of newer, more modern culinary options.

Still, if there's one food that defines the

COURTESY CHRIS HARTLOVE AND WOODBERRY KITCHEN

HIGHLIGHTS

LOOK FOR **(** TO FIND
RECOMMENDED RESTAURANTS.

(**Best Breakfast:** Baltimoreans don't like waiting for tables unless the food is brilliant; hence, the long weekend lines outside Fell's Point's petite **Blue Moon Café** are a sure sign that the hearty, homemade breakfasts inside are worth the wait (page 64).

(**Best Bar That's Also a Great Restaurant:** If you're the kind of diner who loves great, unpretentious food, a smashing wine selection, old-time American music, and a happily incongruous crowd, head to Fell's Point's cozy **Peter's Inn** (page 66).

(**Best Burgers:** They're tiny, and technically only an appetizer, but the sliders at Fell's Point's **Salt** pack a serious wallop of flavor. That's because they're made of Kobe beef and topped with foie gras, red onion marmalade, and truffle aioli (page 67).

(**Best Scene: Pazo,** an immaculately designed and executed, vaguely Mediterranean-meets-the-Casbah-themed tapas restaurant and lounge has transformed an old machine shop in Fell's Point (page 70).

(**Best Upscale Italian in Little Italy:** For some of the most indulgent takes on popular Southern Italian dishes, head to **Aldo's,** where chef Aldo Vitale has stocked a fantastic wine cellar to match his culinary creations (page 73).

(**Best Crab House View:** During spring and summer, call ahead early to reserve a table on the west side of the outdoor crab deck at Canton's **Bo Brooks,** where you can look toward the Inner Harbor and watch the pleasure boats coming in for the night (page 76).

(**Best Oysters:** In a town known for crab cakes, getting a good oyster isn't always easy. **Mama's on the Half Shell,** a Canton favorite, dishes them up in many styles, all delicious (page 77).

(**Best Old-School Baltimore Restaurant:** Think of **The Prime Rib** as a downtown, steak-powered time machine: The tuxedoed waiters, leather and cheetah-print decor, and smooth piano player will whisk you back to 1970s-era Charm City (page 84).

(**Best Restaurant Worth Searching For:** Though located in a somewhat off-the-beaten-path location (an old mill center near Hampden), **Woodberry Kitchen** has earned a coterie of feverishly loyal regulars who adore the locally sourced meals, prepared simply but with finesse (page 93).

(**Best Weekend Brunch:** It's not just the care with which everything is made at Hampden's **Golden West Café,** it's that you can get everything from whole-wheat chocolate chip pancakes to *chilaquiles* (tortilla chips with eggs, cheese, and chile sauce) to wild mushroom and Madeira omelettes (page 94).

Mama's on the Half Shell

© GEOFF BROWN

RESTAURANTS

RESTAURANTS

city of Baltimore, it's crabs. You can eat them many ways, but four are the most popular: steamed whole in the shell, which makes for a wonderful social meal; soft shell–style; in crab soup; or served as crab cakes (lump crab meat, seasoned and placed into a patty or ball, and either broiled or fried). These crustaceans are the city's specialty, and though they once came from the bountiful Chesapeake Bay, most of the crab you'll eat in Baltimore is now imported from the Gulf of Mexico or the Far East. If you want to get locals arguing, ask three strangers which restaurant has the best steamed crabs or the best crab cakes: Everyone has their own personal favorite, the

more obscure the better. But you'll want to explore the city's menus on your own, eating your way to your own decision, because it's almost impossible to find a reputable restaurant in town that doesn't offer at least a decent crab cake.

PRICE KEY

- **$** Entrées less than $10
- **$$** Entrées $10-20
- **$$$** Entrées more than $20

Downtown and Inner Harbor   Map 1

AMERICAN
BURKE'S CAFÉ $$
36 Light St., 410/752-4189, www.burkescafe.com
HOURS: Daily 7 A.M.-2 A.M.

Just a block from the Inner Harbor sits Burke's Café, a 1970s-era throwback that still clings to the windowless, dark, medieval design school that was so popular at the time (the place originally opened back in 1934). Miniature barrels and pewter mugs decorate the walls, and the wooden beams and brickwork give the place a decidedly Tower of London feel. The menu is also a throwback, featuring lots of heavy entrées (like meatloaf) and gravies, along with items like grilled hot dogs and salami, onions, and cheese (and that's on the light fare menu). The surprising thing is, the food's not too bad (come for breakfast if you're staying downtown), and their enormous onion rings are a minor city legend. If you like quirky, real-life-Baltimore scenes, there are plenty here.

WERNER'S RESTAURANT $
231 E. Redwood St., 410/752-3335,
www.burkescafe.com
HOURS: Mon.-Fri. 6 A.M.-2 P.M.

Werner's Restaurant is a still-busy Baltimore landmark on a one-way street in the city's

small financial district. The booths and tables and decor (and, frankly, some of the staff) haven't changed in decades, and neither has the menu. This is what restaurants were like back in the 1960s, so stick with basics like tuna salad sandwiches and cheeseburgers. You'll notice a lot of suits and backslapping here—it's a favorite breakfast and lunch spot (no dinner is served) for denizens of City Hall and the surrounding banks. Note that it's only open on weekdays.

ASIAN
BAN THAI $$
340 N. Charles St., 410/727-7971, www.banthai.us
HOURS: Mon.-Sat. 11 A.M.-10 P.M.

This unassuming Thai restaurant is a little gem in a part of town that's dominated at night by empty office towers and a nearby Irish pub. Walk up the long ramp to the dining room, past the portraits of Thailand's royal family, and try to get a seat near the window to watch people heading up Charles Street. The food here is quite good (and can be ordered quite spicy), from the basics like pad Thai to crispy whole fish and soft-shell crabs. There are also a dozen entrées for vegetarians, though some contain fish sauces.

BREWPUB
THE WHARF RAT 😊😊
206 W. Pratt St., 410/244-8900,
www.thewharfrat.com

HOURS: Daily 11:30 P.M.-2 A.M.

Just a block from Oriole Park at Camden Yards, this outpost of the legendary Wharf Rat (the original is a dark, cozy pub in Fell's Point) is a solid place to eat and drink, rather than just a place to hoist a few ales. It's tucked into a brick building that somehow escaped the wrecking balls that claimed much of the old downtown. The menu leans toward English pub favorites, as well as some more refined options like non-battered seafood and salads. Interested in trying their made-on-site Oliver ales? There's a great tasting feature at either location (except during Orioles games, at the Pratt Street shop): the "3 beers for 4 bucks" plan, where you choose different varieties of Oliver ales, served up in 10-ounce mugs.

CRAB HOUSE
PHILLIPS HARBORPLACE 😊😊😊
Light Street Pavilion, 301 Light St., 410/685-6600,
www.phillipsseafood.com

HOURS: Daily 11 A.M.-10 P.M.

The Phillips name is synonymous with crabs in Maryland; from a single crab house on the shore, the family has built what is today a veritable mini-empire on the backs of the Chesapeake Bay's delicious crustaceans. They've got a prime location in the Light Street Pavilion in Harborplace, with lots of window tables overlooking the harbor, as well as plentiful outdoor seating during the warmer months. The friendly servers will help explain how to eat crabs, if you're a neophyte, but there are plenty of more conventional seafood (and meat, and even vegetarian) options on the menu. This is a big, high-volume place, designed to accommodate lots of tourists, but calling ahead for reservations is strongly encouraged.

DINER
HOLLYWOOD DINER 😊
400 E. Saratoga St., 410/962-5379

HOURS: Mon.-Fri. 7 A.M.-2 P.M.

North of City Hall, where cars on I-83

DINER FEVER

Baltimore is the city that made diners famous again. Well, technically, it was the movie *Diner* that did it, but since that 1982 film, Baltimore has been associated with diner culture. And though the city has lost some of its great old joints, there are still plenty of places in town to get some coffee, meat loaf, and a piece of pie while sitting on a chrome stool at the counter.

Start with breakfast at the **Hollywood Diner** in downtown, because that's where the film *Diner* was shot (though the diner was down by Fell's Point in the film). It's the city's last stainless-steel railcar diner, and probably one of the last in the nation. In Fell's Point, there's the 24-hour **Sip & Bite Restaurant,** a lovely and long-lived greasy spoon in a row house on Boston Street that's just across from another Baltimore culinary landmark, the ship-shaped **Captain James Landing.** This has both a small diner-like section and a more all-out menu in the main dining area (there's also a crab deck on the other side of the street); note that the late-night crowds can get a little boisterous and pushy. You can eat early and late (until 2 A.M. on weekends) at Homewood's **Papermoon Diner,** a Technicolor carnival of random weirdness, toys, and garage sale finds (and a huge menu of filling foods, from veggie breakfasts to meatloaf).

---

rumble overhead on viaducts, there's a gleaming chrome rail car diner (a 1954 Mountain View) surrounded by parking lots and warehouses. This is the Hollywood Diner, so dubbed because of its starring roles in *Diner, Sleepless in Seattle,* and other hits of the silver screen. Inside, it's just what you'd expect: chrome, stools, an old-fashioned counter, and booths. The menu features all your diner favorites, from bacon and egg breakfasts to turkey and mashed potato dinners. The weekday-only diner is operated by the Chesapeake Center for Youth Development, so eating here not only does your stomach good, it helps city kids learning work and life skills (so be patient if there are any service hiccups).

SEAFOOD
BLUE SEA GRILL $$$

Power Plant Live!, 614 Water St., 410/837-7300, www.blueseagrill.com

HOURS: Mon.-Sat. 4-10 P.M.

Though it's surrounded by the youthful neon thumping of open-air bar and restaurant complex Power Plant Live!, Blue Sea Grill is for adults (so dress nicely), and it was opened by the local owner of the neighboring Ruth's Chris Steakhouse. Blue Sea Grill is one of the city's top independent seafood restaurants, housed in a modernist, South Beach-ish, and very blue dining room. There's a wide variety of fresh fish that you can have prepared to your liking, as well as shellfish dishes galore. This was one of the first places in Baltimore to serve macaroni and cheese with lobster, and the dish is still a favorite.

FAIDLEY SEAFOOD $$

Lexington Market, 203 N. Paca St., 410/727-4898, www.faidleyscrabcakes.com

HOURS: Mon.-Sat. 9 A.M.-5 P.M.

Don't expect fine silverware and tablecloths here; in fact, don't even expect seats. Guests at Faidley Seafood on the west side of historic, busy, and very un-gentrified Lexington Market eat communally, standing up at long wooden tables—surrounded by a winding line of people waiting to order the city's famous crab cakes. Three styles are available: Skip the cheapest option and decide between the mid-range backfin (which consists of the less-prized meat of the blue crab) and jumbo lump, the Cadillac of crab cakes. The cakes are served fried, adorned only with a little garnish and a two-pack of crackers in a plastic wrapper, and served on red cafeteria trays. It's a humble-looking meal, but once you taste the divinity of these morsels, you'll understand the lines and the legend. The area around Lexington Market is not one

---

THE BEST CRAB CAKES IN TOWN

As simple a concept as the crab cake is – crab meat formed into a patty, with some mild (and secret) seasoning, cooked and served either as a sandwich or in pairs – the variety is astounding. Broiling gives them one flavor; frying them another. Getting a jumbo backfin lump crab cake (which can cost about the same as a good steak, about $20-30) will result in a different, though not always better, crab cake than cheaping out for one made of less top-grade meat, with a little filler. Seasonings vary from restaurant to restaurant as well; one may go light, another heavy. But for those seeking out the ultimate in Baltimore's signature meal (and frankly, you're not going to find a better crab cake outside the city, no matter how much you pay), here's a short list of places that have earned fervent devotees. Note that these are generally unexpected places to find a great crab cake, and places favored by locals. If you're at a premier restaurant and crab cakes are on the menu, you can be 99 percent

that they're going to be quite good: You just can't survive in this town by serving a lousy crab cake.

There's a triumvirate of local, long-time crab-cake sellers that have near-unanimous approval in Baltimore. First is the esteemed **Faidley Seafood,** in downtown's Lexington Market; the delicacy is best eaten at Faidley's long communal tables and washed down with a cold beer. It's a great place to grab a crab cake for lunch (though lines can get a little long) or before a baseball or football game. In Fell's Point, the tidy corner bar **Duda's Tavern** turns out great pub food, including a much-respected, tasty crab cake. Finally, a bit east of Federal Hill is another no-frills local haunt, **Captain Larry's,** where the bar's microscopic kitchen somehow turns out a big, legendary crab-cake sandwich. For a very different take on the dish, head to **Pierpoint** in Fell's Point, where they eschew the normal broiler or frying pan and cook their crab cakes in a smoker.

© GEOFF BROWN

RESTAURANTS

The still bustling Lexington Market serves many residents of the city's less-gentrified neighborhoods.

of the city's best, and visiting after dark is not recommended.

WATERTABLE $$$

Renaissance Harborplace Hotel, 202 E. Pratt St., 410/685-8439, www.watertablerestaurant.com
HOURS: Daily 11 A.M.–11 P.M.

Located on the fifth floor of the Renaissance Harborplace Hotel (a Marriott operation), this sleek, smooth, modern restaurant offers some stunning nighttime views of the harbor and Federal Hill. The menu is very seafood-oriented, and offers both small plates and conventional multi-course dinners, which have drawn solid, if uninspired, reviews; perhaps the fact that the clientele is predominantly tourists and businesspeople spending only a few days in town keeps the kitchen from pushing itself too hard. Having lunch here—for the view more than for the food—is probably your best option.

TURKISH

CAZBAR $$

316 N. Charles St., 410/528-1222, www.cazbarbaltimore.com
HOURS: Mon.-Fri. 11 A.M.–midnight, Sat.-Sun. 11 A.M.–2 A.M.

The cuisine of Turkey—based heavily on Mediterranean ingredients like grape leaves, yogurt, seafood, and lamb—guides this fun, colorful restaurant, but there are plenty of other familiar items on the menu. Still, stick with the Turkish delights for the best the kitchen offers; their Mediterranean takes on pizzas are particularly interesting and very good. It's a great place for couples or small groups, particularly on Friday and Saturday nights. That's when the belly dancers perform, swirling through the dining room and making this well-designed space the most happening place on the block.

RESTAURANTS

Fell's Point

Map 2

AMERICAN

◖ BLUE MOON CAFÉ ⑤

1621 Aliceanna St., 410/522-3940

HOURS: Sun.-Wed. 7 A.M.-3 P.M., Thurs.-Sat. 11 A.M.-3 P.M. and 11 P.M.-7 A.M.

This converted row house has nine tables—and a crowd waiting out front on most weekend mornings. The reason is that this bohemian, seat-of-the-pants operation makes some amazing breakfasts, from homemade biscuits and buttery grits to Cap'n Crunch French toast and even Maryland crab eggs Benedict. Either arrive early in the morning (say, 7 or 8 A.M.), or very, very late: They open at 11 P.M. and close at 3 A.M. the next day on weekends, the better to handle the area's nocturnal, booze-sodden hordes.

CAPTAIN JAMES LANDING ⑤⑤⑤

2127 Boston St., 410/327-8600, www.captainjameslanding.com

HOURS: Restaurant daily 7 A.M.-2 A.M.; crab house Mon.-Fri. 5-10 P.M., Sat.-Sun. 2-10 P.M.; carry-out daily 24 hours

It's not hard to find Captain James Landing; it's the huge white and blue building, shaped like a freighter, on the way from Fell's Point to Canton along Boston Street. What is hard is classifying it in a few words. First, it's a 24-hour carry-out shop, with diner fare like cheesesteaks, sandwiches, and pizza—plus seafood and steak platters. In the ship-shaped, nautically themed dining rooms of the main restaurant, food is served nearly all day long, with menus changing with each meal. Late-night dinner crowds can be a little intimidating, both in size and attitude. Then there's the crab house (more of a patio), across the street by the water, where the food ranges from budget diner fare to expensive surf-and-turf meals.

DU CLAW BREWING CO. ⑤⑤

901 S. Bond St., 410/563-3400, www.duclaw.com

HOURS: Sun.-Thurs. 11 A.M.-10 P.M., Fri.-Sat. 11 A.M.-11 P.M.

Du Claw is a Maryland-based brewing company with four locations in the Baltimore area; the Fell's Point outpost (in the building with "Bond Street Wharf" painted on the

LOCAL EATS

For the most part, if you see a restaurant with a line in Baltimore, it's probably worth getting in that line. Unless you're a very early bird, there's usually a breakfast/brunch queue outside Fell's Point's **Blue Moon Café** – and for good reason. If you're downtown and looking for breakfast or lunch, head to **Werner's Restaurant,** a 1950s-era diner in the bottom of an office building that's a favorite of lawyers, politicos, and blue-collar folks.

Lunchtime means a trip to **Attman's** delicatessen, which has survived Baltimore's good and bad times. It's the most authentic New York City–style deli in the whole city, and is a tightly packed and hungry zoo at lunchtime. For a legendary crab-cake lunch, visit **Faidley Seafood** in the busy, hectic Lexington Market

downtown, and pay for the jumbo lump crab cake; it's worth the extra cost. You'll dine standing up at common tables, so don't be shy.

For dinner, here are two completely different, yet totally Baltimore suggestions. **Peter's Inn** is a small, one-story, husband-and-wife-run restaurant off the beaten path in Fell's Point. It's popular with people who like hearty and inspired meals, boasts an interesting and devoted clientele, and plays great, offbeat music. Things couldn't be less quirky than at **Woodberry Kitchen,** a gleaming new restaurant in a rehabbed factory complex near Hampden and Homeland. Local produce and immense skill have made this one of Baltimore's most instantly adored dining destinations.

west side) is a big draw for its outdoor seating, which looks west toward the Domino Sugars sign and Federal Hill. Though there's plenty of room to dine inside, it's worth the wait to partake of the scenery. Order up a table full of bar grub staples (like burgers and sandwiches) or entrées (like steaks and crab cakes), a few beers, and take in the sunset from the brick patio. You can get all the major beers here, but you'll want to try the house creations—particularly the Misfit Red, an amber ale.

SHUCKER'S $$
1629 Thames St., 410/522-5820,
www.shuckersoffellspoint.com
HOURS: Mon.-Thurs. 11 A.M.-11 P.M.,
Fri.-Sat. 11 A.M.-midnight, Sun. 10 A.M.-11 P.M.

Located at the base of Broadway, Shucker's is a big bar and restaurant that caters to sports fans and tourists with plentiful TVs and party music, respectively. It's their sweeping outdoor dining section that makes this place worth visiting, because the panoramas of the Inner Harbor's interior are quite impressive. The menu does spice up some basic dishes (basil tuna, shrimp-topped rib eye) and offers something for almost every palate (stick with the basics and you'll be rewarded). But the real action's not on the menu; there's no better place to watch the Water Taxis and pleasure boats slowly pull in to the Broadway Pier—or, later in the evening, chuckle at the crowds of intoxicated revelers who flock to Fell's Point on weekend nights.

ASIAN
DING HOW $$
631 S. Broadway, 410/327-8888
HOURS: Sun.-Fri. 11:30 A.M.-10:30 P.M.,
Sat. 11:30 A.M.-11:30 P.M.

In a neighborhood packed with bars, taverns, and seafood restaurants that cater to tourists and weekend foot traffic, Ding How has managed to remain a fixture in Fell's Point. Maybe it's because this always-busy restaurant turns out solidly good, reasonably priced Chinese food, year after year. Maybe it's the fish tank,

the dark red wood pillars, and bamboo-backed chairs. Maybe it's that their more elaborate mixed and tropical drinks come with umbrellas in them. The only thing Baltimoreans—both Fell's Point die-hards and suburban cocktail-seekers out for a night on the town—know for sure is that Ding How is a reliable place to get a lot of food and drinks and not break the bank.

CONTEMPORARY AND NEW AMERICAN
CHARLESTON $$$
1000 Lancaster St., 410/332-7373,
www.charlestonrestaurant.com
HOURS: Mon.-Sat. 5:30-10 P.M.

Owners and operators of four top-notch establishments, chef Cindy Wolf and her husband Tony Foreman are, in many ways, the ultimate restaurateurs in Baltimore. Chef Wolf is a two-time finalist for the James Beard Foundation's regional award, and Charleston is her culinary flagship—and one of the city's top restaurants. It's a beautifully designed, completely unrestrained palace of fine American cooking, guided by the principles of the southern United States' "low country," which includes this establishment's namesake city in South Carolina. Low country–inspired dishes here (available in three- to six-course tasting menus) include pan-roasted squab, grilled veal sweetbreads, and shrimp, andouille sausage, and grits unlike any you've ever tasted.

HENNINGER'S TAVERN $$
1812 Bank St., 410/342-2172,
www.henningerstavern.com
HOURS: Tues.-Sat. 5 P.M.-1 A.M.

It's entirely possible to pass by the mild-mannered exterior of Henninger's a couple of times without noticing it, but make sure you don't give up trying to find it. Inside, there's a popular bar for locals (and a special bar menu, which includes a delicious $10 "TV dinner," served in a surplus military tray), and a charming dining room lined with old photos and older objets d'art. The variable menu takes some chances—such as pomegranate-glazed pork loin and barbecue salmon—without ignoring the standards, like crab cakes and hangar steaks. A trip to the restrooms reveals that the back of the restaurant seems like someone's house, which may help regulars feel even more at home.

◖ PETER'S INN $$

504 S. Ann St., 410/675-7313, www.petersinn.com

HOURS: Tues.-Thurs. 6:30-10 P.M., Fri.-Sat. 6:30-11 P.M.

The short but comprehensive menu here changes weekly, and is written on a chalkboard next to the tiny men's room; there's a huge swordfish mounted on the wall; the music veers from old-school country to alternapop; and the owners live upstairs. Peter's Inn has been one of Baltimore's favorite restaurants for years because it pairs inventive cooking and fresh ingredients with an unpretentious, eclectic bar scene and a petite dining room (there's also outdoor seating). There are always steak, fish, and vegetarian-friendly options, and don't skip the legendary garlic bread. Weekend crowds and no reservations can mean a wait at the bar,

but then again, it's a really great bar (and it's open until 1 A.M.).

PIERPOINT $$$

1822 Aliceanna St., 410/675-2080, www.pierpointrestaurant.com

HOURS: Tues.-Thurs. 5-9:30 P.M., Fri.-Sat. 5:30-10:30 P.M., Sun. 4-9 P.M., brunch Sun. 10:30 A.M.-1:30 P.M.

One of the city's few (yet accomplished) female executive chefs is Nancy Longo; her open-kitchen Pierpoint restaurant, at the eastern outskirts of Fell's Point, has been a city favorite since 1989. She was one of the first in town to focus on using local ingredients, and still does today: Eastern Shore rabbit sausage and vegetables from nearby farms are a constant here, as are poultry, seafood, and an ample selection of vegetarian dishes (she also puts out a fine Sunday brunch). The restaurant's decor hasn't changed much since the 1990s, but it's a warm, modern look that has aged well. Longo is also known for her unique take on crab cakes: She smokes them, rather than broiling or frying.

Peter's Inn offers inventive cooking and a great bar.

© GEOFF BROWN

RESTAURANTS

GREAT BAR-RESTAURANTS

As befits a town with treasured working-class roots, but also a taste for quality, Baltimore has a great proliferation of local bars and taverns that happen to have top-notch kitchens, turning out not great nachos and burgers but real gourmet meals that sometimes surpass the fare at the city's haute eateries. It's also not surprising that tavern-rich Fell's Point is home to many of these establishments. At some of these places, you'll eat right next to (if not at) the bar; others have real dining rooms. But if you want to dine with real Baltimoreans, head to one of these great bars that also happen to be great restaurants.

Start with **Henninger's Tavern,** where the mascot is a pink elephant and the dining room's entrées include Portuguese fisherman's stew and pomegranate-glazed pork loin. You can also eat from a small menu at the bar here; try the special TV dinner, served up in a genuine metal cafeteria tray. **Peter's Inn** has maximized every possible inch of its cozy quarters, but only has a handful of tables for the devoted regulars (you can eat at the bar as well); don't skip the garlic bread. In Canton, **Birches** has a very nice dining room, but it's more fun to choose from the pommes frites menu and wood-grilled entrées (like ahi tuna) in the warm, bustling bar area.

🌙 SALT $$$

2127 E. Pratt St., 410/276-5480, www.salttavern.com
HOURS: Mon.-Thurs. 5-10 P.M., Fri.-Sat. 5-11 P.M.

One of the latest wave of modern upper-crust bistros that opened in Baltimore in the last few years, Salt has become a neighborhood favorite that also draws diners from across the city. The owners spent some money on real interior design (still a bit of a rarity in Baltimore), and concocted a menu that has a bit of experimentation without being too daring. Stick with seafood here, like the coriander- and pepper-crusted tuna, and don't skip the chance to try their famous Kobe beef and foie gras sliders. This is definitely a scene restaurant, and the staff can lean toward accommodating the innumerable regulars over first-timers, but not dauntingly so.

CONTEMPORARY ITALIAN
CINGHIALE $$$

822 Lancaster St., 410/547-8282,
www.cinghiale-osteria.com
HOURS: Lunch Mon.-Fri. 11:30 A.M.-2 P.M., dinner Mon.-Thurs. 5-9 P.M., Fri.-Sat. 5 P.M.-1 A.M.

Though it's built in the ground floor of a new condo and apartment building, Cinghiale could be an 80-year-old Italian restaurant, lifted right out of its beloved little town and placed gently just a few dozen feet from the Baltimore waterfront. There are two separate and beautiful dining rooms here; one is a less-formal, bistro-like *enoteca*, designed for casual diners who want small plates while they explore the immense wine collection. The more serious, mahogany and leather osteria is where the kitchen and menu aim for new heights (such as magret of duck with fennel, and veal tenderloin).

CRAB HOUSE
OBRYCKI'S CRAB HOUSE $$$

1727 E. Pratt St., 410/732-6399, www.obryckis.com
HOURS: Mon.-Sat. 11:30 A.M.-11 P.M., Sun. 11:30 A.M.-9:30 P.M.

The exterior couldn't be less inviting, but inside this almost bunker-like building east of Fell's Point's bustling Broadway, Obrycki's has been satisfying Baltimoreans' and tourists' need for steamed crabs since 1986 (and the Obrycki family has been feeding Charm City's residents since the mid-1940s). The brick-arched dining rooms are usually filled with locals and first-timers (more of the latter than the former) cracking and picking their way through fresh-steamed and seasoned crabs. The staff is more than willing to help novice crab consumers learn the ropes, and there are plenty of non-crab items on the menu as well.

CREOLE
LOUISIANA $$$
1708 Aliceanna St., 410/327-2610,
www.louisianasrestaurant.com
HOURS: Mon.-Thurs. 5-10 P.M., Fri.-Sat. 5-11 P.M.,
Sun. 4-10 P.M.

Though this luxurious restaurant bills itself as being French with a Creole flair, it's best to dine here with New Orleans in mind. The menu is undeniably French, but it's the Louisiana- and Creole-inspired dishes that really stand out here. Simple beginning courses like blackened shrimp, collard greens, and grits lead the way to entrées like grilled quail with andouille Roquefort cornbread. The dining rooms here are heavy on dark woods, thick fabrics, and quiet enjoyment—which is to say, the complete opposite of the Fell's Point bar scene just outside the massive door.

DINERS
JIMMY'S RESTAURANT $
801 S. Broadway, 410/327-3273
HOURS: Daily 5 A.M.-9 P.M.

Though you couldn't tell from the exterior, Jimmy's is a diner, serving breakfast all day and hot, gravy-laden dinners into the evening. Want a beer with breakfast? Not a problem here, though the waitress might eyeball you a little. This is a social hub for lifetime Fell's Pointers, as well as politicians, news anchors, tugboat crews, Hopkins medical staffers— you name it. The room is always alive with buzz, conversations, and action, whether it's romance or heated political debate. The food is genuine diner cuisine served up freshly made and at a bargain price; if you want to eat like a real local, ask for gravy on your French fries.

SIP & BITE RESTAURANT $
2200 Boston St., 410/675-7077
HOURS: Open 24 hours

One of the landmark tiny diners of Baltimore's waterfront is the Sip & Bite, which has been dishing up American classics like grilled cheese sandwiches and turkey and mashed potato platters since 1948. As with most Baltimore diners (many of which are owned by Greek families), you can also get good salads, souvlaki, and gyros—plus a decent, cheap crab cake. This tiny, no-frills eatery (there are tables and a lunch counter) bursts at the seams when the many nearby bars close at 2 A.M. and the hungry crowds realize they need greasy food; if you're planning on stopping in and don't want to face teeming hordes of properly inebriated folks, go early.

EASTERN EUROPEAN
ZE MEAN BEAN CAFÉ $$
1739 Fleet St., 410/675-5999,
www.zemeanbeancafe.com
HOURS: Mon.-Thurs. 11 A.M.-11 P.M., Fri. 11 A.M.-1 A.M.,
Sat. 9 A.M.-1 A.M., Sun. 9 A.M.-11 P.M.

Getting a good pierogi in Baltimore is not as easy as it used to be, but Ze Mean Bean is definitely one place in town capable of producing great examples of these cheese-filled, sautéed Polish staples. There are more than a few other Eastern European items on the menu, including *leckzo* (dumplings), cabbage rolls, and goulash, all served in a medium-sized and cozy living-room-cum-dining-room, which often features music and jazz brunches. But the menu has plenty of surprises on it too, like roasted bison (raised locally) and sea bass with tomato and sage.

ECUADORIAN
LA CAZUELA $
1718 Eastern Ave., 410/522-9485
HOURS: Sun.-Thurs. 11 A.M.-9 P.M., Fri.-Sat. 11 A.M.-11 P.M.

In the past decade, Baltimore has seen a real growth in the population of Latin Americans, many of whom have settled in upper Fell's Point and created their own new communities, much as European immigrants did in the early 20th century. There are now taco wagons, bars, international cash services, churches, and other businesses catering to the Spanish-speaking newcomers. And there are also eateries, like the homey, no-frills La Cazuela—perhaps the easiest for non-Ecuadorians to patronize, as it's a restaurant designed to please newcomers and long-time Baltimoreans of all creeds: beef, pork, seafood, fried plantains, and casseroles (or *cazuleas*), all served in enormous portions.

ITALIAN
BRICK OVEN PIZZA ⑤
800 S. Broadway, 410/563-1600, www.boppizza.com
HOURS: Sun.-Thurs. 11 A.M.-midnight,
Fri.-Sat. 11 A.M.-3 A.M.
Whether it's for a quick lunch, a hearty dinner, or a couple of slices to soak up some beer, this eatery has been serving up extra-crispy pizzas (made in its wood-burning brick oven) for more than a decade. A vast list of toppings lets diners concoct their own exotic pies (clams, pesto, and bacon!), but there are also pastas, salads, and wraps. The dining room is basic pizza shop utilitarian, but when it's bustling with customers, it's a great place to people-watch. Murals on the walls depict the neighborhood in a classic 1980s-style cartoon format, a reminder of the changes that lie outside the big windows.

LEBANESE
LEBANESE TAVERNA ⑤⑤
719 S. President St., 410/244-5533,
www.lebanesetaverna.com
HOURS: Mon.-Thurs. 11 A.M.-10 P.M., Fri. 11:30 A.M.-11 P.M.,
Sat. noon-11 P.M., Sun. noon-9 P.M.
This Baltimore outpost of the Washington, D.C.–based chain is a big, modern, hip dining space (and bustling bar) that is popular with both locals and visitors looking to try new cuisines. There are great views of the water from the open, sweeping dining room (which still retains a few key Middle Eastern touches), making it a great destination for both dates and business. Start with hommos or *kibbeh* (little fried shells filled with meat), then try anything with lamb (the vegetarian kabob is quite good too). Wondering what to pair with *schawarma?* The hot tea here is delightful, as is the lemonade.

SEAFOOD
BERTHA'S ⑤⑤
734 S. Broadway, 410/327-5795, www.berthas.com
HOURS: Sun.-Thurs. 11:30 A.M.-11 P.M.,
Fri.-Sat. 11:30 A.M.-midnight
Perhaps best known for the "Eat Bertha's

Mussels" bumper stickers seen all across America (and in abundance in the dark, welcoming bar itself), Bertha's is a great place to grab a beer and a pound of the aforementioned bivalves and strike up a conversation with the quite possibly fascinating person seated at the next bar stool. Or you could eat in the dining room, choose something from the full menu, and take a quick tour of the bric-a-brac-filled old building. If you just want to hang out at the bar (open until 2 A.M.), the pub food here is great, there's live music most nights (generally blues), and there's always a good crowd in this tavern that many consider the heart of old Fell's Point.

THE BLACK OLIVE ⑤⑤⑤
814 S. Bond St., 410/276-7141, www.theblackolive.com
HOURS: Lunch daily noon-2 P.M., dinner daily 5-10 P.M.
One of the superlative moments when dining at the Black Olive comes when your waiter or waitress asks your table to please proceed to the kitchen in order to personally select the fish that will end up on your plate. It's an act that somehow engages the diner with the food in a more complete way, not that this Mediterranean-influenced restaurant needs it. Inside, the place feels like a small Greek eatery, albeit a very nice one (non-casual dress is recommended here). The fish is almost always spectacularly fresh, and what's on offer changes depending on what's the freshest at the market that week.

KALI'S COURT ⑤⑤⑤
1606 Thames St., 410/276-4700, www.kaliscourt.com
HOURS: Lunch daily 11:30 A.M.-2:30 P.M.,
dinner daily 5 P.M.-close
Kali's Court is one of Fell's Point's truly exemplary seafood restaurants, and the kind of place where it's worth the risk to order something you've never had before. The posh, red-draped, wood-paneled dining room can seat a lot of diners, but the shape and layout keep it from seeming uninvitingly large. There's a strong Mediterranean hand guiding the kitchen here, and amazingly fresh whole fish and fillets alike are deftly executed.

© GEOFF BROWN

Pazo is home to one of the city's most vibrant nighttime dining scenes.

The owners of Kali's have two smaller restaurants on the same street. Next door is **Mezze** (1606 Thames St., 410/563-7600, www.kalis mezze.com, Mon.–Sat. 4 P.M.–close, Sun. 11:30 A.M.–close), a contemporary-styled, two-story tapas eatery. Closer to Broadway is **Meli** (1636 Thames St., 410/534-6354, www.kalis meli.com, lunch daily 11:30 A.M.–2:30 P.M., dinner daily 5–11 P.M., late-night menu until 1 A.M.), which has small plates and a selection of full entrées, and a lounge-like downstairs area.

TAPAS
◖ PAZO $$$

1425 Aliceanna St., 410/534-7296,
www.pazorestaurant.com
HOURS: Sun.-Wed. 5-10 P.M., Thurs.-Sat. 5 P.M.-1 A.M.
Baltimore was a little unsure of what to make

of Pazo when it opened in 2004—there weren't many upscale, beautifully renovated, industrial warehouse/Spanish tapas restaurant and lounges in town, much less in generally dressed-down Fell's Point. But this sprawling former machine shop is now one of the city's hottest places to both eat and drink and pose and be noticed. The city's well-dressed young turks come here to be seen while sipping wine from stemless glasses and noshing on grilled pork tenderloin pinchos, and relaxing on circular couches beneath massive windows, iron chandeliers, and luxurious wall hangings. Less hedonistic city (and county) residents come to Pazo because of the food: There's a full menu of traditional Spanish-influenced entrées, best eaten at one of the upstairs tables across from the humming bar, giving foodies a fine perch from which to people-watch.

Little Italy
Map 2

CLASSIC ITALIAN

AMICCI'S 💲💲

231 S. High St., 410/528-1096, www.amiccis.com
HOURS: Daily 11:30 A.M.-midnight

Many Little Italy restaurants have a signature dish: Amicci's features *pane rotundo,* a round, flat loaf of Italian bread that's been hollowed out and filled with garlic butter and scampi sauce, and then topped with enormous shrimp. Despite the daunting challenge presented by this and the other entrées here, this is perhaps the only restaurant in Little Italy where you can get a quick dinner and be on your way in 30 minutes. It's a casual, friendly eatery, decorated with large-size Italian film posters (of both Hollywood and Italian origin) and, in the front dining room, an at-home feel; Amicci's is perfect for those who don't have time for a two-hour, multi-course production.

CAESAR'S DEN 💲💲💲

223 S. High St., 410/547-0820, www.caesarsden.com
HOURS: Daily 11:30 A.M.-10 P.M.

This is a restaurant that embodies what a traditional Little Italy restaurant should look like: warm colors, big paintings, and candles and flowers on the tables (though the exterior is a little more over the top). The mood is somewhere between casual and formal (the waiters wear tuxedos), and it's a good fit, because while the menu offers few deviations from the standards you'll find in other restaurants, you can see and taste the difference that a concerned, skilled kitchen makes. From the simplest pastas to the veal saltimbocca, the food here is well executed. Also, the bocce ball courts are right across the street.

DA MIMMO 💲💲💲

217 S. High St., 410/727-6876, www.damimmo.com
HOURS: Sun.-Thurs. 11:30 A.M.-11 P.M., Fri.-Sat. 11:30 A.M.-midnight

Named for Domenico "Mimmo" Cricchio Sr., the late founder of this Little Italy landmark, this is a restaurant for those who eschew the subtle. The exterior is festooned with awnings, faux stones, and paint; the interior boasts plush red chairs, large paintings, and gilded everything. The signature dish here is the veal chop alla Fiorentina, and it shares the decor's extravagance: a nearly three-inch thick slab of veal. Movie and stage stars have dined here in years past, which is fitting—as dining at Da Mimmo is an event unto itself.

GERMANO'S TRATTORIA 💲💲💲

300 S. High St., 410/752-4515,
www.germanostrattoria.com
HOURS: Lunch daily 11:30 A.M.-2:30 P.M., dinner Sun.-Thurs. 4:30-10 P.M., Fri.-Sat. 4:30-11 P.M.

Though Germano's is a strictly traditional Italian restaurant, it's a Tuscan-influenced kitchen, so the dishes may seem unfamiliar to those expecting the usual marinara and pasta selections (though they offer those, too). Olive oil and lighter pastas are a staple in Tuscan cooking; the lasagna here is made with *besciamella* sauce, not marinara, and the seafood risotto is an appreciated change of pace. The dining rooms' interiors (exposed brick, warm Tuscan orange-yellows and blues, large vintage posters) are also less ponderous than those of the more august neighboring eateries, but Germano's still maintains the ambiance of a serious restaurant, albeit one where fun is encouraged (there's even a cabaret on Thursday nights).

SABATINO'S 💲💲

901 Fawn St., 410/727-9414, www.sabatinos.com
HOURS: Sun.-Thurs. 11:30 A.M.-midnight, Fri.-Sat. 11:30 A.M.-3 A.M.

There's a charming, homey feel at this legendary restaurant that keeps diners returning for decades and decades. Things are done simply at "Sab's," from the basic house-made pasta dishes to the monstrous *brasciloe,* beef filled with veal, prosciutto, egg, and cheese, then topped with marinara. The experienced wait staff here has seen it all (there's a brisk post-bar-closing weekend business here during the busy season, since

LITTLE ITALY AND ITS RESTAURANTS

As Baltimore became the nation's second-largest intake port for European immigrants in the 1800s, each arriving group – Germans, Poles, Irish – naturally moved into tenements and houses near people from their own home country. Around 1849, many Italians who had decided to stay in Baltimore chose to settle in the neighborhood just east of President Street, a couple of blocks from the waters of the Inner Harbor. Those Italian American Baltimoreans went on to produce two Baltimore mayors, Thomas D'Alesandro Jr., and his son, Thomas D'Alesandro III; one of Tommy Jr.'s other children, Nancy D'Alesandro Pelosi, moved to California and became the first female Speaker of the U.S. House of Representatives.

Today, though many of the Italian American families who called this neighborhood home for generations have moved on, it's still the site of a small group of storied Italian American families and about 20 Italian restaurants, ranging from basic pasta-and-tomato-sauce places to top-dollar purveyors of decadent seafood and veal. It's long been a destination for tourists, even before the city's renaissance in the 1980s, and as such some restaurants can have a slightly impersonal and insincere feel, especially during the busy summer weekends when these eateries are trying to turn their tables over as fast as possible. Though you won't find all of the city's absolute finest Italian dining here (the splendid Cinghiale, a two-room palace of marble, wood, and brass in nearby Harbor East, just a few blocks from Little Italy, is one of the newest and best in town), there are plenty of perfectly good options here, and the mood and scenery of the neighborhood can't be beat.

The best way to enjoy Little Italy, then, is to not focus too intently on the food, but rather to take everything as part of a whole, from pre-dinner drinks to people-watching at the restaurant to lingering over a decadent dessert. Stroll the streets: You might see grandmothers watering their flower boxes at night, lifelong residents getting their tosses ready for a game of bocce on the neighborhood's court (902-904 Stiles St.) late on a Saturday after-noon, or people packing around a parking lot to watch an outdoor movie on a Friday. On weekends, the place is abuzz with diners from all over the city and the nation; young couples on dates, birthday parties, wedding anniversaries, along with groups of tourists, all wandering around, trying to decide which restaurant to enter. Red, green, and white lighted stars and banners hang above one-way streets packed with limos and cabs and valet parking crews. The sidewalks can be filled with diners wearing everything from slinky cocktail dresses and $800 Jimmy Choos to T-shirts and $5 flip-flops. So go for the scenery and the characters and the experience, and have a good dinner while you're there. And don't forget to grab a cannoli or tiramisu for dessert at Vaccaro's (222 Albemarle St.) on your way home.

© GEOFF BROWN

Sabatino's, one of the nearly 20 Italian restaurants in Little Italy

it's one of the few places to serve late dinner), so they're happy to deal with pleasant inquiries and give recommendations. They can also handle anything from a couple to a large group with just a little advance notice.

CONTEMPORARY ITALIAN
🄲 ALDO'S $$$

306 S. High St., 410/727-0700, www.aldositaly.com
HOURS: Daily 5-10 P.M.

It may look like a grand row house on the outside, but the inside of this upscale Little Italy restaurant is pure Italian piazza, with lots of natural light, marble, and open space. This is a special occasion restaurant, with all of the excelsior service, fantastic wine selection, and rich, immaculately prepared food (like the tournedos Rossini) that such an excursion entails (or with a bill to match). There's also a great bar here, which provides a great reason to arrive a little early and admire the handmade cabinetry and woodwork of the place (it was built by the restaurant's owner, namesake, and executive chef, Aldo Vitale).

DELLA NOTTE $$$

801 Eastern Ave., 410/837-5500, www.dellanotte.com
HOURS: Daily 11 A.M.-10 P.M.

From the broad, sweeping, window-filled dining room overlooking President Street to the huge (but artificial) tree in the center of the room to the busts of Roman senators and emperor to the wine atrium, this is a place to indulge your taste for grandeur. Though the menu offers many expected Italian dishes, there are also some surprises here, like duck breast with beets. The dining room has a great energy to it when full, and the aproned wait staff is always ready to suggest a wine pairing (wine is a fully recognized equal to the entrées here) or dessert.

LA SCALA $$$

1012 Eastern Ave., 410/783-9209,
www.lascaladining.com
HOURS: Mon.-Thurs. 4:30-10 P.M., Fri.-Sat. 4-11 P.M.,
Sun. 4-11 P.M.

A recent renovation has greatly expanded and updated this Little Italy favorite's dining areas and bar—and even created an indoor bocce ball court (with disco ball). The lively interior is now an open, airy mix of levels, stairways, exposed brick, subdued yellows, and warm woods. The real star here, though, is the food: Though the menu adheres to the basics you'll find at other restaurants, the quality of the kitchen here helps lift the fettuccine and spaghetti to delicious heights (simple ingredients used well seem to be the secret). Weekly specials let the chefs really show their mettle, though they can be very pricey. Make sure to save room (and money) for some cannoli, which are outstanding as well.

LA TAVOLA $$$

248 Albemarle St., 410/685-1859, www.la-tavola.com
HOURS: Daily 11:30 A.M.-10:30 P.M.

This is one of the newest restaurants in Little Italy, which means it's only about a decade old. The casual modern decor (lots of warm contemporary earth tones and matching furniture) is punctuated with tributes to classic Italy (check out the re-creations of vintage Italian ads on the walls), much like the menu. While many places offer a standard review of Italian American favorites, La Tavola has its own classics: Think linguine with truffles, taleggio cheese, and pioppini mushrooms, or grilled calamari served atop black squid-ink linguine. This is a great place to go to sample modern takes on Italian food, though the basics are also available in fine form here.

DELI
ATTMAN'S $

1019 E. Lombard St., 410/563-2666,
www.attmansdeli.com
HOURS: Mon.-Sat. 8 A.M.-6:30 P.M., Sun. 8 A.M.-5 P.M.

Downtown's once-vibrant delicatessen culture has, alas, faded into distant, smoked and pickled memory. A few stalwarts survive; king of the bunch is Attman's, a modest deli and always-crowded, well-worn dining area (the no-frills Kibbitz Room). There's a panoply of meats, cheeses, side dishes, and breads to choose from. Corned beef here is always on the money—and a sign helpfully reminds you how to order it (on rye with mustard only). Or you can order a combo sandwich, from the sedate New Yorker to the wackier Tongue Fu. Jars offering pickled and preserved items line the back walls, and if you're overwhelmed by all the choices, you can always order a kosher hot dog.

DESSERTS
VACCARO'S ●

222 Albemarle St., 410/685-4905,
www.vaccarospastry.com

HOURS: Mon. 9 A.M.-10 P.M., Tues.-Thurs. and Sun 9 A.M.-11 P.M., Fri.-Sat. 9 A.M.-1 A.M.

Though many of the restaurants in Little Italy excel at traditional Italian desserts, it's a tradition to take a short stroll from wherever you ate dinner to Baltimore's temple of tiramisu and its cathedral of cannoli: Vaccaro's. The decor is more ice cream parlor than romantic nightcap stop, but that's because of the volume they do here, mostly in their two stalwart sweet treats. There are plenty of other cake and sugary options as well.

INDIAN
INDIA RASOI ●●

411 S. High St., 410/385-4900, www.india-rasoi.com
HOURS: Mon.-Sat. 11:30 A.M.-2:30 P.M., 5-10 P.M.

Yes, tucked among the pasta emporiums and marinara palaces of Little Italy, there is a single non-Italian restaurant…and it's an Indian restaurant. And it's actually a pretty good Indian restaurant, serving up all the usual fare like chicken tikka masala and lamb vindaloo, as well as a tasty mulligatawny soup. It's a cozy, colorful, and casual place that does a bustling lunch buffet business, and if for some reason you're in the neighborhood and can't bear the thought of tortellini, it's worth stopping by.

SEAFOOD
McCORMICK & SCHMICK'S ●●●

Pier 5, 711 Eastern Ave., 410/234-1300,
www.mccormickandschmicks.com

HOURS: Sun.-Thurs. 11:30 A.M.-10:30 P.M., Fri.-Sat. 11:30 A.M.-11:30 P.M.

The Inner Harbor branch (just a block from Little Italy) of this national chain of seafood restaurants has some of the best real estate in town—and is a convenient place to dine with two or 20 people. There are dozens of outdoor tables that fill up fast on sunny days, all with good to great views of the water and Federal Hill. Inside, there's a big, casual bar area, with a massive wood and mirrored bar, and several large, more formal dining rooms, where eating in a T-shirt and shorts might feel a little funny. The seafood dishes, from scallops and oysters to halibut and salmon, are best here; other meats and poultry are fine, but not that memorable.

Canton
Map 3

AMERICAN
ANNABEL LEE TAVERN ●●

601 S. Clinton St., 410/522-2929,
www.annabelleetavern.com

HOURS: Mon.-Sat. 4 P.M.-1 A.M.

Only in Baltimore do you get a restaurant and bar with an Edgar Allan Poe theme. The walls here are purple and inscribed with the words of this tragic author (the bar is named for his last poem), and there is just the tiniest hint of the gothic here. But it's also a warm, fun place to grab a drink and eat at the bar, or head back to the small dining room and sample some of the bolder menu items, like half duckling barbequed with cayenne and Jack Daniel's, with French fries cooked in duck fat.

BIRCHES ●●

641 S. Montford Ave., 410/732-3000,
www.birchesrestaurant.com

HOURS: Mon.-Thurs. 5-11 P.M., Fri.-Sat. 5 P.M.-midnight

Half warm, well-used bar, half candlelit romantic dining room, Birches manages to pull off the best of both worlds. You can dine on a whim with some friends in the rich, wooden bar and tables at the front of the house, or make a reservation and take a seat in the cozy dining room for a more formal experience. Most meats and seafood are wood grilled, which gives them a great smoky taste, and there are gourmet versions of favorites like crab dip and risotto (with shrimp and scallops). There's even a French fry menu (Mon.–Thurs. only), with eight different ways to devour Birches' delicious spuds.

CLADDAGH PUB $$

2918 O'Donnell St., 410/522-4220,
www.claddaghonline.com
HOURS: Mon.-Fri. 11 A.M.-11 P.M., Sat.-Sun. 9 A.M.-11 P.M.

Many Canton taverns can get away with serving good pub grub and still pack in the customers every night. But Claddagh—while an immensely popular bar (open until 2 A.M., and opening early for critical European soccer matches)—is also a genuine restaurant. You can tell someone in the kitchen cares about the food, even if it's just a burger or a Caesar salad; if you're feeling bold, try the trio of "bistro filets"—three little prime cuts of beef topped with bleu cheese, Dijon gratinée, and a raspberry reduction. There are a few good outdoor tables and a few good indoor seats right by the big windows overlooking O'Donnell Square (and lots of other perfectly nice tables, too).

HELEN'S GARDEN $$

2908 O'Donnell St., 410/276-2233,
www.helensgarden.com
HOURS: Lunch Tues.-Sat. 11:30 A.M.-4 P.M.,
dinner Tues.-Thurs. 5-9:30 P.M., Fri.-Sat. 5-10 P.M.,
Sun. 5-9 P.M., brunch Sun. 10 A.M.-2 P.M.

It's one of the more intriguing entrances to a Baltimore restaurant—you'll head down a long, narrow, brick hallway before turning left and heading back into the spacious and artful dining room, or right into the large bar area. You can dine in either space, though be aware that on Wednesdays, many of the entrées are available at a reduced cost, which draws big crowds. Start with the portobello mushroom topped with crab and red pepper aioli; then move on to entrées like curried salmon, roman lamb, or spicy tenderloin au poivre. Table turnover here follows an oddly strict schedule, especially for large parties.

THREE $$

2901 E. Baltimore St., 410/327-3333,
www.myspace.com/threerestaurant
HOURS: Mon.-Thurs. 5:30-10 P.M., Fri.-Sat. 5:30-11 P.M.

The Patterson Park area was one of the beneficiaries of Baltimore's early 21st-century rejuvenation; lots of young couples and singles moved into the area to be near the sprawling park's green space. They make up the regulars at Three, a vibrant bistro and tavern on the east side of the park. Exposed brick and hardwood floors make for a loud, exciting environment here, but that's the idea (there's also limited outdoor seating in the front of the restaurant). Both small plates (like asparagus bundles and blackened venison) and entrées (like Cajun-fried rabbit) are offered here; it can get crowded on weekends, as this is one of the few modern dining options in this section of town.

BARGAIN BALTIMORE: RESTAURANTS

Baltimore was made famous by the movie *Diner;* the diner in which the film was shot is now the **Hollywood Diner,** off the beaten path near City Hall, but it's worth a detour if you want to say you ate there (and ate cheaply). Two other bargain faves are **Jimmy's Restaurant** in Fell's Point and **Werner's Restaurant,** near the Inner Harbor.

Vegans should head to **The Yabba Pot** for excellent cheap chow. Canton's **Nacho Mama's** serves huge portions of Mexican food that will fill you up for hours of walking.

And with all the money you saved, if you're in town on a Tuesday, you should head to **Gertrude's** in the BMA for $10 Tuesdays. Any other day of the week, go to Hampden's **Angelo's Pizza,** and get a hot, delicious slice that's the size of an airplane wing, and only about $3.

RESTAURANTS

Look for the lighthouse to find Canton's best waterfront crab house.

CRAB HOUSE
BO BROOKS $$$
2701 Boston St., 410/558-0202, www.bobrooks.com
HOURS: Mon.-Thurs. 11:30 A.M.-9 P.M., Fri. 11:30 A.M.-10 P.M., Sat. 12:30-10 P.M., Sun. 12:30-8 P.M.

Head for the once-operational lighthouse along Canton's waterfront—home to yachts and condos—and don't wear your best shirt or blouse, because you're going to be working for your dinner. Crabs are available year-round at Bo Brooks, steamed and then seasoned with spices, then brought to your brown-paper-wrapped table, along with wooden mallets and knives and lots of napkins (there are other menu items to chose from as well). The great crabs and the stellar view mean this is one of the few restaurants in town that's popular with both locals and tourists, and it's hard to find an unhappy customer here. Reservations for one of the prime outdoor seats on the side of the restaurant are a must, especially during nice weather.

DESSERTS
CAKELOVE $
2500 Boston St., 410/522-1825
HOURS: Mon.-Fri. 8 A.M.-8 P.M., Sat. 8 A.M.-9 P.M., Sun. 10 A.M.-7 P.M.

The Baltimore outpost of Washington, D.C. celebrity-baker Warren Brown, Cakelove offers supremely rich cakes featuring ingredients like mocha, buttercream, and carrot—as well as a splendid selection of gourmet cupcakes (orange and strawberry are always a hit) and even ice creams. This big, modern space is very industrial and clean, though there are a couple of mod sofas in the front to tuck into with your cupcakes; or you can order a whole, decadent cheesecake to take with you. Customers range from in-the-know hipsters to seasoned sugar mamas and papas.

ITALIAN
MATTHEW'S PIZZERIA $$
3131 Eastern Ave., 410/276-8755, www.matthewspizza.com
HOURS: Mon.-Thurs. 11 A.M.-10 P.M., Fri.-Sat. 11 A.M.-11 P.M., Sun. noon-8 P.M.

Sometimes, it's the humble little kitchens that make some of the most unforgettable, better-than-home cooking, and Matthew's Pizzeria is one of those places. Opened back in 1943 by Matthew Cacciolo, this pizza shop makes a very good and very classic pie, one best ordered with only a few choice toppings (the Crab Pie, with jumbo lump crab meat, cheese, and caramelized onions, is a favorite of Baltimoreans), and eaten fresh out of the oven at one of the tables in the small, bright dining room. They also serve a variety of other Italian dishes, but it's the pizza that makes this place a city treasure.

PY $$
2917 O'Donnell St., 410/483-8015, www.pypizza.com
HOURS: Mon.-Wed. 11 A.M.-11 P.M., Thurs.-Sat. 11 A.M.-3 A.M., Sun. 11 A.M.-midnight

A relative newcomer to the Baltimore pizza scene, Py has quickly earned a sizeable contingency of fans by doing something that's sadly hard to find here: making consistently excellent pizza. Nothing too flashy here (though they do serve a crab pizza and a chicken tikka pie)—their strength comes from doing something simple very well. The crust is just right (not too thin, not too thick, not too crunchy), the tomato sauce has a great flavor, and the toppings are fresh and generous. There's also a selection of calzones, sandwiches, and subs. Recently added tables have gained Py some regulars, and the exposed brick and modern decor make it a good place to recharge and have a quick bite.

TUTTI GUSTI $$

3102 Fait Ave., 410/534-4040

HOURS: Mon.-Thurs. 11 A.M.-10 P.M., Fri.-Sat.

11 A.M.-11 P.M., Sun. noon-10 P.M.

Purveyors of probably the most New York City–like pizza in Canton, Tutti Gusti's owners celebrated their Italian (Neapolitan, specifically) roots by commissioning a huge pop-art mural of famous Italians on one interior wall. This place is a few blocks from the high-density O'Donnell Square area, so you're certain to bump into locals here; regulars know where to get a great pizza, calzones, panzarotti, and cannoli, and the quattro stagione pizza (ham, red peppers, artichokes, and mushrooms) is a favorite.

MEXICAN
GECKO'S $$

2318 Fleet St., 410/732-1961, www.geckosonline.com

HOURS: Mon.-Wed. 3:30 P.M.-1 A.M., Thurs.-Sat.

11 A.M.-1 A.M., Sun. 11:30 A.M.-1 A.M.

Away from the other restaurant-rich areas of Canton, Gecko's is tucked into the middle of a residential area, which turns out to be its greatest strength. Devoted and vocal regulars mean that the kitchen (and bar, which is open until 2 A.M.) have to keep their game up, and Gecko's does that with some intriguing Southwestern fare, including daily specials like quesadillas filled with roast duck, shiitake mushrooms, and goat cheese. There are roughly two floors of dining past the always-

popular bar in the front, and the exposed-brick walls and casual vibe here keep the bar stools full.

NACHO MAMA'S $$

2907 O'Donnell St., 410/675-0898,

www.nachomamascanton.com

HOURS: Daily 11 A.M.-12:30 A.M.

Elvis was big in Baltimore—he embodied much of the city's white, Southern, working-class sensibility—and The King lives on today at Nacho Mama's, out front (as a statue) and on the walls (in velvet). The food here is Mexican, served with a wink (chips and salsa arrive in old hubcaps, as do some of the margaritas) but also with a real eye toward balancing quality and quantity. Fajitas (from veggie to tenderloin) are popular, as are the enormous burritos, quesadillas, and enchiladas. There is also beer aplenty; to blend in, order a "Natty Boh," shorthand for National Bohemian, a once-locally-brewed cheap, cold brew that's still a big seller.

SEAFOOD
◖ MAMA'S ON THE HALF SHELL $$

2901 O'Donnell St., 410/276-3160

HOURS: Mon.-Thurs. 11 A.M.-11 P.M., Fri.-Sat.

11 A.M.-midnight, Sun. 9 A.M.-11 P.M.

Owned by the same proprietor as Nacho Mama's a couple of doors down, this more upscale (though not uptight) seafood restaurant is done up in New England–oyster house decor. There's nothing fake about the food here, though: the selection of oysters (available in preparations ranging from iced to oysters Rockefeller to stew) has quickly gained favor as the city's favorite. In fact, all the seafood here is exceptionally good, from crab cakes to shrimp to rockfish and salmon. Save room, though, for a slice of gooey, chocolate-oozing Derby pie. Despite two levels of seating and outdoor tables, this place is almost always packed (the raw bar serves until 1 A.M. and the bar is open until 2 A.M.), so plan accordingly.

Federal Hill Map 4

AMERICAN
HARVEST TABLE ❺
1000 Hull St., 410/837-0073,
www.myharvesttable.com
HOURS: Mon.-Fri. 7 A.M.-5 P.M., Sat.-Sun. 9 A.M.-4 P.M.

Go past the final brick row houses and warehouses of Locust Point, to the end of Hull Street, and you'll find Tide Point, a repurposed former detergent production facility that's now home to high-tech offices and the sleek, glass-enclosed Harvest Table, a strictly breakfast-and-lunch bistro that offers lots of outdoor seating for sunny mornings. Breakfast and brunch specialties (like the Carolina layered breakfast, full of eggs, grits, bacon, and cheese, and their Grand Marnier French toast) are hearty, and fresh ingredients make basic lunch standards shine. This place is very, very popular, particularly on bright spring and summer days, so be prepared to wait if you arrive at, say, 11 A.M. on a Saturday.

HULL STREET BLUES ❺❺
1222 Hull St., 410/727-7476, www.hullstreetblues.com
HOURS: Mon. 11 A.M.-10 P.M. (light fare only),
Tues.-Thurs. 5-10 P.M., Fri.-Sat. 5-11 P.M., Sun. 4-9 P.M.,
brunch Sun. 10 A.M.-2 P.M.

A local favorite long before the Locust Point neighborhood was awash in new condos and townhouses, this big, well-aged restaurant (named for the street it's on and the 1980s TV show *Hill Street Blues*) is still a fixture in this part of town. Ample, hearty Sunday brunches in particular draw crowds of Locust Point lifers and newcomers, so plan accordingly. At other times, you can stop by this inviting tavern and restaurant (it started as a saloon back in 1889) for lunch or dinner, from big sandwiches and burgers to steaks and seafood. Meals are best taken in the nautically themed Commodore Room, the adjoining formal dining area named for Commodore Isaac Hull, one of the heroes of the War of 1812.

OUTSTANDING OUTDOOR DINING

Not all of the best outdoor dining in Baltimore is at the Inner Harbor (though the views there are pretty darn great). There's also plenty of people-watching to be done around town in some of the city's historic neighborhoods.

At the Inner Harbor, those looking for the quintessential Baltimore experience should book an outdoor table at **Phillips Harborplace** and get a couple of dozen crabs, which should be devoured while watching the nighttime water traffic skim across the waters of the harbor. There are lots of other restaurants at Harborplace with outdoor dining as well, so if Phillips is overbooked, you should be able to find a substitute. (The second-floor restaurants of the Pratt Street Pavilion are a good bet for a great view; a quieter option is

McCormick & Schmick's, on the far eastern side of the harbor.)

In Fell's Point, you can get a great street-level table along Thames Street at two bars: **Duda's Tavern** and **John Steven,** each at opposite ends of the (mostly) waterfront thoroughfare. There's also local upscale brewpub chain **Du Claw Brewing Co.,** across the street from Duda's in the Bond Street Wharf; it's close enough to count as waterfront. **Shucker's** has the best view in the neighborhood, though the feel is less "salty dog" than at Duda's or John Steven. On warm weekend nights, you'll get to see the rowdy crowds roll in with the evening tide, so don't think of this as a romantic Saturday night destination.

Federal Hill has only a few options, but they're quite good. First is **Regi's,** a longtime

ASIAN

MATSURI $

1105 S. Charles St., 410/752-8561, www.matsuri.us
HOURS: Mon.-Fri. 11:30 A.M.-2:30 P.M. and 5-11 P.M.,
Sat.-Sun. 5-11 P.M.

Matsuri has one of the best locations in Federal Hill. Sushi here is very fresh and cut generously, and it's one of the city's best sushi bargains (which are generally two words you don't want to see together). They're imaginative here: Take their shiitake and carrot sushi roll, topped with spiced mayonnaise and then baked. Other Japanese dishes, such as the lightly done tempura, are also prepared well. The spacious second floor, replete with origami cranes, has a much less hectic vibe than the bustling first floor and outdoor patio seats.

TEN-O-SIX $$

1006 Light St., 410/528-2146, www.ten-o-six.com
HOURS: Tues.-Sat. 5-9:30 P.M., Sun. 4-9 P.M.

Located right next to the popular Regi's Bistro on Light Street, Ten-O-Six offers up a menu of gourmet Thai dishes, along with a few more American and European entrées for those who foolishly don't want crispy, very spicy soft-shell crab or massamun lamb. The kitchen is the first thing you see when you enter this former row house; the attendant small dining rooms are not the most stylish in town (new ownership has yet to update the bland 1990s-era "modern" decor), but the sins are of omission. If you're looking for a different take on Thai classics—and traveling with someone who needs a steak—there's no other place in Baltimore that can satisfy both needs under one roof.

CONTEMPORARY AND NEW AMERICAN

THE BICYCLE $$$

1444 Light St., 410/234-1900, www.bicyclebistro.com
HOURS: Sun.-Tues. 5:30-9 P.M., Wed.-Sat. 5:30-10 P.M.

It's hard to get the combination of a serious restaurant and an amusing dining experience to work together, but that's exactly what brings so many diners to The Bicycle. The wood-and-metal interior is sleek and modern, and there's also a great little outdoor patio that holds several tables. The menu, on first glance, doesn't

fixture on Light Street that serves classic American dishes. On the water, the Baltimore location of the **Rusty Scupper** chain doesn't have the city's most inventive menu, but the view (especially for brunch) is probably the best in the city. The innovative **The Bicycle** has an interior, brick-lined courtyard for dining; the almost-waterfront **Little Havana** is a loud, raucous bar and club where you can sip marvelous mojitos in the glow of the Domino Sugars sign; and south of Federal Hill proper is **Nick's Fish House,** a hard-to-find little waterfront bar and restaurant that overlooks an inlet of the Patapsco (think Tampa, more than Miami).

There are some other outdoor dining gems in Baltimore, scattered across town. In Mount Vernon, **Donna's** gives its diners a look at Charles Street's bustle through the neighborhood, while **Sascha's 527 Café** offers a great view of the Walters and the Washington Monument. In the small Station North arts district, and right next to the Charles movie theater, **Tapas Teatro** may not have a waterfront view, but it's a thriving, bustling scene for dinner and drinks (and great small plates). In Hampden and Homewood, **The Ambassador Dining Room** has a magnificent backyard lawn/dining area that offers seclusion among the neighboring apartment towers. At the Baltimore Museum of Art, the modern, tented patio at **Gertrude's** overlooks the museum's sculpture garden. And the lauded **Woodberry Kitchen** offers dining among the repurposed and restored mills and buildings of Woodberry's Clipper Mill complex of dwellings and stores.

The Bicycle is one of Federal Hill's best restaurants.

seem particularly inventive—grilled salmon, short ribs, gnocchi—but notice the details of the dishes (and the artistic presentation). There's parmesan flan, and goosefat-roasted potatoes, which explains some of the enthusiasm for this eatery. Don't skip dessert here (they're made in-house): The lemongrass crème brûlée and brioche bread pudding are worth saving room for.

CORKS $$$

1026 S. Charles St., 410/752-3810,
www.corksrestaurant.com
HOURS: Daily 11:30 A.M.-11:30 P.M., light fare until 1:30 A.M., brunch Sun. 10 A.M.-4 P.M.

Once one of the city's no-holds-barred restaurants and a favorite of foodies from across the region, Corks recently underwent a fairly major transformation. Now, the dining room is simpler and more relaxed, while the food selections are generally much smaller and less ambitious—but

the ingredients and care that goes into making them remains top-notch. Sandwiches are the new feature here, but taken to a higher plane; the burger is bison, served with grilled Vidalia onion; the BLT is made with braised pork belly, tomato confit, and fancy frisée; and more traditional entrées are also available. The well-planned and comprehensive wine selection, thankfully, remains in place, as does Corks' popular in-house sommelier.

JUNIOR'S WINE BAR $$

1117 S. Charles St., 410/727-1212
HOURS: Tues.-Sun. 5:30 P.M.-1 A.M.

Federal Hill attracts lots of young people on weekend nights, which doesn't leave lots of places for older (read: over 29) folks to go out and not get jostled or feel the need to bump and grind in order to have a good time. That's probably why there are always few empty spaces at Junior's Wine Bar, which is more of a restaurant with a lot of wine than strictly a wine bar. It's a big, modern space, with copper and marble tables and a great menu of mostly Mediterranean and American entrées. This is a straightforward place for thirtysomethings who want to eat, have some wine, and talk without having to yell—or lean against a crowded and rowdy bar.

REGI'S ⑤⑤
1002 Light St., 410/539-7344,
www.regisamericanbistro.com
HOURS: Mon.-Thurs. 11 A.M.-midnight, Fri.
11 A.M.-1:45 A.M., Sat. 9:30 A.M.-1:45 A.M.,
Sun. 9:30 A.M.-11 P.M.

This always-hopping bistro has been popular since before Federal Hill became one of the city's thriving next-generation neighborhoods, and part of the reason has been the consistently satisfying food. Mundane items like tater tots (a minor sensation in Baltimore these days) take on a new life when covered with brie and bacon—as do huge slabs of meatloaf served with onion straws and a demi-glaze. (There are also plenty of lighter entrées here.) The dining room is very cozy, but the outdoor seating right on busy Light Street is where the real social scene can be found (especially at Sunday brunch). One of the neighborhood's notable residents, Jenna Bush (daughter of former President George W. Bush), is a semi-regular here.

SOBO CAFÉ ⑤
6 W. Cross St., 410/752-1518
HOURS: Daily noon-4 P.M. and 6-10 P.M.
If you are a fan of a restaurants run by a gleeful group of creative and skilled misfits (instead of stern, talented taskmaskers), you'll love SoBo (short for South Baltimore) Café. Be aware that this place can be very seat-of-the-pants, particularly on weekends when hungry crowds can swamp the staff, but the food is so good (indulgently rich macaroni and cheese, chicken pot pies, pork loins, fish like wahoo, and steaks) that you should gird yourself for the idiosyncrasies of this popular

neighborhood café. If something goes screwy, be ready to change your mind on the fly—and have another glass of wine while you wait. Besides, there's always a good selection of works by local artists hanging on the brightly painted walls to admire.

THE WINE MARKET ⑤⑤
921 E. Fort Ave., 410/244-6166,
www.the-wine-market.com
HOURS: Mon.-Thurs. 11 A.M.-11 P.M., Fri.-Thurs.
11 A.M.-midnight, Sun. 11 A.M.-9 P.M.

Located in a renovated old foundry complex on Fort Avenue, this popular, modern restaurant (with exposed brick, bright corrugated air pipes) is the kind of place that wouldn't have flourished without Baltimore's recent influx of young urban professionals, particularly into the surrounding neighborhoods. You'll find a generally youthful crowd here that's as interested in hanging out as it is the food, and a few foodie diehards who are all about the kitchen's creations (and the massive wine selection). There are a lot of lighter seafood entrées here worth trying, or you can create a meal from small plates. Brunch here is a popular, well-booked event, particularly on nice days, when the outdoor patio is packed with happy eaters.

CRAB HOUSE
L. P. STEAMER'S ⑤⑤
1100 E. Fort Ave., 410/576-9294, www.lpsteamers.com
HOURS: Sun.-Thurs. 11:30 A.M.-10 P.M.,
Fri.-Sat. 11:30 A.M.-11 P.M.

This is a tavern that's devoted to making great, basic seafood, most notably steamed crabs. Thus, it can be counted a crab house (particularly since there's a rooftop crab deck), though it's unlike the others in town. All the seafood here is good, from crab soup to steamed shrimp to fried clams (just stick with the basics and you'll be thrilled). And even though gentrification is sweeping through this part of town, L. P. Steamer's remains a genuine, working-class-and-proud-of-it Baltimore joint, where locals go for a few beers and a dozen delicious crabs.

RESTAURANTS

STEAMED CRABS 101: A PRIMER

Gathering a group of friends, a few pitchers of beer, a couple dozen crabs, and sitting around pulling, smashing, and feasting on the steamed, seasoned critters is a nearly sacred Baltimore tradition, whether it's in a backyard or on a waterfront crab deck.

If you've never attempted to eat a steamed, hard-shell crab before, you're going to be pretty stumped about how to even start. The first hurdle you'll have to leap: What kind of crabs do you want? Mediums? Jumbos? Males? Females? And how many do you need?

Here are some good rules of thumb to use when ordering steamed crabs. Technically (and environmentally), it's better to order males only; the females need to be spared for future reproduction and harvests. For all the work you'll do cracking open a crab, there's not much meat, so figure on about four or five crabs per person. A crab's size determines the amount of meat and its cost. The price fluctuates with that week's harvest; at press time, a dozen large males went for about $38.

After you place your order, you'll be presented with a huge, hot heap of the crustacean critters, dumped in the center of a table wrapped in brown craft paper. You'll be issued a mallet and perhaps a knife, a roll of paper towels, and a stack of wet napkin packs. Now what?

Start with the claws (though some people save them for last, we'll start here). Tear them off and use the knife as a fulcrum to crack the shell open about one-quarter of the way down the claw, using the mallet to whack the knife and shatter the shell. Crack open the claw and get the meat out – you can eat everything in the claw.

Now comes the body. Flip the crab over and notice the "key," a long tab on the belly of the crab; the male's looks like the Washington Monument in D.C., while the female's looks like the Capitol dome. Lift it up and use it to remove the top shell, exposing the interior of the crab. You'll notice some yellowish, fatty material on the sides and the crab's "lungs," more or less, which are also yellow. Do *not* eat anything yellow; scrape that stuff out! Crack open the shell some more, breaking the crab in half, and eat the white crab meat.

Some of the best meat of the crab is the backfin meat; to get at it, notice the two small rear legs that have paddle-like flaps on them. The backfin meat is above those legs, in the crab's body.

Here are a few other tips from experienced eaters: Use plastic cups or cans for your beers (and drink beer or iced tea with crabs, please; chardonnay is preposterous). Don't accidentally wipe your eyes during crab eating; the spices and salts of the seasoning will hurt terribly. And don't wear a nice outfit or a bib (this ain't lobster) when eating crabs. It's going to be a delicious, loud, wonderful mess.

Here's a little secret: These days, the crabs you'll eat in Baltimore are almost definitely not from the Chesapeake Bay at all, but rather from the Gulf of Mexico or even farther afield. The Bay's crab population is too low for major harvests right now; rejuvenation efforts continue to make small strides, but there's still plenty of work to be done.

© TIM TADDER AND MARYLAND OFFICE OF TOURISM

Baltimore's signature crustacean, the steamed crab

DESSERTS
BALTIMORE CUPCAKE COMPANY ⓢ
1433 E. Fort Ave., 410/783-1600,
www.baltimorecupcakecompany.com
HOURS: Mon.-Fri. 9 A.M.-6 P.M., Sat. 9 A.M.-5 P.M.

The resurgent fascination with cupcakes (taken to gourmet levels and prices) that has swept the nation also made it to Baltimore; this local cupcake emporium has won over many fans with their rich, sweet treats. Pinks and whites are abundant in this gorgeous little shop on Fort Avenue in Locust Point, from the paint scheme to the cupcakes themselves. Flavors change daily, which encourages return visits. Plus, it's on the way to Fort McHenry, which makes stopping by for another cupcake almost a patriotic endeavor.

ITALIAN
PAZZA LUNA ⓢⓢ
1401 E. Clement St., 410/962-1212, www.pazzaluna.us
HOURS: Lunch Tues.-Fri. 11:30 A.M.-2 P.M., dinner Tues.-Thurs. 5-10 P.M., Fri.-Sat. 5-11 P.M.

Now run by the owner of the sleek, modern Sotto Sopra in urbane Mount Vernon, Pazza Luna is a completely different type of Italian restaurant—at least in terms of atmosphere. It's tucked away on a side street in working-class (if you ignore the new waterfront condos) Locust Point, and in past incarnations has been a favorite of locals and visitors to Federal Hill. The new menu here is geared to keep it as that type of restaurant: thoughtful execution of standards, with a little creativity on top, like grilled tuna on phyllo dough with red pepper mousse.

MEXICAN
BLUE AGAVE ⓢⓢ
1032 Light St., 410/576-3938,
www.blueagaverestaurant.com
HOURS: Tues.-Sun. 5-10:30 P.M.

This is a pretty serious Mexican restaurant, where seafood, chicken, *cotija* cheese, and handmade moles rule; even better, it's also a serious tequileria, with about 100 tequilas on hand, including the mighty 1800 Reposado, which goes for about $35 a shot. The long, tiled bar dishes out libations until 2 A.M. It's easy to focus on the delicious margaritas and tequilas here, but the exposed-brick and wood dining room is inviting, and the food here is worth paying some attention to as well; the small plates and basics are stronger here than some of the more grandiose entrées, and you shouldn't miss the in-house flan and *tres leches* cake for dessert.

SEAFOOD
NICK'S OYSTER BAR ⓢⓢ
Cross Street Market, 1065 S. Charles St., 410/685-2020, www.nicksoysterbar.com
HOURS: Mon. 11 A.M.-7 P.M., Tues.-Thurs. 11 A.M.-10 P.M., Fri.-Sat. 10 A.M.-midnight, Sun. 11 A.M.-7 P.M.

Located in the renovated west end of the historic Cross Street Market, this staple of Federal Hill living (and dining) has been serving up huge piles of mussels, steamed shrimp, fish and chips, and more for decades. Pull up one of the many stools and eat your catch at the counter (don't forget to order a big beer, served in a plastic cup). There's a fully stocked raw bar, as well as a sushi bar. Take in the loud, sometimes-raucous small crowd that gathers at Nick's operation, watch sports on one of the many TVs, or just dig in to a big plate of deliciously spicy shrimp.

RUSTY SCUPPER ⓢⓢⓢ
402 Key Hwy., 410/727-3678,
www.selectrestaurants.com/rusty
HOURS: Sun.-Thurs. 11:30 A.M.-10 P.M., Fri.-Sat. 11:30 A.M.-midnight, brunch Sun. 11 A.M.-2 P.M.

At the base of Federal Hill rises this longtime Inner Harbor eatery, which was one of the first big restaurants to take advantage of the great views of the then-new Harborplace gained from the south side of the harbor. The view is still the main reason to come to this big, corporate operation, though the (expensive) food can be surprisingly well-handled, and the Sunday brunches are a favorite of many locals. The best views are from the upper patio deck, so pass through the nautically themed main dining rooms and head for the stairs. There's live music most weekends (generally piano), and this is a lively, bustling place, so don't plan on a quiet, sedate evening here.

RESTAURANTS

RYLEIGH'S OYSTER $$
36 E. Cross St., 410/539-2093, www.ryleighs.com
HOURS: Daily 11 A.M.-2 A.M.

This is one of the two best places to get seafood like oysters and steamed shrimp in Federal Hill (the other is Nick's Oyster Bar, in the Cross Street Market). Unlike the no-frills Nick's, Ryleigh's is a real restaurant, so in addition to their popular, blue-slate oyster bar (and the oysters here, no matter which variety you pick, are always very fresh), there's a full menu of gourmet seafood dishes, all artfully plated, along with hearty sandwiches and salads. It's also a great historic space, with lots of wood, exposed brick, large windowed dining areas that look out on bustling Cross Street, and an upstairs loft dining room.

Mount Vernon   Map 5

AFGHAN
THE HELMAND $$
806 N. Charles St., 410/752-0311
HOURS: Sun.-Thurs. 5-10 P.M., Fri.-Sat. 5-11 P.M.

Few restaurants in Baltimore can boast of the family ties of The Helmand's owner, Quayum Karzai: His brother Hamid is president of Afghanistan. The Karzai name has been cherished in Baltimore for years, mostly because of the amazing, basic-yet-complex Afghan food served in this simple, white-walls-and-tablecloths restaurant. One of the city's most beloved appetizers is the *kaddo borawni:* fried and baked baby pumpkin served on garlic yogurt; popular entrées include lamb and beef meatballs and grapes and *mantwo,* hand-made pastries with onions and beef. There are plenty of vegetarian options here as well.

AMERICAN
◖ THE PRIME RIB $$$
1101 N. Calvert St., 410/539-1804,
www.theprimerib.com
HOURS: Mon.-Thurs. 5-11 P.M., Fri.-Sat. 5-11 P.M.,
Sun. 4-10 P.M.

If you want to know what going out to a no-holds-barred prime rib steak dinner with the boys in 1973 Baltimore was like, head to this well-preserved but still vital luxurious steakhouse in an unassuming building east of Mount Vernon. The chairs are huge leather thrones; the waiters are tuxedoed and battle-tested; the floors are cheetah-print; the piano lid is Lucite; the drinks are stiff and the wine list decadent. But the beef here (as well as the other food) is excelsior, and The Prime Rib was recently anointed by *Esquire* magazine for producing one of the best 20 steaks in America. It's a place worth dressing up for, which is good, because jackets are required.

ASIAN
MINATO $$
1013 N. Charles St., 410/332-0332,
www.minatosushibar.com
HOURS: Lunch Mon.-Fri. 11:30 A.M.-2:30 P.M., dinner
Mon.-Thurs. 5:30-10 P.M., Fri.-Sat. 5-11 P.M., Sun. 5-10 P.M.

It's uncommon in Baltimore for a very good sushi restaurant to also be a very good bar, but Minato does both. The historic row house manages to incorporate modern, interesting design that doesn't wreck the original space (though the huge lighting fixture is rather dominant). Maybe it's the confluence of these feats that makes Minato so popular, but it's probably the quality of the sushi and sashimi here; freshness is a constant, and the presentation (unless the place is swamped) is charming. There's a good selection of sake as well, making this a favorite for Mount Vernon residents and a destination for other Baltimoreans.

THAI LANDING $$
1207 N. Charles St., 410/727-1234
HOURS: Lunch Mon.-Fri. 11:30 A.M.-2:30 P.M., dinner
Mon.-Thurs. 5-9:40 P.M., Fri.-Sat. 5-10:10 P.M.

The neighborhood may have changed—new,

Minato serves up great sushi and more in a modern, vibrant row house setting.

upscale apartment and condo construction has embraced Thai Landing's much older three-story building—but this restaurant is still going strong, having earned loyal customers from all across the city. The decor in both the first- and second-floor dining rooms is un-assuming, with several large Thai items and statuary, and a small shrine to family members in the back is particularly intriguing. The food is solid, if not the best Thai in town, and the staff is helpful and pleasant. Still, Thai Landing will cook up some mettle-testing spicy food (if requested, and double-checked if they don't know you), like the *goong khob pho* (grilled shrimp) appetizer or *pet prad kra-pao* (roast duck with vegetables).

THAIRISH $$

804 N. Charles St., 410/752-5857
HOURS: Lunch Tues.-Fri. 11:30 A.M.-3 P.M., dinner Tues.-Fri. 4:30-9:30 P.M., Sat.-Sun. 4:30-10 P.M.
Combine Thai and Irish and you get Thairish,

a cozy little Thai restaurant/service counter with a tiny handful of tables. This is a one-man shop, for the most part, run by white-haired Thai native Kerrigan Kitikul (he's married to an Irish woman, and took an Irish-sounding name), and it's a personal dining experience to place your order with him from Thairish's small but complete menu. Curries are the way to go here, as are any of the Thai staples (like panangs and pad thai). Be warned: There's a no-cell-phones policy here, enforced with vigor that would make the East Germans envious.

CONTEMPORARY AND NEW AMERICAN
ABACROMBIE $$

58 W. Biddle St., 410/837-3630, www.abacrombie.net
HOURS: Wed.-Sat. 5-10 P.M., brunch Sun. noon-7 P.M.
Depending on what kind of night you visit this charming, minimalist, slightly-below-ground-level restaurant, you might think it's either the hottest table in town or a place that forgot to

advertise. Business here ebbs and flows with the performance schedule at the nearby Meyerhoff Symphony Hall and Lyric Opera House. No shows mean you may have the room to yourself—which is a win for you, because the kitchen turns out some fantastic food, like pork confit and lamb leg steak, using lots of local ingredients. The room is very white, and the upholstered chairs are very plush; stop by for their popular and tasty Sunday brunches, which include delicious omelettes and pancakes.

B $$

1501 Bolton St., 410/383-8600, www.b-bistro.com
HOURS: Tues.-Sat. 5-10 P.M., Sun. 5-9 P.M., brunch Sun. 10 A.M.-2 P.M.

The Bolton Hill section of town has lots of grand and stately row homes and, sadly, very few places to eat. Luckily, it has b, a bright, tidy city bistro that is a cornerstone for the neighborhood's residents. The restaurant has a great, warm feel, and you'll see lots of people on dates—and long-time lovers having a great dinner. The menu features some particularly nice salads and seafood entrées, and delicate, inventive pastas and pizzas round out the bill. Sunday brunch (with omelettes, eggs, and pancakes) is immensely popular here, and reservations are highly recommended.

THE BREWER'S ART $$

1106 N. Charles St., 410/547-6925,
www.belgianbeer.com
HOURS: Mon.-Sat. 4 P.M.-2 A.M., Sun. 5 P.M.-2 A.M.

Though there are two outstanding bars in the building, the dining room at The Brewer's Art is a sometimes-overlooked star. Imaginative takes on old favorites are the standard fare here, often using the house-brewed ales in reductions or in even more interesting ways. The deep, inviting dining room retains the early-20th-century charms of this once-grand mansion, with wood details and floors and grand fireplaces, updated with modern art hangings. The staff is generally friendly and knowledgeable, and the wine list is solid and not ridiculously marked-up. The rosemary garlic fries absolutely

must be ordered; they are one of the city's most beloved snacks.

CITY CAFÉ $$

1001 Cathedral St., 410/539-4252,
www.citycafebaltimore.com
HOURS: Mon.-Fri. 11 A.M.-10 P.M., Sat. 10 A.M.-10 P.M., Sun. 10 A.M.-7 P.M.

Even if the food here weren't as good as it is—from lamb burgers and eggplant sandwiches to steaks, roasted chickens, tuna, and not-to-be-missed sweet potato fries—there are other reasons to come to this longtime Mount Vernon favorite. There's a great morning rush for coffee and bagels in the café section, which is more informal than the bar/restaurant area. It's a good place to come before going to a performance at one of the nearby theaters and concert halls. And few restaurants in Baltimore cater to as diverse a clientele, which makes the people-watching scene here almost as interesting as the food.

DONNA'S $$

800 N. Charles St., 410/385-0180, www.donnas.com
HOURS: Mon.-Thurs. 7:30 A.M.-9 P.M., Fri. 7:30 A.M.-10 P.M., Sat. 9 A.M.-10 P.M., Sun. 9 A.M.-9 P.M.

A very local chain of coffee shops and cafés, Donna's handful of outposts have long been hangout staples for many city residents; they predated the Starbucks that have, inevitably, appeared around town. This, the original location, filled a niche that Baltimore sorely needed; reasonably priced, well-thought-out café food, from zippy salads to great takes on comfort food (the mac and cheese is addictively good) and modern entrées and vegetarian options. You can get in and out of Donna's in 25 minutes, or you can linger for an hour, if there's not a huge wait.

IXIA $$$

518 N. Charles St., 410/727-1800, www.ixia-online.com
HOURS: Tues.-Thurs. 5-9:30 P.M., Fri.-Sat. 5-10:30 P.M.

Dining at Ixia is an experience for more than just your sense of taste. There's the almost lapis lazuli–like blue color of the walls, the white and yellow beads and wall hangings and chandeliers, the 40-foot-long black marble bar in the back, and the Warhol-ized portrait of Jackie Kennedy over the dining room's mantelpiece. Design like this leads to an expectation of equally daring meals, and the menu rises to the challenge: Kona kampachi sashimi and lobster and crab macaroni and cheese to start, crispy-skin Scottish salmon with four different preparations and tempura soft-shell crab for main events. Service can be great, if occasionally distracted, but the food excuses some of these lapses. Note that the hours listed here end with final seating times, not closing times.

JOE SQUARED ⑤⑤

133 W. North Ave., 410/545-0444,
www.joesquared.com

HOURS: Mon.-Fri. 11 A.M.-2 A.M., Sat.-Sun. 4 P.M.-2 A.M.

Another newcomer to Baltimore's short list of good pizza purveyors, Joe Squared lives up to its name by serving squared-off pizzas topped with everything from traditional pepperoni and vegetables to corned beef and Granny Smith apples. Owing to the eclectic live music, a great jukebox and CD selection,

and cheap prices, this is a popular joint with cool, college-aged kids, though the only nearby school is the Maryland Institute College of Art. Specials carry sometimes-painful famous musician names (Ike Turner's Black and Blue tilapia sub, Bob Dylan's Winey Chicken linguini). This is not the best neighborhood after dark, alas; there's a seedy motel across the street that was used in *The Wire*.

SASCHA'S 527 CAFÉ ⑤⑤

527 N. Charles St., 410/539-8880, www.saschas.com

HOURS: Lunch Mon.-Fri. 11 A.M.-3 P.M., dinner Mon.-Thurs. 5:30-11 P.M., Fri.-Sat. 5:30 P.M.-midnight

The production begins with the entrance to Sascha's, which involves massive red velvet drapes that conceal an enormous, chandeliered Mount Vernon row house, with ceilings some 16 feet high and a red and gold color scheme that exudes warmth even in the dead of winter. A good selection of small plates is popular here (their take on the BLT: fried lobster, bacon, and tomato, on a slice of grilled semolina), but the entrées have some strong contenders as well (scallops with grits and Andouille sausage, and "deconstructed" eggplant lasagna). Sascha's is a place for those who like to eat and

---

PIE HOPES: FINDING BALTIMORE'S BEST PIZZA

Baltimore's lack of fantastic pizza is, regretfully, one of the city's glaring culinary shortcomings. Despite all the headway that the town has made on the dining front in recent decades, there are still only a few places that serve good pizza – and fewer still where you can grab just a slice.

For those looking to sit down and savor a pie, here are some very different suggestions. First is **Matthew's Pizzeria,** on the outskirts of Canton. Opened in 1943, the pizza you'll get here is nothing like the flat, thin pizzas Americans are used to. It's a thick, hearty disc, almost like a real pie. If that's not your style, head a few blocks south and you can get a traditional New York City-style pizza (among other authentic Italian dishes) at Canton's **Tutti Gusti.** A very differ-

ent, thin, gourmet-topping Neapolitan pie can be found at the self-serve, no-frills, but still charming **Iggie's** in Mount Vernon. And for a square deal on a square pizza, try hipster haven **Joe Squared,** on the outskirts of Mount Vernon.

If you want a slice to go, and you're in Fell's Point, the crispy creations of **Brick Oven Pizza** are found right on the plaza at the foot of Broadway (you can also get a whole pie to eat as you watch the crowds circulate through Fell's Point). In Hampden, it may not be the best, but it is the biggest: the monster 30-plus-inch slice at **Angelo's Pizza** is literally almost an entire pizza unto itself. And one of the best pizzas in town – made by Mount Vernon's **Neo Viccino** – can be eaten in-store or (even better) picked up for home consumption.

be seen eating, especially when it involves red velvet. Note that lunch is served here as well, but it's very light, with lots of salads, and done cafeteria-style.

XS ⑤⑤

1307 N. Charles St., 410/468-0002,
www.xsbaltimore.com

HOURS: Mon.-Thurs. 7 A.M.-midnight, Fri.-Sat.
7 A.M.-2 A.M., Sun. 9 A.M.-midnight

This sleek, exposed-brick café (the name is pronounced "excess") and dessert favorite is the city's most vertical dining establishment; once you enter, you can continue to climb riserless stairs, choosing from one of the four floors of seating. This is a popular place with students from the nearby University of Baltimore; there are DJs every day of the week, and the crowd is young, cool, and energized. The first floor is home to the coffee bar, desserts, sushi bar, and a small outdoor dining area. The rest is restaurant and lounge, with a broad menu that covers everything from sushi to panini.

CONTEMPORARY ITALIAN
BRASS ELEPHANT ⑤⑤⑤

924 N. Charles St., 410/547-8485,
www.brasselephant.com

HOURS: Daily 5:30-9 P.M.

Baltimore has embraced a lot of new cuisine trends and movements—local producers, tapas, even some fusion—but there are still a few classic Baltimore restaurants that stick to the tried and true, usually in a exquisite setting. The Brass Elephant is one of these stalwarts. Tucked within a grand old Mount Vernon mansion, the ambiance here is robber-baron Baltimore (note the many elephant-themed items in the building), and the food is Italian/Continental with modern American inspirations (such as parmesan-crusted rockfish, placed in a bowl of minestrone soup). This is an "occasion" sort of restaurant, so dress accordingly; then have an after-dinner drink and dessert at the great Tusk Lounge upstairs.

IGGIE'S ⑤⑤

818 N. Calvert St., 410/528-0818, www.iggiespizza.com

HOURS: Tues.-Thurs. noon-9 P.M., Fri.-Sat. noon-10 P.M.

Any pizza place named for a dog is probably going to be good, and Iggie's is—just not in the ways you might expect. It's a bare-bones operation: You place your order, get your silverware and glassware, set your own table, open your own bottle of wine (bring-your-own only), and clean up your own mess. But it's worth the effort, because it makes you feel like you helped prepare the thin, gourmet pizzas made in Neapolitan style, with toppings like *soprasatta,* roast duck, blue cheese, and fennel. It's a great environment, too, with lots of exposed ductwork, intriguing customers, and a few inexplicable pipes and big wheel valves springing out of the floor and ceiling.

SOTTO SOPRA ⑤⑤⑤

405 N. Charles St., 410/625-0534,
www.sottosoprainc.com

HOURS: Lunch Mon.-Sat. 11:30 A.M.-2:30 P.M., dinner Tues.-Thurs. 5:30-10:30 P.M., Fri.-Sat. 5:30-11:30 P.M., Sun. 5-9 P.M.

For a city used to a certain type of Italian restaurant—that is, the kind in Little Italy—the arrival of Sotto Sopra was a bit jarring. Here was a modern, hip, exciting, and youthful-feeling restaurant, in a strange part of town for an Italian restaurant, serving interesting, delightful dishes with top-notch presentation. Their take on calamari comes served with tarragon-caper remoulade and red pepper coulis. Huge murals portraying diners line the expansive main dining room, curtains and gold-painted pillars accent the room, and there's a more intimate back bar as well.

ETHIOPIAN
DUKEM ⑤⑤

1100 Maryland Ave., 410/385-0318,
www.dukemrestaurant.com

HOURS: Daily 11 A.M.-11 P.M.

Though the sign out front doesn't say it, this is Dukem #2; the flagship location is in Washington, D.C. The Baltimore outpost is in a building barely two blocks from the Meyerhoff Symphony Hall and the Lyric Opera House. The oddly shaped first-floor dining room (very narrow and not very long) has been joined, thankfully, by a more traditionally laid-out second-floor room. Seating is provided both in traditional Ethiopian style (small stools and woven basket-tables to hold the communal tray) and with conventional tables and chairs. The food is delectably garlicky and designed to be eaten using pieces of a spongy sour bread called *injera;* utensils take away from the fun.

INDIAN
AKBAR $$

823 N. Charles St., 410/539-0944,
www.akbar-restaurant.com
HOURS: Lunch Mon.-Fri. 11:30 A.M.-2:30 P.M.,
Sat.-Sun. noon-3 P.M., dinner Sun.-Thurs. 5-11 P.M.,
Fri.-Sat. 5-11:30 P.M.

This place puts out a massive and renowned lunchtime buffet that always packs them in. But go at dinner, when the kitchen is not so focused on quantity, and you'll get even better versions of the Indian standards, like tandoori, palak paneer, and chicken tikka masala. The restaurant is in the basement of a large row house, so while it's a decent-enough sized room, it's doesn't have the greatest views. But when the place is full, the candles are burning brightly, and the Indian music is rolling, there's a very good mood and feel here.

INDIGMA $$

802 N. Charles St., 410/605-1212,
www.indigmarestaurant.com
HOURS: Lunch Tues.-Fri. 11:30 A.M.-2:30 P.M., Sat.-Sun.
noon-3 P.M., dinner Tues.-Thurs. and Sun. 5-9:30 P.M.,
Fri.-Sat. 5-10:30 P.M.

A relative newcomer to the Baltimore Indian-food scene, Indigma (and its lush dining room bathed in deep hues of purples, reds, and yellows) takes a couple of detours from the usual bill of fare, adding in more dates, raisins, and Eastern Indian dishes to the standard offerings. There are also some more adventurous meals to be had here, like *machi addraki,* a tangy,

spicy grouper filet, though the food here, like most ethnic food in Baltimore, may be a little sedate to those used to traditional preparations. But Indigma is more about the entire experience, unlike at some more modest tikka masala joints; this is an upscale eatery, with professional waiters who know how to make a meal into an evening out.

ITALIAN
NEO VICCINO $$

1317 N. Charles St., 410/347-0349, www.viccino.com
HOURS: Mon.-Sat. 11 A.M.-11 P.M., Sun. 11 A.M.-9 P.M.

Just one of the several eateries on this stretch of Charles Street across from the University of Baltimore (and a block from Amtrak's Pennsylvania Station), there's not much on the outside (or the inside) to distinguish this contemporary Italian restaurant. So why is it worth a visit? The pizza. This place makes its own dough, and while so much of the city's pizza is average at best, this well-crafted pie— with just the right thickness and crunch, plus slightly better-than-normal toppings—is a real stand-out. Want the pizza, but can't find the time to stop in for a sit-down meal? They deliver, and offer most of their menu (including the great pizza) for carry-out.

NEPALESE
KUMARI $$

911 N. Charles St., 410/547-1600,
www.kumaricuisine.com
HOURS: Lunch Mon.-Fri. 11:30 A.M.-2:30 P.M.,
Sat.-Sun. 11:30 A.M.-3 P.M., dinner Mon.-Fri. 5-10 P.M.,
Sat.-Sun. 5-10:30 P.M.

Baltimore's only Nepalese restaurant opened in 2003, and diners have supported it enough to keep it going. The menu includes a number of Indian standards, which are abundant in their popular lunchtime buffets. While the Indian staples are good here, take at least a small chance and order something you've never had before, like the *khaja* (bean, soybean, potato, and vegetables) appetizer or *bhojan* (Nepalese lamb curry) entrée. The views of Charles Street are great from the second-story tables, which lie behind large plate-glass windows, and the decor is a mish-mash of old Baltimore rowhouse-meets-restaurant and a simple white, red, and black color scheme.

SPANISH
TIO PEPE $$$

10 E. Franklin St., 410/539-4675

HOURS: Lunch Mon.-Fri. 11 A.M.-3 P.M., dinner daily 4-10 P.M.

A beloved Baltimore institution, this subterranean Spanish restaurant has been in business since 1968, and hasn't done much to change the decor or menu since. The walls are white stucco and brick, there are plenty of wrought-iron sconces, and brightly painted sangria pitchers adorn many tables. Waiters in red tuxedo jackets glide through the room and linger at your table. The classic Spanish cuisine emphasizes seafood, starting with excellent shrimp in garlic and ending with two tours de force: whole suckling pig and a massive paella. Dining at the expensive Tio Pepe is an event;

jackets are required for men, reservations are a must, and you'll need to let them know in advance if you want the pig or the paella.

TAPAS
TAPAS TEATRO $$

1711 N. Charles St., 410/332-0110, www.tapasteatro.com

HOURS: Tues.-Fri. 5 P.M.-2 A.M., Sat.-Sun. 4 P.M.-2 A.M.

Once, the only reason to come to this stretch of Charles Street, just north of Pennsylvania Station, was to see a movie at the Charles Theatre or maybe grab a cocktail at the Club Charles across the street. But Tapas Teatro has become another social anchor here, drawing hungry and thirsty crowds, especially during the warmer seasons for their expansive outdoor dining section and bar. It's a great place to stop before or after catching a film at the Charles, or to go just to eat. The plates are generally of Spanish and Mediterranean origin, and while quite good, dining at Tapas Teatro is about more than the food: It's about the scene.

Hampden and Homewood   Map 6

AMERICAN
ANGELO'S PIZZA $

3600 Keswick Rd., 410/235-2595

HOURS: Mon.-Thurs. 11 A.M.-10 P.M., Fri.-Sat. 11 A.M.-11 P.M., Sun. noon-5 P.M.

This corner pizzeria and sub shop (owned by two brothers named Pizza) has been serving pizzas and cheesesteaks to hungry Hampdenites for generations, but most people know Angelo's for one reason: their monstrous slices of pizza, cut from a colossal 30-inch pie. Best of all, it's not just quantity: Angelo's pizzas are among the city's better pies (although, alas, that's not saying much). There are a few outdoor tables that make for good people-watching and scene-observing, especially during the warmer months, and you can eat inside, but the basement-like space can get a tad claustrophobic and is a bit overstuffed with the kitchen, tables, pillars,

equipment, and video poker machines—and that's all before you add people.

CAFÉ HON $$

1002 W. 36th St., 410/243-1230, www.cafehon.com

HOURS: Mon.-Thurs. 7 A.M.-10 P.M., Fri.-Sat. 9 A.M.-10 P.M., Sun. 9 A.M.-8 P.M.

The two-story pink flamingo on the front of Café Hon is a tribute to local director John Waters' film of the same name and the "hon" culture that the restaurant's owner has helped build into a city-wide brand (see June's HonFest). The café is always busy, serving up diner-style staples like meat loaf, slightly more upscale dishes like salmon, and Baltimore-peculiar entrées (like sour beef on Mondays, and fries with gravy every day). There's even an adjacent tavern (Hon Bar) with live music on Wednesdays and most Sundays.

© GEOFF BROWN

Beneath the pink flamingo lies Café Hon, a Hampden institution.

ASIAN

SUZIE'S SOBA 💲💲

1009 W. 36th St., 410/243-0051

HOURS: Daily 5-10 P.M.

If you're in Hampden and looking for Asian food, this is your best (and basically only) bet, unless you want to stop in one of the two basic Chinese food joints on 36th Street. A noodle house that doesn't play favorites, Suzie's has noodle dishes from Japan, China, Korea, and Vietnam, and lots of vegetarian and vegan options—which can be welcome in meat-centric Baltimore. The decorations are a mix of modern, leftover, and Asian, a conglomeration that might not make much sense, except that it fits the menu plan here. There's also a great little back patio and garden, perfect for grabbing a quick bite between rounds of shopping on The Avenue.

CAFÉS

A COMMON GROUND 💲

819 W. 36th St., 410/235-5533

HOURS: Daily 7 A.M.-5 P.M.

Wedged into an exposed-brick row house that seems a little tight even by Baltimore standards, this homegrown coffee house and café is worth the squeeze. Great java and other drinks are their specialty, plus they have huge muffins, bagels, and freshly made sandwiches. If you can't find a seat in the tiny front area, there's another dining room in the back, and an outdoor deck past that. The small tables are usually taken by typical coffee house denizens—writers, students, artists, teachers, layabouts—and the songs selected by the staff, from every musical era, are always worth listening to.

DONNA'S 💲💲

3101 St. Paul St., 410/889-3410, www.donnas.com

HOURS: Mon.-Thurs. 6:30 A.M.-10 P.M., Fri. 6:30 A.M.-11 P.M., Sat. 7 A.M.-11 P.M., Sun. 7 A.M.-9 P.M.

The Homewood (Charles Village, technically) branch of this local coffee house/café chain is one of the few places in the neighborhood to linger over a glass of wine and dine on pumpkin cannelloni (or perhaps a lamb burger) in a modern, TV-free environment. There are plenty of students from nearby Johns Hopkins

FARMERS MARKETS

Baltimore may be one of the nation's 25 largest metropolises, but just outside the I-695 Beltway that loops around the city, there are miles and miles of fields, dairies, orchards, and livestock farms. A century ago, the city used to have a thriving municipal market system, with huge indoor and outdoor markets in the most populous neighborhoods; changes in population and shopping habits have hurt many of them or turned them into places to grab a quick bite or a beer, rather than do a daily produce run. Today, the still-thriving markets include Federal Hill's **Cross Street Market,** downtown's **Lexington Market,** and Fell's Point's **Broadway Market.**

Today, market culture is back, though not at the traditional city stalls. With the increasingly popularity of locally grown and raised foods, some of Baltimore's most popular outdoor farmers markets have seen a surge in crowds and purveyors, selling everything from fresh-baked multigrain bread to obscure varieties of peaches to unprocessed, naturally raised meats.

On Saturdays, head east of Homewood to the **Waverly Farmers Market,** held in a parking lot at the corner of Barclay and 32nd Streets, where more than 40 vendors sell fruits, vegetables, nuts, breads, coffee, and more, all year long (7 A.M. to roughly noon). You can even grab some smoked fish or freshly steamed shrimp for a snack during your shopping expedition. A new **Freshfarm Market,** also held on Saturdays (June-October, 9 A.M.-1 P.M.) is tucked between the new office, condo, and retail towers of Harbor East (between the Inner Harbor and Fell's Point). This progressive chain of farmers markets operates across the Baltimore and Washington, D.C., region, and insists on local farmers and products. On Sundays from May through December, head downtown and under I-83, where Holiday and Saratoga Streets intersect, for the **Baltimore Farmers Market.** Though the location's not terribly scenic, crowds descend each Sunday (8 A.M.-noon) on the dozens of vendors here, selling all manner of foods from Maryland, Pennsylvania, and Delaware farms; there's lots of prepared food to nosh on while shopping, too (and you won't want to miss the freshly fried mini-donuts).

here, but they're the kind more interested in food and conversation than partying—this is an appropriate place to bring their parents for a quick, metropolitan meal. There's a popular (and small) outdoor sidewalk patio, too.

CONTEMPORARY AND NEW AMERICAN
DOGWOOD $$$

911 W. 36th Street, 410/889-0952,
www.dogwoodbaltimore.com

HOURS: Mon.-Thurs. 11:30 A.M.-10 P.M.,
Fri.-Sat. 11 A.M.-11 P.M.

Take the unassuming staircase down from 36th Street into Dogwood and you'll find a sleek, modern dining room and bar that has garnered a reputation as one of the city's most promising new restaurants. Large artworks adorn the walls, and eclectic lighting and objets d'art are sprinkled around the room. The menu uses local, seasonal produce and meats, so it changes often and unpredictably. Count on about seven entrées, which veer from tender beef cuts (teres major, a less well-known cut, is a menu staple) to local poultry and seafood (from oysters to rockfish) whenever possible. Desserts, made in house, can be a work in progress, which is the only caveat at this highly recommended gourmet destination.

GERTRUDE'S $$$

The Baltimore Museum of Art, 410/889-3399,
www.gertrudesbaltimore.com

HOURS: Tues.-Fri. 11:30 A.M.-9 P.M., Sat. 5-9 P.M.,
Sun. 5-8 P.M., brunch Sat.-Sun. 10:30 A.M.-3 P.M.

Located in the Baltimore Museum of Art, Gertrude's (named for chef John Shields' grandmother) is a showcase for classic Chesapeake Bay dishes, like oysters and fish, as well as Asian-style entrées, steaks, and even burgers. There's also a "make your own entrée" menu system, which is great for both the indecisive and the adventurous. The restaurant's gorgeous, tented patio, overlooking the BMA's sculpture garden and grounds, with the city bustling just beyond the trees, is a local favorite. The patio fills up fast on fair-weather weekends and nights, so reservations, especially for brunch, are a necessity.

ROCKET TO VENUS $$

3360 Chestnut Ave., 410/235-7887,
www.rockettovenus.com

HOURS: Mon.-Sat. 5-11 P.M., Sun. noon-7 P.M.

"RTV" has become one of the city's most popular and interesting places to eat, drink, and hang out. The menu seems to have been designed by a committee of hungry party-goers at 4 A.M. (fried pickles, pierogies, mini-burgers) and then burnished by inventive chefs (duck confit, tenderloin skewers with peppers and lemon ancho aioli). A great jukebox and free entertainment—there's a thriving see-and-be-seen scene at the bar—are two other reasons to visit.

◀ WOODBERRY KITCHEN $$$

2010 Clipper Park Rd., No. 126, 410/464-8000,
www.woodberrykitchen.com

HOURS: Sun.-Thurs. 5-10 P.M., Fri.-Sat. 5-11 P.M.

The brains and talent behind Woodberry Kitchen belong to one of Baltimore's few culinary superstars, Spike Gjerde. This latest venture—a big, contemporary/rehabbed late-1800s-era industrial space with an open kitchen, in an old mill complex just west of Hampden—has quickly become one of the city's favorites (and hardest to get into on a weekend night). Completely seasonal menus, based on as-local-as-possible purveyors, mean hearty regional dishes like roasted pears, cider-brined pork chops, shrimp and spoonbread, and wood-oven-roasted oysters. Some of the crowd comes for the social status points, but is often distracted by the quality of the food. On weekend nights, the small bar is packed with slightly younger folks, along with hopeful walk-ins without reservations who will never

© GEOFF BROWN

RESTAURANTS

Inside Woodberry Kitchen is a contemporary renovation and locally sourced cuisine.

see an empty table; there are a lot of serious eaters from across the region who plan their dinners here weeks in advance.

DINER
PAPERMOON DINER $$

227 W. 29th St., 410/889-4444,
www.papermoondiner24.com

HOURS: Sun.-Thurs. 7 A.M.-midnight,
Fri.-Sat. 7 A.M.-2 A.M.

This colorful, eclectic diner is adorned (on nearly every surface of the house-like space) with garish paint schemes, toys, mannequins, bric-a-brac, and junk. Take a stool at the long dining counter, or head for one of the utterly mismatched tables in one of two dining rooms. The sprawling menu covers almost every culinary base (though it's best with breakfasts and sandwiches), and this is one of the few places in town where the decor is more interesting than the clientele (a mix of moms, kids, artists, students, and businesspeople). The wait on weekend mornings can be severe, so come either early or late.

ECLECTIC

☾ GOLDEN WEST CAFÉ $$

1105 W. 36th St., 410/889-8891,
www.goldenwestcafe.com

HOURS: Mon.-Fri. 9 A.M.-3 P.M. and 5-9:45 P.M., Sat.
9 A.M.-2:30 P.M. and 5-9:45 P.M., Sun. 9 A.M.-2:30 P.M.
and 5-8:45 P.M.

The decor is American Western Kitsch (note the looming mounted moose head and barbed wire samplers), the wait staff is unapologetically hipster, and the menu is...well, it's all over the place, but in the best way. Tex-Mex is sort of the guiding principle here (fantastic polenta with carne, Frito pie, and enchiladas), but there are also Asian influences, and other dishes inspired by a multitude of cuisines—all made fresh, to order, and with care. Huge and wholesome breakfasts are a specialty here, which makes the waits for Sunday brunch long but worthwhile. Also note that the kitchen closes midday, every day, before reopening for dinner; on weekends, it's brunch only until 5 P.M.

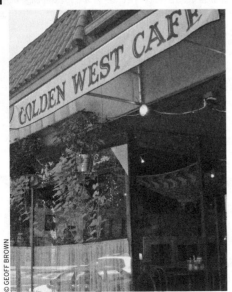

© GEOFF BROWN

Golden West Café, one of the city's favorite restaurants (especially for brunch)

INDIAN

THE AMBASSADOR DINING ROOM $$$

3811 Canterbury Rd., 410/366-1484,
www.ambassadordiningroom.com

HOURS: Lunch Mon.-Fri. 11:30 A.M.-2:30 P.M.,
Sat.-Sun. noon-3 P.M., dinner Sun.-Thurs. 5-10 P.M.,
Fri.-Sat. 5-11 P.M.

In the back of a grand, gothic apartment building just north of Johns Hopkins University is, surprisingly, a grand, semi-upscale Indian restaurant, where wait staff in tuxedos and saris watch over a sprawling, stately dining room. Best of all, though, is the back yard, where—during warm months—the restaurant expands onto the green lawn behind the building, and guests sit in large chairs as they dine on tandoori and naan. It's still worth a visit here in the winter, as well: There's a large gas fireplace in the back patio, which makes for a relaxing evening. The lunch buffet is a big hit with locals and is a much less formal event than dinner.

VEGETARIAN

THE YABBA POT $

2431 St. Paul St., 410/662-8638,
www.theyabbapotcafe.com

HOURS: Mon.-Sat. 11 A.M.-9 P.M., Sun. 2-7 P.M.

While more and more restaurants offer some vegetarian options, this is basically the only option in town for a completely meat-free dining experience (though the food here is enjoyed even by non-vegetarians, particularly the "I Can't Believe There's Not Pork in Here" Queen Greens). Run by the wonderful Chef Mama Skai Davis, this isn't just a restaurant; it's a warm, welcoming place for people to hang out, read about cultural and activist causes, and interact over some great food. Bright colors and homemade signs ("Eat More Kale") create an oasis effect here, encouraging folks to linger and try some more food. Everything at The Yabba Pot is vegetarian; many items are vegan, as well.

Greater Baltimore   Map 7

ASIAN
SUSHI HANA 💲💲
6 E. Pennsylvania Ave., 410/823-0372,
www.sushihanatowson.com
HOURS: Tues.-Thurs. 11 A.M.-10 P.M., Fri. 11 A.M.-11 P.M.,
Sat.-Sun. 3-11 P.M.

The exterior is, somehow, more Mexican-restaurant than Asian (perhaps it's the neon and beige combination), but the interior is utterly perfect, with lots of light-colored woods, paper and wood light fixtures, and a welcoming sushi bar (there's a full menu of Asian specialties available). Located in downtown Towson, a place rife with quick and easy dining options, Sushi Hana has a good reputation as one of the area's better sushi purveyors. The fish here is always very fresh, and while connoisseurs won't be wowed, it's a solid choice. It's popular with the younger crowd on the weekends (who go as much for the sake and Sapporo as the sushi).

FRENCH
THE CHAMELEON CAFÉ 💲💲💲
4341 Harford Rd., 410/254-2376,
www.thechameleoncafe.com
HOURS: Tues.-Thurs. 5-9 P.M., Fri.-Sat. 5-10 P.M.

Located in the culinary hinterland of northern Baltimore City, which looks like the suburbs, this popular restaurant lures rigidly downtown folks into their cars and up Harford Road to a family-run French bistro that is consistently filled with happy diners. Walk through the front of the house, where the kitchen and supplies reside, to the single dining room, painted in a faded light rust red. It can be a wonderfully boisterous place on a weekend night (and on Wednesdays, when wines are 20–50 percent off) as customers dine on grilled lettuce salad, escargot, oysters, and coq au vin. The staff is young (in age or "at heart"), and diners range from youthful sweethearts to silver anniversary couples.

PETIT LOUIS BISTRO 💲💲💲
4800 Roland Ave., 410/366-9393, www.petitlouis.com
HOURS: Lunch Tues.-Fri. 11:30 A.M.-2 P.M.,
dinner Sun.-Thurs. 5-10 P.M., Fri.-Sat. 5-11 P.M.,
brunch Sun. 10:30 A.M.-2 P.M.

Roland Park is one of Baltimore's most prestigious neighborhoods, but it's one where the concept of neighborhood hasn't been lost; people know one another and interact on a regular basis. And a lot of that interaction goes on at Petit Louis Bistro, located in one of the nation's first tiny shopping centers. Though the restaurant looks like a century-old Parisian bistro—marble topped-tables, wrought-iron details and filigree—it's actually a modern installation. The service here is well dressed and well informed, and always willing to help and fulfill any request. The menu is, unsurprisingly, hard-core French bistro, with lots of fresh local ingredients and produce, an amazing selection of cheeses, and upscale fish, meat, and casserole dishes.

SEAFOOD
NICK'S FISH HOUSE 💲💲
2600 Insulator Dr., 410/347-4123,
www.nicksfishhouse.com
HOURS: Sun.-Thurs. 11 A.M.-9 P.M., Fri.-Sat. 11 A.M.-10 P.M.

Owned by the man behind the popular Nick's Oyster Bar in Federal Hill's Cross Street Market, this peculiar restaurant and watering hole is a short drive south of that neighborhood in an industrial area of the waterfront that doesn't get much tourist traffic. This bright yellow seafood house is popular with the young drinking enthusiast set and can get boisterous at night—but it's also a great place for an outdoor lunch with a view of the Hanover Street Bridge. The menu isn't noteworthy in concept or execution, so stick with the basics. After all, you're here for some cocktails and a bite to eat on the big deck, and to get the feel of being far from downtown—which is only a five-minute drive north.

NIGHTLIFE

Going out on the town in Baltimore is easy; all you need to do is figure out what kind of evening you're looking to experience. Decadent cocktails and dancing to house music? Hot jazz upstairs at a music store? Innovative modern music in an art gallery? A huge megaclub or a tiny dive bar? With the city's rejuvenation has come a wide variety of nightlife options to meet any taste or thirst—a big improvement over the (still charming) shot-and-a-beer joints that proliferated throughout the city for years.

Two neighborhoods are real standouts for their often over-lively nocturnal scenes: Fell's Point and Federal Hill. The waterfront bars and restaurants of Fell's Point entertain all sorts of folks, from those looking for a glass of wine and some dessert to college kids out for serious revelry. Federal Hill is very similar

in character, though as there are a few less restaurants, there are more folks just out for some drinks. Closing time in both places (which is 2 A.M. in Baltimore) can be a little hectic, especially on warm summer nights, so plan wisely. Also note that Canton's small O'Donnell Square area is very similar to Fell's Point and Federal Hill in character and crowd make-up.

The rest of the city can be categorized in some broad strokes: Downtown is where the city's big, sprawling clubs and bar complexes are found; more sophisticated-feeling lounges are located in stately Mount Vernon; and Hampden and Homewood have a few well-populated hipster bars and taverns. Unlike some cities, where music venues are congregated into certain areas, Baltimore's live music scene is scattered all over town, which makes

HIGHLIGHTS

LOOK FOR  TO FIND RECOMMENDED NIGHTLIFE.

🌙 **Best Serious Jazz Club:** There are some places where the musicians are stuck in a corner so people can focus on their drinks and food and each other; upstairs at **An die Musik Live,** the audience is there to listen, and the performers respond with knockout sets (page 98).

🌙 **Best Alternative Music Venue:** If you like being so close to a performer that their sweat can drip on you, the resolutely indie **Ottobar** is the joint for you; there's also a great upstairs bar/jukebox/pool scene (page 99).

🌙 **Best One-Stop Club: Sonar** is what every big Baltimore club should be like: different rooms with different vibes, people having fun and not being aggressive, and a constant stream of cutting-edge music, both live and DJ-driven (page 99).

🌙 **Best Atmospheric Bar:** The murals are wonderful faux-WPA style, the chairs and booths are Art Deco, the bartenders are charming and make a mean martini, and you can go to a play or a movie across the street, all at the venerable **Club Charles** (page 101).

🌙 **Best Old-School Baltimore Corner Bar:** One visit to Fell's Point's tiny **Duda's Tavern** and you'll wonder why the once-ubiquitous corner bar has faded into history: there's cold beer, great bartenders and waiters, old-school rock tunes, local sports on the TV, and some fantastic food (page 102).

🌙 **Best Wine Bar with a View:** The views of the Inner Harbor, the Broadway City Recreation Pier, and the historic buildings on Thames Street are made so much nicer with a glass of Riesling and some Jarlsberg cheese at Fell's Point's **V-NO** (page 107).

🌙 **Best Lounge:** Though it was one of the first modern lounges to come to town, **Red Maple** is still one of the best, from the great bar and space and music selections, to the outdoor back patio, to the very appealing small plates menu (page 108).

🌙 **Best After-Hours Club:** In the dark shadows of elevated roadways and warehouses lurks **Paradox,** Baltimore's unstoppable, 13,000-square-foot late-night dance club (and restaurant and half-size basketball court) for the city's cool kids (18 and over) (page 110).

© GEOFF BROWN

Club Charles

NIGHTLIFE

NIGHTLIFE

wandering into a club and hearing a great local band a bit tough; check the websites of some of the listed locations to find out what kind of music you'll find on each stage. So whether it's a night listening to traditional Irish music and hoisting a few Guinnesses, raising a well-shaken martini, or slipping into a small art gallery to catch a buzz-laden new band, nighttime in Baltimore is a great time to experience a different side of the city.

Live Music

AN DIE MUSIK LIVE

409 N. Charles St., 410/385-2638 or 888/221-6170, www.andiemusiklive.com
COST: Cover varies
Map 5

This is a fantastic classical and jazz CD and LP store, and it's also one of the most enchanting places to catch a jazz show. It's no smoky subterranean groove cellar, though; it's the second floor of a cool, modern renovation in the heart of downtown. Big, comfortable chairs are the standard here, and the acoustics of the room are outstanding. Owner Henry Wong also manages to lure a very high caliber of players here, which draws the real cognoscenti.

CHARM CITY ART SPACE

1729 Maryland Ave., no phone, www.ccspace.org
HOURS: Doors open approximately 1 hour before showtime
COST: Cover varies
Map 5

This is not a quiet, subdued art space; it's a working, serious, do-it-yourself building for art and generally loud, unrestrained music. Upstairs are artworks and offices; rock shows take place in the totally rocker-friendly wood-paneled basement, which rapidly turns into an overheated swamp during well-attended gigs, but it all fits in with the ethos of the place. This is a DIY joint, so don't expect frills of any sorts, but do expect that, by coming to a show

B'MORE BEATS: FROM BALTIMORE CLUB TO WHAM CITY

There are two new(ish) schools of music in Baltimore, created by two different communities, that provide excellent examples of the music the city likes right now. First is Baltimore Club, a specific type of hip-hop club and dance music that originated in the early 1990s. It's fast: 130-beats-per-minute fast, which means you better know how to dance if you hit the floor. It's not terribly complex in terms of composition or structure, and the same sampled phrases or lyrics are repeated a lot, but if there's a good crowd and they like the song, it's a sight to behold as they all move in a sort of jittering unison.

More recently, a new group of young musicians and artists have gained attention. Bands like Beach House, Double Dagger, and Wye Oak have devoted and interested followings. One group of like-minded folks came together to form an operation known as Wham City, headed by Dan Deacon, who is something of a darling of the independent music press. This group is composed of artists and performers who like to include both costumes and strange sonic events in their shows, and they encourage crowd participation. As unlikely as it might sound, a lot of what comes out is really immediately fun and engaging; live shows are more like big parties than anything else.

here, your money is going right to the artists and the space.

8x10
10 E. Cross St., 410/625-2000, www.the8x10.com
HOURS: Doors open approximately 1 hour before showtime
COST: Cover varies
Map 4

Though this rock and roots club has changed names and philosophies a few times over the years (it's back to the original 8x10 now, reflecting the addresses of the two buildings it occupies), this is still one of the city's great little venues that can pull in a full house with a mid-sized name band or performer. It's a no-frills rock club, so don't expect anything too grandiose, but the beers are relatively cheap and the sound is not bad for such a narrowly shaped space.

METRO GALLERY
1700 N. Charles St., 410/244-0899, www.themetrogallery.net
HOURS: Doors open approximately 1 hour before showtime
COST: Cover varies
Map 5

Metro Gallery began as a basic art gallery; it's since evolved into a performance space and bar, and a great place to see some of the town's best new young bands. It's a nice big room, which hosts readings and art performances in addition to visual artworks. Best of all, there's a great big picture window behind the bands that let crowds watch the traffic on busy Charles Street blur by (though sometimes the management shuts the drapes) as the music plays.

THE OTTOBAR
2549 N. Howard St., 410/662-0069, www.theottobar.com
HOURS: Doors open approximately 1 hour before showtime; upstairs bar opens at 5 P.M.
COST: Cover varies
Map 6

It takes a special venue to host both underground rap and metal bands as well as '80s nights and more mainstream rock bands, but it all makes a strange sort of sense at the Ottobar. Upstairs is a great bar that's open before and during shows, with lots of pool tables and a phenomenal jukebox; downstairs is a (relatively) huge stage (for a Baltimore rock club), a big main floor, and a side balcony with tables and chairs.

RAM'S HEAD LIVE
20 Market Pl., Power Plant Live!, 410/244-1131, www.ramsheadlive.com
HOURS: Mon.-Sat. from 10 A.M.; doors open 2 hours before showtime
COST: Cover varies
Map 1

This is the Baltimore outlet of a long-popular Annapolis-based nightspot; located in the bar/restaurant party complex called Power Plant Live! (and yes, the exclamation point is part of the official name), this venue filled a most-needed niche in the Baltimore music scene. It's a medium-sized performance space that can draw medium-sized acts (and even top-name acts on their way down) and provide a slick, well-managed experience for everyone involved.

SONAR
407 E. Saratoga St., 410/783-7888, www.sonarbaltimore.com
HOURS: Daily 9 P.M.-2 A.M.
COST: Cover varies
Map 1

If you're looking for a generally relaxed and always interesting night out, mixing up drinks and dancing and maybe live music, Sonar is your best bet. DJs are the mainstay here, but there are also plenty of great live gigs (one recent three-show lineup included Gwar, Method Man and Redman, and Alejandro Escovedo); fittingly, there's no dress code or hassle about things like that. Three rooms of increasing size can accommodate bands of various popularity, and there are plenty of places to just hang out and dance.

Dance Clubs

CLUB ONE
300 E. Saratoga St., 410/230-0049,
www.onebaltimore.com
HOURS: Wed. 7 P.M.-12:30 A.M., Thurs. and Sat.-Sun.
10 P.M.-2 A.M., Fri. 9 P.M.-2 A.M.
COST: Cover varies
Map 1

A lot of dance clubs have come and gone in downtown Baltimore, but One has managed to retain the crown as the city's king of get-dressed-up-to-get-down nighttime fun (there's a serious dress code here; no athletic attire permitted). It also helps that the club (in a renovated ancient building near City Hall) is huge, with four levels of themed rooms and music. The cover charge can be a little ridiculous, considering that it's Baltimore and all, but for a club to last in this town it has to have happy, repeat guests, and One has managed to build that base.

CLUB ORPHEUS
1003 E. Pratt St., 410/276-5599
HOURS: Daily 9 P.M.-2 A.M.
COST: Cover varies
Map 2

For those who enjoy slipping into leather, black lipstick, fishnet, and sorrow, Baltimore offers Club Orpheus, a very goth-centered venue just east of the candlelit pasta dinners of Little Italy. Fans of similar genres, like industrial and punk, will generally feel at home here as well; the sound system is not bad, and the atmosphere is relatively welcoming to new, like-minded people. Decor in this large, joy-free space is, unsurprisingly, black, minimal, and functional. There are parties on different nights of the week: every Friday is Ascension, every Saturday is Rapture (each has its own MySpace page).

THE DEPOT
1728 N. Charles St., 410/528-0174,
www.myspace.com/thedepotbaltimore
HOURS: Wed.-Sun. 9 P.M.-2 A.M.
COST: Cover varies
Map 5

If you miss the big hair and synthesizer-rich stylings of the 1980s music scene, The Depot is for you. Most nights, the sugary hits of the '80s are on heavy rotation in this dark, neon-lit, no-frills dance club; live bands and more modern DJs round out the bill the other nights. There's no food, and you should wear something you'll feel comfortable sweating through as you jump and twist the night away; it's a place for happy people with simple needs, not a place to show off your Jimmy Choo shoes.

Bars

BARTENDER'S
2218 Boston St., 410/534-2337,
www.bartendersbaltimore.com
HOURS: Daily 11:30 A.M.-2 A.M.
Map 3

Most of Boston Street in Canton is populated by clubs or hipster lounges; this home-grown establishment is run by gregarious local semi-celebrity Danny Coker, a lifelong bar and restaurant saint. The crowd at this well-sized, wood-rich bar is devoted, and they're open to strangers who appreciate the place as much as they do; the bargain-priced pizzas also have many devotees (try the Big Bill). It's a place that's popular with locals who want to grab a drink and some food and watch a little sports, or listen to another hilarious tale or theory from Coker.

THE BREWER'S ART
1106 N. Charles St., 410/547-6925,
www.thebrewersart.com
HOURS: Mon.-Sat. 4 P.M.-2 A.M., Sun. 5 P.M.-2 A.M.
Map 5

There are two completely different kinds of

bars here (as well as a popular and inventive restaurant that you shouldn't miss). In the upstairs lounge, beneath an elaborate chandelier, you can have a cocktail and watch traffic glide past on Charles Street. After that, you can dine in the expansive, wood-paneled dining room, hung with contemporary paintings (don't skip the rosemary fries!). Then head downstairs to the dark, catacomb-like basement bar, and sample the beer that made this place infamous: Resurrection, a potent dubbel-style ale. This bar has gotten national attention as a must-patronize tavern, and once you're tucked into a dark, medieval brick corner with a well-crafted ale, you'll understand why.

CAPTAIN LARRY'S
601 E. Fort Ave., 410/727-4799,
www.captainlarrys.com
HOURS: Mon.-Fri. 11:30 A.M.-2 A.M., Sat.-Sun.
4 P.M.-2 A.M.
Map 4

The legendary founder and namesake of this South Baltimore watering hole may have sailed for warmer shores (Florida), but his fine bar and tiny restaurant still thrives, discovered by a new generation of residents. One room is a cluttered, eclectic bar; the other is the dining room, where your entrée of choice is the crab-cake sandwich, served on a roll or with Saltine crackers. A visit to this institution is a trip into the real South Baltimore, where pretension is forbidden and rooms filled with nautical memorabilia, random junk, and neon beer signs are celebrated.

THE CAT'S EYE PUB
1730 Thames St., 410/276-9866, www.catseyepub.com
HOURS: Daily noon-2 A.M.
Map 2

With the advent of new condos and upscale wine bars around Fell's Point, the survival of places like The Cat's Eye was sometimes in doubt. Never fear: This ramshackle, holiday-light-festooned tavern is a remnant of the older, grittier Fell's Point, where sailors, bikers, and boozers all mingled among the then-

The Cat's Eye Pub

© GEOFF BROWN

NIGHTLIFE

dirty wharves and streets. The Cat's Eye's tiny but serviceable stage is a great place to catch live music. It's a bar that wouldn't seem out of place in New Orleans, especially in the summertime.

☾ CLUB CHARLES
1724 N. Charles St., 410/727-8815
HOURS: Daily 6 P.M.-2 A.M.
Map 5

One of Baltimore's premier, old-fashioned watering holes for discriminating drinkers, this Art Deco bar has hosted generations of city residents looking for some fine drinks, good music, and an artsy, metropolitan scene. The light here is very, very low, making it a great place to grab a booth and canoodle and people-watch over some martinis, either before or after a film at the Charles Theatre. The marvelous bartenders are unflappably kind, even when the crowds get two deep.

(DUDA'S TAVERN

1600 Thames St., 410/276-9719

HOURS: Mon.-Sat. 11 A.M.-1 A.M.

Map 2

This is what most of the bars in Fell's Point used to look like back in the pre-gentrification 1980s—well, actually, it's nicer than that, but Duda's is part of a vanishing breed of excellent old-school taverns (with great food, by the way). Grab a bar stool (or an outside table), order a beer, and tuck in to a huge burger, fantastic crab crake, or some crab soup to watch an Orioles game (note the tablecloths). It's a small enough place that you can listen in on the conversations of the nearby patrons; this place seems to be a favorite of National Aquarium workers. If you're a suds fan, Duda's has a fairly broad beer selection for a corner joint.

EXPLORER'S LOUNGE

InterContinental Baltimore, 550 Light St., 410/234-0550, www.harborcourt.com/restaurants/explorers_lounge.cfm

HOURS: Daily 11 A.M.-2 A.M.

Map 1

Though there's a slightly Hollywood-set feel to this wonderful drinking establishment—owing to the fact that it's in the 1970s-era architectural bore that is the InterContinental hotel—it's still one of the city's best places to have a civilized cocktail or two. That's because it's got a spectacular, second-story view of Baltimore's Inner Harbor, enjoyed from your choice of stately chairs in a room filled with rugs, bookcases, huge plants, and murals depicting animals and scenery from Africa. There's often live jazz, and seats near the windows can go fast on weekends, so act quickly if you're looking to start your evening here.

FRIENDS

1634 Aliceanna St., 410/732-3885

HOURS: Mon.-Thurs. 5 P.M.-2 A.M., Fri.-Sun. 4 P.M.-2 A.M.

Map 2

This well-worn old bar is one of the larger watering holes in Fell's Point, and it's a wonderfully lived-in space, from the chipped floor to

---

BARGAIN BALTIMORE: NIGHTLIFE

A "happy hour" can, at some places in Baltimore, last up to three hours, which is happy news indeed. There are plenty of great microbrews to try, but they're pricey; order a "Natty Boh" (National Bohemian), and you're probably looking at $2, tops, for a cold, perfectly adequate pilsner that's a Charm City staple during hot summers.

Most Baltimore bars – bars, mind you, not clubs or lounges – are going to be relatively cheap; so are indie clubs like **The Ottobar.** Baltimore's young, resurgent music scene plays at places like **Metro Gallery** and **Charm City Art Space.**

People-watching is also a great, free option, and Baltimore's got plenty of characters: pull up some stools at bars like **Club Charles, The Brewer's Art,** and the **Mount Royal Tavern** and enjoy the show.

---

the rickety coolers to the general sense of happily inebriated dereliction. A devoted crowd of regulars, generally of the tattooed and rock-band variety, patronizes Friends—but there's a little of everything in this place come Saturday night. There's a great, short menu of entrées if you get hungry, there's pool in the back, and the jukebox isn't bad either. The only problem can be a wait for the bathrooms, but that's a minor quibble.

JOHN STEVEN

1800 Thames St., 410/327-5561, www.johnstevenltd.com

HOURS: Daily 11 A.M.-2 A.M.

Map 2

There's a particular skill to getting the most out of a visit to this venerable, authentic, and well-used Fell's Point bar, where the crowd is a mix of lifers and tourists. First, get a couple of seats at the big bar (or one of the tables next to the small windows). Next, order from the ample, well-planned beer list. Third, order a pound of mussels or steamed shrimp. As you eat and drink, look around the room at the great wooden details on the bar and the pressed tin ceiling. Repeat until pleasantly full. Sure, there's a nice dining room and an enticing outdoor (and out back) dining patio, but the real fun is in the front bar (or at the outdoor tables).

J. PATRICK'S IRISH PUB

1371 Andre St., 410/244-8613,
http://home.netcom.com/~leemarsh/jpatrick.html
HOURS: Daily 9 A.M.-2 A.M.
`Map 4`

It's not much to look at from the outside—or from the inside, for that matter. But this popular bar in Locust Point might be one of the most traditional Irish pubs you'll ever set foot in, not only because of the fantastic musicians who play Irish standards most nights, but also because it's such a welcoming and warm place. (The great crab cakes don't hurt, either.) There's Irish dancing many nights at this barebones bar, where posters and flags constitute most of the decor, and many a new friend to meet (and buy a Guinness) here in this quiet residential neighborhood just a few blocks from the Inner Harbor.

LITTLE HAVANA

1325 Key Hwy., 410/837-9903, www.littlehavanas.com
HOURS: Mon.-Thurs. 4 P.M.-2 A.M., Fri.-Sat.
11:30 A.M.-2 A.M., Sun. 11 A.M.-2 A.M.
`Map 4`

Overlooking a couple of parking lots—and the Inner Harbor—this Federal Hill bar has been packing in crowds for years. The big, rear waterview deck is an ideal spot to partake of some cool mojitos and carnitas tacos under the glow of the Domino Sugars sign (and it's a great place to watch the fireworks that occasionally illuminate the Inner Harbor). Inside, this industrial-strength establishment has a huge central bar, lots of seats and TVs, and a fauxrickety "old Cuba" feel. If you're over 35, you might be in the minority here some weekends, but you won't be alone.

MAHAFFEY'S

2706 Dillon St., 410/276-9899,
www.mahaffeyspub.com
HOURS: Sun.-Thurs. 3 P.M.-2 A.M., Fri.-Sat. noon-2 A.M.
`Map 3`

It's nowhere near the often-boisterous O'Donnell Square that's the heart of Canton's nightlife scene, which may explain why this small corner pub has such a devoted following. (The great tin ceiling, huge back-room mural of an 1800s cityscape, and friendly atmosphere help, too.) Mahaffey's takes care to serve great beer correctly (not too cold, not too warm) from its often-rotated menu. There's also a grill right behind the well-stocked bar, where the chef may be turning intoxicatingly seasoned steaks over the fire.

MAX'S ON BROADWAY

737 S. Broadway, 410/675-6297, www.maxs.com
HOURS: Daily 11 A.M.-2 A.M.
`Map 2`

Do you like beer? Really, *really* like beer? Do you like beer enough to brave an enormous

Max's on Broadway

© GEOFF BROWN

It isn't much to look at on the outside (or the inside), but Mum's is one of Federal Hill's last cheap and atmospheric local independent bars.

mini-complex of three separate taverns, with 80 draft beers and more than 500 bottled beers that will challenge your beer stamina? This brick and wood palace of hops and barley—located in the heart of Fell's Point, just a block from the water—has a huge assortment of TVs, along with pool and foosball, a huge menu of burgers and sandwiches, and a regulation darts room (there's also a "lounge" upstairs that's a bit less beer-hall-like).

MOUNT ROYAL TAVERN

1204 W. Mount Royal Ave., 410/669-6686
HOURS: Daily 10 A.M.-2 A.M.
Map 5

There's really one reason to stop in at this well-worn and frankly dirty bar, long a favorite for the generations of art students from neighboring Maryland Institute College of Art, and one reason only: the ceiling. Rather, what's on the ceiling, which is a stunningly faithful recreation of Leonardo da Vinci's ceiling mural from the Sistine Chapel. Don't snicker: The quality and craftsmanship on this project is

astonishing. Rotate around on your bar stool as you sip a beer and study the technique, the focus, and the preposterousness of the endeavor. Think it was a waste of time? Local legend has it that the mural's creator drinks for free, for life, here at the Mount Royal Tavern.

MUM'S

1132 S. Hanover St., 410/547-7415
HOURS: Mon.-Fri. 2 P.M.-2 A.M., Sat.-Sun. 1 P.M.-2 A.M.
Map 4

A town like Baltimore is going to have a few bars that are, to be polite, low-rent dives. Mum's is one of the city's greatest, meeting all of the requirements of a great cheap dive. Live music in a cramped back room? Check. Cheap drinks? Check. Surly, hilarious bartenders? Check. Great jukebox featuring exactly zero Top 40 hits of the past 10 years? Check. Located a couple of blocks from Federal Hill's more tony lounges, wine bars, and polished taverns, Mum's is where seasoned locals go for a drink and a stool near the TV to watch the O's or Ravens game.

ONE EYED MIKE'S

708 S. Bond St., 410/327-9823,
www.oneeyedmikes.com
HOURS: Mon.-Sat. 11 A.M.-1 A.M.
Map 2

Some bars sell particularly large amounts of whiskey, or beer, or shiraz. One Eyed Mike's sells Grand Marnier, and lots of it. Enough to cover many of the walls with bottles. Enough to have not a mug club, but rather a Grand Marnier club (complete with newsletter and bylaws), in which people keep personal bottles of the liqueur in vast glass cases. One Eyed Mike's also serves food (which tends toward well-done, slightly upscale pub grub) to a loyal crowd, with a dining room in between the busy front bar and a popular back patio.

POWER PLANT LIVE!

34 Market Pl., 410/752-5483, www.powerplantlive.com
HOURS: Hours vary; most bars open at 5 P.M.
Map 1

It's best to consider Power Plant Live! as a single entity, rather than trying to separate it into its many various food-and-alcohol-serving parts. This is a planned, managed congregation of eateries and bars, with a large center plaza area that hosts bands, DJs, and warm-weather crowds. There are restaurants here (like Babalu Grill, Mondo Bondo, MEX, and a Ruth's Chris Steakhouse), along with large bars (Angels Rocks Bar, Luckie's Tavern), and even a dueling-pianos establishment (Howl at the Moon). It's a reasonable option for an early dinner, but as the night goes on, the crowd gets younger and younger, and the music volumes and social high jinks increase.

THE PUB DOG

20 E. Cross St., 410/727-6077, www.pubdog.net
HOURS: Daily 5 P.M.-2 A.M.
Map 4

Formerly one of the city's most popular "bring your dog while you go drinking" establishments (a now-outlawed practice), this bar, cozy and dark with lots of exposed brick, is still packing in regulars. Locals are drawn to the fireplace and brick-oven gourmet pizzas and

NIGHTLIFE

COURTESY BALTIMORE AREA CONVENTION AND VISITORS ASSOCIATION

Power Plant Live! hosts bands and DJs in its large plaza area.

the good, cheap, micro-brewed beer. Well-used booths and bar stools and a shuffleboard pub game upstairs let newcomers know that this place stays busy, especially on weekends.

THE 13TH FLOOR
1 E. Chase St., 410/347-0888,
www.trufflescatering.com
HOURS: Wed.-Sat. 5 P.M.-2 A.M.
Map 5

Atop the looming historic Belvedere building, which rises at one of the city's highest points, is this storied bar, which has survived a number of themes, crazes, and economic roller coasters. The main reason it's still around is the view; enormous picture windows provide amazing views of nighttime Baltimore from most directions; the skyscrapers and Inner Harbor lie to the south. There are some decent small plates and pizzas to be had if you want to grab a bite and enjoy the view. Live bands appear many nights during the week; DJs spin and mix the rest of the time.

THE TUSK LOUNGE
The Brass Elephant, 924 N. Charles St., 410/547-8485,
www.brasselephant.com/tusk_lounge.html
HOURS: Mon.-Sat. 5 P.M.-2 A.M., Sun. 4:30-8:30 P.M.
Map 5

The Tusk Lounge is one of those splendid old fin de siècle bars that somehow escaped ill-considered disco-era renovations and remodeling. From the long marble bar to the tall ceilings dangling elaborate chandeliers, to the tiny tables and romantic corner nooks and quiet jazz on the stereo, this is a great place to grab a fancy cocktail or single malt scotch (and some food from the brief but tempting bar menu) before heading out to one of Mount Vernon's cultural venues. Note that the bar is located on the second floor of the old-school Brass Elephant restaurant; head right upstairs as soon as you enter the building.

THE WHARF RAT
801 S. Ann St., 410/276-9034, www.thewharfrat.com
HOURS: Daily 11:30 A.M.-2 A.M.
Map 2

This Baltimore institution has undergone

© GEOFF BROWN

One of Fell's Point's best bars, the Wharf Rat is also one of its best-looking.

some changes over the years; originally just another well-worn waterfront tavern, it's now got a much larger sister on Pratt Street near Oriole Park at Camden Yards (that's where they make their house-brand Oliver ales). But this is the original and favorite of many Baltimoreans, probably because of the character this dark, Colonial-era room possesses: old wooden chairs and round tables decorated with beer caps and nautical charts, low ceilings filled with rowing oars and exposed wooden beams, and a grand back bar with a working fireplace. The crowd (which ranges from young to old) is a mix of regulars here for the beers and company, and tourists who peeked inside, saw the great atmosphere, and pulled up a chair.

Wine Bars

THE CHESAPEAKE WINE COMPANY

2400 Boston St., 410/522-4556,
www.chesapeakewine.com
HOURS: Mon.-Wed. 11 A.M.-9 P.M., Thurs.-Sat.
11 A.M.-11 P.M., Sun. 11 A.M.-6 P.M.
Map 3

One of the many businesses retrofitted into the Can Company, a former canning facility turned into offices, shops, and restaurants, this open, airy wine and liquor store is also home to one of Canton's more popular little wine bars, located at the back of the store. There's a bar, good music, and lots of tables, often filled with neighbors (and their strollers) partaking of a pinot noir or a chardonnay, along with small plates of cheeses and fruit. Drinks are available by the glass or bottle.

GRAND CRU

527 E. Belvedere Ave., 410/464-1944,
www.grandcrubaltimore.com
HOURS: Mon.-Thurs. 11 A.M.-10 P.M., Fri.-Sat. 11 A.M.-1 A.M.,
Sun. noon-8 P.M.
Map 7

On weekends and summer nights, the crowds descend on this popular wine bar and store, found in the Belvedere Square market, to sample the grape, nosh on some cheese and meats (don't miss the smoked meat sampler from Neopol, another market favorite), and mingle with neighbors and newcomers. It's a modern space, with dramatic lighting and sleek design that's still warm and inviting, and there is regular live music.

☾ V-NO

905 S. Ann St., 410/342-8466
HOURS: Tues.-Wed. from 4:30 P.M.,
Thurs.-Sun. from 11:30 A.M.
Map 2

A relative newcomer to the Baltimore wine bar scene, this small oenophile's outpost has some of the best real estate in town—waterfront in Fell's Point, best viewed from one of the cute outdoor tables. Inside, blonde-wood seating sections and an inviting bar are regularly filled with locals discussing the affairs of the historic neighborhood. Most wines for sale run under $30 per bottle (glasses are also available), and there's a good assortment of cheeses, breads, salads, and desserts to cleanse your palate.

OENOPHILE'S METROPOLIS

Baltimore's turned into a bit of an oenophile's metropolis in the past few years. It's been rated as one of the best wine cities in the nation, and a number of restaurants now specialize in broad selections and presentation at special-purpose areas within the main dining room, while a few specialized wine bars and stores have opened as well.

Of the restaurants that do double-duty as premier places to sample the grape, Federal Hill's **The Wine Market** is in a marvelous old rehabbed foundry building, and its massive selection draws a lot of fans. In Fell's Point, both **Charleston** and **Pazo** are great places to have an amazing meal, as well as sample the astute wine selections of Tony Foreman.

Three small, comfortable wine bars (and stores) have opened around town in recent years. North of town, near the historic Senator Theatre, **Grand Cru,** located in the bustling Belvedere Square market, is a great place to learn about some different vintners and then grab some food. **The Chesapeake Wine Company,** in Canton, has a loyal contingent of regular visitors to the rear of the shop, where tables and a bar encourage lingering. And in Fell's Point, cozy **V-NO** has a great location on the water, a selection of cheeses and desserts, and a smart range of affordable varieties.

NIGHTLIFE

Lounges

EDEN'S LOUNGE

15 W. Eager St., 410/244-0405, www.edenslounge.com
HOURS: Mon.-Tues. 7 P.M.-midnight, Wed.-Sat.
5 P.M.-2 A.M., Sun. 8 P.M.-2 A.M.

Map 5

Located in Mount Vernon, this club and lounge is bustling and packed with Baltimoreans of all races (predominantly African American), a diverse party that is sadly still not too common. There's a traditional bar area in the front of the house, with the rest devoted to combinations of booths, tables, back bars, and a DJ-driven dance floor. What unites the patrons of this popular hotspot is the generally chill atmosphere; the calming, vaguely Arabic decor and pleasant staff don't hurt either. It's also a large enough club for people to have enough room to have their own kind of party without disturbing others.

HAVANA CLUB

600 Water St., 410/468-0022,
www.havanaclub-baltimore.com
HOURS: Daily 6 P.M.-2 A.M.

Map 1

Following the passage of the citywide (statewide, too) smoking ban, this richly appointed club and lounge—located above a Ruth's Chris Steakhouse, just a few steps from the monstrous Power Plant Live! complex—has become one of the very few places in town for smokers. And they come here in droves to puff on stogies from the club's ample selection, as well as to hang out in the big, leather chairs, have a few drinks, and get moving on a small dance floor.

MOSAIC

4 Market Pl., Power Plant Live!, 410/262-8713,
www.mosaic-baltimore.com
HOURS: Thurs.-Sat. 5 P.M.-2 A.M.

Map 1

Somewhat hidden at the back of the west side of the sprawling Power Plant Live! bar and restaurant complex is Mosaic, a medium-sized lounge and club for those looking to get away from the hordes of beer-swilling patrons the venue attracts. This is a space to relax, have an adult cocktail, recline on some pillows, and let some ambient house music unwind (or entice) you. Later in the evening, the beats per minute accelerate, and there is a lot more energy.

◖ RED MAPLE

930 N. Charles St., 410/547-0149,
www.930redmaple.com
HOURS: Mon. 9 P.M.-2 A.M., Tues. 5:30 P.M.-2 A.M.,
Wed.-Fri. 5 P.M.-2 A.M., Sat.-Sun. 6 P.M.-2 A.M.

Map 5

Longevity in a lounge is something rare, especially in Baltimore, which has always favored bars or mega-clubs and little in-between. But Red Maple succeeded because it got the basics right: great music, both from DJs and small live performances; a well-designed and nicely-appointed building with different areas for sitting, eating, and dancing; a tasty, modern

Havana Club

© GEOFF BROWN

Don't look for a sign; just head for the telltale tree icons to find the Red Maple.

menu (mostly Asian tapas) that's just right for the space; and even an out-back smoking patio featuring the club's namesake tree. Even the bathrooms, where many Baltimore lounges will cut corners, have smart design. Live flamenco bands and belly dancing balance out the house and trance DJs.

ZEEBA LOUNGE

916 Light St., 410/539-7900, www.zeebalounge.com
HOURS: Wed.-Thurs. and Sun. 6 P.M.-midnight, Fri.-Sat. 6 P.M.-4 A.M.

Map 4

This beautiful Federal Hill hookah bar and lounge really comes alive toward the end of the night, as it's one of the only late-night (until 4 A.M. on Fridays and Saturdays) options in the bar-heavy neighborhood. Lots of warm woods, rugs, tapestries, and pillows add to the vibe here, along with the heady smell of hookah smoke (which is the only kind of smoking allowed). There are belly dancers and live drumming, a pleasantly pre-inebriated crowd, and a great Mediterranean menu to help ward off a hangover. Note there are bottle fees; bringing a single bottle for a group interested in post-2 A.M. drinking is the best idea.

After Hours

Baltimore's 2 A.M. closing time means that those looking for some further nocturnal festivities will need to leave the bars and head elsewhere; note that these places do not sell alcohol, and they do not allow it to be brought in after 2 A.M., although some may permit BYOB before that hour. In Federal Hill, **Zeeba Lounge** is one of the city's few establishments that is a regular-hours bar and restaurant that turns into an after-hours destination allowing alcohol consumption after 2 A.M. (guests can drink their BYO libations, for a charge).

CLUB 1722

1722 N. Charles St., 410/547-8423, www.club1722.com
HOURS: Fri.-Sat. from 1:45 A.M.
COST: Cover varies
Map 5

Inside this unassuming Mount Vernon club, a stalwart of the Baltimore late-night party scene, there are two stories of rooms, dance areas, and couches. If there's a particularly popular DJ or themed party going on, there may even be a line out front. Generally speaking, this is a gay club, but the scene is tolerant of everyone who can follow the rules (this place is for grown-ups, and people sporting the youth "street" look are not allowed in). One of the biggest draws is Sugar, a regular Friday night event hosted by Baltimore's own Ultra Naté, a singer/producer whose popularity in the States is eclipsed a hundredfold by her fan base in Europe.

◖ PARADOX

1310 Russell St., 410/837-9110, www.thedox.com
HOURS: Fri. 11 P.M.-5 A.M., Sat. midnight-6 A.M.
COST: Cover varies
Map 1

In the always-mercurial after-hours industry, Paradox has managed to survive for nearly two decades; it has done so by figuring out what the hordes of young people (it's an 18+ club) who head to this dark, industrial part of town want to do when their parents are asleep. They want to dance (two floors, lots of lights, smoke, and lasers), they want to eat (there's a full restaurant serving pizza, chicken, and more), and they want to hoop (a half-court basketball area is always packed, until the dancing gets going). Depending on the DJ and event, crowds here can vary from googly ravers to intimidating thugs, so a drive-by is recommended to see who has shown up.

Gay and Lesbian

CLUB BUNNS

608 W. Lexington St., 410/234-2866
HOURS: Daily 3 P.M.-2 A.M.
Map 1

This dance club and bar is a popular hangout for gay and lesbian African Americans, though all are welcome here. The music tends toward more hip-hop and R&B tracks than the usual club and house music played at the city's other gay clubs. The neighborhood is not one of the city's best when visited after dark, so use caution and prudence when parking in the area.

COCONUTS CAFE

311 W. Madison St., 410/383-6064
HOURS: Tues.-Sat. 6 P.M.-2 A.M.
Map 5

This small club is home to the city's largest African American lesbian scene, and offers the usual blend of drinking, dancing, and music. There's pool and karaoke, too, all in a kind of small building decorated (as the name implies)

in a Polynesian/Hawaiian-themed mix of palm tree iconography, lights, leis, and other island paradise items. What's a little different is that the food here is really good, particularly their chicken wings, which come in a variety of flavors and heat intensities (be sure to check out the inside jokes on the menu).

THE DRINKERY

207 W. Read St., 410/225-3100
HOURS: Daily 11 A.M.-2 A.M.
Map 5

This Mount Vernon institution is a gay bar in the most basic sense of the words: there's no glitz or glamour or club atmosphere here. It's just a regular city bar that happens to have purple walls and a gay clientele. There's a good jukebox, karaoke on the weekends, and a loyal crowd of regulars (most of whom are past their 20s and 30s). Drinks are cheap, the people are friendly, and there's no production required before a visit.

© GEOFF BROWN

The Hippo is housed in a wonderful building from the 1930s.

GRAND CENTRAL

1001 N. Charles St., 410/752-7133,
www.centralstationpub.com
HOURS: Daily 4 P.M.-2 A.M.
Map 5

One of the two big gay and lesbian scenes
in Charm City convenes nightly in this very
large three-story bar and dance club in Mount
Vernon. There are three separate areas in
Grand Central (much like The Hippo across
the street): a large bar area downstairs with
karaoke and DJs; a massive dance floor with
requisite light show and effects (plus a great
sound system); and Sapphos, a second-floor,
ladies-mostly area with a deck, pool, and
dancing.

THE HIPPO

1 W Eager St., 410/547-0069, www.clubhippo.com
HOURS: Daily 4 P.M.-2 A.M.; dance club opens at 10 P.M.
Map 5

The Hippo is the other major gay and lesbian
nexus of Baltimore; it's in a wonderful old building built as a nightclub in the 1930s. There are
three main rooms here: a huge dance floor, where
DJs and a sophisticated light show work the
crowds into non-stop motion; a more traditional
bar area, with pool tables; and a third lounge-ish
area that's sometimes a piano bar, sometimes a
video bar. Gay Bingo on Wednesday nights has
become a favorite for patrons of all persuasions,
as it's generally led by a no-nonsense-tolerated,
wickedly witted drag queen.

ARTS AND LEISURE

Baltimore has long supported a variety of outstanding museums and collections, as well as talented artists, musical and theater companies, and bona fide legends. Lately, the city has gained fresh acclaim for its new wave of young artists. Singers, songwriters, rappers, DJs, painters, collectives—there's a real, legitimate scene going on in Baltimore now, one that's being covered more and more by the national press. There are also plenty of things to do after dark; Baltimore's artists and musicians are working hard to make things happen, and to entertain and engage the public.

After years of having only a few outlets for young artists, there are more and more galleries (both traditional and ad hoc) displaying new and exciting works, and maybe having a band or two to liven up the party. The music being made by Baltimoreans is inventive, and the city's gritty nature and do-it-yourself attitude can be heard in the final product, no matter what genre of music.

But Baltimore's established artists and musicians—from the symphony to classical pianists like Leon Fleischer to modern abstract painters like the late Grace Hartigan—remains just as vital, if not more so now, because of the city's rising young stars. The Baltimore Museum of Art and the Walters Art Museum are world-class institutions, and the big-name venues like Pier 6 and Ram's Head Live and the 1st Mariner Bank Arena draw a variety of national and international performers.

Spring and summer are when the small neighborhood festivals and larger big-scale events are held around town, creating up to

COURTESY BALTIMORE AREA CONVENTION AND VISITORS ASSOCIATION

HIGHLIGHTS

LOOK FOR (TO FIND RECOMMENDED ARTS AND ACTIVITIES.

(**Best Theater:** For more than four decades, **Center Stage** has produced thoughtful, powerful performances – with a range of classic, re-imagined, and contemporary shows (page 117).

(**Best Venue for a Broadway Show:** It's now the jewel of the west side of downtown, and the immaculately restored **Hippodrome Theatre** is once again a city landmark (page 119).

(**Best Independent Cinema:** The fare at **The Charles Theatre** can include foreign films, classics, and even a minor Hollywood hit or two (page 121).

The Hippodrome Theatre

© GEOFF BROWN

(**Best Strange Fund-Raising Event:** It's actually over two nights, and there aren't 100 performers, but **The Night of 100 Elvises** in December is one of the most unexpectedly wonderful ways to spend an evening in Baltimore (page 125).

(**Best Huge Festival:** It's the festival that eats Baltimore every steamy July, but the performers, artists, and culinary delights at **Artscape** make the imposition worthwhile (page 128).

(**Best Woodland Estate Stroll:** The beautiful trees, well-manicured lawns and gardens, and the gorgeous Cylburn Mansion make a jaunt through the two-and-a-half miles of trails at the 200-acre **Cylburn Arboretum** a bucolic joy (page 132).

(**Best Serious Bike Ride:** Get to BWI Airport (the Dixon Observation Area, to be specific) with your bike, and you can cruise down the (relatively) flat 25 miles from there to beautiful downtown Annapolis along the **Baltimore-Annapolis Trail;** the way back is uphill, but not dauntingly so (page 133).

(**Best Baltimore Tour Guide:** It's not just that **Zippy Tours with Zippy Larson** knows things about Baltimore that almost no one else does, it's that her quirky, unstoppable personality can get her tour groups into places no one else can go (page 146).

(**Best Urban Golf Course:** The drive into **Clifton Park** may not be like rolling into Augusta or Pebble Beach, but the golf at this historic course is darn good, and the views of downtown from the last holes on the back nine are regal (page 148).

(**Best Yoga Studio:** Need a break from the hectic pace of sightseeing and fine dining? Try the bright, airy Fell's Point location of **Charm City Yoga** – and get out on the roof deck if the weather's nice (page 149).

two months' worth of event-rich weekends. There are longtime favorites, like the many neighborhood ethnic festivals, and new, totally independent shows, like the musical mayhem of Whartscape, held (in whatever spaces, halls, or alleys the bands can secure) on the same weekend as the massive and city-sponsored Artscape.

Baltimore also has two major league sports teams (the Orioles in baseball and the Ravens in football), lots of great college action (particularly in lacrosse, a regional favorite), and plenty of ways for you to work up a sweat on your own. The Baltimore Running Festival and Marathon is growing into a major annual event; there's sailing on the harbor and the bay; and lots of places to bike, hike, and otherwise stretch your legs. Speaking of legs, if you like to see the city on foot rather than from the back of a bus, there are a variety of great walking tours. It's just another benefit of visiting a town where the citizens take a great deal of pride in being resolutely independent.

The Arts

Ever since Baltimore's early days as a burgeoning metropolis, the arts have played an important role in the life of the city. From opera houses to art colleges to conservatories and art museums, Baltimore has always managed to maintain artistic voices, despite economic issues and changing tastes and mores. The city's biggest outdoor festival, Artscape, is a celebration of art and music that lasts for three days and draws a crowd of more than 100,000 each year. And there's recently been a resurgence in Baltimore's appreciation of the classical arts as well, particularly since the addition of maestra Marin Alsop to the Baltimore Symphony Orchestra. Her ascendance to the podium of the BSO—and her enthusiastic cheerleading for Baltimore, the BSO, and music—has garnered the city a lot of positive attention.

Mount Vernon is the cultural heart of Baltimore City. From its elegant, European-influenced architecture and landscaping to the symphony hall, opera house, and Walters Art Museum—not to mention the prestigious Peabody Institute, one of the finest music schools in the nation—it's impossible to not be influenced and affected by the arts in this wonderful neighborhood. And Mount Vernon is rich with art galleries and more modern takes on the concept of what a museum can be, especially at the Contemporary Museum, located just a few steps from the Walters.

As to contemporary art and music, Baltimore's East Coast location, urban energy, and low rents have attracted a variety of creative people to the city. This new vanguard of artists and musicians have set up their own spaces, galleries, and performance areas in the Station North arts district just north of Mount Vernon and in parts of the city where buildings and rents are still very affordable—mostly because no one else wants to inhabit those areas, though that's changed a bit. Another locus of the contemporary arts scene is Highlandtown's Creative Alliance, located a little north of Canton; this converted movie theater hosts art exhibitions, performances, films, and bands on a regular basis, as well as offering classes and lectures on the arts.

The new artists and performers who are shaping Baltimore's cultural scene are making waves across the nation. *Rolling Stone* magazine named Baltimore the next big thing back in 2008; bands like Beach House, musicians like Dan Deacon, and performer/producers like Blaqstarr are getting attention and garnering fans from all over. Not that Baltimore is slacking in the classical musician department; celebrated violinist Hilary Hahn is a Charm City native.

Many of Baltimore's independent musicians and artists have formed loose (or more solid) collectives to help each other get shows and exhibit their works. They've even organized their own response to the massive,

MENCKEN TO MO'NIQUE: FAMOUS BALTIMOREANS

A city with the peculiar personality of Baltimore is bound to produce some unique artists, performers, writers, and scientists. The city's most famous man of letters, Henry Louis "H. L." Mencken (1880-1956), set a high bar through his pointed criticism and voluminous output, but he also put Baltimore on the map as the home of some of the nation's best artistic and intellectual talent. Though some of these folks are from outlying suburbs, here's a short list of the city's most preeminent sons and daughters who are proud to call themselves Baltimoreans:

Musical artists abound, starting alphabetically with singer and songwriter **Tori Amos,** classical pianist **Leon Fleischer,** minimalist composer **Philip Glass,** "Thong Song"-singer **SisQó,** singer and songwriter **Ultra Naté,** and the late outsider rocker **Frank Zappa.**

Actors and on-screen personalities include **John Astin,** who played Gomez in the original TV version of *The Addams Family;* **Charles "Roc" Dutton,** who is also a fine director; *Baywatch, Knight Rider,* and reality-show star **David Hasselhoff;** plus-sized comedienne **Mo'Nique Imes-Jackson;** serious actor and film force **Edward Norton;** Howard Stern straight-woman **Robin Quivers;** and singer-actress (and Mrs. Will Smith) **Jada Pinkett Smith.**

Directors **Barry Levinson** and **John Waters** are the best-known Baltimore filmmakers.

commercial Artscape; Whartscape is a DIY, back-alley, semi-underground music and arts festival that runs concurrently with the more accessible Artscape, and generally just a few blocks away from it.

This is a great time to explore Baltimore's arts and cultural landscapes, as rarely before has there been so much energy, talent, and enthusiasm at both ends of the scale, from the classical to the experimental. The high quality of artists in Baltimore these days makes taking a chance on a show or event not only a worthwhile risk; it should be considered a requirement.

GALLERIES
THE ANTREASIAN GALLERY
1111 W 36th St., 410/235-4420,
www.antreasiangallery.com
HOURS: Wed.-Sat. 11 A.M.-7 P.M., Sun. noon-5 P.M.
Map 6

Though it's located in Hampden, a neighborhood that's practically made quirkiness a marketable commodity, the artwork at this gallery is almost refreshingly mainstream. Landscapes and portraiture, as well as sculpture and some less traditional media, fill this large space; there are plenty of abstract and realist works as well. Shows change relatively frequently here, which makes the changing exhibits a draw for window shoppers.

C. GRIMALDIS GALLERY
523 N. Charles St., 410/539-1080,
www.cgrimaldisgallery.com
HOURS: Mon.-Sat. 9 A.M.-6 P.M., Sun. 10 A.M.-5 P.M.
Map 5

Open since 1977, this renowned Mount Vernon stalwart (named for owner Constantine Grimaldis) is the grande dame of Baltimore's contemporary art gallery scene. Grimaldis exhibits many paintings and sculptures by several of the city's most prominent artists (like Raoul Middleman, Tony Shore, and the late Grace Hartigan), as well as a wide range of European and American modern artists. There's also intriguing work by new young painters and sculptors on display here.

CURRENT GALLERY
30 S. Calvert St., 410/244-7003,
www.currentspace.com
HOURS: Fri.-Sun. 11 A.M.-3 P.M.
Map 1

Just a short walk from the commercial glare and glaze of the Inner Harbor is this experimental and (relatively) unpretentious art gallery/performance space, where you may look at paintings or be asked to join in on some manual labor as part of a performance. Because it's run as an artists' cooperative, there's less interest in doing things that make financial sense and more interest in doing things that are interesting; expect to see and experience some risk-taking work here.

GALLERY IMPERATO

921 E. Fort Ave., Ste. 120, 443/257-4166,
www.galleryimperato.com
HOURS: Tues.-Sat. 11 A.M.-6 P.M.
Map 4

Tucked into a huge former foundry building on the way to Fort McHenry from Federal Hill, this contemporary art gallery likes to work with and display art made in slightly different ways (think painted photo collages, string and metal and photos, abstract paintings, reclaimed and recycled items). One pleasant surprise here is the number of out-of-town artists (and even those from outside America) represented in the collections.

GOYA CONTEMPORARY

3000 Chestnut Ave., Mill Center, Studio 214,
410/366-2001, www.goyacontemporary.com
HOURS: Tues.-Fri. 10 A.M.-5:30 P.M., Sat. by appt.
noon-5 P.M.
Map 6

This is the gallery side of Martha Macks' Goya operations (the other is Goya Girl Press, geared toward artists in need of high-quality printing options); located in an old mill building at the base of Hampden, this brick-and-wood gallery shows works by all sorts of artists (females are well-represented) working in paint and print, but photography and sculpture are also part of the palette here.

THE G SPOT

2980 Falls Rd., 410/889-6767, www.gspotavp.com
HOURS: Hours vary
Map 6

It's a little tough to find this warehouse space, located on the weird and wonderful stretch of Falls Road that's next to the Jones Falls and surrounded by woods and cliffs. Inside, the large space hosts everything from traditional visual arts to rock bands to movies. The gallery calls itself an audio-visual playground, and it's an apt moniker. Some events here are small, while some are standing room only, depending on the artists.

MEREDITH GALLERY

805 N. Charles St., 410/837-3575,
www.meredithgallery.com
HOURS: Tues.-Sat. 10 A.M.-5:30 P.M.
Map 5

Another long-lived veteran of the Baltimore art gallery community, this charming two-story building focuses on furniture and home furnishings made by artists (there are also ceramics and paintings), often pushing the expected forms to interesting limits. The pieces on display here succeed when they make visitors look at an artwork that's ostensibly a chair or a table, but through innovative design or materials, it becomes something quite different and intriguing.

SCHOOL 33 ART CENTER

1427 Light St., 410/396-4641, www.school33.org
HOURS: Tues.-Fri. 10 A.M.-4 P.M., Thurs. 10 A.M.-7 P.M.,
Sat. noon-4 P.M.
Map 4

This former city school building—a sturdy brick Richardsonian Romanesque structure in Federal Hill—is now a city-sponsored collection of artists' studios, exhibition areas, and classrooms for art lessons. The contemporary art on display is often abstract and made of found and created materials, though traditional paint and sculpture is also regularly featured. Regular special events, and a great annual fundraiser held every April ("Lotta Art"), make this a feature on the art social circuit.

SUB-BASEMENT ARTIST STUDIOS

118 N. Howard St., 410/659-6950,
www.subbasementartiststudios.com
HOURS: Sat. 11 A.M.-5 P.M. and by appt.
Map 1

A collection of modern artists working in paint, sculpture, and found-object art, this gallery features some of the best work in the city, much of which is being made by African American artists. Despite the truth-in-advertising name of this operation (it really is a sub-basement), this is a big space—some 13,000 square feet and very tall ceilings—that lets the works (and visitors) have space to breathe and establish their presence.

THEATER
❿ CENTER STAGE

700 N. Calvert St., 410/986-4000,
www.centerstage.org
Map 5

Baltimore's premier theater is also the official state theater of Maryland. Started more than four decades ago by local actors and performance enthusiasts, Center Stage is now a treasured civic jewel, and a theater where the seats are often filled and the playbill is a smart mix of standards, crowd favorites, and even a few offbeat shows. The plays and performances here also reflect the city's diversity in a way that feels organic and welcoming. Another reason for this venue's popularity: low ticket prices, a tribute to their mission to expose as many people, from as many social strata, to the theater as possible. The theater itself was built in the mid-1970s after a fire destroyed the then-small company's North Avenue home; its age and design era is apparent, but not unpleasantly so.

CREATIVE ALLIANCE AT THE PATTERSON

3134 Eastern Ave., 410/276-1651,
www.creativealliance.org
Map 3

Housed in the former Patterson movie theater—and, thankfully, still under its massive neon marquee—the Creative Alliance is a community-based arts group that works to both help local artists pursue their goals and get non-artist Baltimoreans to get involved with the arts. Their HQ is this wonderful re-purposed space, which includes a theater that holds about 200 people for movies, performances, and lectures; two galleries for artworks; and a variety of labs, offices, and other rooms for the Alliance's artists, staff, and students who study here.

EVERYMAN THEATRE

1727 N. Charles St., 410/752-2208,
www.everymantheatre.org
Map 5

An intimate Actors' Equity theater in what's now known as the Station North Arts District, this popular venue frequently fills nearly every seat during its roughly five-play season, and has been staging top-notch productions of both

BARGAIN BALTIMORE: THE ARTS

Start by perusing one of the city's free papers with good event listings: **b,** put out by the *Baltimore Sun,* is printed every weekday; while *City Paper* comes out weekly. Also check out Baltimore's visitor website, **baltimore.org,** for happenings and bargains.

During most of the year, you'll find live music all over town on **First Fridays,** which takes place (obviously) on the first Friday of the month. Most museums and gathering places will have some sort of special events, bands, or entertainment, and many shopping districts stay open late.

Scholars, artists, and authors frequently give shows and performances across town at universities and libraries. For just $15, you can get a "best available" seat to see the acclaimed **Baltimore Symphony Orchestra** under conductor Marin Alsop.

Free outdoor movies have become a Baltimore tradition, and they're available in several flavors: Little Italy's well-attended summer series, from July through August, shows (generally) tried-and-true Hollywood hits, all (generally) with an Italian or Baltimore theme or protagonist. At Federal Hill, the American Visionary Art Museum screens a broader range of Hollywood classics and more recent hits of the quirkier variety, projected on the side of the museum in June and July. And Johns Hopkins University shows family-friendly films in June and July on its main quadrangle.

ARTS AND LEISURE

venerable classics and Baltimore debuts of interesting new works at this Charles Street location since 1994. Though their current venue is doing well, it's so small (just 170 seats) that the theater plans to be in a new building (a former movie theater) at 315 West Fayette Street by 2010 or 2011.

THE 14KARAT CABARET

218 W. Saratoga St., 410/225-0706, www.normals.com/14k.html

Map 5

This subterranean performance venue hosts a wide variety of fringe, weird, peculiar, delightful, and (rarely) rather normal artists and shows, ranging from performance artists to bands to vaudeville-like revues to dance parties. It's a non-profit venture run and organized by artists, so the program schedule is generally pretty interesting. There are more than a few regular performers (like founder Laure Drogoul) and shows (like Shattered Wig Night).

THEATRE HOPKINS

410/516-7159, www.jhu.edu/theatre

Map 6

The name of this troupe can be a little confusing when you learn the details: though it is supported and housed by Johns Hopkins University, it does not perform there all the time (when it does, it's often at the Swirnow Theater, at the campus's Mattin Arts Center). And despite the Hopkins name, the actors are not students, but professional performers; this is a semi-professional community theater group (formed back in 1921, it's the second-oldest in the city) that performs modern plays and famous classic readings and scenes across the area.

THEATRE PROJECT

45 W. Preston St., 410/539-3091, www.theatreproject.org

Map 5

This is the Baltimore theater where, often, risks are taken and boundaries are pushed (though not to unreasonable ends). Performances here at this 150-seat theater range from drastic re-imaginings of traditional tales to experimental

Theatre Project, one of Baltimore's many local theater companies

works, sometimes dances, that aim to break new ground. The stage itself is a simple wooden platform that's about 35 feet on each side; that and the small size put the performers and audience in very close company. There's a good selection of more accessible works, some that will amaze through their inventiveness, and then a few that will prove challenging to all but the most avant-garde.

VAGABOND THEATER

806 S. Broadway, 410/563-9135, www.vagabondplayers.org

Map 2

Among the bars and taverns and boutiques of Fell's Point is this enchanting little shoebox theater, whose performers have been taking to this and other local stages for more than 90 years. The Vagabond stages about five plays each season, leaning toward easily enjoyed fare like light comedies and musicals, but there are some heavy dramas on the bill as well. Best of all, after the show, you've got about two-dozen options nearby for a nightcap.

CONCERT VENUES
1ST MARINER BANK ARENA
201 W. Baltimore St., 410/347-2020,
www.baltimorearena.com
`Map 1`

Long known as the Baltimore Arena, this mid-sized stadium/performance venue was built way back in 1962, and though a series of upgrades and improvements have been made, this place is showing its age. Still, at 13,500 seats, it's the only game in town for a variety of performers. Four decades ago, the arena hosted bands and performers like the Beatles, the Rolling Stones, the Supremes, and Led Zeppelin. Today, the bigger names in country, hip-hop, and rock stop here on tours geared toward second-tier cities; it's also where the TV-created next generation of performers (like Miley Cyrus) stop as they head across America.

◖ THE HIPPODROME THEATRE
12 N. Eutaw St., 410/837-7400,
www.france-merrickpac.com
`Map 1`

In the 1940s, the western side of downtown was home to the city's thriving arts scene, with movie theaters, stages, music halls, and nightclubs on every street. As Baltimore declined, this neighborhood was particularly hard hit, but recent rebirths have included wonderful rehabs like this project. The original Hippodrome theater, which opened in 1914 as a movie house and vaudeville palace, saw stars like Frank Sinatra, Bob Hope, and Benny Goodman take the stage. In 2004, a larger complex (The France-Merrick Performing Arts Center) was opened here, and the heart of the operation is the gorgeously renovated and rebuilt Hippodrome. There's an enormous mural above the stage, incredible detail in everything from the seats to the ceiling, and a sense of ceremony for the audiences who fill the 2,286-seat

© GEOFF BROWN

the beautifully restored Hippodrome Theatre

auditorium for musicals, holiday performances, comedians, and other entertainers.

THE JOSEPH MEYERHOFF SYMPHONY HALL

1212 Cathedral St., 410/783-8000, www.bsomusic.org

Map 5

Opened in 1982, this graceful building, a series of rising, curved structures, is named for one of the Baltimore Symphony Orchestra's most generous patrons and officers. The curves on the exterior carry over to the interior, as the outer areas and hallways gently sweep around the 2,443-seat concert space. The BSO has been playing to packed houses of late because of the excitement created by the addition of acclaimed music director Marin Alsop, the first woman to be named as head of a major U.S. orchestra. Rave reviews for her conducting, and the performances of the BSO under her guidance, have been given by the national and international press, and her presence has reignited interest in and appreciation of the BSO both in Baltimore and beyond.

THE LYRIC OPERA HOUSE

140 W. Mount Royal Ave., 410/685-5086, www.lyricoperahouse.com

Map 5

It's difficult to appreciate the splendor of this opera house from the drab, 1980s-era exterior that was constructed around the original 1894 building. But get past the unappealing brown stone and glass and inside this civic treasure, and you'll be swept back to an era of grand theaters, red velvet chairs, and detailed craftsmanship. This has been the home of the Baltimore Opera Company, a very respected performance group that, throughout its history, has staged roughly four operas each season, including some amazingly complex productions and sets. The venue also hosts a variety of solo performers, comedians, traveling companies, and even high-definition simulcasts of performances from New York City's Metropolitan Opera.

© GEOFF BROWN

the sweeping curves and arcs of the Joseph Meyerhoff Symphony Hall

THE BSO'S MAESTRA: MARIN ALSOP

In 2005, the Baltimore Symphony Orchestra announced that Marin Alsop would become the symphony's music director. It was a tremendously important hire that drew international attention to the BSO, for it marked the first time a woman had been chosen to lead a major American orchestra. The BSO had been going through a rough patch when Alsop was hired, and through her will and work, the symphony has regained stature, morale, and momentum. She frequently conducts, and has introduced a wider variety of performances, from audience-friendly pops and contemporary music shows to more obscure and challenging pieces. In 2007, the *New York Times* wrote of her conducting style: "Ms. Alsop is a dynamo on the podium, an incisive technician who moves and grooves much like [Leonard] Bernstein, her mentor." Check the BSO's website for performance schedules, and if Alsop is wielding her baton, by all means get over to Joseph Meyerhoff Symphony Hall.

PIER 6 CONCERT PAVILION
731 Eastern Ave., 410/783-4189,
www.piersixpavilion.com
Map 2

The large, white wave-meets-tent-like structure you may glimpse in your travels around the Inner Harbor is this waterfront performance venue. The 4,200-capacity space (there is also lawn seating) plays host to a variety of smaller big-name acts during the season (as it's an outdoor space, shows run normally from spring to fall each year). These have included all kinds of performers, from country to rap, and include names like James Taylor, Erykah Badu, and Duran Duran. The acoustics can be less than stellar here, as with most outdoor venues, but the location—right on the water, with views of Baltimore's downtown in every direction—somehow excuses any sonic sins here.

CINEMA
◖ THE CHARLES THEATRE
1711 N. Charles St., 410/727-3456,
www.thecharles.com
Map 5

Once a cable car barn and a powerhouse, the two Beaux-Arts buildings that are now the Charles Theatre are a great warren of open, exposed-brick spaces—with winding hallways into four smaller theaters that hold from 115 to 230 people, and one large auditorium that accommodates 485 people. Independent, art-house, and revivals are the staples at this popular theater, with a smattering of more popcorn-oriented fare as appropriate. There's a popular Cinema Sundays series that includes bagel breakfasts and guest speakers. This was once (along with the Club Charles and the Everyman Theatre) the only reason to come to this part of town; now, the renamed Station North Arts District has added options for dinner and post-show drinks.

IMAX THEATER AT MARYLAND SCIENCE CENTER
601 Light St., 410/685-5225,
www.mdsci.org/shows/imax.html
Map 1

There's nothing like walking into a five-story tall, 400-seat IMAX theater and preparing to have your senses blown away by surreally clear building-high images and gut-shaking sound. Like most IMAX theaters that are associated with science centers, this venue shows a healthy slate of nature and science documentaries, blended with kid-friendly Hollywood fare like animated films and Disney features. This theater can also show IMAX 3-D films, making for an even more engrossing experience. Most showings are in the morning and afternoon, with occasional Friday 7 P.M. screenings.

LANDMARK THEATRES
645 S. President St., 410/624-2622,
www.landmarktheatres.com
Map 2

Tucked into one of the new towers of the Harbor East neighborhood, this seven-screen

ARTS AND LEISURE

art-house chain theater shows both standard Hollywood fare as well as more thoughtful films, from documentaries to foreign features. This is a theater for grown-ups who like their movies; there's a full bar where cocktails can be purchased and taken into the theater, the projection and sound is spectacular, and the plush leather seats are some of the best in town.

MICA BROWN CENTER

1301 Mt. Royal Ave., 410/669-9200,
www.mica.edu/programs/bfa/video/blog.cfm
Map 5

Part of the Maryland Institute College of Art, this dramatic, angular, green-glass building is home to the school's new media department; it's also the site of a 550-seat auditorium in the basement that shows all sorts of interesting films throughout the year. Documentaries, propaganda features, classics, avant-garde experiments, and cult favorites all make the quirky cut here; check the MICA website's

events section for a current listing of films. Admission is generally free, but bring some cash just in case. This theater also serves as one of May's Maryland Film Festival screening sites (most films are shown at the nearby Charles Theatre).

THE ROTUNDA CINEMATHEQUE

711 W. 40th St., 410/235-4800, www.senator.com
Map 6

Operated by the same owner as the massive Senator Theatre, this smaller two-screen theater is located at the northern edge of Hampden in the Rotunda, a large, historic office and retail complex that looks more like a college hall than a shopping mall. There's usually one mainstream film and one independent or art-house film being shown at any given time here. Both theaters are cozy, with about 120 seats each. It's not a great choice for a big-budget blockbuster, but smaller films and character-driven movies fit perfectly.

ARTS AND LEISURE

© GEOFF BROWN

The Maryland Institute College of Art's Brown Center hosts films and speakers.

CINEMA AL FRESCO: OUTDOOR MOVIES

It started in 1999, in Little Italy, on a bare billboard hung in a parking lot; now, free outdoor film festivals are a staple of Baltimore summers.

The elder statesman of the bunch, and most popular, is the **Little Italy Open Air Film Festival** (www.littleitalymd.com), held on eight Friday nights in July and August. Beginning at sundown, films from *Moonstruck* to *Cinema Paradiso* are projected right out of the window of a row house. Crowds form early (bring a lawn chair) and fill the streets around the parking lot.

Wednesdays now offer **Films on the Pier** (www.cdjoint.com/filmsonthepier.cfm), shown on a 300-foot screen at the Broadway Pier in Fell's Point; the series runs all summer long. On Thursdays in June and July, head to the other side of the Inner Harbor, to Federal Hill Park; bring a blanket and pack a picnic for the American Visionary Art Museum's **Flicks from the Hill** (www.avam.org/cgi-bin/Events.cgi), projected on the west side of the museum. Uptown, the five-week-long, Friday-night series of **Johns Hopkins Summer Outdoor Films** (www.jhu.edu/summer/films) in June and July features opening bands playing on the bucolic Upper Quad in front of Gilman Hall, followed by the feature.

COURTESY BALTIMORE AREA CONVENTION AND VISITORS ASSOCIATION

Film fans pack the streets of Little Italy for summer outdoor movies.

THE SENATOR THEATRE

5904 York Rd., 410/435-8338, www.senator.com

Map 7

Just south of the city line with Baltimore County is this civic treasure: an enormous, single-screen movie theater that's led a charmed life, escaping demolition, repossession, financial strife, and a myriad of other disasters. Thankfully, this wonderful old Art Deco movie palace (900 seats) shows major Hollywood blockbusters and often hosts Baltimore premieres of films shot in the city, or those that star (or were directed by) Charm City natives or fans, like John Waters and Edward Norton. In front, check out the mosaic of tributes—a collection of hand and footprints in cement—to premieres and events at this historic theater.

ARTS AND LEISURE

Festivals and Events

Baltimore's parks and streets are host to a surprising array of beloved annual events, from tiny neighborhood block parties to enormous three-day extravaganzas like Mount Vernon's Artscape. Many of the various ethnic groups who moved to Baltimore in the 19th century and set up their own little enclaves—like Poles, Lithuanians, Greeks, Ukrainians, and Italians—host festivals featuring the traditional foods, music, and dances of their home countries. These sorts of neighborhood events occur all spring and summer long, and are held on the neighborhoods' streets or at nearby parks. Stop by any of them to get some great food and hear some obscure music and learn a little bit about Baltimore's treasured ethnic neighborhoods.

At the other end of the spectrum are the city's blockbuster festivals, which attract hundreds of thousands of visitors to see national musical acts, enjoy the arts, or just hang out. The biggest of these is July's Artscape, but the

Preakness Stakes also brings huge crowds to town each May. Watch out for the collateral effects of some special goings-on: Newly popular events like the Baltimore Marathon close down the city for most of a Saturday, and stranger events like the Kinetic Sculpture Race also shut down part of some city streets.

And there are lots of intriguing, weird, peculiar, and captivating festivals, gatherings, and events across the city all year long. There's Otakon, a national convention of Asian anime fans; the Night of 100 Elvises, which actually takes place over two nights, each packed with Elvis tribute artists; and the High Zero Festival of experimental music, where the concepts of songs and melodies are totally rewritten (or just destroyed). These are the kinds of only-in-Baltimore events that make the city so fascinating, not only for visitors, but for the people who call Charm City home.

WINTER
THE MAYOR'S CHRISTMAS PARADE
Hampden, www.mayorschristmasparade.com
Map 6

Every first Sunday of December (most years), the streets of Hampden are filled with a peculiar collection of high school cheerleaders and marching bands, floats, classic cars, Elvis tribute artists, Santa Claus, a woman dressed like Underdog, and maybe even some brightly costumed Bolivian marchers. Oh, and the mayor of Baltimore will be there, too, waving from the back seat of a convertible. It's a fitting event for quirky Hampden, and during the medium-sized parade, the streets are lined with families, hipsters, and assorted other local characters.

MIRACLE ON 34TH STREET
Hampden, 34th St. between Keswick Ave. and Chestnut Ave., www.christmasstreet.com
Map 6

Taking its name from the classic holiday film, this Hampden tradition—in which every resident on one block of 34th Street takes holiday

Imani Edu-Tainers African Dance Company performing at Artscape, described as "America's largest free public arts festival"

© MIDDLETON EVANS FOR THE BALTIMORE OFFICE OF PROMOTION & THE ARTS

the Miracle on 34th Street in Hampden, a local sightseeing tradition during the winter holidays

COURTESY BALTIMORE AREA CONVENTION AND VISITORS ASSOCIATION

light decoration to an unreal level—begins around Thanksgiving, and the lights don't go out until after New Year's Day. Tens of thousands of people drive countless miles to either cruise through the street or stop and enjoy it on foot. The sidewalks are packed with bundled-up visitors drinking hot chocolate and gawking at the snowmen built from hubcaps, gigantic glowing Santa Clauses, and rivers of colored lights that flow over the houses and even across the street itself.

◖ THE NIGHT OF 100 ELVISES

410/494-9558 or 888/494-9558,
www.nightof100elvises.com

Map 7

This annual event, which raises money for the Johns Hopkins Children's Center, is actually held on two nights, owing to its popularity (inevitably on the first Friday and Saturday in December). This massive homage to everything Elvis features a massive array of Elvis tribute artists (don't call them impersonators), bands playing Elvis songs, fried peanut butter and banana sandwiches, dancing—as well as a lounge, a bar and karaoke area, and a building packed with happy guests mingling with Elvises and Santa Claus and Vegas-style showgirls. It's been covered by the Discovery Channel and Japanese television, and there's nothing else like it in America.

ST. PATRICK'S DAY PARADE

Downtown, www.irishparade.net

Map 1

Baltimore's proud Irish American citizens have helped make this one of the city's biggest events (held on the Saturday closest to St. Patrick's Day, not the actual day). The spectacle features bagpipe-brandishing marching bands, St. Patrick–honoring floats, and a popular 5K race that has thousands of runners hurdling through downtown streets packed with pleasantly inebriated parade-goers. Irish bars across town have all-day music and Irish dancing, along with Guinness and corned beef. Downtown is basically closed off to car traffic for this day-long celebration

ARTS AND LEISURE

of the patron saint of Ireland; plan any trips accordingly.

WASHINGTON MONUMENT LIGHTING
Mount Vernon Place, 410/244-1030
Map 5

In early December each year, on a chilly Thursday night, Mount Vernon Place overflows with more than 5,000 onlookers as the city's mayor and assembled VIPs flip the switch that turns on the colored strings of lights that adorn the Washington Monument. There's also a small but impressive fireworks display, as well as vendors selling seasonally appropriate hot cider and roasted chestnuts. Dubbed "A Monumental Occasion," it's a popular event with families, and an adored city tradition that really marks the beginning of the holiday season in Baltimore.

SPRING
FLOWER MART
600 N. Charles St., 410/323-0022,
www.flowermart.org
Map 5

Perhaps the most civilized city festival, this family-friendly event takes place around the Washington Monument in Mount Vernon; regular attendees arrive in a riot of colorful attire that blends in with the elaborate floral displays. Enormous, gaudy hats are de rigueur at this early-May floral festival (there's a contest for the most impressive), and vendors sell all manner of live and cut plants and flowers, along with food and drinks. The traditional treat to get at this event is the lemon stick: a lemon cut in half with a peppermint stick stuck into it. Suck on the peppermint stick to get the de-soured lemon juice. It's another "only in Baltimore" tradition, one that lasts for two days (Friday and Saturday).

HIGH ZERO FESTIVAL
Theatre Project, 45 W. Preston St., 410/752-8558,
www.highzero.org
Map 5

Held at the end of spring, this is not a festival for everyone, unless everyone likes experimental and improvisational music, often made using non-traditional instruments...like rocks, metal, and furniture. Plenty of traditional instruments are used as well, but in very untraditional ways, creating atonal, oddly structured music that can be very difficult to understand or comprehend. Still, that doesn't mean it's not worth going to a performance or two, as this peerless festival has drawn international attention from people looking to push the boundaries of conventional sound and music.

HONFEST
Hampden, 36th St., www.honfest.net
Map 6

Back in 1994, the owner of Hampden's Café Hon decided to put on a tribute festival to the colorful local residents who were thought to be fading away as times changed—like the strong working-class white women who wore beehive hairdos and greeted everyone as "hon." Now a two-day-long weekend event in mid-June that takes up Hampden's main drag (36th Street, or "The Avenue"), there are lots of activities for kids, as well as bands and food and beer—plus the crowning of Miss Hon, where faux-hons don their biggest wigs, cat's-eye glasses, and best "Bawlmer" accent to vie for the title.

JOHNS HOPKINS UNIVERSITY SPRING FAIR
3400 N. Charles St., www.jhuspringfair.com
Map 6

An annual spring (late April) event for nearly 40 years, JHU's Spring Fair opens up the campus to the public for a weekend mix of music, food, crafts, and art, as well as a healthy contingent of non-profit and socially active booths and displays. There's a big section for kids, but in addition to the usual rides and activities, the college kids sneak in some fun motivational education projects for children to encourage reading and learning. The big draw comes on Friday night, when a major alternative performer (maybe hip-hop, maybe rock, maybe something weirder) takes the stage.

KINETIC SCULPTURE RACE

Starts at the American Visionary Art Museum, 800 Key Hwy., 410/244-1900, www.kineticbaltimore.com

Map 2

If it's early May and Saturday, and you see a giant pink poodle about the size of a U-Haul rolling down the streets of downtown Baltimore, you've stumbled upon the Kinetic Sculpture Race, a smile-inducing and whimsical combination of mechanical engineering, artistic creativity, pedal power, and buoyancy. Teams build people-powered sculptures of varying sizes and structural integrity levels, then pedal them all over the city, braving a series of muddy, off-road challenges as well as a water obstacle course in Canton. Winners and losers—that's not the point of this preposterous carnival. The point is just being a part of it.

LATINOFEST

Patterson Park, www.latinofest.org

Map 3

With the surge in Baltimore's Latino population in recent years, the area of north Fell's Point has gone from being somewhat underpopulated and sparsely occupied to thriving with new immigrants who have brought their own cultural outlets to the city. LatinoFest, once a smaller city festival, is now one of the larger ones. Held at Patterson Park on a weekend in June, there are plenty of art, food, and drink vendors, and some great performances from Latino musicians both local and international.

MARYLAND FILM FESTIVAL

The Charles Theatre and the MICA Brown Center, 410/752-8083, www.mdfilmfest.org

Map 5

For a city with such a stellar cinematic history, it took a while for Baltimore to host a film festival; this four-day event didn't start until 1998. Still, it's been worth the wait, as the festival now attracts a great mix of local, national, and international films, speakers, and even a super-secret sneak preview every year, the content of which audiences are sworn to not reveal. Shorts, animation, documentaries, and a couple mondo oddballs make up the bulk of the schedule for this three-day event held in early May.

MARYLAND HUNT CUP

Worthington Valley, Baltimore County, www.marylandsteeplechasing.com

Map 7

First run back in 1894, the Maryland Hunt Cup is the grandfather of the state's steeplechase racing series, as well as the oldest steeplechase race in America. Though most people (rightly) think of Kentucky as the nation's premier horseracing state, horses have played a big part in northern Baltimore County's history, both as farm animals and as racers. This race celebrates the latter role in an all-day event held at Worthington Farms in Hunt Valley, where the country squires and dames assemble in their finery to drink, dine, and hobnob. There are plenty of regular folks here, too, as the excitement of this four-mile, 22-gate steeplechase draws crowds from all walks of life to the valley on a Saturday in late April.

THE PREAKNESS STAKES

Pimlico Race Course, 5201 Park Heights Ave., 410/542-9400, www.preakness.com

Map 7

On the third Saturday in May, Baltimore's Pimlico Race Course is host to the middle jewel in horse racing's Triple Crown (the first is the Kentucky Derby; the last is the Belmont Stakes). For the week before the race, Baltimore hosts all sorts of parties, events, festivals, and other activities for the tens of thousands of visitors who descend on the city for pre-race fun. Hot-air balloons fill the skies, and it seems like there's a hospitality tent on every patch of ground around the Inner Harbor. Race day itself brings traffic on I-83 to a halt as the throngs head for Pimlico (the infield alone groans under the beer-sodden feet of some 104,000 people), and the evenings usually see bars and restaurants filled with tired, sunburned folks.

ARTS AND LEISURE

ST. ANTHONY ITALIAN FESTIVAL
Exeter and Stiles Sts., Little Italy, 410/675-7275
Map 2

When the Baltimore Fire of 1904 destroyed much of downtown, the residents of Little Italy gathered at the St. Leo the Great Catholic church and prayed to St. Anthony for the salvation of their neighborhood. The fire never made it across the Jones Falls and Little Italy was spared; to thank St. Anthony, a festival was held that year, and every year since. Now, for a weekend in early June, there's lots of great Italian food, dancing, music, and a Sunday bocce tournament.

SUMMER
AFRICAN AMERICAN HERITAGE FESTIVAL
333 Camden St., 410/235-4427, ext. 211, www.aahf.net
Map 1

This three-day festival, which takes place in late June, was first held in 2002, and quickly became a major success, luring crowds and big-name musical acts to Baltimore to celebrate African American culture and also take part in a great event. Food, crafts, vendors, and children's activities are the other attractions at the festival, held in the sprawling parking lots between Oriole Park and M&T Bank Stadium in Camden Yards. Though the success of the initial few years of the festival has dimmed slightly, it's still a popular event, and one that was overdue for a city where 65 percent of the population is African American.

❰ ARTSCAPE
Mt. Royal Ave. and Cathedral St., www.artscape.org
Map 5

Described as "America's largest free public arts festival," Artscape is a pretty amazing thing for several reasons. First, it's a festival that literally everyone in the city—no matter what economic, social, or cultural background—goes to, making it a rare place for city residents to interact with one another. Second, it's an art

Art Car exhibition at Artscape

festival, which makes its popularity even more astonishing. And third, it's always really hot on the July Artscape weekend, but the crowds—estimated at about 500,000 over Friday, Saturday, and Sunday—keep coming, and everyone manages to stay cool. Held on Mount Royal Avenue near the Maryland Institute College of Art, this huge event draws more than 150 vendors, as well as some top-notch musical acts that perform all weekend long.

BILLIE HOLIDAY & CAB CALLOWAY VOCAL COMPETITION
Meyerhoff Symphony Hall, 1212 Cathedral St.,
410/752-8632, www.artscape.org
Map 5

Held during the three-day Artscape festival, this long-running female vocalist competition is named for one of Baltimore's favorite adopted artists, the incomparable Billie Holiday; a male component, named for Cab Calloway, was added a few years ago. Unknown and up-and-coming young singers take the stage at the wonderful Meyerhoff to partisan, cheering crowds and blow audiences away with their professional-level performances. The winner is chosen on Saturday and performs on Sunday with the Baltimore Symphony Orchestra.

FOURTH OF JULY
Inner Harbor, events start at 3 P.M.
Map 1

Join a crowd of several hundred thousand as people flock from all over the Baltimore region for the huge fireworks show, launched from barges in the center of the harbor. There are plenty of vendors, bands, and things to do starting in the afternoon, and the fireworks display itself is a big-budget spectacular that looks great reflected on the windows of the waterfront office towers. In places like Fell's Point and Federal Hill, folks start staking out spaces well before sundown, so plan accordingly if you're trying to get in or out of the Inner Harbor area that night—parking can be non-existent, and the traffic jams out of the area can be frustrating.

OTAKON
Baltimore Convention Center, 1 W. Pratt St.,
610/577-6136, www.otakon.com
Map 1

An *otaku* (it's a Japanese word) is a person who is a devoted follower of Asian pop culture, including (but not limited to) anime, video games, comics, and movies. Otakon, then, is a convention of *otaku*, and it's fitting that a slightly off-center city like Baltimore would get a slightly off-center convention like this. It's one of the largest in the nation (over 26,000 people came in 2008) for people whose devotion to anime involves creating elaborate homemade costumes and props—which leads to some strange sights around the convention center, as suited businesspeople wait to cross the street with people in enormous white PVC helmets, boots, and plastic swords. It's held for three days, beginning on a Thursday, in early August.

WHARTSCAPE
Various locations, www.whamcity.com

Put together as an avant-garde response to the more mainstream Artscape festival (and held the same weekend in mid-July as that massive Mount Vernon event), Whartscape is the brainchild of a collective known as Wham City, made up of some of Baltimore's most intriguing and motivated independent musicians and artists. New, exciting, and buzz-worthy musicians and bands from Baltimore (and a few other cities) play in non-traditional venues and at outdoor shows all weekend long. Primarily held in the Mount Vernon area, Whartscape's big Saturday night lineup has moved to downtown's Sonar club, where the headlining acts draw major crowds.

FALL
BALTIMORE BOOK FESTIVAL
Mount Vernon Place, 600 N. Charles St.,
410/752-8632, www.baltimorebookfestival.com
Map 5

A two-and-a-half day celebration in late September of Baltimore's literary history, from authors to books and libraries, this event is a bibliophile's dream. The fun includes lots of book vendors hawking interesting reads, from expensive rarities to cheap bulk books, and a variety of panels, speakers, readings, and discussions featuring local and national writers. There's also the usual assortment of food and music, all found around the Washington Monument in Mount Vernon.

THE BALTIMORE RUNNING FESTIVAL & MARATHON

Begins and ends at Camden Yards, 410/605-9381, www.thebaltimoremarathon.com

Map 1

Many cities have had successful marathons for years; though Baltimore's early October marathon was started only in 2001, it's quickly become a big hit with prominent runners, especially with the addition of larger purses and route improvement that removed some seriously unpleasant hills. Nearly 18,000 ran either the marathon or half-marathon in 2008, and a new course record of 2:11:56 was set by Kenyan runner Julius Keter. The course winds all over the central part of the city, making travel impossible in those areas during race morning and early afternoon.

FREE FALL BALTIMORE

Citywide, 410/752-8632, www.freefallbaltimore.com

Thanks to this simple and brilliant promotion, sponsored by the city and some corporate partners, many of Baltimore's best attractions, museums, and venues are free throughout the month of October. In addition, unique events ranging from music performances to festivals are held, all free of charge. To get free passes to specific events, and to find out about all the available gratis entertainment, go to the Free Fall Baltimore website.

THE GREAT HALLOWEEN LANTERN PARADE

Patterson Park, Pulaski Monument, Eastern and Linwood Aves.

Map 3

The beauty of this community-based art project is hard to capture in words, but picture some 1,000 children and adults walking through the chilly autumn air, trekking across the winding and dark paths of Patterson Park's fields and woods, carrying candlelit lanterns, and wearing costumes ranging from simple capes to enormous papier-mâché skeletons and fantastic beasts. Some parade-goers play instruments, some clang bells, some walk in spooky silence. It all adds up to an amazing experience for spectators and participants alike.

THANKSGIVING PARADE

Pratt St. downtown, www.bop.org

Map 1

An annual Baltimore tradition, held on the Saturday after Thanksgiving, this three-hour-long parade takes to Baltimore's biggest street (Pratt St.) each year for a crowd of about 17,000 people who line the route. There are floats and marching bands both formal and way more funky (a Baltimore high school and youth orchestra tradition; bands and dance squads to watch for include the Westsiders, Showstoppers, and New Edition). Plus you'll see historic vehicles, local celebrities, horses, and Santa Claus. The fun begins at the corner of Pratt and Eutaw Streets and heads 10 long blocks east through downtown, along the Inner Harbor, and finally winds up at Market Place.

TOUR DU PORT

Starts at the Canton Waterfront Park, 410/235-3678, www.onelesscar.org/TDP

Map 3

Organized by Maryland's largest pedestrian and bicycling advocacy group, this popular bike event lets riders take one of several long rides through the city and parts of the Port of Baltimore, from a long 45-mile ride to a brisk 15-mile jaunt. On a Sunday in early October, some 1,500 riders begin their morning at this annual event, which covers territory from the Inner Harbor all the way out to North Point State Park in Baltimore County. Proceeds go to help make the state safer and easier for people looking to ditch their driving habits.

Recreation

Whether it's cheering the Orioles in the landmark Oriole Park at Camden Yards, learning the difference between a jib and a tack while sailing on the Inner Harbor, or taking a serious bike trip down to Annapolis, there are countless ways to get out and enjoy the lands and waters that surround Baltimore City. There are also several brand-new, high-tech gyms and athletic centers that have opened up across town if you're looking for an indoor workout that will challenge your limits. And there are even a couple of unique city golf courses worth checking out.

If you're the kind of person who prefers to watch the pros handle all the sweating, there's the storied Baltimore Orioles baseball team (the lifelong squad of Hall of Famer Cal Ripken, Jr.) and the new but perhaps even more beloved Baltimore Ravens (winners of Super Bowl XXXV in 2001). There's also the multiple-championship-winning Baltimore Blast of the National Indoor Soccer League. Lacrosse is Maryland's state team sport, and the high schools and universities around Baltimore play some of the best "lax" in the world. And there's the Pimlico Race Course, where you can play the ponies and spend the day at the track, catch some rays and sip on a Black-Eyed Susan cocktail while the horses and jockeys do all the work.

For gym rats and road runners, there's plenty of options in Charm City. The lands around the Inner Harbor are nice and flat, making for a great 10-mile run, and the Baltimore Marathon draws some 18,000 runners a year for a long course that ambles throughout most of the city. Bicyclists have some great new paths and trails, including the NCR Trail that runs from Baltimore County into Pennsylvania and the Baltimore-Annapolis Trail. Swimmers can head to several local gyms or aquatic centers (including the same pool where 14-Olympic-gold-medal-winner Michael Phelps once trained). And there are several great city parks for simple walks, tennis, or jogs. State and county parks outside the city offer great opportunities for hiking and trail running.

Baltimore's been rated (somewhat surprisingly) as one of the fittest cities in America (by *Men's Fitness* magazine, back in 2006); though it doesn't totally jibe with first-hand observations, this is a city and region that's really improved its health in the past few years. No matter what kind of physical challenge you prefer—from aerobics to trail riding to yoga—there's a place in Baltimore where (with all due respect to the late, great Baltimore sportscaster Jim McKay) you can pursue the thrill of victory, and hopefully avoid the agony of defeat.

PARKS

Unlike many great cities, Baltimore is without a single defining park. Patterson Park, in Canton, has become the city's favorite park in many ways, but it's not quite the same as New York City's unsurpassed Central Park. And while Federal Hill Park offers some great views of the city (and has a great playground for toddlers), it's not large enough to be Baltimore's main park. Druid Hill Park has the size and the majesty to have been the city's premier

---

BARGAIN BALTIMORE: RECREATION

Take a hike through bucolic **Robert E. Lee Park** (and meet a lot of happy canines). During spring, you can have a day at the races at **Pimlico Race Course,** the home of the Preakness, for a paltry $3 – and you don't even have to place a bet. Tuesday nights are $8 upper deck nights at **Oriole Park at Camden Yards.** And an old sport has gained fresh legs and a wicked forearm check – go see a **Charm City Roller Girls** roller-derby match, where 10 bucks gets you two furious bouts.

park, but with much of the surrounding neighborhoods having fallen into disrepair over the past 40 years—and the physical separation created by I-83—the park, while popular (and home to the Maryland Zoo and Rawlings Conservatory), is not a central public space.

Despite this, many neighborhoods have smaller parks that are important parts of those communities, offering some needed green space to row-house dwellers who may have a backyard made of concrete. And in many ways, the Inner Harbor area serves as an unofficial (and very concrete-laden) main public space for Baltimoreans, as does much of the waterfront. The green lawns and shade trees of Fort McHenry are popular for picnicking and just lying under the sun (no ball- or Frisbee-playing is allowed; it's a hallowed national shrine, after all). Patterson Park is the main sports park in town, if that's what you're looking for; it includes tennis courts, a covered ice rink, a public pool, and lots of space for softball, football, and—more and more often—soccer games between Latin American immigrants.

◖ CYLBURN ARBORETUM
4915 Greenspring Ave., 410/367-2217,
www.cylburnassociation.org
Map 7

No, it's technically not a park, but the lovely grounds of this 207-acre arboretum make it one of the city's most beautiful urban retreats. There are more than two miles of paths running through the rolling hills and dense woods here (guided tours are available, or you can stroll on your own), and the majestic, Victorian-era Cylburn Mansion (1888) provides a strong anchor for the site's superlative grounds. There are gentle lawns and well-tended gardens around the mansion, while tall trees provide shade for the pathways that wind around the property.

DRUID HILL PARK
900 Druid Park Lake Dr., 410/396-7900,
www.ci.baltimore.md.us/government/recnparks
Map 6

Covering some 745 acres of woods, fields, ball fields, tennis courts, and paths, Druid Hill Park is also home to a large lake, the Maryland Zoo in Baltimore, and the Howard P. Rawlings Conservatory. This one of the oldest major parks in the United States (along with New York City's Central Park and Philadelphia's Fairmount Park), and though it's showing its age in some places, it's still a major part of the lives of west Baltimoreans. Not all of the park is open, and that's probably for the best, as this is not a place to visit after dark. During the day, however, it's perfect for jogging around the reservoir and the main, open areas.

FORT McHENRY NATIONAL MONUMENT AND HISTORIC SHRINE
2400 E. Fort Ave., 410/962-4290, www.nps.gov/fomc
Map 7

With a couple of acres of flat, green lawns and tall, shade-giving trees overlooking the Inner Harbor as it becomes the Patapsco River again and heads toward the Chesapeake Bay, the grounds surrounding historic Fort McHenry are a favorite for Federal Hill residents, who bike, jog, and picnic here regularly (but no ball playing). It's one of the most peaceful spots in town (except for the heliport across the water), and a great way to escape the heat and noise of downtown Baltimore. Do take a look around before you put your blanket down, however; the large geese who make their homes around the fort tend to use the grassy areas as their toilet.

RIVERSIDE PARK
1800 Covington St., 410/396-8059
Map 4

This small park is a big hit with the many residents of this neighborhood south of Federal Hill, where the row houses are a little less stately and the streets a little less crowded. There's a popular public pool here that draws sweltering residents from all around, and the paths are popular for the many dog owners who call this area home. There are also some ball fields, a good little playground, and a pavilion that hosts small community gatherings and other events. Lots of big, broad trees make for great shade in the summer.

ROBERT E. LEE PARK

302 Woodbrook Ln.

Map 7

This is *the* city park (though it lies in Baltimore County, Baltimore City owns it) for dog lovers, despite what you might think having been to some other parks. Acres of wooded trails and the Jones Falls (plus the shores of Lake Roland) are a paradise for a stroll and a frolic, though the light rail trains blow through the park and are not behind a fence, so use caution when crossing the tracks. If you're not a fan of dogs, this is probably not the best place to get away from it all, as this park is usually teeming with happy-go-lucky (and often illegally unleashed) canines and their owners. And yes, it's named for the Confederate general; Baltimore's Confederate-sympathizing proclivities are always lurking around.

BICYCLING

The past few years have marked some dramatic gains for Baltimore's die-hard bike community. New bicycle lanes have been added to many streets, more buses have been outfitted with bicycle carrying racks, and even more places to lock up a bike have been added at major area attractions and throughout the city. Still, this ain't Portland, Oregon; many main streets are narrow enough with two lanes of traffic, and the addition of a bicyclist can lead to honking horns (at best) and peril (at worst).

It's a relatively easy city to get around in by bike, though heading north to Mount Vernon and Homewood is a long uphill trip that can take a cumulative toll on the less-than-fit. But just pedaling around the waterfront, from Canton over to Federal Hill, is predominantly flat and often doesn't even involve crossing major thoroughfares. Tour du Port is the city's big bike event, held in early fall and offering a few different routes.

North and south of the city are two great trails, both of which are pretty flat and cover some serious ground. To the south, there's the Baltimore-Annapolis Trail, which runs from BWI Airport all the way to the state capital, about a 25-mile trek. And to the north is the NCR Trail, a rail-to-trail bike path that starts in Baltimore County and rolls northward into Pennsylvania. If you're looking for a shorter ride, there's the Gwynns Falls Trail. Find out about riding in Baltimore at Baltimore Spokes (www.baltimorespokes.org).

Trails

◖ BALTIMORE-ANNAPOLIS TRAIL

www.aacounty.org/RecParks/parks/aacotrails_park

Map 7

This trail technically starts in the town of Glen Burnie, so plan to begin your ride at BWI Airport, and take the BWI Trail about 12 miles to the northern end of the 13-mile long Baltimore-Annapolis Trail (the URL included in this listing will get you to maps of both trails). The ride crosses only a few roads, and mostly takes you through woods and behind lots of residential areas. Built on a former railroad line, this is a flat trail that challenges riders with distance, not elevation gain. There are plenty of places to stop for food and drink along the way, including (during the summers) a great snowball stand at the halfway point of the B-A Trail.

GWYNNS FALLS TRAIL

410/396-0440 or 410/448-5663, ext. 113, www.gwynnsfallstrail.org

Map 7

What's coolest about this 15-mile trail, which starts on the west side of town, is that if you ride it from its beginning at the I-70 Park & Ride near the I-695 Beltway and follow its winding paths across bridges, past baseball fields, and through deep woods, you'll have passed through some 30 city neighborhoods. At the end, you'll be in the heart of the city, long past the trees and streams, but the voyage from wilderness to concrete jungle is transformative in a lot of ways. This is part of two greenways projects: the East Coast Greenway and the Chesapeake Bay Gateways Network. The trail does pass through some less-than-thriving sections of town, but there's never been any trouble for riders on this trail.

ARTS AND LEISURE

Federal Hill bikers, enjoying a view of the skyline

LAKE MONTEBELLO
Between Harford and Hillen Rds. at 32nd St.
Map 7

This brand-new bike and pedestrian path follows the shoreline of this 54-acre lake (actually one of the city's reservoirs) and is popular with joggers, inline skaters, and bicyclists. The loop is 1.35 miles, and the smooth, low-traffic road that hugs the bike path is no worry for bikers. During the early morning and early evening, many residents take their daily constitutionals around the waters of the lake.

NORTH CENTRAL RAILROAD TRAIL
Ashland, 410/592-2897,
www.dnr.state.md.us/greenways/ncrt_trail.html
Map 7

This trail, which connects with the York (Pennsylvania) Heritage Trail after it crosses the border some 20 miles from its start point in Ashland in rural northern Baltimore County, is extremely popular with Baltimore bicyclists. If you take the trail all the way to York, it's a 41-mile ride one-way, mostly flat until you hit the Pennsylvania border; then, it's a long gradual climb uphill (which becomes a pleasant downhill on the way home). A former railroad bed, this trail runs through almost entirely rural countryside, with big shade trees and beautiful scenery. There aren't many facilities around, though, so you'll need to pack all your own food and water.

Bike Rentals
LIGHT STREET CYCLES
1015 Light St., 410/685-2234, www.lightstcycles.com
HOURS: Mon.-Fri. 10 A.M.-8 P.M., Sat. 10 A.M.-6 P.M., Sun. 11 A.M.-4 P.M.
Map 4

The city's premier bicycle shop is also the only place near the Inner Harbor to rent a ride; you can pick it up at their bustling Federal Hill location, or (if you're nice and need help) they'll deliver and pick-up, for an extra fee. Costs vary according the type of bike rented (all rentals come with helmets, and they try to accommodate pedal choices too): Mountain bikes and road bikes are $45 for the first day, $35 for each additional day, while hybrids are $25 for the first day and $15 each day after.

PRINCETON SPORTS
6239 Falls Rd., 410/828-1127,
www.princetonsports.com
HOURS: Mon.-Fri. 10 A.M.-8 P.M., Sat. 10 A.M.-6 P.M., Sun. 11 A.M.-4 P.M.
Map 7

Head north to the outskirts of the city on Falls Road, past the Mount Washington neighborhood, and you'll find this big, well-stocked sporting goods store in a bucolic little office building in the woods. Rentals available here include road, mountain, and hybrid bikes (all come with helmets). Rates are $25 per day, with Thursday–Monday weekend rentals for $45 and week-long rentals for $75.

Resources
VELOCIPEDE BIKE PROJECT
4 W. Lanvale St., 410/244-5585,
www.velocipedebikeproject.org
Map 5

This collective non-profit group of bicyclists, mechanics, and socially minded folks in the Station North Arts District works to repair, restore, and provide bicycles to people who want to use them for transportation. The main goal is to get bikes into the hands of low-income folks who need to get to work or get around the city. To that end, this group rescues bikes from all sorts of near-fatal ends, spiffs them back up, and makes them available to Baltimoreans who need them.

SPECTATOR SPORTS
Baltimore's glory days were heady times indeed; both major sports teams—baseball's Orioles and football's Colts—regularly went to the playoffs and notched their share of championships. Players lived around town, weren't paid sums that dwarfed many countries' GDPs, and there was a (perhaps) naive joy taken by Baltimoreans in their star athletes and teams.

Times are different today, though not as grim as they were back in the mid- to late 1980s; the Orioles couldn't get back to the playoffs, and even worse, the Colts were moved by their owner in the dead of night to Indianapolis, where they continue to play today. While the Colts are still loathed in town, the Baltimore Ravens (nee the Cleveland Browns, and first playing in Baltimore under the Ravens moniker in 1996) have become the city's number-one sports franchise, making tickets a little tough to come by. The Orioles logged 11 straight years of losing baseball in 2008; once-packed Camden Yards is now regularly half-empty—which means that it's easy to walk up to a game and get decent tickets. The Baltimore Blast of the National Indoor Soccer League regularly vie for the title, and play in the friendly confines of the 1st Mariner Bank Arena.

Baltimore has no major colleges or universities (save one, but it's Johns Hopkins), so NCAA Division I basketball and football is only watched via TV here. There is one sport, however, where several local schools—not sports powerhouses by any means—compete at the nation's top level: lacrosse. Rivalry games between Johns Hopkins, Towson University, Loyola College, and the University of Maryland Baltimore County, can draw tens of thousands of fans; the NCAA Division I Men's Lacrosse Championships, often held at M&T Bank Stadium, last drew some 48,000 fans for the championship game.

Baseball
BALTIMORE ORIOLES
333 W. Camden St., 888/848-2473,
http://baltimore.orioles.mlb.com
Map 1

There have been a couple of incarnations of the Baltimore Orioles throughout baseball history; this current club came to Baltimore in 1954 from St. Louis, where they had been the Browns. The American League East Orioles have won three World Series, in 1966, 1970, and 1983. The last World Series win was the first (and only) for a young shortstop named Calvin Edwin Ripken, Jr.; Cal would go on to break the Major League Baseball consecutive game streak in 1995, a milestone and

BALTIMORE'S HOMERS: CHARM CITY SPORTS HEROES

Not only has Baltimore given the sporting world some amazing athletes, it's also contributed some great sportscasters and sportswriters. Obviously, the most well-known athlete of them all is celebrated baseball "Ironman," hall of famer, and lifelong Baltimore Oriole **Cal Ripken, Jr.** – but note that he is technically from Aberdeen, a small town about 25 minutes north east of Baltimore, though he's called Baltimore home for most of his adult life. Late sportscasting legend **Jim McKay** (who famously intoned the intro of the *ABC Wide World of Sports* that touted "the thrill of victory and the agony of defeat") was a Philadelphia native who moved to Baltimore in 1935 and never left. On a more recent note, NBA All-Star and Olympic gold medalist **Carmelo Anthony** hails from New York City originally, but moved to Baltimore at age eight; and 14-time Olympic gold medalist swimmer **Michael Phelps,** grew up just north of the city.

Here are some more well-known men and women from the Baltimore area who have distinguished themselves on the fields of sport (or chronicled those who have done so):

- Tyrone "Muggsy" Bogues – Former NBA player
- Frank DeFord – Prominent sportswriter and broadcaster
- Juan Dixon – NBA player
- Antonio Freeman – Former Pro Bowl NFL player
- Joe Gans – Legendary boxer, died 1909
- Rudy Gay – NBA player
- Al Kaline – MLB Hall of Famer
- Mel Kiper, Jr. – Television football analyst
- Bucky Lasek – Skateboard superstar
- Kimmie Meissner – Olympic figure skater
- Anita Nall – Olympic gold medal-winning swimmer, 1992
- Travis Pastrana – Motocross magician
- Bill Ripken – Cal's brother; had 12 seasons in the major leagues
- Cal Ripken, Sr. – Cal's dad; spent 36 years with the Orioles, three as manager
- George Herman "Babe" Ruth, Jr. – Possibly the greatest baseball player of all time
- Mark Teixeira – MLB player
- Bernard Williams – Olympic gold medal-winning relay runner, 2000

celebration that many critics cite as the first step baseball took back into America's hearts after the players' strike of 1994 (a year in which there was no World Series).

The early years of the Orioles (known affectionately as the O's) were a mixture of good and bad, with the majority of their games played in the now-demolished Memorial Stadium. Loyal crowds packed the house during the team's glory years, which ran from that 1966 championship year until the next World Series in 1983. The team was made up of All-Stars who played hard and led by a mean, foul-mouthed, happy-go-lucky and fearless manager of short stature and massive confidence named Earl Weaver; naturally, they had the undying loyalty of the city's fans.

The opening of Oriole Park at Camden Yards in 1991 was a revelation to American baseball fans; the stadium wasn't one of the typical huge, monolithic, concrete bowls that had became de rigueur throughout American cities. It was a throwback to storied stadiums like Wrigley Field in Chicago and Fenway Park in Boston—built downtown, and not out in the suburbs where the fan base lived, designed to hold about 48,000 fans, and crafted of brick and wrought iron, meant to evoke the feeling of old-time baseball and Americana (and this was done even before the steroid scandals of the early 2000s). A few years after the Orioles moved downtown, they became the powerhouse of the A.L. East, reaching the American League Championship Series in both 1996 and 1997, but falling short both times.

Recent years have been less kind to this club. After losing 93 games (and winning only 68) in 2008, the Orioles marked 11 straight years of losing records, and finished last in their division for the first time in 20 years. Hopes continue that the team will eventually compete again, but the once-devoted fan base that used to sell out the park has been cut by two-thirds. The stadium is packed, however, when the in-division rival Boston Red Sox or New York Yankees come to town; their boisterous, proud fans take over the seats, providing their teams with an away-from-home advantage.

If you're planning to pay a visit to the park, take some time for a behind-the-scenes tour of the facility ($7 for adults, $5 for kids), including the luxury boxes, the press box, and the Orioles dugout. Getting to see the stadium from the field is a real thrill, no matter how old you are.

Now, to attend an Orioles game like a real Baltimorean, here's a simple guide. First, pay a visit to the Babe Ruth statue outside the main gate on Camden Street. Notice anything strange about this tribute to George Herman Ruth? If you did, you're a real seamhead: the sculptor gave Ruth a left-handed glove, but Ruth was a lefty. Owing to the team's decade of dismal performances, you can get a decent ticket (prices run from $9 on bargain nights for nosebleeds to $80 for the primo behind-the-dugout seats) at the ticket booth right before the game. Once inside, stop by former Oriole great Boog Powell's pit beef stand (just follow the plume of beefy smoke) and grab a traditional Baltimore pit beef (it's roast beef cooked over a very hot flame) sandwich and a beer. Then head to Uncle Teddy's (also on your way in, but in the stadium proper) and grab a handmade cinnamon pretzel. Get to your seat in time for the national anthem;

© GEOFF BROWN

the entrance to the beloved Oriole Park at Camden Yards

there's a peculiar Baltimore tradition to follow during the song, which was written here. When the singer reaches the "O say does that Star-Spangled Banner" line, everyone in the stadium yells "O!" in tribute to the beloved, if currently hapless, O's.

Football
BALTIMORE BURN
443/983-3713 or 202/253-4707,
www.baltimoreburnfootball.com

Baltimore's representatives in the National Women's Football Association are the hard-hitting women of the Baltimore Burn. There are roughly 40 teams across America that play in the NWFA, and while some teams have a decent level of support and even some perks, the women of the Baltimore Burn do it on a shoestring budget and for the love of the game. Check their website for schedules and game locations.

BALTIMORE RAVENS
1101 Russell St., 410/261-7283,
www.baltimoreravens.com
Map 1

Baltimore football fans' hearts were broken one snowy night in 1984 when the Colts stole away into the dark and reappeared in the exotic city of…Indianapolis. Sure, Baltimore ended up getting a Canadian Football League team (the Baltimore CFL Stallions won the Grey Cup in 1995), but the black hole where NFL football had once lived was a wound that wouldn't heal for many residents. So it was with bittersweet rapture that, in 1995, it was announced that the Cleveland Browns—another beloved blue-collar football team—would be moving to Baltimore to take advantage of a big new taxpayer-financed stadium, one that Cleveland would not provide.

While that gridiron structure (now M&T Bank Stadium) was being built, the Ravens played at Memorial Stadium, which is now only a memory (a retirement community and a YMCA stand on the site). They stunk those early years, but it wasn't for lack of fan support, as the city got used to not only the return of

Rub Johnny's left foot for a Ravens win.

real NFL action, but the black and purple uniforms, and the fact that their team was named, in part, to honor a poem by the tragic figure of Edgar Allan Poe.

The team gradually improved under new coach Brian Billick, and the Ravens defense quickly became one of the most devastating of the late 1990s and early 2000s. Led by Ray Lewis, the Ravens' defense shut down many a high-flying offense, and despite anemic scoring, Baltimore began to rack up the wins (though scores of 16–3 were common). The 2000 team would be the one where, with a mix of hungry veterans and talented youngsters, all things seemed possible. After a strong start, the Ravens went five games without an offensive touchdown—but lost only three of those contests. A regular season record of 12 wins and four losses got them into the playoffs, where they beat the rival Tennessee Titans and Oakland Raiders to make it to Super Bowl XXXV. Their drubbing of the New York Giants in that match (winning 34–7) earned them a special place in the city's heart, and despite their ups and downs since 2001, the fans stay devoted, selling out M&T Bank Stadium regularly and turning downtown purple on many fall and winter Sundays.

Game day (single tickets range from $50–345) at M&T Bank Stadium (most locals still call it Ravens Stadium) begins with tailgating, whether or not you've driven. Just wander through the cars, SUVs, vans, and customized RVs in purple and black, meeting some very happy, beverage-hoisting fans who are cooking up some great-smelling foods. There's usually an "NFL Experience" set up outside the stadium, on the walkway to Oriole Park, where fans can try their hand at accurately throwing a football, or have their face painted, or get some free giveaways. Before heading inside, wish for luck for the Ravens and rub the left foot of the Johnny Unitas statue located at Unitas Plaza, on the north side of the stadium. Once inside, it might be a long walk to your seats; as the stadium was wedged into a tight urban footprint, it's quite steep, and if you've got nosebleed seats, you might want to get in shape before hiking up to the top of the stadium. Fans here also cheer with the "O" in the "O say does that Star-Spangled Banner" line in the national anthem, though not at heartily as at Orioles games.

Horse Racing
PIMLICO RACE COURSE
5201 Park Heights Ave., 410/542-9400, www.pimlico.com
Map 7

The nation's second-oldest horse-racing track (behind New York's Saratoga) opened in 1870, covering 70 acres of what was then countryside north of Baltimore City. Although there was a period (1889–1904) when there was no flat-track racing here, Pimlico has now been running the horses for more than 104 years. The first Preakness Stakes was run here in 1873, two years before the first Kentucky Derby. "Old Hilltop," as it's called by old-timers, runs races throughout the spring, sharing the state's racing season with another track in Laurel, south of Baltimore (check the website for schedules). Weekday attendance is pretty sparse, so if you're looking for a quiet day at the races, Pimlico is a lock. Crowds erupt, however, on the third Saturday in May, when the Preakness draws over 100,000 fans.

Indoor Soccer
BALTIMORE BLAST
1st Mariner Bank Arena, 201 West Baltimore St., 410/732-5278, www.baltimoreblast.com
Map 1

The Baltimore Blast are perennial contenders in indoor soccer, a bit of a niche sport, which is played in small arenas across the country; they're now in the new five-team National

LACROSSE

Known as the "fastest game on two feet," this physically demanding and violent yet finesse-filled sport – a favorite at Baltimore prep and public schools – reaches its pinnacle at the college level. (There are some semi-pro leagues, but NCAA lacrosse is the best, as the young players are fighting for school pride.) Played on a large field, "lax" is similar to hockey, except instead of a puck, there's a hard rubber ball about the size of a pool ball that's passed around using sticks with small nets at the top. There's plenty of hitting and beautiful passing, and goals are scored a lot more often than in hockey. Four local schools play some of the best lacrosse in the country: **Johns Hopkins University** (www.jhu.edu), which won the NCAA championship in 2005 and 2007 (that last game, against Duke University, was watched by a crowd of 48,000); **Loyola College** (www.loyola.edu); **Towson University** (www.towson.edu); and **University of Maryland Baltimore County** (www.umbc.edu). Check each school's schedule to see when they play each other if you want to experience what the excitement is all about.

ARTS AND LEISURE

Indoor Soccer League (there's one team from Monterrey, Mexico). The Blast have been in existence since 1980, with a few years on hiatus here and there as various indoor soccer leagues have come and gone. The team plays fast, captivating soccer, using boards to keep the action going and the scoring high (a typical indoor soccer game score can be 11–8).

Roller Derby
CHARM CITY ROLLER GIRLS
www.charmcityrollergirls.com
This four-team league of talented young ladies plays to packed houses across Baltimore, and fields an All-Star team that goes up against the crème de la crème from other cities. Founded in 2005, this rejuvenation of the concept of all-female roller derby (a hit in the 1950s and '60s) mixes the thrill of competition, the knowledge that the matches aren't rigged, and a black-fingernailed dose of punk rock fearlessness and pride in the ability to perform a thunderous take-down without drawing a penalty.

WATER ACTIVITIES
Baltimore came into existence thanks to the waters of the Patapsco River (the Inner Harbor) and the Chesapeake Bay; it's a shame that, for so many years, the city thanked those giving waters by dumping pollutants and garbage into them. Recent efforts to get the Inner Harbor back to decent quality have had some good effect, but as many of the city's storm sewers empty into the Inner Harbor during torrential downpours, you may see a few floating islands of debris following a storm.

The water is perfectly fine to boat on, however, and on warm, sunny spring days, you'll see all sorts of sailboats, motorboats, and other watercraft taking to the waters of the Inner Harbor (but no personal watercraft, as it's not the best water in which to plunge). If you want to join them, you can take a spin on a kayak or sailboat, but it will cost you (in both time and money). There are currently no facilities to rent anything more impressive

than a paddleboat at the Inner Harbor, but the following organizations will let you use their vessels if you join their clubs or sign up for lessons.

PORTS OF BALTIMORE

Arriving in Baltimore via the water is a special experience that not everyone gets to savor. If you're a boater (or know one) and plan on coming into town on the Patapsco River, there are several public marinas you can try to dock at. Be warned that during beautiful summer days, spaces can go fast; you may have to venture farther out of the Inner Harbor to areas like Canton, which will require a cab ride to reach downtown (unless you have a smaller dinghy, which you can probably fit anywhere along Fell's Point's several piers).

As you enter the Northwest Harbor area, heading west toward the city, the first marina you'll come upon is Canton's **Anchorage Marina** (2501 Boston St., #200, 410/522-7200, www.anchorage marina.com). Farther along into the harbor is **Henderson's Wharf Marina** (1001 Fell St., 410/732-1049, www.hendersonswharf .com), which conveniently also offers an inn, and is in Fell's Point. Across the water, near Federal Hill, is the **Harborview Marina and Yacht Club** (500 Harborview Dr., 410/528-1122, www.harborview community.com), part of the new housing developments along the waterfront. On the other side of the harbor, between Fell's Point and downtown, is the new **Inner Harbor East Marina** (801 Lancaster St., 410/625-1700). And finally, right in the heart of the Inner Harbor, is the **Baltimore Inner Harbor Marine Center** (400 Key Hwy., 410/837-5339, www.baltimoreinner harbormarinecenter.com), though if you have any inadequacy issues about docking your 25-foot fishing boat next to a 300-foot luxury yacht, this might not be the best dock for you.

Kayaking and Rowing
BALTIMORE ROWING CLUB
3301 Waterview Ave., 410/355-5649,
www.baltimorerowing.org

`Map 7`

From a boathouse in the shadow of the Hanover Street Bridge in south Baltimore, this group of rowers (and coxswains) takes to the waters of Baltimore in a collection of shells ranging from singles to fours and eights. The club competes against other groups at regattas up and down the East Coast, and offers serious, weeks-long lessons to newcomers ($200) and the chance to row with the pros.

CANTON KAYAK CLUB
Four Inner Harbor locations (Canton, Fell's Point, Harbor East, Locust Point),
www.cantonkayakclub.com

Founded in part by a major city developer and renovator and a prominent restaurateur, who figured that kayaks would be a perfect way to cross the generally calm waters of the harbor, the Canton Kayak Club now has more than 400 members. These avid paddlers regularly take to the Patapsco in their plastic and fiberglass shells, using them almost like bicycles to cross back and forth. Members are allowed to use the club's 60 or so kayaks, which are scattered across four Inner Harbor docks (there's another one outside of the harbor). It's a great and popular program, but the annual membership fee ($135) may make it impractical for those only visiting for a couple of days.

Sailing
DOWNTOWN SAILING CENTER
1425 Key Hwy., Ste. 110, 410/727-0722,
www.downtownsailing.org

`Map 4`

Located a few dozen yards east of the Baltimore Museum of Industry, this non-profit organization exists to teach sailing and provide sailboats to anyone who wants to learn, but with an eye toward letting city residents who can't afford sailing get a chance to try their hand aboard a real sailboat. The fleet consists primarily of fast, safe J-22s and Sonars; visitors can sign up for $75 "social" membership, which allows you to be aboard

© GEOFF BROWN

sailing past Fell's Point, on the Inner Harbor

a boat but not take part in the actual sailing. Real lessons start at $325 for the first of six sessions.

Fishing
CAPT. DON'S FISHING CHARTER
Henderson's Wharf Marina, Fell's Point, 410/342-2004, www.fishbaltimore.com

COST: Two-hour sightseeing cruise, $220; three-, six-, and eight-hour fishing tours, $250, $425, $475

Map 2

You don't want to fish, much less eat, anything from the Inner Harbor; that said, there is a lot of great fishing to be done in the waters of the upper Chesapeake Bay—all you need to do is get out of the city. Captain Don will take out groups of up to six people on two-, three-, six-, and eight-hour fishing (or just sightseeing) charters that leave right from Henderson's Wharf in Fell's Point. His boat, the *Lady Luck* is a 46-foot Chesapeake Bay–built, low-slung and wide-beamed fishing vessel, designed to be able to handle the rough chop that can spring up on the bay. This is the only major all-day, full-time fishing charter in town.

Boating Supplies and Facilities
TIDEWATER YACHT SERVICE
321 E. Cromwell St., 410/625-4992, www.tysc.com

Map 7

If you're a boater in need of some service or repair, Tidewater is your best bet in town, though they're located well to the south of the Inner Harbor, in the industrial area of Port Covington, south of Federal Hill. This marine shop offers everything from engine and hull repair and electrical work to painting and woodworking. They can handle craft ranging from small boats to huge yachts (they've got a 77-ton crane), and have even implemented environmentally friendly business practices.

WEST MARINE
2700 Lighthouse Pt. E, #100, 410/563-8905, www.westmarine.com

HOURS: Mon.-Sat. 9 A.M.-6 P.M., Sun. 10 A.M.-5 P.M.

Map 3

This Canton store, part of the nationwide West Marine boating supply chain, sells just about every piece of boating gear you might need in case you forgot it or broke it. From basics to more obscure gear, Baltimore's busy boating community keeps this shop busy and well stocked. They're also just a short drive (or sail) from the Inner Harbor.

GYMS AND HEALTH CLUBS
Baltimore has been lauded as being one of the fittest cities in America—an honor the city is proud to accept, even though a look at some of the less-healthy citizens and their lifestyles doesn't explain the kudos. Still, over the past decade, Baltimore has gotten noticeably more toned, lean, and active; there's a Baltimore Marathon now, and joggers, bikers, and swimmers are common sights around town. The gyms listed here are some of the best in the city as rated by regulars and local gurus, but by no means constitute a complete listing.

MAC HARBOR EAST
655 President St., 410/625-5000, www.macwellness.com

HOURS: Mon.-Thurs. 5:30 A.M.-10 P.M., Fri. 5:30 A.M.-9 P.M., Sat.-Sun. 7 A.M.-6 P.M.

COST: $25 for single-day guest pass

Map 2

This cosmopolitan palace of fitness offers just about every conceivable piece of exercise equipment, instructor-led class, and even a five-lane, 25-meter lap pool, which is impressive as this new gym is located on the second floor of one of Harbor East's new towers. There are kinesis stations and four squash courts here, plus a Whole Foods supermarket right across the street for some post-workout healthy eats.

MERRITT ATHLETIC CLUBS CANTON
3401 Boston St., 410/563-0225, www.merrittclubs.com

HOURS: Mon.-Thurs. 5:30 A.M.-10 P.M., Fri. 5:30 A.M.-9 P.M., Sat. 8 A.M.-7 P.M., Sun. 9 A.M.-6 P.M.

COST: $16.50 for single-day guest pass

Map 3

An enormous facility on the outskirts of Canton, this hugely popular gym (run by a local chain with 10 locations) has so many

SUPREME COURT: BALTIMORE'S BEST STREETBALL

Basketball and Baltimore have long been intertwined, even though the city does not currently have an NBA team (or even a minor league squad, or a WNBA franchise, for that matter). The Washington Wizards used to be named the Washington Bullets, which used to be the Baltimore Bullets until they left town in 1973.

But Baltimore players have lit up the courts at all levels of play: a short list of some of the city's finest modern-era ballers includes Carmelo Anthony, Tyrone "Muggsy" Bogues, Sam Cassell, Juan Dixon, Rudy Gay, and the late, great Reggie Lewis. These stars got their start on some of the city's best neighborhood courts; if you're looking to see some future talent before they make it big, or some prime-time NBA players take on the city's finest street magicians, there's really only one place to go: **The Dome.**

The Dome is the nickname for the covered court located behind the Madison Square Recreation Center (1401 E. Biddle St., 410/396-9284, www.baltimorecity.gov/government/recnparks) in East Baltimore. This court is to Baltimore what Rucker Park is to New York City: a legendary field of battle between up-and-coming young stars, street ballers known only by nicknames, and NBA stars looking to improve their games and maintain their street credibility. Knowing when to come to catch a game is the tricky issue. The truly epic games operate under the radar, known only to neighborhood mavens and to Charm City basketball cognoscenti. There are frequent Midnight Madness tournaments, held on Monday and Wednesday nights beginning at 10 P.M., but frankly this is a not a great neighborhood to be in after dark, much less at midnight.

pieces of equipment that waiting is almost never a concern. There's a full-size basketball court, three squash courts, and a good-sized outdoor lap pool (covered with a heated tent in winter), in addition to several classrooms and a yoga studio. A day spa and massage area are also available for those who want to relax after they feel the burn. This is also a popular place for young urban professionals to meet one another, which can be both amusing and frustrating to those trying to get in a real workout.

MERRITT FORT AVENUE

921 E. Fort Ave., 410/576-2004, www.merrittclubs.com
HOURS: Mon.-Thurs. 5:30 A.M.-10 P.M., Fri. 5:30 A.M.-8:30 P.M., Sat. 8 A.M.-7 P.M., Sun. 9 A.M.-6 P.M.
COST: $16.50 for single-day guest pass
Map 4

The lap and exercise pool is out back and outdoors, a welcome change from the inside swim centers of many local gyms (though it means no swimming in the winter months, alas). This long, well-stocked Federal Hill gym is always busy, stocked with young professionals from the neighborhood who are hitting

the huge assortment of treadmills, Lifecycles, Stairmasters, and free weights—or playing on the two squash courts. A nice variety of classes is offered (including Pilates), and regular lunchtime sessions are available.

MERRITT'S DOWNTOWN ATHLETIC CLUB

210 E. Centre St., 410/332-0906, www.merrittclubs.com
HOURS: Open 24 hours
COST: $16.50 for single-day guest pass
Map 5

The local Merritt Athletic Club chain now operates this venerable health club, which is one of the city's two 24-hour gym facilities (the other is also a Merritt operation, in Tide Point east of Federal Hill). This sprawling building (66,000 square feet) was once a train depot, and has been a gym for decades, though it's been renovated repeatedly. There are plenty of machines, plus basketball and squash courts, group work-out classrooms, an indoor track, a golf "driving range" practice room, and a small aquatic center.

ARTS AND LEISURE

Aquatic Center
MEADOWBROOK AQUATIC CENTER
5700 Cottonworth Ave., 410/433-8300,
www.mbrook.com

`Map 7`

This Mount Washington pool complex, located under a bridge, doesn't give visitors much to see from the outside, but within these walls (and in these waters), Olympic gold has been forged. These lanes are home to the phenomenal Michael Phelps, as well as other swimming gold medalists like Katie Hoff, Teresa Andrews, Anita Nall, and Beth Botsford. The center has indoor and outdoor pools (including one for kids), and indoor exercise facilities as well as outdoor tennis courts. Alas, you can't just walk in and use the pool for a day; you've got to purchase a season pass.

GUIDED AND WALKING TOURS

A waterfront city as old as Baltimore has so much history, so many secrets, and so many tall tales associated with its neighborhoods and residents that it's worth considering signing up for a guided tour (or at least one of the self-guided walking tours) of the city's neighborhoods. Head to the new Baltimore Visitors Center in the Inner Harbor—it's the building with the roof that looks like a wave—and consult with one of the staffers there for suggestions about which tour is best for you, and pick up some brochures detailing the routes through neighborhoods like Fell's Point and Mount Vernon. Though it's an easy city to walk, you can also take a powered tour, either about the historic, amphibious "ducks" that tour the harbor area, or aboard a Segway personal transporter.

If you're looking for a really personalized way to learn about the city, there are two famous people to consider: first is historian Zippy Larson, whose Zippy Tours take you wherever you want to go, and often into private homes and places the general public can't access. Then there's Wayne Schaumburg, another historian of renown who can reveal many of the city's hidden mysteries and legends on his own guided tours; he's the recognized expert on Green Mount Cemetery.

FREDERICK DOUGLASS "PATH TO FREEDOM" WALKING TOUR
Fell's Point, 410/783-5469, www.bbhtours.com
COST: $18 adult, $12 child

`Map 2`

As a young slave sent to Baltimore to work for a relative of his owner, Frederick Douglass grew into early manhood along the same streets and buildings of Fell's Point that you can visit today. Fell's Point was an important town in African American history during the 18th century, populated by free blacks, slaves, and fugitive escapees who used Baltimore as a launching point for the free northern states. Learn about Douglass and his life from tour guide Lou Fields, who has run this excursion for many years. This tour was recently added to the Network to Freedom Program of tours and walks by the National Park Service. The 90-minute tour runs year-round and reservations are required.

HERITAGE WALK
Inner Harbor Visitor Center, 443/514-5900,
www.heritagewalk.org
COST: $30

`Map 1`

From May through November, this free guided walking tour leaves from the Inner Harbor Visitor Center at 10 A.M. and heads for many of the city's greatest neighborhoods and landmarks. The 90-minute walk covers about half of the entire Heritage Walk (about three miles), and is led by an Urban Park Ranger. Featured areas and stops include the Inner Harbor, Little Italy, Jonestown, the Carroll Mansion, and the Star-Spangled Banner Flag House. Private group tours can be scheduled.

MOUNT VERNON WALKING TOURS
Starts in Peabody Court Hotel (612 Cathedral St.),
410/889-0894, www.mvcd.org
COST: $10

`Map 5`

This 90-minute tour, organized by the Baltimore Architecture Foundation, begins in the ornate

Learn about the ornate architecture of Mount Vernon on a walking tour.

lobby of the Peabody Court Hotel and takes visitors through the history of the charming Mount Vernon Place. Tales of the families who built these grand homes, like the Garretts and the Walters, are blended with a close study of the architecture and construction of the buildings. This 10 A.M., Saturdays-only tour runs April–November, and reservations are required.

RIDE THE DUCKS BALTIMORE
25 Light St., Ste. 300, 410/727-3825 or 877/887-8225, www.baltimoreducks.com
COST: $25 adult, $15 child
Map 1

Call it part of the peacetime dividend: the same amphibious vehicle design that is now used to create these new "duck" vehicles (it's an easy way to pronounce DUKW, their military designation) once was used by the U.S. Army as an invaluable invasion and transportation tool during World War II. Today, the big, funny-looking white trucks take tourists on a 50-minute ride through the downtown neighborhoods and into the Inner Harbor itself for a 20-minute jaunt around the waterfront (tours run year-round). You'll also be issued a quacking device, and instructed to use it liberally during your tour.

SECRETS OF A SEAPORT WALKING TOUR
1732 Thames St., 410/675-6750
COST: $10 (reduced group rate available)
Map 2

Held every other Saturday morning at 10 A.M. from April until November (and some Thursdays during the summers), this tour—led by a living history performer—takes visitors on a 90-minute stroll through the stone streets of Fell's Point. The history of the region, from its upstanding merchants and captains to its more scurvy seadogs, is revealed with flourish; other historic characters, including shipwrights, immigrants, and the less-fortunate members of 18th-century Fell's Point life are also discussed.

ARTS AND LEISURE

© GEOFF BROWN

SEGS IN THE CITY
2003 Fleet St., 410/276-7347 or 800/734-7393,
www.segsinthecity.com
COST: $45 for one-hour tour, $70 for two-hour tour
Map 2

Based in Fell's Point (and part of a regional chain), this Segway-based tour operation takes visitors on two tours (or "safaris," as they call them): a one-hour roll through Fell's Point and the Inner Harbor, and a longer two-hour trip that includes Little Italy and more of downtown. Tours leave at 10 A.M. and 2:30 P.M.; guides use headset microphone systems to discuss historical and important sights. Learning to ride a Segway takes about two minutes, and while you may draw some chuckles from the "cool" Baltimore kids as you go whirring past, you'll cover a huge amount of ground in no time flat.

WAYNE SCHAUMBURG
410/256-2180,
http://home.earthlink.net/~wschaumburg
COST: $15

Wayne Schaumburg is one of those little-appreciated civic resources that makes a city a better place to live, even if few people know about him or what he does. Though he's most famed for his fascinating walking tours of Green Mount Cemetery, his knowledge of the city doesn't end with its dead; let him know what you're interested in, and maybe you can work out a personalized tour that might mix walking and a little driving. His website is also one of the best ways to find out about the various tours, open houses, lectures, and historic walks that are taking place in Baltimore in upcoming months.

(ZIPPY TOURS WITH ZIPPY LARSON
410/522-7334, zippy@zippytours.com
COST: About $60 per person (includes a meal)

When you sign up for a guided tour with Zippy Larson, you're getting one of the city's great personalities to go along with the city's history. Larson offers about 36 different kinds of tours (most involve driving from place to place, but she will do concentrated walking tours); these range from specialized voyages like that through the sites that inspired *Hairspray*, and

the Duchess of Windsor Tour (Wallis Warfield Simpson was a Baltimore girl) to more standard Fell's Point and Mount Vernon visits. Larson has access to lots of one-of-a-kind areas, and her irrepressible charm and demeanor open those few doors that are initially closed to her.

OTHER RECREATION
Adventure Sports
TRAPEZE SCHOOL OF BALTIMORE
300 Key Hwy., 410/459-6839,
www.baltimore.trapezeschool.com
Map 1

Made famous (infamous?) after an appearance on *Sex and the City*, urban trapeze schools reached new heights in recent years. Baltimore's trapeze school benefits from its great location on Rash Field on the south end of the Inner Harbor, giving new students some great views of the waterfront as they contemplate the wisdom of leaping from a perfectly good swing into the arms of a stranger. Plenty of safety nets and harnesses help ensure the safety of students and gawkers; cost for the two-hour class runs $45–55.

Duckpin Bowling
This unique version of bowling was once of the city's most popular pastimes: it features much smaller balls and pins, and three throws instead of two. It's also dirt cheap: figure on about $5 per game per person, plus another couple of bucks for shoe rental; bring your own beverage of choice (except at Charm City Bowl), and order a pizza or fries from the snack bar, and you've got a fun evening of bargain entertainment you can experience only in Baltimore.

CHARM CITY BOWL
3540 South Hanover St., 410/355-2196
HOURS: Mon.-Wed. 11 A.M.-9 P.M., Thurs.-Sat.
11 A.M.-midnight, Sun. noon-8 P.M.
Map 7

Head south—far south—from Federal Hill down Hanover Street, almost to the city line, and the working-class neighborhood of Brooklyn to find this bowling palace. Located on the second floor of a furniture warehouse, this refurbished, semi-modern alley has 14

A BALTIMORE TRADITION: DUCKPIN BOWLING

Visualize a standard bowling ball and 10 pins. Now reduce them in size so that the pins are under a foot high and much tubbier; shrink the ball to the size of a big grapefruit and fill in the finger holes. Instead of two throws, take three. You've now gotten the basics of duckpin bowling, a variant of the American recreation activity that was once so popular that, in the early 1960s, there were not one but *two* local Baltimore television shows devoted to the sport.

Alas, like so many other strange and wonderful Baltimore traditions, duckpin bowling has faded from its glory days – but it hasn't completely vanished. There are, as of press time, still two die-hard duckpin bowling lanes in Baltimore City, and one close by in Baltimore County; the bowlers at these facilities will be either old-timers still tossing the ball or kids who like the oddball fun and scale of it (and also the BYOB policy at these establishments).

If you decide to challenge the duckpins, one word of caution; the pin-setting machines are very, very old, and frequently jam. Be patient. Have another National Bohemian beer, order a pizza, and remember that you are taking part in a nearly extinct social activity. And keep this in mind: No one has ever bowled a perfect game (score of 300) in regulation duckpin play. Could you be the first?

lanes, and sells beer (a rarity at duckpin facilities) and food together, meaning you need only to bring your wallet. While the people are friendly and the food is good and greasy, it's a bit of haul from downtown Baltimore.

PATTERSON BOWLING CENTER

2105 Eastern Ave., 410/675-1011,
www.pattersonbowl.com
HOURS: Mon.-Tues. 11 A.M.-9 P.M., Wed.-Thurs. 10 A.M.-9 P.M., Fri. 10 P.M.-midnight, Sat. 11 A.M.-11 P.M., Sun. noon-9 P.M.
Map 2

The only downtown duckpin bowling alley remaining in Baltimore, Patterson Bowling Center—which opened in 1927—is right on the Fell's Point/Canton border, just a few blocks west of Patterson Park. A relatively recent upgrade brought duckpin here into the 21st century (mostly), with the addition of electronic scoring for all 12 of its lanes (there are two levels here). A full-duty snack bar churns out great salty snacks, and a tavern across the street conveniently sells carry-out beer and wine.

STONELEIGH LANES DUCKPIN BOWLING CENTER

6703 York Rd., 410/377-8115,
www.stoneleighlanes.com
HOURS: Mon. noon-9 P.M., Tues. 9 A.M.-11 P.M., Wed. noon-11 P.M., Thurs. 10 A.M.-11 P.M., Fri.-Sat. 10 A.M.-midnight, Sun. 10 A.M.-8 P.M.
Map 7

Of the dedicated duckpin lanes that remain in the Baltimore area, this one is probably in the best shape; the decor, lanes, and equipment are all wonderfully retro and in kind-of good repair. Located in the basement of a 1950s-era shopping strip, Stoneleigh is like a time capsule of crazy carpeting and jet-age industrial design—and 16 lanes of duckpin action.

Golf

Heavily built-up and urbanized Baltimore is, surprisingly, home to some very interesting public golf courses, where the greens fees are ridiculously cheap and the quality of play is good. Operated by the Baltimore Municipal Golf Corporation (www.bmgcgolf.com), Baltimore's "classic five" courses are spread across the city (one, Pine Ridge, is actually in north Baltimore County) and offer very different experiences for both the beginner and the pro.

CARROLL PARK

2100 Washington Blvd., 410/685-8344
COST: Weekdays $17, weekends $18
Map 7

Carroll Park, just a short drive west from downtown, is a modest nine-hole course that's

ARTS AND LEISURE

CHARM CITY TENNIS

Tennis has been a part of Baltimore's recreational history for over a century; it even played a part in the city's desegregation movement. (At Druid Hill Park, in 1948, four black players and four white players took to a whites-only tennis court to protest segregation; all were arrested, but three years later, the city parks department ended the whites-only policy.) And tennis legend Pam Shriver is a Baltimore native who still lives in the area.

Baltimore City has 60 open-play (no reservations required or accepted) tennis courts at its various parks (410/396-7019, www.ci.baltimore.md.us/government/recnparks). Both of the city's largest downtown parks, **Druid Hill Park** and **Patterson Park,** have 10 tennis courts available.

perfect for getting in a few quick holes. Located next to the lumbering, recently-rehabbed Montgomery Park office building right off of I-95, this is a quirky course that is often used by office workers to fire off a few quick drives during conferences and lunchtimes.

⟨ CLIFTON PARK
2701 St. Lo Dr., 410/243-3500
COST: Weekdays $28, weekends $33
Map 7

Though the course is not as good as Mount Pleasant, Clifton Park (formerly the site of Johns Hopkins' summer mansion) is a favorite because it provides some amazing views of the city, particularly as you play back to the clubhouse. Challenges here include some unforgiving out-of-bounds—and the occasional city resident who stops on a walk past the course to provide blunt criticism of your game.

FOREST PARK
2900 Hillsdale Ave., 410/448-4653
COST: Weekdays $29, weekends $33
Map 7

On the far west side of the city is Forest Park, a short course that makes up for lack of distance with an increase in obstacles and hazards. The front nine are tight, tough holes, while the back nine are more modern and open. There's a brand-new clubhouse here, with locker rooms, a pro shop, and a small restaurant.

MOUNT PLEASANT
6001 Hillen Rd., 410/254-5100
COST: Weekdays $36, weekends $42
Map 7

The pinnacle of Baltimore City's golf courses is Mount Pleasant, a four-star-rated course by *Golf Digest;* it's also *Golf Week*'s pick as the 12th-best municipal course in the country. It's also the most expensive weekend morning course, at $42—but that's still peanuts compared to what most courses charge. Arnold Palmer won a tournament here (his second) back in 1956, and throughout the 1950s and '60s, this course was host to many major tournaments. It's aged well (it was built back in 1934), and is a good example of early pro golf course design and tests.

Ice Skating
DOMINIC "MIMI" DIPIETRO FAMILY ICE SKATING CENTER
200 S. Linwood Ave., 410/396-9392, www.pattersonpark.com/Park Information/skatingrink.html
HOURS: Tues. noon-2 P.M., Fri. 7-9 P.M., Sat. 3-5 P.M. and 7-9 P.M., Sun. 3-5 P.M., closed Mon., Wed., and Thurs. for league use
COST: $4; skate rental $2
Map 3

Dubbed "The Mimi Dome" by wise-acre city wags, this inflated, pale yellow structure on the eastern side of Patterson Park contains a large rink (big enough for hockey games) beneath a latticework of metal arms. So while the view's not much, the skating is sure fun, and after you leave the ice, the concession stand has hot chocolate and a fireplace.

Skateboarding
CARROLL PARK SKATEBOARDING AND BIKE FACILITY
1500 Washington Blvd., 410/396-9177 or 410/396-7019, www.ci.baltimore.md.us/government/recnparks
HOURS: Wed.-Fri. 4-8 P.M., Sat. noon-8 P.M., Sun. (bikes only) noon-9 P.M.
COST: $2 per day
Map 7

Baltimore City built this all-concrete course to give city skaters—and bikers, who have the park on Sundays—a place to go besides the downtown area (which has some great jumps, to be honest). Anyway, there's an eight-foot quarter pipe here, as well as a selection of smaller quarter pipes, rails, and a ledged pyramid. Hours (and bike-only days) vary in spring; helmets and pads required.

CHARM CITY SKATE PARK
4401 O'Donnell St., #D, 410/327-7909, www.charmcity.tv
HOURS: Mon.-Sat. 12:30-8:30 P.M., Sun. noon-6 P.M.
COST: $10 before 5 P.M., $5 after
Map 3

This semi-respectable private skatepark is in an old warehouse under a highway overpass (which is pretty punk rock). Charm City Skate Park has re-created (in plywood and metal) a mini-city of steps, ramps, and rails, then decorated the walls with top-flight tags and artwork. Regular events and pro skaters on tour stop by this Canton fixture.

Yoga
BIKRAM YOGA
911 W. 36th St., 410/243-2040, www.bikramyogahampden.com
COST: $17 for a drop-in class
Map 6

This Hampden center is dedicated to the practice of Bikram yoga (the hot kind); the 8,000-square-foot studio can accommodate many practitioners, and there's a nice recovery room to help re-acclimate to normal temperatures. The studio also offers One, a wellness spa that can provide hot-stone massage as well as facials and pedicures; acupuncture is available by appointment.

(CHARM CITY YOGA
901 Fell St., 410/276-9642, www.charmcityyoga.com
COST: $15 for a drop-in class
Map 2

One of Baltimore's most popular yoga studios is Charm City Yoga; this Fell's Point location is their newest, and while it's not huge, it has a great view of the neighborhood and water. There's also an outdoor deck for practicing during the nice months, a great and rare opportunity in Baltimore. Charm City Yoga does a version of hot yoga, as well as other routines, and there's a midtown location (107 E. Preston St., 410/234-8967) if you're staying in Mount Vernon.

ARTS AND LEISURE

SHOPS

There are two great reasons to set aside some time to go shopping in Baltimore: The city has lots of cool stuff, and it's all still pretty cheap. That's not always true, of course—there are plenty of boutiques, galleries, and high-end stores throughout town. In fact, that's a third great reason to make shopping part of your trip: New retail districts have literally sprung from the ground in the past few years. Harbor East's upscale stores are a very welcome addition to a downtown shopping scene that was, to put it kindly, sparse, and South Charles Street in Federal Hill has welcomed some popular boutiques and salons. But part of Baltimore's charm for shoppers is also found in its quirky, independently owned shops, especially in neighborhoods like Hampden (where a large percentage of the stores are owned and operated by women) and in Belvedere Square, a recently revitalized shopping hub in the north part of the city that's also become a social scene.

Downtown, shoppers looking for a single location to handle lots of shopping need head no farther than the Gallery, located at the corner of Pratt and Calvert Streets just across the street from Harborplace, which has its own collection of shops and gift stores. Outside of the city, there are a few truly massive palaces of retail wonder. First and foremost is the Arundel Mills Mall, located south of BWI Airport: not only does it have more than 225 stores, there's a Muvico 24 Egyptian theater, which sometimes ranks as the nation's number-one theater in terms of ticket sales. To the north of town is Towson Town Center, a more upscale mall that's recently undergone yet another expansion.

HIGHLIGHTS

LOOK FOR ◖ TO FIND
RECOMMENDED SHOPS.

◖ **Best Bookstore that Also Sells Art Toys:** Need one store to sell you the latest Chuck Palahniuk novel, a new Dark Knight compendium, and a limited-run Frank Kozik vinyl art doll? Head to Hampden's **Atomic Books** (page 156).

◖ **Best Music Store Run by Musicians:** Motor down to Fell's Point's **The Sound Garden** for not only the big new sounds, but the obscure old ones (page 159).

◖ **Best Traditional Men's Clothing:** If you want to dress like a Baltimore gentleman, acquit yourself to **Jos. A. Bank** for a proper selection of suits, tweeds, and overcoats (page 159).

◖ **Best Cool Men's Clothing:** Find exclusive brands of shirts, jeans, limited-run sneakers, and jackets, plus skater and biker apparel, at the awesome **Shop Gentei** in Mount Vernon (page 160).

◖ **Best Place to Buy a Dress and Gifts:** The generally (but not exclusively) Latin-themed selection at Hampden's **Milagro** spans great print dresses, handmade jewelry and trinkets, and fair-trade pottery and crafts (page 162).

◖ **Best Women's Clothing:** Urban Chic, in Harbor East, is a locally founded mini-chain that features some of the best and hippest bets in denim, footwear, and tops (page 163).

◖ **Best Enormous Furniture Store:** From French country to English manor to Italian modernist, there's no other store in town like the enormous **Shofer's** in Federal Hill (page 165).

◖ **Best Day Spa:** If you need a break from a grueling schedule of brunch, sightseeing, and shopping, you should take the edge off at **Studio 921 Salon & Day Spa,** near Federal Hill (page 167).

◖ **Best Kids' Furnishings:** From charming cribs to envy-inducing beds and dressers and everything in-between, if you don't want to subject your kids to boring design, head to **Bratt Decor** in Belvedere Square (page 168).

◖ **Best Pet Shop:** From luxurious little coats to delicious treats and chew toys, Canton's **Dogma** has everything for your precious pooch or kitty (page 168).

© GEOFF BROWN

Atomic Books

It's pretty easy to find what you're searching for in Baltimore, whether it's an item of apparel, jewelry, art, or a unique handmade gift. Between the big-name stores at the malls, the upscale boutiques around town, and the charming little single-proprietor shops tucked into neighborhoods, shoppers have a great hunt waiting for them in Baltimore.

SHOPPING DISTRICTS
Downtown and Inner Harbor

Pratt Street, which runs through downtown and along the north side of the Inner Harbor, is the prime shopping artery in this part of the city. There is the Gallery, a small shopping center with clothiers and apparel merchants located directly across from Harborplace, which itself is filled with gift shops and locally themed stores that are perfect for souvenirs and mementos. Farther east lie some newer additions, including a huge Barnes & Noble bookstore in the old Power Plant building (look for the four tall smokestacks). On the other side of the street are some national retailers (such as Best Buy and Filene's Basement).

Fell's Point

One of the city's most popular shopping areas, the charming waterfront and paving-stone streets of Fell's Point are perfect for an afternoon of poking into the wide variety of shops that line both the main thoroughfares and the tiny side streets. From jewelry to clothing to home goods to music, this quirky, busy neighborhood has a store for every shopper, from high-end connoisseurs to bargain hunters.

Federal Hill

Along Charles Street and Light Street, small clothing boutiques and housewares stores have found a happy home in this historic

New and renewed blend together in Fell's Point.

© GEOFF BROWN

COURTESY BALTIMORE AREA CONVENTION AND VISITORS ASSOCIATION

shopping in Hampden

neighborhood, making it not only a popular social destination but also a cool place to shop. There are lots of places to pick up some hot new styles, from jeans to dresses and shoes, plus some fun gifts for friends. For those looking for something old, there's the huge Antique Center at Federal Hill, located a few blocks east on Key Highway. And there are plenty of weird finds at the American Visionary Art Museum's interesting gift shop.

Hampden

Hampden's 36th Street—known as "The Avenue"—is one of Baltimore's best shopping areas for several reasons. There are four blocks of stores, selling everything from clothing to furniture, from high-end name brands to cut-rate quirky. No matter your style, you'll find at least three stores that match your aesthetic,

and since they're all locally run and owner-operated, you can get great service and ideas. There's a real buzz on the sidewalks as people flock to Hampden for antiques, health and beauty products, clothes, and just to be part of the shopping scene.

Belvedere Square

Far from the waterfront (and far from the peculiar charms of Hampden) is Belvedere Square, a now-thriving shopping center that's become a social anchor for the far northern part of Baltimore City (where there are far more single-family homes, lawns, and wide avenues). Clothing and housewares are in abundance here, and the food options at Belvedere Market make this a great place to spend an afternoon before catching a show on the huge screen at the historic Senator Theatre.

Architectural Salvage

Renovators, rehabbers, and other folks who've come to Baltimore to fix up and live in old row houses (and larger buildings) have helped create a fledgling business trend: architectural salvage, where cast-offs from demolished or decrepit buildings are saved from the garbage and re-used or re-purposed.

the spooky catacomb-like basement, there are neon signs, store relics, decorative sconces and lights, and all sorts of peculiar wonders. Many items are huge and carry similar price tags, but there are also amazing finds for around $20. If it's a neat or cool or interesting piece of a house or building, it's probably in this store.

HOUSEWERKS

1415 Bayard St., 410/685-8047,
www.housewerksalvage.com
HOURS: Tues.-Sat. 10 A.M.-6 P.M., Sun. noon-4 P.M.
`Map 7`

This delightful store lives up to its mission by inhabiting a former natural gas pumping station (Bayard Station), a beautifully decaying old building with an enormous cupola-topped center room where many of the store's salvaged items reside. Outside are huge signs, marble pieces, and sculpture; downstairs, in

SECOND CHANCE

1645 Warner St., 410/385-1101,
www.secondchanceinc.org
HOURS: Mon.-Sat. 9 A.M.-5 P.M.
`Map 7`

This sprawling complex of four warehouses spreads out south of M&T Bank Stadium in the southern part of the city; even if you're not in need of antique toilets, claw-foot bathtubs, glass doorknobs, or pieces of the Philadelphia Civic Center's facade, take a tour of warehouse one, then skip over to one and three (they're

The selection of architectural salvage at Housewerks ranges from majestic to eccentric.

© GEOFF BROWN

connected), where there's a huge selection of antiques, and even some leftover sets and props from the HBO series *The Wire*. You'll also find plenty of smaller items that make great keepsakes, like brass items and Art Deco curiosities and detail pieces.

Arts and Crafts

BALTIMORE CLAYWORKS
5707 Smith Ave., 410/578-1919,
www.baltimoreclayworks.org
HOURS: Mon.-Sat. 10 A.M.-5 P.M.
Map 7

A working studio and gallery and school, Baltimore Clayworks has 13 resident artists and 30 member artists who take humble clay and transform it into everything from working home furnishings to fantastic, creative visions. Located in the New England–like village center of Mt. Washington, this store/gallery/education center has a great home in an old library surrounded by tall pines, right by the waters of the Jones Falls. Demonstrations, classes, and lectures are held throughout the year and draw healthy crowds. There's even a tiny outdoor community space that has a great mosaic and clay fountain.

CORADETTI GLASSWORKS
2010 Clipper Park Rd., Ste. 119, 410/243-2010,
www.coradetti.com
HOURS: Call for hours
Map 6

Anthony Coradetti is one of several artists who have set up shop in the sturdy, stone, late-1800s-era mill buildings of Clipper Mill. His beautiful and innovative glass sculptures and creations are renowned throughout Baltimore and the region. This large, reclaimed industrial

artist Chun Lan Li's solo exhibition during Baltimore Clayworks' Taiwanese Artist Exchange Program

space is both his rough and tumble studio (complete with Hades-hot furnace) and sedate gallery; as such, hours vary wildly, and a quick phone call is the best way to make sure he'll be there when you want to visit.

A GOOD YARN
1738 Aliceanna St., 410/327-3884,
www.agoodyarn.com
HOURS: Wed.-Sun. 10 A.M.-7 P.M.
Map 2

The resurgence of knitting in America—picked up by a new generation of needle-twirlers, and re-embraced by their parents—has led to the opening of a couple of great yarn and knitting shops. This is Fell's Point's center of knit culture; yarns both pedestrian and exotic are available at this cozy little shop (which always smells divine), and the helpful staff has an astonishing array of tricks and tips available for both newcomers and old purlers.

LOVELYARNS
846 W 36th St., 410/662-9276, www.lovelyarns.com
HOURS: Wed.-Fri. 11 A.M.-5:30 P.M., Sat. 11 A.M.-6 P.M.,
Sun. 11 A.M.-4 P.M.
Map 6

This Hampden store is the city's other fine knitting supply shop. A bit less polite than A Good Yarn (there's a regular Saturday "Stitch N Bitch"), this is where the more "punk rock" knitters head for their yarns, patterns, and supplies, though many perfectly upstanding knitters also do their shopping here. There's a great front living room area for folks to sit and stitch, the selection of yarns and other craft essentials is wide and varied, and the owner and staff are full of great suggestions and ideas.

Books and Music

AN DIE MUSIK
409 N. Charles St., 410/385-2638
HOURS: Mon.-Sat. 10 A.M.-9 P.M., Sun. noon-5 P.M.
Map 5

Located (fittingly) within a couple of blocks of the Peabody Institute, Baltimore's renowned music school, An die Musik is the city's finest store for classical, jazz, and world music. No rock, no rap, no country or western here—just the finest highlights in the recorded canon of classical music and the milestone moments in jazz. And it's all sold and discussed without any attitude, which makes this a great place to either start exploring these great genres or continue your journey. The second floor hosts a wide variety of jazz and classical performances all year long.

▐ ATOMIC BOOKS
3620 Falls Rd., 410/662-4444, www.atomicbooks.com
HOURS: Mon.-Sat. 11 A.M.-7 P.M., Sun. 11 A.M.-6 P.M.
Map 6

This alternative, independent bookstore features tomes on culture, politics, humor, and music, as well as a thorough compendium of graphic novels and books, plus gag gifts, 'zines, CDs, crafts, and outsider DVDs. It's also where director (and frequent shopper) John Waters gets his fan mail delivered—be sure to look at the collection of charmingly unnerving holiday cards he's sent the store. They also stock an amazing selection of limited-run art toys and figures from creators like Kid Robot and Rocket World. The store is large enough to have separate sections: toys and new books are in the front, graphic novels and crafts are toward the back, and in the very back (behind a discrete curtain) are mature-themed domestic and foreign publications, some artsy, some not.

THE BALTIMORE CHOP
625 Washington Blvd., 410/752-4487,
www.myspace.com/baltimorechop
HOURS: Mon.-Fri. 7:30 A.M.-6 P.M., Sat.-Sun.
8 A.M.-2 P.M., open late on live music nights
Map 1

Named for a unique type of infield hit

© GEOFF BROWN

limited-run toys, eclectic tomes, and obscure wonders at Atomic Books

in baseball that was made popular by the Baltimore Orioles, this eclectic bookstore, coffeeshop, and live performance space does all of its jobs quite well. The book selection is very, very heavy on baseball tomes, as the store is just a long fly ball away from Oriole Park, so if you're looking to kill an hour before the first pitch and don't want to face the beer-guzzling hordes at the pubs, try this civilized oasis instead.

DAEDALUS BOOKS AND MUSIC

5911 York Rd., 410/464-2701, www.daedalusbooks.com
HOURS: Sun.-Thurs. 10 A.M.-8 P.M., Fri.-Sat. 10 A.M.-9 P.M.
Map 7

Just across the street from the historic Senator movie theater is this sprawling and popular discounted book and music outlet (it's located in a former department store). Unlike many discounters, Daedalus actually has lots of books

you'll want to buy; art, literature, history, and fiction are good bets here, and they stock the latest and greatest bestsellers (with an eye toward quality). There's a large CD selection, as well as books on tape, DVDs, and periodicals. The discounts range from minor to major, putting huge, folio-sized art books within the budget of even the most starving artists. There's even a Starbucks next door, if you're planning on browsing for a while and need some caffeine for the journey.

DIMENSIONS IN MUSIC

233 Park Ave., 410/752-7121, www.dimensionsinmusic.com
HOURS: Mon.-Sat. 10 A.M.-6 P.M.
Map 5

Be it on CD, tape, or wax, Dimensions in Music has the best selection of hip-hop, R&B, rap, and house music in town, along with plenty of jazz, gospel, and oldies recordings.

This three-story store keeps bargain records on the third floor, a huge selection of records on the second floor, and DJ gear on floors one and two. If you're looking to grab some homegrown Baltimore music, ask one of the staffers—or maybe one of the DJs browsing the vinyl, though they're not always up for sharing their inside info on Charm City's best beats.

EL SUPRIMO
1709 Aliceanna St., 443/226-9628, web.mac.com/elsuprimo/iWeb/Site/Home Page.html
HOURS: Mon.-Fri. 1-7 P.M., Sat. noon-7 P.M., Sun. noon-6 P.M.
Map 2

This basement-based vinyl paradise mostly eschews the CD in favor of racks and racks of black (and sometimes other hued) vinyl, covering the weird, the awesome, and the inexplicable (the store's label issued a title called "Cambodian Psych-Out"). There are also turntables for sale, along with other DJ equipment, books, and even some musical instruments. Call to make sure they're open before stopping in, and if you want to bring a beer or two with you into the store, that's OK too.

THE KELMSCOTT BOOKSHOP
34 W. 25th St., 410/235-6810, www.kelmscottbookshop.com
HOURS: Mon.-Fri. 10 A.M.-6 P.M., Sat. by appt. only
Map 6

Baltimore's tiny fine books district—numbering less than a half-dozen shops—lies along a stretch of 25th Street where most residents and passersby favor loud hip-hop music instead of rare first editions. Kelmscott is the largest of the group, though all are worth a browse for the dedicated bibliophile. This isn't an old London bookshop, dark and dusty and encased in dark woods; it's bright, clean, and simple. Within this store's selection are some 30,000 rare, unique, and fascinating books (there are many first-edition H. L. Mencken tomes), and some rarer works dating back to the 1600s. Kelmscott also sells prints, manuscripts, and assorted book-reading paraphernalia (they also repair and re-bind books);

and, of course, there is a resident cat, named Madeline.

NORMAL'S BOOKS AND RECORDS
425 E. 31st St., 410/243-6888, www.normals.com
HOURS: Daily 11 A.M.-6 P.M.
Map 7

Located about seven blocks east of Johns Hopkins University, Normal's has survived every literary and musical trend of the past two decades and continues to persevere in a world it feels has gone utterly corporate and foul. The collectively run shop (run by the legendary writer/creative guru "Blaster" Al Ackerman) has stacks of used books, from classics to obscure oddities. There's also music galore (spanning the range of must-have hits to never-heard-of-'em obscure tunes), and the Red Room, a performance space for generally non-standard music.

READ STREET BOOKS
229 W. Read St., 410/669-4103, www.readstreetbooks.com
HOURS: Mon.-Fri. noon-8 P.M., Sat.-Sun. 10 A.M.-8 P.M.
Map 5

Located on an appropriately named street, this independent bookstore carries a little bit of everything, as long as it's not expected. There's a big selection of used paperbacks, new books of note, and even vintage magazines and art folios. There's also a good selection of lesbian works. And like most smart bookstores in Baltimore, Read Street has branched out to offer coffee and, on Fridays and Saturdays, singer/songwriter performances, all inside a European-feeling and charming, historic Mount Vernon storefront.

REPTILIAN RECORDS
2545 N. Howard St., 410/327-6853, www.reptilianrecords.com
HOURS: Daily noon-9 P.M.
Map 6

Baltimore's long been home to this legendary indie punk and rock recording label; their retail shop is now in Charles Village, after a long stay in Fell's Point (and now it's just down the street from the most appropriate venue for Reptilian artists, The Ottobar). The record and CD bins here are packed with serious, earnest, not-screwing-around bands that probably don't break out the acoustic guitars that often. It's not all woofer-crushing rock; there's some calmer bands and even some emo. But don't come in here looking for Hootie and the Blowfish, or you'll get your ass kicked.

◖ THE SOUND GARDEN

1616 Thames St., 410/563-9011, www.cdjoint.com
HOURS: Sun.-Thurs. 10 A.M.-10 P.M.,
Fri.-Sat. 10 A.M.-midnight
Map 2

Getting the name out of the way first: This store is not associated with the famed Seattle grunge band. What they are associated with is a very broad selection of CDs and a decent vinyl selection, covering both the big hits of the day, but also more obscure rock, hip-hop, and country artists. There's a big used CD collection, which can be full of dreck but also contain some hidden gems. The DVD wall has a lot of really fantastic finds, from TV boxed sets to strange foreign films to anime and horror. There are a few listening stations to try before you buy, and the in-store music selection is usually right on.

THE TRUE VINE

3544 Hickory Ave., 410/235-4500,
www.thetruevinerecordshop.com
HOURS: Tues.-Sat. 11 A.M.-8 P.M., Sun.-Mon. 11 A.M.-6 P.M.
Map 6

If you're the kind of music lover who, instead of the latest Top 40 pop CD, would rather find a treasure trove of obscure Turkish recordings from the 1930s, psychedelic Japanese pop from the 1970s, or underground new crazy blues from some Baltimore musicians, the True Vine is for you. The weirder the better is the mantra here, but the music is always good, even if the provenance is peculiar. In-store performances at this off-the-Avenue Hampden shop are frequent and often captivating.

Clothing and Accessories for Men

◖ JOS. A. BANK

100 E. Pratt St., 410/547-1700, www.josbank.com
HOURS: Mon.-Sat. 9 A.M.-8 P.M., Sun. noon-6 P.M.
Map 1

For Baltimore's upper class, the sensible khakis, blue blazers, tweed suits, and tattersall shirts of Joseph A. Bank clothiers (not as fancy as Brooks Brothers, but just as preppy) have been de rigueur since 1905, when the company was founded. After some lean years in the recent past, this clothing company has become a real mover in the U.S. men's clothing world, and while you won't be setting any trends with the conservative attire here, you will be able to gain entry into any of the city's more elite restaurants and clubs. This is the city's flagship store, located in the same building as one of Baltimore's most storied financial companies (T. Rowe Price), which means while it's no marble and walnut shopping Shangri La, you can feel the heavy billfolds of some of the shoppers here.

SAMUEL PARKER CLOTHIER

Lake Falls Village, 6080 Falls Rd., 410/372-0078,
www.samuelparker.com
HOURS: Mon.-Fri. 10 A.M.-6 P.M., Sat. 10 A.M.-5 P.M.
Map 7

Travel up Falls Road, past Mount Washington's tree-canopied stores, and you'll find this Baltimore institution for traditional men's clothing in a tasteful little shopping center. This is the kind of quiet, sturdy store that's a bit like a private club; once you're done relaxing and browsing, you'll actually want one of the knowledgeable salesmen to help you figure out your sartorial style, and be walked through a variety of suits, materials, and cuts to find the piece of haberdashery that is "you." You won't find any Prada or Hugo Boss here; brands tend toward the conservative qualities of Polo Ralph Lauren and Samuelsohn of Canada.

☾ SHOP GENTEI

1010 Morton St., 410/244-8961, www.shopgentei.com
HOURS: Mon.-Sat. 10 A.M.-8 P.M., Sun. noon-5 P.M.
Map 5

How typical of Baltimore: You can't buy a fancy Italian suit downtown, but you can find a store that's stocked with the latest Japanese street wear—shirts and coats so cutting-edge that you'll fit in anywhere the cool kids hang out.

Looking like a semi-evil secret agent's massive closet (note the huge, assault-rifle Shop Gentei seal on the wall behind the counter), this store likes spotlights and dark recesses, plus small, well-selected displays. You'll find shirts, coats, hats, shoes, and accessories from Mastermind, No. 9, Y-3, and Sag, as well as an array of skater and street gear. Given the rarity and limited runs of these items, prices are very reasonable. Bring home something like a Fiberops hoodie from your trip to Baltimore, and get massive cool cred (plus, you'll increase Baltimore's).

Clothing and Accessories for Women

BABE

910 S. Charles St., 410/244-5114,
www.babeaboutique.com
HOURS: Wed.-Fri. noon-8 P.M., Sat. 11 A.M.-6 P.M.,
Sun. 11 A.M.-3 P.M.
Map 4

Opened by a former fashion buyer, this hip and youthful Federal Hill store was designed for cost-conscious (but fashion-starved) Baltimoreans who wanted better clothing options without the SoHo prices. You'll find tops, pants, and dresses by Free People, Rebecca Beason, and Ya, plus handbags by makers like Lulubella, and shoes by Chinese Laundry and Luichiny. There are also extras like metal picture frames, cards, and aromatic candles.

BLU VINTAGE

823 N. Charles St., 410/547-9335, www.bluvintage.com
HOURS: Mon.-Sat. 11 A.M.-7 P.M., Sun. noon-4 P.M.
Map 5

The name's a little misleading, as there's almost no vintage here; this modern, cosmopolitan Mount Vernon store is all about cutting-edge names and designers not normally found in Baltimore women's clothing stores. Founded by a former graphic designer and a model, this store leans toward apparel lines like Supreme Being and C-Label; their shoe selection (featuring Missoni and Ashley Dearborn) is also worth a look. The lines

range from work outfits to a few out-on-the-town selections.

CLOUD 9

The Can Company, 2400 Boston St., 410/534-4200
HOURS: Mon.-Thurs. 11 A.M.-7 P.M., Fri.-Sat. 11 A.M.-8 P.M.,
Sun. noon-5 P.M.
Map 3

This Baltimore-based women's (and some men's) clothing and accessories merchant has built a loyal following because they've got great taste and don't charge a fortune for their wares. There are two Baltimore locations; this Canton outlet, and another in Belvedere Square (546 E. Belvedere Ave., 410/435-2400). In addition to denim and tops, there are dresses for work, play, and special events; handbags and jewelry round out the options here. This is a fun, airy store, with good music playing. Allow plenty of time to browse and discover items on the racks and tables.

CUPCAKE

813 S. Broadway, 410/522-0941,
www.cupcake-shop.com
HOURS: Mon.-Sat. 11 A.M.-8 P.M., Sun. 11 A.M.-6 P.M.
Map 2

Right on Fell's Point's main square, at the foot of Broadway, this boutique draws regulars for its upscale selection, which includes labels like BCBG, J Brand, and Nicole Miller. This clean,

Hampden's Form offers a more upscale women's clothing alternative.

sunny, and unobtrusively decorated store (with white walls and neutral decor) is the perfect place to look for a great little dress destined to liven up an event or a night on the town. If you're not in the market for a knockout outfit, there are plenty of jeans and more day-to-day apparel here as well.

DOUBLEDUTCH BOUTIQUE

3616 Falls Rd., 410/554-0055,
www.doubledutchboutique.com
HOURS: Mon.-Thurs. 10 A.M.-6 P.M., Fri.-Sat.
10 A.M.-7 P.M., Sun. 11 A.M.-5 P.M.
Map 6

Featuring an excellent range of women's modern design lines from well-known designers and even some local talent, this shop stocks contemporary clothing, handbags, and accessories. This airy space is in an old storefront just steps from Hampden's main shopping drag (36th Street, or "The Avenue" as the locals call it), and it's worth the slight detour to check out designs by makers like Orla Kiely and Penguin, and shoes by Jeffrey Campbell.

FORM

1115 W. 36th St., 410/889-3116,
www.formtheboutique.com
HOURS: Mon.-Thurs. 11 A.M.-6:30 P.M., Fri.-Sat.
11 A.M.-7 P.M., Sun. noon-4 P.M.
Map 6

The opening of Form marked a definitive step up for Hampden's retail game. Form is a sleek, upscale boutique (with exposed brick and well-tended display racks) that offers women's clothing, accessories, and shoes from makers like Vera Wang Lavender, Anna Sui, Bensoni, and Cynthia Steffe. If you're looking for a complete wardrobe retooling, the store offers a personal shopper and second-floor studio for one-on-one service.

HANDBAGS IN THE CITY

840 Aliceanna St., 410/528-1443,
www.handbagsinthecity.com
HOURS: Mon.-Fri. 11 A.M.-7 P.M., Sat. 11 A.M.-8 P.M., Sun.
noon-5 P.M.
Map 2

There's more to life than purses, to be sure, but if handbags are a big part of your life, it's

© GEOFF BROWN

worth a visit to this modern boutique along Harbor East's main shopping drag. Expect to find handbags (and clothing) from must-have labels like Kooba, Michael Kors, Longchamps, Boktier, and Jill Stuart. There's a second location in Mount Washington, north of Hampden, as well (5614 Newbury St., 410/601-0096).

HOLLY G.
1018 S. Charles St., 410/962-1506, www.hollyg.com
HOURS: Daily 11 A.M.-7 P.M.
Map 4

This small but well-stocked Federal Hill boutique was one of the first to help establish the section of the neighborhood (South Charles Street) as one of the city's better shopping destinations. The shop is adorned with great blouses and dresses from makers like Dace and Linea O, and denim by Rosner, Frankie B., and Red Engine. There's a wonderful chandelier by which to do your browsing, and plenty of places to eat and drink are within just a few steps. Like many Baltimore stores, Holly G. also has a Mount Washington outpost; it's at The Wheel House (1340 A Smith Ave., 410/433-3389).

KASHMIR IMPORTS
830 Aliceanna St., 410/209-2700, www.kashmirimports.com
HOURS: Mon.-Sat. 10 A.M.-8 P.M., Sun. 11 A.M.-6 P.M.
Map 2

Amidst the sleek boutiques and offerings in the new towers of Harbor East, this small shop provides an unexpected and exotic selection of goods handmade in the Kashmir Valley (the store is a member of the Fair Trade Federation). Incredibly lavish hand-stitched clothing, carves, and coats are all offered at surprisingly affordable prices. There are also pashmina scarves and some home items, including pillows and wall hangings.

MILAGRO
1005 W. 36th St., 410/235-3800
HOURS: Mon.-Sat. 11 A.M.-6 P.M., Sun. 11 A.M.-5 P.M.
Map 6

Milagro (Spanish for "miracle") features modern, hip clothing, handbags, and accessories from

Mexico and all over the world, almost always from fair-trade makers and suppliers. There are plenty of items for your home, too, from pottery to mirrors to wall hangings. Baltimore's savvy shoppers are particularly fond of the dresses and extensive jewelry selection in this warm-colored, whimsical, and friendly store: the cash register station is in a large, hand-carved wooden cantina from Mexico.

A PEOPLE UNITED
516 N. Charles St., 410/727-4471, www.apeopleunited.com
HOURS: Mon.-Sat. 10 A.M.-6 P.M., Sun. 11 A.M.-6 P.M.
Map 5

Designed to both showcase and help craftspeople from developing nations, A People United features handmade and small-scale production clothing for women in a variety of ethnic styles and formality levels. In addition to clothing, there's also a selection of Tibetan and Indian furniture, and rugs and statuary from several cultures. The store is a treat for senses besides the eyes and touch, too, as there's always incense burning, and exotic scents from teas and aromatic products. The store's longevity (it was opened by a Johns Hopkins public health expert and his photographer wife in 1994) shows that being able to learn about the people who made your clothes definitely helps foster sales, which directly helps the creators of the clothing, not a multinational corporation.

SHINE COLLECTIVE
1007 A W. 36th St., 410/366-6100, www.shopshinecollective.com
HOURS: Mon.-Sat. 11 A.M.-7 P.M., Sun. noon-5 P.M.
Map 6

Though this hip, sleek store offers a little of everything—men's clothes, home decor, and even art posters—Shine Collective's selection of women's clothing and accessories is the real reason for its popularity. Check out dresses by Rodebjer and Margarita Sapala, jeans, jewelry, handbags, and more—including lots of charming small objects that make great gifts. The music in this well-designed store is always a treat (and on some nights, a DJ may even spin some wax).

SOUTH MOON UNDER

815 Aliceanna St., 410/685-7820

HOURS: Mon.-Sat. 10 A.M.-8 P.M., Sun. noon-5 P.M.

Map 2

If you find yourself in need of a swimsuit—either for the pool or a trip to the beach on Maryland's Eastern Shore—you'd be smart to head straight to the bright, sunny corner occupied by South Moon Under, where you'll find suits from classic makers like Quiksilver and Billabong as well as new creations from Shoshanna and Juicy Couture. There's also a wide variety of casual clothes for men and women, including denim and shoes. If you're in need of a small gift, South Moon Under has plenty of great options (it's a big, modern store with several well-stocked sections).

TRIXIE'S PALACE

1704 Thames St., 410/558-2195,

www.trixiespalace.com

HOURS: Mon.-Thurs. 11 A.M.-6:30 P.M.,

Fri.-Sun. 11 A.M.-7 P.M.

Map 2

This Fell's Point institution (you'll know it by the bright, blue and red, carnival-like paint job on the exterior) is a perfect place to pick up some small, inexpensive gifts for the people

back home—or for yourself. There are lots of fun finds in this eclectic but smart shop, from rhinestone-bedecked sunglasses and kitschy accessories to Hello Kitty rarities, as well as plenty of cheap, useful clothing from Free People, Riot Apparel, and from the local T-shirt geniuses at Squidfire. There are also some more serious goods here, including imported fabrics, pillows, and more from Asia.

◖ URBAN CHIC

811 Aliceanna St., 410/685-1601,

www.urbanchiconline.com

HOURS: Mon.-Sat. 10 A.M.-8 P.M., Sun. noon-5 P.M.

Map 2

This small local chain gained popularity for stocking modern clothing brands that weren't always easy to find in Baltimore. Their sleek, modern, yet warm store (there are some nice real-world objects tossed in as decor to keep things grounded) features denim from makers like Hudson, Joe's Jeans, and Paige. Urban Chic has a good variety of men's and women's apparel and shoes (including Hunter Wellington Boots), featuring brands like Vineyard Vines, Tibi, and Nanette Lepore. There's also a good assortment of skin and beauty products from makers like Bliss, and even kids' clothes.

© GEOFF BROWN

fresh denim, shoes, and designs at Urban Chic, near Fell's Point

SHOPS

Furniture and Home Decor

NOUVEAU
Belvedere Square, 514 E. Belvedere Ave.,
410/962-8248, www.nouveaubaltimore.com
HOURS: Mon.-Sat. 10 A.M.-6 P.M., Sun. 11 A.M.-4 P.M.
`Map 7`

This is a big, modern furniture store, but one
geared toward modern furniture that is practi-
cal, inspired, and actually usable. Various room
configurations—living rooms, dining rooms,
bedrooms—are set up throughout the large
showrooms of the store. You won't find much
in the way of abstract chairs or for-display-
purposes-only tables here; everything is built for
regular everyday use and enjoyment, from overstuffed couches to icy, sleek dining room sets.
Nouveau's furniture, artworks, and other home
goods adorn many a Baltimore house, and they
provided the whimsical contemporary furniture
for the Pier 5 Hotel in the Inner Harbor.

PAD
1500 Thames St., 410/563-4723,
www.calligarisshop.com/pad
HOURS: Mon.-Wed. 11 A.M.-8 P.M., Thurs. 11 A.M.-9 P.M.,
Fri. 11 A.M.-10 P.M., Sat. 10 A.M.-10 P.M., Sun. 11 A.M.-7 P.M.
`Map 2`

Opened by the owners of nearby Su Casa in
2005, this furniture and home goods store is
almost entirely a Calligaris store; the modern, very Italian design house's creations fill
the bright, open store. Living room sets, dining rooms, and bedrooms show off a variety of
ultra-modern designs and materials (white
plastic, chrome, etc.). There aren't many (if
any) other modern furniture stores offering
this level of European style in Baltimore, so if
contemporary is your thing, Pad is your store.

PATRICK SUTTON HOME
1000 Light St., 410/783-1500, www.patricksutton.com
HOURS: Mon.-Fri. 10 A.M.-6 P.M., Sat.-Sun. 11 A.M.-5 P.M.
`Map 4`

This is the retail home goods store of Patrick
Sutton, perhaps Baltimore's most acclaimed and
sought-after architect and interior designer. There

© GEOFF BROWN

**Great items for home (and gifts) are on
display at Federal Hill's Patrick Sutton Home.**

are the usual decorative and functional pieces here
(lots of metal, glass, and textiles) cleanly displayed
under track lighting, white walls, and hardwood
floors, but the best pieces are the antiques and
odd artifacts that Sutton and his staff have chosen to use as both decoration and art. There are
enormous, weighty pieces of well-used furniture
and work tables, lots of un-gussied-up old bowls,
urns, and pots, and one-of-a-kind wonders like
saddles and waterman's tools.

RED TREE
921 W. 36th St., 410/554-0055,
www.redtreebaltimore.com
HOURS: Mon.-Wed. 11 A.M.-7 P.M., Thurs.-Sat.
10 A.M.-8 P.M., Sun. 11 A.M.-6 P.M.
`Map 6`

Two stories display new, traditional-yet-cool
furniture, decorations, lamps, and even jewelry and art. Part of Hampden's latest, more
upscale wave of merchants, this sprawling retailer offers everything from tiny earrings to
enormous wardrobes and beds, all in well-

thought-out displays that might make you want to redo your own bedroom and living room. The owners and staff and well known for their friendliness.

◖ SHOFER'S
930 S. Charles St., 410/752-4212, www.shofers.com
HOURS: Mon. 10 A.M.-9 P.M., Tues.-Sat. 10 A.M.-5:30 P.M., Sun. noon-5 P.M.
Map 4

Many of Baltimore's storied companies of yore—Hamburger's, Hochschild Kohn—have long vanished. But Shofer's, first opened in 1914 in part of the same Federal Hill location (now some 70,000 square feet) it occupies today, has managed to hang on, probably because it's helped establish Baltimore's taste in furniture and home decor for almost a century. No matter your style, be it over-the-top leopard print or staid, proper leather, Shofer's probably has something for you. Looking for a bargain? Don't miss checking the outlet center, located across the street.

SU CASA
901 S. Bond St., 410/522-7010, www.esucasa.com
HOURS: Mon.-Thurs. 10 A.M.-9 P.M., Fri.-Sat. 10 A.M.-11 P.M., Sun. 10 A.M.-8 P.M.
Map 2

One of the first stores to embody the new Fell's Point—one where people can walk from their house to a contemporary furniture store, instead of having to drive somewhere—Su Casa has a vast array of home goods, most in the modern Americana school of design, with faux distressed pressed tin stars and heavy wooden construction. Su Casa is packed with beds, lamps, tables, love seats, armchairs, and all sorts of objects for decorating. There are also dishes and glassware.

Gifts

AMERICAN VISIONARY ART MUSEUM EYE SHOP
AVAM, 800 Key Hwy., 410/244-1900, ext. 236, www.avam.org
HOURS: Tues.-Sun. 10 A.M.-6 P.M.
Map 4

As befits a museum like AVAM that celebrates the genius of the off-kilter, the gift store (known as the "Eye Shop") here is run by Chicago's legendary Uncle Fun (Ted Frankel), who travels from the Second City to Charm City to keep the place stocked. You won't find boring old coffee cups and coasters here; instead, be prepared for original folk art, hand-painted Indian movie banners, strange antique castoffs, junky bric-a-brac, gimmicks, jokes, puns, and all sorts of other perfectly peculiar items.

GLARUS CHOCOLATIER
644 S. Exeter St., 410/727-6601, www.glaruschocolatier.com
HOURS: Mon.-Sat. 10 A.M.-8 P.M., Sun. 11 A.M.-5 P.M.
Map 2

Opened in 2004 to provide Baltimore with a high-quality, Swiss-style boutique chocolate maker, Glarus today is one of the city's best purveyors of things cocoa. This new, small, dark-wood-clad store offers chocolate and cocoa delights in small displays, to be ordered almost like sushi, as well as a wide variety of travel-friendly packs of truffles, bars, and "bark" (slabs of dark chocolate festooned with nuts or espresso beans).

IN WATERMELON SUGAR
3555 Chestnut Ave., 410/662-9090
HOURS: Mon.-Thurs. 10 A.M.-6 P.M., Fri.-Sat. 10 A.M.-7 P.M., Sun. noon-6 P.M.
Map 6

Like many of Hampden's successful stores, this charming, warm shop has stocked a little bit of everything—skin care and beauty products in the big bright front room, while the back room contains glassware, decorative boxes, pet snacks and trifles, pottery, candles and holders, and more. Be sure to spend some time ogling the great window displays that change throughout the year to reflect the seasons.

LE PETIT COCHON

1030 S. Charles St., 410/528-6001,
www.lepetitcochon.biz
HOURS: Tues.-Sat. 11 A.M.-6 P.M.

Map 4

This delightful little Federal Hill store with the purple and pink exterior is the ideal place to find a special gift. One of the owners is a former museum shop buyer, which helps explain the high level of quality (lots of stuff from the Continent) and intelligence of the goods here; there are all sorts of cards and notepads, toile boxes, ceramics, bakeware, candles, napkins, beautiful fabric flowers, and corners and crannies filled with equally wonderful items.

MAJA

1744 Aliceanna St., 410/327-9499,
www.majacollections.com
HOURS: Wed.-Sun. 11 A.M.-7 P.M.

Map 2

Jewelry, clothing, bags, and masks from all over the world, but primarily the United States, Africa, and East Asia, line the walls and fill the cases of this inviting Fell's Point store. The owner regularly travels to Mali to obtain new goods, particularly a special woven fabric that's not available elsewhere. There are also blouses, handbags, and hats, from places like Madagascar and Cambodia. Incense is also a big part of this store; you can buy everything from sticks to Buddhist holders, plus soaps and oils.

2910 ON THE SQUARE

2910 O'Donnell St., 410/675-8505,
www.2910onthesquare.com
HOURS: Tues.-Thurs. noon-9 P.M., Fri. noon-10 P.M.,
Sat. noon-11 P.M., Sun. 10 A.M.-4 P.M.

Map 3

This whimsical store, located on Canton's O'Donnell Square between the bars, restaurants, and hair salons, is a good place to find gifts for a wide range of people. There are lots of fun toys and clothes for kids, for example, and chewable goods for pets, glassware boxes for the office, and so on. This multi-colored, multi-ethnic shop is also one of the only places in the area for Judaica, so if you're in need of a Jewish-themed gift or maybe a mezuzah, this is probably your best bet.

Health and Beauty

ABOUT FACES

Canton Crossing, 1501 S. Clinton St., 410/675-0099,
www.aboutfacesdayspa.com
HOURS: Mon.-Tues. 10 A.M.-7 P.M., Wed. 8 A.M.-8 P.M.,
Thurs. 8 A.M.-9 P.M., Fri. 8 A.M.-7 P.M., Sat. 8 A.M.-6 P.M.,
Sun. 11 A.M.-5 P.M.

Map 3

This locally run chain of hair salon and day spa centers has been around for more than three decades, giving them the claim to the title of grande dame of the Baltimore spa circuit. There are roughly nine kinds of massages, five types of spa treatments (from mud soaks to green coffee wraps), and a vast array of hair, nail, and makeup services available. This is a huge, blonde-wood and glass filled facility, with lighting plans and flow decisions to help guide the traffic between the stations. The location, on the third floor of a new Canton office tower, gives clients some great views of the city as they get a manicure or soak in a huge whirlpool tub.

KISS N MAKE UP

827 W. 36th St., 410/467-5477,
http://kissnmakeup.netfirms.com
HOURS: Tues.-Wed. 11 A.M.-5 P.M.,
Thurs.-Sat. 11 A.M.-6 P.M., Sun. noon-5 P.M.

Map 6

This Hampden shop offers a broad selection of top contemporary cosmetic lines (Beauty Buffet, Pop Beauty, Too Faced) to cleanse, buff, cover, and improve just about every place on your epidermis, as well as a great bunch of gag items (such as Happy Childhood Memories Breath Spray). The festively decorated and fun store—there's an oversized lip sculpture, bright fabrics and colors everywhere, and inventive little displays, though all have a down-to-earth feel—also provides a complete line of cosmetic services, from facials and manicures to waxing.

M SALON

1131 S. Charles St., 410/685-0089,
www.msalonfederalhill.com
HOURS: Tues. by appt only, Wed.-Fri. 10 A.M.-8 P.M.,
Sat. 8:30 A.M.-4 P.M.
Map 4

This is Federal Hill's most popular salon for getting a haircut that looks as good in the boardroom as it does at a nightclub—or just a regular trim and highlights, if that's all you need. A variety of other hair and beauty services (like extensions and eyebrow waxing) are available at this luxe-appointed power salon (gold walls, cranberry drapes). There's even an in-salon store, M Vanity, that stocks a huge variety of beauty products from all the major makers.

SEEDS

3600 Roland Ave., Ste. 4, 410/235-1776,
www.seedswellness.com
HOURS: Call for appt.
Map 6

A collection of five practitioners of natural medical arts have joined forces at this Hampden location to offer services like acupuncture, cranio-sacral therapy, several more conventional types of massage, naturopathy, and reiki. There are also regular lectures, workshops, training sessions, and classes held at this calm, tranquilly decorated space located in the building with the pink flamingo on it (the Café Hon restaurant is on the first floor).

SOBOTANICAL

1130 S. Charles St., 410/234-0333,
www.sobotanical.com
HOURS: Tues. 12:30-5:30 P.M.,
Wed.-Thurs. noon-7:30 P.M., Fri.-Sat. 11 A.M.-6 P.M.
Map 4

Natural botanicals, aromatherapy, personalized fragrances, all-natural therapeutic creams—not exactly the kind of products and philosophy one would normally associate with blue-collar Baltimore. But this Federal Hill–based company, set up in a sunny, New Age-y apothecary space, with hundreds of ingredients in great little jars and boxes, creates a wide range of health, skin, and hair products from all-natural ingredients that are gaining space on store and salon shelves all over the country. You can work with a consultant to mix up your own perfumes and scents here, or take a turn at the aromatherapy bar.

SPROUT

925 W. 36th St., 410/235-2269, www.sproutsalon.com
HOURS: Tues.-Fri. 10 A.M.-7 P.M., Sat. 10 A.M.-5 P.M.
Map 6

In a bright space filled with exposed brick and wood, this all-natural hair salon really goes the extra mile to make sure everything used on your hair and head is as chemical-free as possible—including making their own line of products. The staff here is young, talented, and artsy (you'll see plenty of gorgeous tattoos), but they can cut, dye, highlight, extend, and spruce up any kind of hair, whether you're going on a power job interview or a month-long stint at a New Mexico painter's colony.

(STUDIO 921 SALON & DAY SPA

921 E. Fort Ave., 410/783-7727, www.studio921spa.com
HOURS: Tues.-Thurs. 11 A.M.-8 P.M., Fri. 10 A.M.-7 P.M.,
Sat. 9 A.M.-5 P.M., Sun. 10 A.M.-5 P.M.
Map 4

This popular full-service salon and spa occupies the same former foundry building as an art gallery (Gallery Imperato) and a restaurant (The Wine Market), creating the potential for an entire day spent wandering the huge, sunlit rooms of this enormous historic brick and wood building. The hair salon area is large, with lots of chairs and stations, so there's never a long wait. There are eight spa treatment rooms, offering everything from massages to microdermabrasion, hair removal, and even Botox treatments; the comprehensive services list is one reason for Studio 921's popularity. The other is the staff, who have developed rabidly loyal (and satisfied) customers and clients that keep the store bouncing and busy.

Kids' Stores

BEDIBOO
4321 Harford Rd., 410/444-6060, www.bediboo.com
HOURS: Sat.-Sun. 11 A.M.-4 P.M., Mon.-Fri. appt. only
Map 7

The residential neighborhood of Lauraville, about a 10-minute drive northeast of Homewood, has become the site of a mini-craze of infant and child shops, offering everything from onesies to books. Bediboo goes even further, as it offers a full range of clothes from the hippest designers for expecting moms as well as kids, plus custom fittings for baby slings, and too-cute shoes and accessories. It's open on weekends only, but you can call to see if they'll open during the week.

BRATT DECOR
Belvedere Square, 548 E. Belvedere Ave., 410/464-9400, www.brattdecor.com
HOURS: Mon.-Thurs. 10 A.M.-6 P.M., Fri.-Sat. 10 A.M.-7 P.M., Sun. 11 A.M.-5 P.M.
Map 7

This immensely popular infant and tot furniture design shop has stocked the nurseries of countless Hollywood stars, artists, and others who think cribs and changing tables don't have to be dreary and dull. It's easy to see why this local store is so popular; the designs vary from playful and unexpected to more traditional, but all of their work is fully functional and never ignores the main job, which is keeping babies safe and happy.

CORDUROY BUTTON
1628 Thames St., Ste. 1, 410/276-5437
HOURS: Mon.-Fri. 10 A.M.-7 P.M., Sat. 10 A.M.-7 P.M., Sun. noon-5 P.M.
Map 2

Looking for some cool kids' clothes and toys for your cool friends (or for your own kids)? This funky Fell's Point infant and toddler shop has plenty of traditional, high-quality apparel choices, as well as a great selection of the clothes you wish you could have worn as a youth, from local makers like Squidfire and other national hipster clothiers. Fun graphic prints, great hats and jackets, and lots of other gear for the cool kids in your life.

Pet Supplies and Grooming

DOGMA
3600 Boston St. #20, 410/276-3410, www.dogmaforpets.com
HOURS: Mon.-Fri. 10 A.M.-8 P.M., Sat. 9 A.M.-6 P.M., Sun. 11 A.M.-6 P.M.
Map 3

Though most pets will never appreciate just how cute any of these chew toys, food bowls, jackets, or collars are, owners go ga-ga over the huge selection of colorful, fuzzy, and sleek items at this Canton emporium of pet accessories (they also sell lots of brands of healthy food and snacks). Bright corrugated metal, pastel colors, and industrial touches like exposed I-beams and ductwork surround displays filled with more leashes and collars than you have ever seen. There are also self-serve baths here, as well as groomers, if your little Fido needs a sprucing up before leaving town.

HOWL
3525 W. Chestnut Ave., 410/235-2469
HOURS: Mon.-Sat. 11 A.M.-7 P.M.
Map 6

You won't find any Snausages here: This bare-bones pet food store stocks the most popular non-corporate and naturally made brands of dog and cat food, as well as a good array of treats, toys, dietary supplements, and other animal accessories. Folks bring their dogs in to chat with the owner and other customers, so plan on making some new canine friends if you stop by. Plus, there's a self-serve pet washing area in the back of the building (also out back: plenty of free parking).

PRETENTIOUS POOCH
1017 Cathedral St., 443/524-7777,
www.pretentiouspooch.com
HOURS: Tues.-Fri. 10 A.M.-8 P.M., Sat. 10 A.M.-7 P.M.
Map 5

In a neighborhood where being fabulous is a valued trait in architecture, personality, and life, this Mount Vernon pet store fits right in, as it's the only dog and cat shop in town with a massive four-foot-high chandelier and a marble-topped check-out station. A wide variety of toys, beds, blankets, healthy snacks, designer leashes, and other wearable and chewable items fill this bright, very city-animal oriented store (small dogs will find plenty of goodies here).

Shoes

BENJAMIN LOVELL
618 S. Exeter St., 410/244-5359, www.blshoes.com
HOURS: Mon.-Thurs. 10 A.M.-7 P.M., Fri.-Sat.
10 A.M.-8 P.M., Sun. 11 A.M.-6 P.M.
Map 2

A regional six-store shoe shop found across Maryland, New Jersey, and Pennsylvania, this is a store for hot new looks and stylishly casual footwear, as well as a few high-end fashion finds. There are plenty of Uggs and other comfort shoes here, plus more exciting designs in footwear and handbags from Ariat, BZ Moda, Dansko, Hobo, and Mephisto. The staff here is as mellow as the shoes, which makes shopping here a pretty great experience.

JOANNA GRAY OF LONDON
Village of Cross Keys, 5100 Falls Rd., 410/435-2233
HOURS: Mon.-Sat. 11 A.M.-6 P.M., Sun. noon-5 P.M.
Map 7

Despite the name, you'll find very little in the way of English footwear at this high-end, high-heel-friendly shoe boutique. Italian is the guiding spirit and mantra here, and the challenging, elaborate designs and architecture of the shoes here will get your feet noticed no matter where you are. This store, in the upscale Cross Keys shopping center that's about a five-minute drive from Hampden, is your best bet for finding footwear from the big-name and big-price-tag premier shoe designers.

MA PETITE SHOE
832 W. 36th St., 410/235-3442,
www.mapetiteshoe.com
HOURS: Mon.-Sat. 11 A.M.-7 P.M., Sun. 11 A.M.-5 P.M.
Map 6

It's a combination so obvious that it's surprising no one else in town came up with it. Talk about a brilliant retail concept: Sell women's shoes and gourmet chocolate. Sure, they have men's and kids' shoes, too, and accessories, but their selection of footwear for the ladies (think John Fluevog and Miz Mooz) and their chocolate delights (from makers like Lake Champlain and Vosges) make this a paradise for many Baltimore shoppers. Displayed on pedestals, mantels, racks, and stands, the offerings at this tiny two-room store (it's in a converted row house with a nice front porch) are treated like the artistic designs they are.

MATAVA TOO
Belvedere Square, 521 E. Belvedere Ave., 410/235-1830
HOURS: Mon.-Sat. 10 A.M.-6 P.M., Sun. 11 A.M.-4 P.M.
Map 7

Another home-grown mini-chain, this three-store-strong collection of women's shoe stores covers Annapolis, Baltimore County's horse country, and their sole (pun intended) Baltimore City location, in the popular and bustling Belvedere Square. Featuring brands of shoes, sandals, clogs, heels, and boots as diverse as Jessica Bennett, Dansko, John

perhaps the greatest store concept ever: women's shoes and chocolate, at Ma Petite Shoe

Fluevog, and Frye, this busy footwear shop manages to still provide great customer service when things get hectic.

POPPY AND STELLA
728 S. Broadway, 410/522-1970,
www.poppyandstella.com
HOURS: Tues.-Sat. 11 A.M.-7 P.M., Sun. noon-5 P.M.
Map 2

This newcomer to the Fell's Point footwear scene has already attracted a loyal clientele thanks to the small but well-stocked store's welcoming vibe and the broad selection of not only shoes but also handbags and accessories. It's the shoes, though, that keep people coming into this shop; from perilous and artsy heels to sneakers and boots, from cobblers like BCBG Max Azria, Jeffery Campbell, Coclico, and

Puma, this shrine to the shoe is worth walking into.

SASSANOVA
805 Aliceanna St., 410/244-6376,
www.sassanova.com
HOURS: Mon.-Sat. 10 A.M.-6 P.M., Sun. 11 A.M.-4 P.M.
Map 2

A shoe lover's paradise, featuring high-end models from houses like Loeffler Randall, Hollywould, and Tory Burch. Mid-price shoes from makers like Seychelles and Sam Edelman round out the footwear selection, and there are also handbags, jewelry, accessories, and kids' shoes. Shoppers (and guests) can relax and browse magazines while seated in the plush couch or armchairs that surround the store's mirrored mantel.

Shopping Centers

ARUNDEL MILLS MALL

7000 Arundel Mills Circle, 410/540-5100,
www.arundelmillsmall.com

HOURS: Mon.-Sat. 10 A.M.-9:30 P.M., Sun. 11 A.M.-7 P.M.

`Map 7`

About 20 minutes south of downtown on Route 295 (the Baltimore-Washington Parkway), this huge shopping center draws people from across the state. One of the national chain of "Mills" malls, it's home to more than 225 stores, including Neiman Marcus Last Call, H&M, White House/Black Market, and a Banana Republic outlet, plus everything from jewelry kiosks to the massive Bass Pro Shops Outdoor World facility, where you can climb a rock wall, practice some archery, or gawk at the 23,000-gallon aquarium. There's also a Best Buy, an Old Navy, and a Medieval Times. Still not sold? Visit the Muvico Egyptian 24 movie theater, one of the busiest cinema palaces in the nation.

BELVEDERE SQUARE

518 E. Belvedere Ave., 410/464-9773,
www.belvederesquare.com

HOURS: Shops: Mon.-Sat. 10 A.M.-7 P.M., Sun. noon-5 P.M.;
Market: Mon.-Fri. 10 A.M.-7 P.M., Sat. 9 A.M.-7 P.M.,
Sun. 9 A.M.-4 P.M.

`Map 7`

This collection of outdoor shops, boutiques, home decor stores, and the popular Market at Belvedere Square has become a social hub for this northern city neighborhood (the county line lies just a few blocks north). There are regular music events on spring and summer Friday nights, and there's a real family-friendly feel to the whole place; the crowd is also diverse and reflects the neighborhood. The Market is home to great produce-sellers, soup-makers, delis, and other food and gourmet purveyors. The historic Senator Theatre is across the street, making this a great destination if you're looking to get out of the city...without actually leaving the city.

THE GALLERY

200 E. Pratt St., 410/332-4191, www.harborplace.com

HOURS: Mon.-Sat. 10 A.M.-9 P.M., Sun. noon-6 P.M.

`Map 1`

Across Pratt Street from the waterfront pavilions of Harborplace is the Gallery, an open, airy, indoor mall that caters to both tourists and downtown office workers with a mix of shops and even a food court (with some great views of the city). Shops here include Ann Taylor, Banana Republic, Brooks Brothers, Coach, Forever 21, Nine West, and Talbots—your typical mall basics. There's also a Bluemercury spa, and a few other personal grooming shops and stores. If you're staying downtown, the convenience of this shopping center can't be beat, even if it's all national chains.

TOWSON TOWN CENTER

825 Dulaney Valley Rd., Towson, 410/494-8800,
www.towsontowncenter.com

HOURS: Mon.-Thurs. 10 A.M.-9:30 P.M.,
Fri.-Sat. 10 A.M.-10 P.M., Sun. 11 A.M.-7 P.M.

`Map 7`

Once a small, intimate mall serving the quiet town of Towson (about a 15-minute drive north of downtown), this massive shopping complex is now one of the busiest malls in the region, and parking can be a bit of a pain—despite the addition of several attached garages. There are about 200 stores here, including anchors like Macy's and Nordstrom, plus the only local Apple store and a trio of upscale cosmetics shops (Lush, MAC, and Sephora). In 2008 several new restaurants opened (including P.F. Chang's China Bistro and a Cheesecake Factory), even more parking was added, and some stores (like Crate & Barrel) expanded into new, much-larger digs.

VILLAGE OF CROSS KEYS

5100 Falls Rd., 410/323-1000,
www.villageofcrosskeys.com
HOURS: Mon.-Sat. 10 A.M.-6 P.M., Sun. noon-4 P.M.
Map 7

This interesting little upscale mall is just one part of the Village of Cross Keys, a planned mini-community located north of Hampden. Tucked into the ground level of a sprawling building, there are about 30 shops and boutiques here, almost all upscale, ranging from shoes to ladies apparel (both classic and trendy) to jewelry to cookware (including a Williams-Sonoma Grand Cuisine). There are also a couple of cafés and restaurants for hungry shoppers, and the tree-lined grounds are a pleasure to stroll through.

Vintage and Antiques

ANOTHER PERIOD IN TIME

1708 Fleet St., 410/675-4776, www.anotherperiod.com
HOURS: Mon.-Thurs. 9 A.M.-5 P.M., Sat. 10 A.M.-6 P.M.,
Sun. noon-5 P.M.
Map 2

A consortium of some 15 antiques and collectibles dealers, this big space is worth a browse because of the volume of stuff you'll find in its roughly 6,000-square-foot warehouse. The store's best items are on the first floor, the better to lure in customers; there's lots of furniture, art, and glassware on display. There's always something peculiar here, from taxidermied animals to old signs, as well as lots of early-20th-century pop culture items, along with costume jewelry. Head upstairs to see the dealers' other, generally more reasonably priced finds.

ANTIQUE CENTER AT FEDERAL HILL

1220 Key Hwy., 410/625-0182
HOURS: Tues.-Sat. 11 A.M.-6 P.M., Sun. noon-5 P.M.
Map 4

Unlike some of the other antique operations in town, this enormous warehouse (some 30,000 square feet) doesn't mess with old beer trays and yellowed Orioles programs. The furniture here is European, American, large, and expensive; it's also beautiful enough, and so resplendent with Old World craftsmanship, that the prices don't seem that ludicrous. In addition to the well-arranged and -displayed items and rooms from the 30 or so dealers here, there is a good selection of smaller items, from porcelain and silverware to clocks and watches.

ANTIQUE ROW STALLS

809 N. Howard St., 410/728-6363,
www.antiquerowstalls.com
HOURS: Wed.-Mon. 11 A.M.-5 P.M.
Map 5

Look for the red awning (and big sign on the building) on Howard Street; it signals the entrance to this sprawling 10,000-square-foot showcase for more than 20 different antiques dealers. One plus about this collaboration is that, unlike at some antique superstores, there's not a great deal of overlap in the offerings here; instead, most of the dealers stick to their specialties, though decorative arts and objects are in abundance. Pottery, porcelain, and paintings are also prevalent, but there are also textiles, furniture (from the past two centuries, including some great 1960s Mod finds), and toys.

AVENUE ANTIQUES

901 W. 36th St., 410/467-0329
HOURS: Mon.-Fri. 11 A.M.-6 P.M., Sat. 10 A.M.-7 P.M.,
Sun. noon-5 P.M.
Map 6

A vast, three-story collection of wares offered by multiple antique dealers, this sprawling shop offers everything from Victorian jewelry and glassware to pop art collectibles and Americana. There are some good items from Baltimore's past here (old Preakness memorabilia, for example), as well as furniture, signage, and clothes. The basement is home to Decades, a mid-century-modern wonderland of groovy furniture, "art," and clothing.

VINTAGE AND ANTIQUES **173**

SHOPS

ANTIQUING ON HOWARD STREET

This broad, once-vital avenue through the western side of downtown used to be one of the city's finest shopping districts. Department stores and specialty retailers lined the streets, which buzzed for decades with nattily attired men and women, until the city's decline began in the 1960s. It fell into such disrepair that planners decided to run the Baltimore area's light-rail cars and tracks right down the middle of it, since it would be the least disruptive place to put a mass transit rail line. But there's one good reason to still venture over here: antiques.

A steadfast group of dealers have held their ground and continue to serve a devoted public, many of whom journey from across the region for a trip to Baltimore's famous Howard Street. The 800 block is where the action is these days; heading north up Howard Street, from the corner of Madison and Howard, start at **Crosskeys Antiques** (801 N. Howard St.), which specializes in decorative items and furniture from Europe. Across the street is **Dubey's Art and Antiques** (807 N. Howard St.), which showcases Chinese Export and Japanese ceramics. Next door is **Antique Row Stalls** (809 N. Howard St.), a large multi-dealer (more than 20) exhibition space featuring all sorts of antiques from all sorts of eras, with a concentration on porcelain and paintings. Vintage and first-edition children's and illustrated tomes and other printed treasures are well represented at **Drusilla's Books** (817 N. Howard St.). And you can resolve troublesome incomplete family silverware patterns at **The Imperial Half Bushel** (831 N. Howard St.), which sells amazing collections of 18th- and 19th-century American and English silverware, including a good array of famous Maryland silverware from the same time period. Not sated? There are lots of other small stores scattered along the 800 block that are worth peering into as well. Check each store's closed days, as they vary between Sundays, Mondays, and Tuesdays.

CRAIG FLINNER GALLERY

1117 W. 36th St., 410/727-1863, www.flinnergallery.com
HOURS: Mon.-Sat. 10 A.M.-6 P.M., Sun. noon-4 P.M.
Map 6

Baltimore's best store for antique and vintage posters, maps, paintings, prints, and other graphic arts, this venerable shop moved to Hampden recently after spending decades in Mount Vernon. The gallery specializes in prints and maps, and has a vast selection organized by subjects and eras, which makes shopping for gifts a real breeze. (Shopping for a flower lover? A fan of 19th-century maps? No problem.) The staff is discretely able to help any request, and they'll even frame your purchase. There are some interesting antiques in stock as well.

CROSSKEYS ANTIQUES

801 N. Howard St., 410/728-0101,
www.crosskeysantiques.com
HOURS: Sat. 10 A.M.-4 P.M., Sun. 11 A.M.-3 P.M.
Map 5

The splendors of continental Europe and England are the stock in trade of this multi-story stalwart of Baltimore's famed (if somewhat sagging) Howard Street antiques district. This is the southernmost of the antiques stores that make up the district, and is a great place to start your shopping, though the items here are large, resplendent, and expensive (they'll ship it to you anywhere in the world). Large furniture (often ornately detailed) and decorative items like mirrors and lamps make up the bulk of the goods here in this very proper shop, though there are more reasonably priced reproductions too.

DRUSILLA'S BOOKS

817 N. Howard St., 410/225-0277,
www.drusillasbooks.com
HOURS: Tues.-Sat. noon-5 P.M.
Map 5

Antique books—mostly for children, but of all other sorts as well—line the shelves and walls of this cozy shop, owned and operated by the store's namesake, Drusilla Jones. Illustrated

Drusilla's has classic, rare children's books and other literary finds.

books, whether with full-color plates or intricate black and white drawings, get special attention here in Drusilla's tidy shop, and careful browsing is perfectly acceptable. There are also vintage and new cards, as well as prints of literary favorites both real (authors) and imaginary (think of famous talking elephants or dogs).

DUBEY'S ART AND ANTIQUES
807 N. Howard St., 410/383-2881,
www.dubeysantiques.com
HOURS: Wed.-Mon. 11 A.M.-5 P.M.
Map 5

Dubey's collections focus on elegant ceramics from the world's best makers in Asia and Europe, from delicately painted vases to ornately festooned plates and other tableware (the Japanese selections are often the most visually striking). The big, sprawling store showcases mixes its porcelain offers in with its other wares in simple tableaus; there generally are also many pieces of early American furniture,

chandeliers, and European paintings on display at this quiet storefront.

THE IMPERIAL HALF BUSHEL
831 N. Howard St., 410/462-1192,
www.imperialhalfbushel.com
HOURS: Mon.-Sat. 10:30 A.M.-5 P.M.
Map 5

One of Baltimore's lesser-known accomplishments began back in the 1800s, when the city joined the ranks of the finest silver-crafting cities in America (Kirk-Stieff, one of the last great Baltimore manufacturers, closed its business in 1999). The Imperial Half Bushel specializes in the great heyday of the city's silverware makers, making it an important resource for people looking to replace specific items in sets, pick up an antique platter for a gift, or even acquire an entire silver service for 12 in one fell swoop. You can learn more about the city's great craftspeople from the helpful owners and staff, and see some of the great items here (like the personalized silver business and calling card holders).

HOTELS

From the massive, looming big-name hotels that line the waters of the Inner Harbor to the cozy owner-operated inns and bed-and-breakfasts scattered throughout Baltimore's classic neighborhoods, there are enough lodging options here to satisfy any traveler. The most commanding views of the city can be found on the top floors of the downtown mega-hotels, and these venues also offer some of the best locations from which to set out and explore the city. Just a few blocks away from the Harbor, though, it's possible to tuck into a historic B&B in a neighborhood like Fell's Point or Federal Hill, and spend your mornings wandering narrow streets and waterfronts.

Baltimore recently added over 1,000 new downtown hotel rooms to help lure more national conventions to town, and most of the rooms were supplied by the huge new Hilton located just north of Oriole Park at Camden Yards. Baltimore's big hotels are designed to provide lots of rooms, rather than make an artistic statement. Still, the Kimpton hotel chain recently opened a modernist Hotel Monaco Baltimore right downtown, and the Pier 5 Hotel is a locally grown boutique lodging choice. Looking for opulence? Though the Inner Harbor's InterContinental Baltimore isn't much to look at from the outside, the interior appointments are some of the best in town. Green-conscious guests may consider the new Fairfield Inn & Suites that opened in spring 2009; it's the city's first LEED-certified (Leadership in Energy and Environmental Design, the standard for eco-conscious construction) hotel, bringing lodging in an

© GEOFF BROWN

HIGHLIGHTS

LOOK FOR ◖ TO FIND
RECOMMENDED HOTELS.

◖ **Best Grand Hotel:** It's hard to top the **InterContinental Baltimore** for opulence (check out the enormous floral bouquet in the lobby), size, location, and the wonderful Explorer's Lounge that overlooks the Inner Harbor (page 180).

◖ **Best Fell's Point Hotel:** If you want to stay in this charming waterfront neighborhood, head for **The Inn at Henderson's Wharf,** a small independent hotel in a huge old warehouse (it's mostly condos now) at the far east end of Fell Street (page 183).

◖ **Best-Located Boutique Waterfront Hotel:** When you pull up in front of the tucked-away **Pier 5 Hotel,** you'll be happy to be just off the beaten path of the bustling waterfront – but still a short walk to the Inner Harbor, Little Italy, and Fell's Point (page 184).

◖ **Best Contemporary Boutique Hotel:** Just a block off of Canton's busy O'Donnell Square is a plain-looking corner row house with an intriguing green door. Behind it lies a modern, cozy, five-room mini-hotel: the **Inn at 2920** (page 185).

◖ **Best Historic Inn:** If you're planning on spending a lot of time among the cultural wonders of Mount Vernon, plan on staying at the historic **4 East Madison Inn,** a massive 1845 townhome full of mahogany, stained glass, and period furniture (page 186).

© GEOFF BROWN

The Inn at Henderson's Wharf

environmentally friendly building to a great location on President Street, between downtown and Little Italy.

Away from the busy Inner Harbor, Baltimore offers several interesting and unique hotels and a handful of B&Bs scattered in some of the city's prettiest neighborhoods. Fell's Point has the widest variety of small hotels, with Mount Vernon a close second. Staying in these neighborhoods has some benefits (you'll really get to experience Baltimore city life) and some downsides (you're pretty far from other attractions, though not prohibitively so). One other bright spot—for young backpackers and bargain hunters—is Baltimore's International Youth Hostel. Renovated and revamped in 2007, this 19th-century brownstone now has fully modern sleeping and bathing quarters. The bad news is that, in many of the other neighborhoods covered in this guide, there are at most one or two lodging options: It's not that there are others that aren't recommended, it's that they don't exist.

Travelers do have options in Baltimore, from brand-new, modern lodging in the heart of downtown to charming little inns and B&Bs tucked into the city's most fashionable and beloved neighborhoods. Take some time to figure out what you want to do in Baltimore, and let that plan help you chose the best place to stay.

PRICE KEY

$ Under $100

$$ $100-200

$$$ Over $200

CHOOSING A HOTEL

The first rule of real estate applies to Baltimore's selection of hotels, inns, and few bed-and-breakfasts: it's all about location, location, location. That means waterfront, preferably, and downtown. The views and convenience of staying at one of the big chain hotels facing the Inner Harbor can't be beat, though you'll pay for both. If you're looking for a centrally located hotel, you'll probably want to stay around the Inner Harbor and downtown, as it makes it much, much easier to travel to other parts of the city. Just be ready to fork over a hefty fee; most of these hotels are geared toward convention and business travelers with expense accounts and big budgets. Also note that parking can add considerably to your costs (free parking at downtown hotels is non-existent, unless there's a special), and that some hotels charge you whenever you enter and exit the lot, so carefully research each hotel's policy. Some of the smaller hotels don't have parking, so you may be on your own in looking for a lot or space. Also note that a lot of the major chain hotels have put HDTV wide-screen sets into the rooms, but have not yet run an HD signal to them.

Fell's Point is a solid choice for those looking to experience a bit of real Baltimore. There are two small, independent hotels here, as well as a couple of bed-and-breakfasts. Staying here gives you the chance to leave your lodging and walk along the working waterfront, watching pleasure boats, tugs, and the Water Taxis scoot across the water—it's an opportunity you shouldn't pass up.

Mount Vernon is another old city neighborhood with a large chain hotel and a few independent options too; it's a great place to walk around during the day, it's loaded with cultural

Staying in Mount Vernon puts you close to lots of cultural attractions.

attractions, and Charles Street has lots of restaurants and bars for evening activities.

Finding a bargain hotel in Baltimore can be a little tricky; do your due diligence on discount websites like www.priceline.com, which can cut the list price of some rooms by more than 50 percent (which makes a merely acceptable $250 room a *fantastic* $109 room). Also check the city's official tourism website, www.baltimore.org, for regular specials and bargain packages. That site—run by the Baltimore Area Convention and Visitors Association, or BACVA—also has a very user-friendly search

function for hotels all across the city, and even points beyond, including BWI Airport. Weekend rates are always higher, so consider a mid-week stay if you're trying to save some cash. There are a few great inns out in northern Baltimore County's horse country, about 20 minutes from downtown Baltimore.

The rates you'll find listed here are summer season rates, the highest charged by each hotel. These top rates may also apply during holidays and major weekend-long events (like May's Preakness Stakes horse race and weeklong celebration).

Downtown and Inner Harbor   Map 1

The best part about staying downtown, or (better yet) in the Inner Harbor, is the central location—allowing easy exploration of the rest of the city with, at most, a 10-minute car ride. Yet there's so much to do in this part of town that guests might not even need to leave. It's the easiest place to find a cab, and Harborplace has a wide selection of restaurants and bars for nighttime diversions.

BALTIMORE HOSTEL $

17 W. Mulberry St., 410/576-8880,
www.baltimorehostel.org

This newly renovated 1857 brownstone has gained positive reviews from all sorts of travelers—mostly those looking for a cheap, clean place to spend a night or two. Located just across the street from the Basilica of the Assumption, this modern Hostelling International–affiliated lodging has 44 beds in various-sized rooms, a lot of great perks (free Wi-Fi, free pancakes, free coffee and tea all day long) and a solid location that makes accessing both the Inner Harbor and Mount Vernon a breeze for motivated walkers.

BROOKSHIRE SUITES $$

120 E. Lombard St., 410/625-1300, www.harbormagic
.com/brookshire/brookshire_default.asp

Just a block from the Inner Harbor, this semi-

boutique hotel is one of three that operates as Harbor Magic Hotels (the other two are the Admiral Fell Inn in Fell's Point and Pier 5 near Little Italy). This 11-story, 97-room hotel has one of the most recognizable exteriors in the city, a geometric pattern of horizontal white and black plates. Though the common spaces have some interesting modern touches, the rooms are pretty traditional. Prices here tend to be fairly low, so it's a good option for the bargain hunter who wants to stay downtown.

DAYS INN INNER HARBOR $$

100 Hopkins Pl., 410/576-1000,
www.daysinnerharbor.com

A bargain-priced hotel with a very good location, this Days Inn is especially convenient for people coming to town for a convention (the Baltimore Convention Center is right across the street), or an Orioles or Ravens game at Camden Yards. This is a basic hotel, with 250 perfectly fine rooms (some of which have pretty great views of the city—ask for a south-facing room) and a heated outdoor pool that's not particularly picturesque.

HAMPTON INN AND SUITES
INNER HARBOR $$$

131 E. Redwood St., 410/539-7888 or 800/426-7866,
www.baltimorehamptoninn.com

A modern hotel retrofitted into a historic old

downtown building (the lobby and entryway were restored and preserved, thankfully), this is a hotel that scores points on location and amenities. There are 116 rooms here (the suites include a wet bar and sofa bed), most of which look out over the heart of Baltimore's downtown district, a place that is pretty deserted after dark. But the Inner Harbor is just three blocks south, and there are plenty of attractions and destinations within walking distance. Note that there is a basic Hampton Inn just across from Oriole Park at Camden Yards; cab drivers sometimes confuse the two.

HILTON BALTIMORE ⑤⑤⑤
401 W. Pratt St., 443/573-8700, www.hilton.com
Baltimore's newest major hotel was built with city-backed bonds to help boost convention business (and it has a connecting walkway to the Baltimore Convention Center). Though the new structure added 757 rooms to the city's hotel stocks (making it the biggest downtown hotel), the boxy metallic building has drawn flak for being too boring and big—as well as for blocking the great views of downtown

many people in Oriole Park used to enjoy. All that aside, the main lobby is awash in natural woods and modern art and furniture, and it's so new that the entire building is relatively immaculate; when you exit the south lobby, you're greeted with a wonderful view of Oriole Park, which is literally a couple dozen steps away.

HOTEL MONACO BALTIMORE ⑤⑤
2 N. Charles St., 888/752-2636,
www.monaco-baltimore.com
This majestic old 13-story Beaux Arts building, built in 1906 as the headquarters for the B&O Railroad company (right after the devastating fire of 1904), lies at the "center" of the city on the corner of Charles and Baltimore Streets. The marble entryway is watched over by a massive chandelier, and while there are numerous other grand, century-old architectural touches, guestrooms at this 202-room Kimpton hotel are completely modern, and feature all the usual 21st-century amenities (Wi-Fi, in-room spa and wellness, and some eco-friendly operating systems)—plus some unusual ones (a hosted wine hour in the lobby and a companion goldfish, upon request).

HOTELS

© GEOFF BROWN
Hilton Baltimore, the city's biggest downtown hotel

BEST WATER VIEWS

If you're willing to pay for it, there are some truly spectacular views of Baltimore's Inner Harbor available at many of the big downtown hotels. Starting on the west side of the water, the luxurious **InterContinental Baltimore** has one of the most commanding views of the entire waterfront, and lots of rooms facing Harborplace. To the north, the **Hyatt Regency Baltimore** also boasts lots of water views, and it's much taller than the InterContinental, so you can get some great birds'-eye panoramas. Moving east down Pratt Street, the **Renaissance Harborplace Hotel** (it's a Marriott) is also tall enough (12 stories) to offer some outstanding scenery; just make sure you're high enough to not end up staring at the pavilions of Harborplace. And on the other side of the harbor, in Harbor East (near Fell's Point), a newer Marriott, the **Baltimore Marriott Waterfront** isn't as close to downtown, but at 31 stories, it offers some of the best vantages in the city; if you're in Baltimore during one of the several weekends when there's a fireworks show at the Inner Harbor, this is one of the most Olympian heights from which to behold the colorful spectacle.

HYATT REGENCY BALTIMORE ⑤⑤⑤

300 Light St., 410/528-1234, www.baltimore.hyatt.com
This is another of the Inner Harbor's original wave of major hotels that went up in the 1980s—not that the mirrored exterior and dated architecture of the building gives it away. Get past that, and inside you'll find one of the city's top upscale chain hotels. Unlike the exterior, the interior is up-to-date and modern, from the lobby to the newly upgraded Bistro 300 restaurant (though the exposed concrete pillars are a bit dated). There are 488 guest rooms here, all appointed with upscale contemporary furniture. Location is the big sell here; the entire Inner Harbor is steps from the door, and Federal Hill is a short walk to the south.

ⓒ INTERCONTINENTAL BALTIMORE ⑤⑤⑤

550 Light St., 410/234-0550 or 888/424-6835, www.intercontinental.com/baltimore
It's a shame, really, that the uninspired 1980s design of this hotel (sort of a boring brick box married to a utilitarian vision of a Parisian apartment building) does so little to proclaim that it's one of the finest lodging options in the city. Renovated in 2005, the InterContinental has a lot going for it: The 195 rooms are really big, and (in all but the most basic rooms) the furniture is old-world European and sturdy. There are 22 suites as well, offering various degrees of luxury (and cost). The lobby features a changed-daily floral bouquet that's the size of a Volkswagen Beetle, and the rooftop health club has great views and everything from free weights to StairMasters. Best of all, the Explorer's Lounge is one of the city's best places for an opulent cocktail while overlooking the Inner Harbor.

RENAISSANCE HARBORPLACE HOTEL ⑤⑤⑤

202 E. Pratt St., 410/547-1200 or 800/535-1201, www.marriott.com/renaissance-hotel/travel.mi
This 622-room building, clad in green glass and a few dozen steps from all of the attractions of the Inner Harbor, is a favorite for many regular Baltimore visitors. Let's start with location: There's no other hotel that puts guests so close to everything, from the National Aquarium to the Maryland Science Center. Next are the views: On the upper floors, the panoramic views of the Inner Harbor are unbeatable. Guest rooms are modern in decor, the comforters are down, and the fully loaded gym has huge windows overlooking Pratt Street and the waterfront—as does Watertable, the property's upscale restaurant.

SPRINGHILL SUITES BY MARRIOTT ⑤⑤

16 S. Calvert St., 410/685-1095, www.marriott.com
This is another relative bargain that, even though it's just a short walk from the Inner Harbor, demonstrates how prices drop off as you move away from the waterfront. An all-suite

hotel, the 99 rooms here use some tricks (like wall-mounted flat-screen TVs) to maximize space, and have basic kitchen facilities. Built in a former bank building, one of the conference rooms is called "The Vault"; entry is gained between two enormous half-round vault doors.

TREMONT PLAZA $\text{\textcircled{S}\textcircled{S}}$

222 St. Paul Pl., 410/727-2222,
www.tremontsuitehotels.com
One of two Tremont Hotels in Baltimore (the other is the Tremont Park, an older, smaller building just a block away), the 303-room Tremont Plaza is the more deluxe of the two. These are all suites, ranging from 450 square feet in the basic configuration to 1,200 square feet in the Chairman's Suite. The suites offer the usual amenities, such as coffee makers, refrigerators, microwaves, and free Wi-Fi. It's a bit of a walk to the Inner Harbor, which means prices here are lower. This is the city's tallest hotel, at 37 stories.

Fell's Point   Map 2

The cultural opposite of downtown, this delightful, real-life, working waterfront neighborhood is perfect for visitors who want to get some real Baltimore experiences—the sights of boat traffic in the harbor, the sounds of the water lapping against piers and wharves, and the feel of paving stones under your feet.

THE ADMIRAL FELL INN $\text{\textcircled{S}\textcircled{S}}$

888 S. Broadway, 410/522-7377,
www.harbormagic.com/admiralfell/admiral_fell_default.asp
The oldest of the buildings that now constitute the Admiral Fell Inn dates from the late 18th century; such history gives the place a storied feel that the modern upgrades can't obscure. And that's for the best, because this wonderful collection of 80 rooms looks out over the

The Admiral Fell Inn, in the heart of Fell's Point

well-worn stone streets, taverns, and piers of Fell's Point. The decor is early nautical America, with modern touches and improvements. The Water Taxi stops a few yards from the front door, and the shops, pubs, and restaurants of Fell's Point are no more than three blocks away. The only catch? The place is reputed to be haunted by the inn's previous inhabitants, a salty collection of mariners and ne'er-do-wells (there's a ghost tour).

BALTIMORE MARRIOTT WATERFRONT 🌑🌑

700 Aliceanna St., 410/385-3000, www.marriott.com

This 31-story hotel towers over a brand-new mini-neighborhood of new condo towers and office buildings that barely existed five years ago; known as Harbor East, it's tucked between the Inner Harbor and Fell's Point, and every single building here is brand new or still under construction. There are a whopping 733 rooms (and 21 suites) here, making it the second-largest hotel in town. If you're planning on doing a few things at the Inner Harbor and a few in Fell's Point, this might be a good choice, as it's equidistant from both. There are amazing views of the city from the upper floors.

BLUE DOOR ON BALTIMORE 🌑🌑

2020 E. Baltimore St., 410/732-0191, www.bluedoorbaltimore.com

Located a good seven-block walk north of Fell's Point proper in Butcher's Hill, this three-room bed-and-breakfast is worth considering if you're looking for a real Baltimore neighborhood experience. It's a totally rehabbed brick row house (dating from the early 1900s), and the rooms are done in a modest, modern style; all have claw-foot tubs and separate showers, and two have private decks with great views of the water, which lies nine blocks south. Parking in this area can be among the toughest in town, but the owners have some smart tips.

CELIE'S WATERFRONT INN 🌑🌑

1714 Thames St., 410/522-2323 or 800/432-0184, www.celieswaterfront.com

In between the art galleries, bars, restaurants,

GREAT NEIGHBORHOOD STAYS

The views, buzz, and convenience of the big downtown and Inner Harbor hotels are definite enticements. But if you're the kind of traveler who likes to get into the real neighborhoods, where people work and live, consider staying at an inn or hotel in one of Baltimore's storied communities like Fell's Point or Mount Vernon.

On the water (or within a few dozen feet of it) in Fell's Point, there's the looming old warehouse of the **Inn at Henderson's Wharf,** the historic-meets-modern **Admiral Fell Inn** right in the heart of the neighborhood, and **Celie's Waterfront Inn** on Thames Street.

North of Fell's Point, in Butcher's Hill near Patterson Park, is the new **Blue Door on Baltimore.** In nearby Canton, the **Inn at 2920** is a contemporary small hotel hidden within the brick row houses that surround the restaurants and bars of O'Donnell Square. In Mount Vernon, there's the Victorian **4 East Madison Inn,** with its koi-stocked pond. And in Federal Hill, **Scarborough Fair B&B** lets you sample life in the heart of this historic neighborhood, just a short stroll from both the Inner Harbor and Federal Hill Park.

coffeeshops, and other businesses along Thames Street, it's possible to stroll right past the door to this charming little bed-and-breakfast. It's even somewhat hidden behind a tall tree. But inside, there's a warren of brightly painted hallways, rooms, and passageways leading to nine guest rooms. Amenities run from wood-burning fireplaces to whirlpool tubs to private balconies; the common areas of Celie's are furnished with simple, arts-and-crafts-style furniture. The rooms that face Thames Street can get a little loud late on weekend nights, so either request a room in the rear of the building, or stay out late yourself.

The Inn at Henderson's Wharf, on the Fell's Point waterfront

COURTYARD BY MARRIOTT ⑤⑤

1000 Aliceanna St., 443/923-4000, www.marriott.com
Sort of a little sibling to the looming Baltimore Marriott Waterfront that's just two blocks to the west, this smaller Marriott (with only 195 rooms and 10 suites) also features smaller costs, and a similar reduction in amenities. But for basic lodging, this hotel is perfectly fine, and its location is great for walks to Little Italy and Fell's Point, as well as the Inner Harbor. The Harbor East neighborhood has plenty to do, from food to shopping, all within a block or two.

HOMEWOOD SUITES BY HILTON BALTIMORE ⑤⑤

625 S. President St., 410/234-0999,
http://homewoodsuites1.hilton.com
Hilton's brand of all-suite hotels now has a Baltimore outpost, located in the Harbor East neighborhood between the Inner Harbor and Fell's Point. The suites aren't always huge, but they often have separate bedrooms with doors, and all have basically complete kitchens and a generally high level of other amenities. There's plenty to do right outside the door

in the surrounding area, and guests can use the huge, glitzy new Maryland Athletic Club (MAC) gym located in the same building.

◖ THE INN AT HENDERSON'S WHARF ⑤⑤⑤

1000 Fell St., 410/522-7777 or 800/522-2088,
www.hendersonswharf.com/inn
This looming brick building and wharf date back to 1893 and in a way they mark the geographic eastern end of Fell's Point. Today, this huge structure is broken up into condominiums, a conference center, and the inn; there's also a large marina, which gives guests even more to look at from their gorgeous waterfront rooms, decorated with plush, heavy, Colonial-style contemporary furnishings. There's a lovely interior courtyard where guests can have their complimentary breakfasts, and visitors can stroll along the wooden planks of the waterfront promenade into the heart of Fell's Point, close enough to enjoy but far enough to keep the late-night revelers out of your slumber plans. The biggest problem here? With only 38 rooms and a devoted clientele, it's sometimes hard to book a room.

Little Italy Map 2

Though there aren't any hotels or inns actually in Little Italy, there are a couple of options very close by—and some of the hotels in Harbor East, just below Little Italy and west of Fell's Point, are within three blocks of the numerous restaurants and row houses of this historic Italian American neighborhood.

1840S CARROLLTON INN $$

50 Albemarle St., 410/385-1840,
www.1840scarrolltoninn.com

You wouldn't expect to find these historic homes in the shadows of a new office tower and contemporary townhouses—but this part of Baltimore, known as Jonestown, was one of the original settlements incorporated into what became Baltimore Town. This collection of row houses has been turned into an inn; there are 13 rooms ranging from the opulent (like the $395-per-night Annapolis Suite) to the merely very nice (generally ranging $175–250). All are furnished with period antiques or reproductions, and many have fireplaces and whirlpool tubs. There's a large, tree-covered brick patio that backs to President Street, historic Carroll Mansion is next door, and most of the city's popular tourist attractions are within a 10-minute walk.

FAIRFIELD INN & SUITES $$

101 President St., 888/236-2427,
www.marriott.com/fairfield-inn/travel.mi

Baltimore's newest hotel is also the city's greenest; this just-completed (as of spring 2009), 156-room structure aimed for LEED-Silver certification, the first hotel in the city built to attain that high a level of eco-friendliness. The designers helped achieve this by integrating the new construction into the historic row houses and buildings that surround it in the historic Jonestown neighborhood, just a block from Little Italy. Built on the site of the Baltimore Brewing Company and Brewer's Park, the hotel uses some of the materials from that famed business (like bricks, metals, the massive brewing silo, and even the signage); inside, the new construction incorporates basic building materials like wood and brick; amenities include a tavern/restaurant and 26 suites.

PIER 5 HOTEL $$

711 Eastern Ave., 410/539-2000,
www.harbormagic.com/pier5/pier5_default.asp

Keep your eyes peeled for the turn into the Pier 5 driveway from Pratt Street—there's a large sign, but the appearance that you'll be driving on a sidewalk can be tough to override. Part of this independent, modern boutique hotel's charm is that it's off the main thoroughfares and tucked down on the water, surrounded by waterfront walkways. The 66 guestrooms are heavy on purples and golds; the modern, swooping furniture takes some chances without being too risky. There's a Ruth's Chris Steakhouse on premises, but you can also walk to dozens of other restaurants at the harbor and in Little Italy, which is just a few blocks east.

Canton Map 3

There's very little modern about most of Canton; most of the recent improvements are rehabbed brick row houses and taverns, along with repurposed factories and canneries that are now waterfront condos. There aren't a lot of short-term accommodations here, as it's a very residential neighborhood (though it's one with a good variety of dining and nightlife options). If you want to stay relatively far from the bustle of downtown and some of the other neighborhoods, this is a good choice, though you'll be traveling 10–15 minutes for attractions.

© GEOFF BROWN

HOTELS

the modern and cool Inn at 2920 in Canton

☾ INN AT 2920 $$

2920 Elliott St., 410/342-4450 or 877/774-2920,
www.theinnat2920.com

Venture just a block south of bustling, bar-and-restaurant-filled O'Donnell Square and you'll find a regular-looking row house with a white stone corner entrance and a suspiciously contemporary green door; this is the Inn at 2920, a hidden gem of a boutique hotel. The inn's five guest rooms feature lots of exposed brick, sleekly designed (but comfortable) furniture and bedding, and an inviting sitting and common area. There's also free parking, which is a big plus in Canton, which can be a nightmare on Saturday nights. It's probably the coolest little hotel in the entire city, and a great place to blend into Baltimore like a local—one who lives in a fantastic, modern rehabbed row house. It's a short walk to the water, and Fell's Point is a good 15- to 20-minute walk to the west (or a very short, and flat, bike ride away).

Federal Hill
Map 4

Though many people only know the Federal Hill of shops, bars, and Cross Street Market, it's a vibrant neighborhood full of historic homes, devoted residents, and small, tree-lined streets. Real estate in this part of town is so valuable that you won't find many places to stay here—in fact, there's really only one option. This is a great neighborhood to stay in if you're a avid walker, as you can be in the Inner Harbor in five minutes, and even make the long walk to Fort McHenry in about 20 minutes.

SCARBOROUGH FAIR B&B $$$

1 E. Montgomery St., 410/837-0010 or 877/954-2747,
www.scarboroughfairbandb.com

You can sample what living in Federal Hill is like at the Scarborough Fair Bed and Breakfast, located on one of the most historic (and beautiful) streets in the area. The original part of this solid brick home dates from 1801, but later additions have expanded the living and guest spaces tremendously. There are six guest rooms, some of which have private entrances, whirlpool tubs, gas fireplaces, and other high-end touches. There's free off-street parking (which is a *huge* bonus in this area), and guests can use the nearby Federal Hill Fitness center on Cross Street. It's also close enough to the Inner Harbor (about a five-minute stroll) that it's worth considering as your Baltimore base of operations.

Mount Vernon   Map 5

There are a couple of different types of lodging available in this gorgeous neighborhood, which is the city's most architecturally notable area. There are some cultural attractions within walking distance, and the Inner Harbor is a long, downhill walk to the south.

4 EAST MADISON INN 🟡🟡
4 E. Madison St., 410/332-0880,
www.4eastmadisoninn.com
This massive 19th-century home (with a great little patio) is now host to nine guest rooms of varying sizes and opulence (there's an elevator at the rear of the house). Antiques and four-poster beds fill the house, and the wonderful main parlors soothe frazzled travelers with deep-blue walls and ornate fireplaces in brightly lit bays. Taking breakfast in the tree-canopied garden on the east side of the house is a great way to plan a day's adventures, perhaps starting at the Walters Art Museum, which is about two blocks away.

PEABODY COURT BY CLARION 🟡🟡
612 Cathedral St., 410/727-7101 or 800/292-5500,
www.peabodycourthotel.com
Request a corner room (they're some of the largest) with a view of Mount Vernon Place, and you'll have one of the finest views of this European-inspired Baltimore treasure in town. This historic 19th-century building has been a hotel since its construction, and has changed names and brands over the years; a renovation in 2006 upgraded and repaired some of the wear and tear. The marble bathrooms and towel heaters are pleasant surprises, and the room furniture is of an understated Colonial-era design. There are 104 rooms and a restaurant (George's on Mount Vernon Square), and most of all, a great location in the heart of Mount Vernon.

Hampden and Homewood   Map 6

The presence of Johns Hopkins University supports two hotels at very different ends of the economic spectrum. While there's plenty to do (but nowhere to stay) in Hampden, the opposite is true for Homewood, with the notable exception of the amazing Baltimore Museum of Art. Getting to the Inner Harbor by car from this part of town will take about 10 minutes, barring heavy traffic.

HOPKINS INN 🟡🟡
3404 St. Paul St., 410/235-8600,
www.hopkinsinnbaltimore.com
The Hopkins Inn serves as a training hotel for students at the Baltimore International College, a culinary and hospitality school. It's also near a university, and university kids are not the neatest, cleanest people on Earth. If you're willing to overlook some issues that a major hotel

wouldn't allow, it's possible to have a good stay here. There are 26 rooms on five stories—and no elevator. The decor is basic ersatz French, and amenities are slim. But the prices are the cheapest in the zip code, and if you need to stay near Johns Hopkins University, this is your sole bargain option.

INN AT THE COLONNADE $$$

4 W. University Pkwy., 410/235-5400 or
800/222-8733, www.colonnadebaltimore.com

Located across the street from the north end of the Johns Hopkins University campus, this sizeable uptown hotel (run by Doubletree) is a favorite of JHU parents and VIPs for its location and its amenities, like the in-house restaurant, spa, salon, beautiful lobby, valet parking service, and the wonderful pool, which is topped by a huge glass dome. There are 125 guestrooms and suites, filled with modern, stylish beds and other furniture. Parking charges can really add up here, so be aware of the complex parking and valet policies. Some rooms can be on the small side, and occasional hiccups in service occur, but overall this hotel has a solid reputation.

Greater Baltimore   Map 7

If your travels lead you to stay outside the city, you'll probably be in one of two areas: either at BWI Thurgood Marshall Airport or in Baltimore County. It's about a 15- to 20-minute drive to downtown Baltimore City from either destination.

FOUR POINTS BY SHERATON
BWI AIRPORT $$

7032 Elm Rd., 410/859-3300,
www.starwoodhotels.com

There are a lot of options for lodging at BWI, including an entire hotel district a short drive from the terminals; this Four Points, however, is the only hotel that's actually on the airport property itself, which makes it a breeze to get to and from your plane. (The 24-hour shuttle service also helps.) There are 196 rooms, and a perfectly fine restaurant and bar, as well as a nice outdoor pool. If you have to stay by the airport, this is the best and most convenient choice.

RADISSON HOTEL AT
CROSS KEYS $$

5100 Falls Rd., Cross Keys, 410/532-6900 or
888/201-1718, www.radisson.com/baltimoremd

About two miles north of Hampden on Falls Road is Cross Keys, an interesting little gated community of apartments, condominiums, shops, and this hotel. It's incredibly convenient to both Hampden and Homewood, as well as I-83 (which runs right into downtown after a 10-minute drive), but the hotel is in a woodsy, isolated part of the city that doesn't seem like the city at all. The property is a somewhat confusing multi-level collection of floors and small stairs, decorated with unobtrusive, modern furniture and carpet. Rates for most of the 138 rooms are around $150 per night, and there's also a good variety of upscale shopping and a café/bistro here, making Cross Keys a desirable suburban enclave for residents and visitors.

SHERATON BALTIMORE NORTH $

903 Dulaney Valley Rd., 410/321-7400,
www.sheratonbaltimorenorth.com

Towson Town Center, one of the region's largest and most continually expanding malls, rises north of the town of Towson's small downtown shopping area. And just across the street (reachable via a pedestrian walkway) is the Sheraton Baltimore North, a big, brick and concrete, angular structure on the corner, and a fine example of 1980s architecture. This 12-story, 283-room suburban hotel puts visitors within an easy walk of shopping, dining, and Goucher College. If your travels lead you to this part of Baltimore County, this is your best, cheapest lodging bet, as it's also barely a minute to the I-695 Beltway.

HOTELS

EXCURSIONS FROM BALTIMORE

The state of Maryland encompasses some dramatically diverse terrain; to the west are mountains high enough (and snowy enough) to host ski resorts and winter sports. The central part of the state is somewhat hilly and full of suburbs, towns, and the city of Baltimore, but it's also home to farms, fields, and woods that eventually end on the waters of the spectacular Chesapeake Bay. On the other side of the bay, the eastern third of Maryland—the Eastern Shore—is an utterly different (and very flat) country, full of small towns, farms, rivers, marshes, and, eventually, the shores of the Atlantic Ocean and the beach towns that are swamped during the summer (and nearly abandoned over the winter). Though a winter ski trip is a bit much for a quick day trip out of Baltimore (it's three hours to the Wisp Resort in McHenry, Maryland, so it's not impossible), there are still plenty of different places to explore that are less than two hours from the concrete and cobblestones of Charm City.

Head west, and you'll be able to browse warehouses teeming with antiques, dine on local produce prepared by talented chefs, and explore the single bloodiest day of America's Civil War past at Antietam battlefield—all in or near the historic town of Frederick. A short drive south leads to Maryland's stately and gorgeous waterfront capital, Annapolis, which is home to the United States Naval Academy, charming bed-and-breakfasts, and blocks of impressive Colonial-era architecture. Past Annapolis, east across the majestic Chesapeake Bay Bridge, you can explore two distinctly different Eastern Shore towns. Shop for great gifts,

HIGHLIGHTS

LOOK FOR ◖◗ TO FIND RECOMMENDED SIGHTS, ACTIVITIES, DINING, AND LODGING.

◖◗ **Best Campus Tour:** If you think your college's alumni have racked up some impressive achievements, see how they stack up against the deeds of the men and women of the **U.S. Naval Academy.** This sprawling, monumental campus is unlike any other school (page 194).

◖◗ **Best Civil War History Lesson:** It's a placid, quiet place today, full of dense woods, grassy rolling fields, and split-rail fencing, but

© GEOFF BROWN

Antietam National Battlefield

Antietam National Battlefield was the site of the bloodiest day of battle during the U.S. Civil War; some 23,000 troops were killed or wounded (page 199).

◖◗ **Best Antique Shopping:** Bargain and treasure hunters from Baltimore, Washington, D.C., and all over the region descend on the well-preserved and well-stocked old warehouses and **antique shops of Frederick** each weekend (page 202).

◖◗ **Best Preserved Theaters:** If you're in Frederick, check the listings for the **Weinberg Center for the Arts,** built in 1926 (page 201); on the Eastern Shore, Easton's **Avalon Theatre** was built in 1921, and hosts bands, solo artists, and more (page 204).

◖◗ **Best Small-Town Museum:** Working boat-builders, hands-on demonstrations, and living history can be found in the picturesque town of St. Michaels and its **Chesapeake Bay Maritime Museum** (page 208).

◖◗ **Best Way to Experience Life as a Chesapeake Bay Waterman:** Climb aboard the H.M. *Krentz* or the *Rebecca T. Ruark,* two still-working Chesapeake Bay oyster boats (called "skipjacks") that take passengers out on **skipjack tours,** and learn about life as an oysterman (page 208).

EXCURSIONS

dine on crab cakes, and enjoy a concert at the historic Avalon Theatre in charming Easton. Just 15 minutes down the road, you can stay at a world-class resort hotel or tiny B&B, sample haute cuisine, and sail aboard one of two working skipjack sailboat fishing vessels from the waters around romantic, relaxing St. Michaels. Each destination is unique, and offers a completely different experience from the urban hum and buzz of Baltimore.

PLANNING YOUR TIME

If you're going to make any of these trips on the spur of the moment, Annapolis is probably

the smartest bet—it's barely 30 minutes from Baltimore, and the road that leads there (I-97) is almost never congested on weekends. Annapolis is a great city because it's so compact; ditch the car near the visitors center, and you can be strolling the shops of Main Street in about 40 minutes after leaving Fell's Point or Federal Hill. There's plenty to do, see, and eat in Annapolis during a long afternoon, and leaving after dinner won't make you feel like you missed anything.

Traveling to Frederick is a bit more of a commitment, but it rewards those who plan their trip in advance. While there is lots of shopping

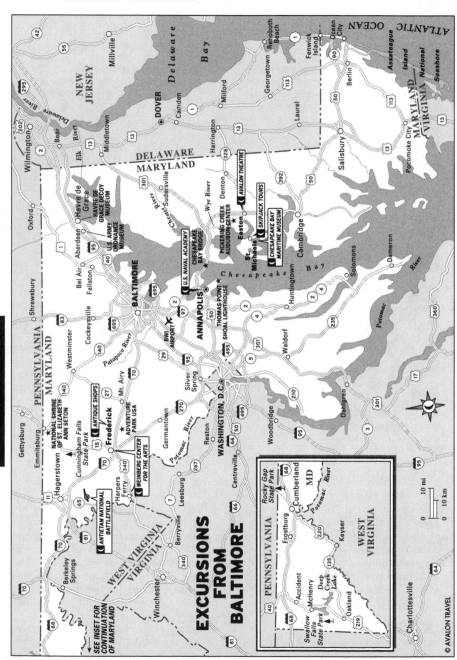

EXCURSIONS FROM BALTIMORE

© AVALON TRAVEL

and eating to be done, visiting the sights will take some forethought, especially if a side trip to Antietam National Battlefield is in order. Some of the other sights near Frederick are a car trip away, so think about what you want to do in town (or outside of it) before you get there.

Though it can be a breeze to get there, the route to Easton and St. Michaels is the most prone to traffic issues, thanks to the Chesapeake Bay Bridge and its propensity to clog up on warm-weather weekends. If you get to the bridge early enough, and there are no accidents, you can make it to Easton in 90 minutes from Baltimore, which is plenty of time to stroll the town's streets and still get in a quick visit to St. Michaels—but the charms of that small waterfront village are so great that many people wish they could spend the night there.

Annapolis

Back in 1649, a group of English Puritan colonial settlers—kicked out of Virginia for being too strident—formed a settlement where the Severn River empties into the Chesapeake Bay. They named their town Providence, and it prospered as a port for the inflow and export of goods, creating affluence and giving rise to stately homes and small estates along the hills surrounding the river—though the source of some of that wealth came from the loathsome trade in slaves. The town was later renamed to honor England's Princess Anne; when she became Queen, she chartered Annapolis as a city, in 1708.

The town grew over the 18th century and managed, somehow, to avoid major modernization and the creep of 1970s urban renewal that wiped out so many historic areas. Today, downtown Annapolis is a strikingly well preserved, Colonial-era waterfront enclave that serves as the state's capital. (Maryland's General Assembly is the longest-serving legislature in the United States; it first met way back in 1634.) The U.S. Naval Academy was built here, on the Severn River; watercraft are measures of wealth and competence for many people in this town, and Annapolis's boating and yachting obsession define this area's cultural landscape. The bustling, jumbled City Dock is home to expensive restaurants, expensive boats, and a see-and-be-seen crowd, but it's still a great place to simply hang out and watch Annapolitan life. The city's location midway between Baltimore and Washington, D.C., makes it a popular day-trip destination for residents of both cities.

SIGHTS
Charles Carroll House
If it seems like there are dozens of houses, roads, documents, and people named for Charles Carroll in Maryland, it's not a coincidence. But they're not necessarily named for the same Charles Carroll. There were at least three prominent Charles Carrolls throughout the state's early history; the Charles Carroll House (107 Duke of Gloucester St., 410/269-1737, www.charlescarrollhouse.com, Jun.–Oct. Sat.–Sun. noon–4 P.M., donation requested) on Spa Creek, belonged to Charles Carroll the settler, whose father came to Maryland to escape persecution as a Catholic (Charles himself would be the only Catholic to sign the Declaration of Independence). The semi-preserved 1670 home now sits behind St. Mary's Church, and is open for limited tours, as the home has been only partially restored. In a way, this makes it even more interesting, and you can see some of the interior structure and age of the house in ways more polished historic homes no longer reveal. Note the original front door, which is now sealed; it's on the second story since the land was re-graded for the construction of the church.

The Kunta Kinte-Alex Haley Memorial
At the bottom of Annapolis's Main Street, along the City Dock lined with expensive yachts and strolling tourists, there's a collection of statues placed in the public walkway. A seated man is

EXCURSIONS

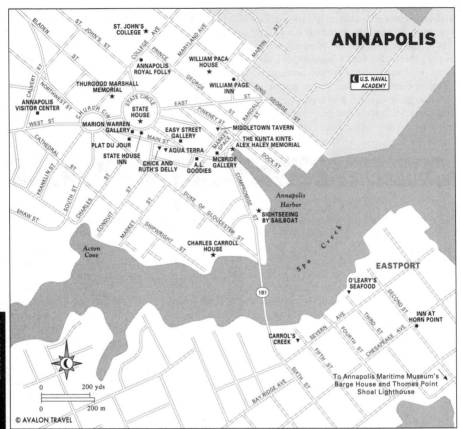

ANNAPOLIS

© AVALON TRAVEL

reading to three young children, who listen intently to him. The man is Alex Haley, the author of the groundbreaking 1976 book *Roots,* which (as both a book and a heavily watched 1977 TV series) did more to advance America's examination of the slavery era, and the repercussions of that time, than any other work in the past century. Kunta Kinte, Haley's direct ancestor, arrived in America as a slave on these very docks; this is the only memorial in the United States that acknowledges the name and place of arrival of an African slave. The memorial scene depicts Haley's explanation to the children of his past and ancestors, as well as the story of Annapolis's place as a center for slave trade in the 18th century.

Maryland State House

Construction on the original section of this historic building began in 1772, but wasn't finished until 1779, owing to a little interruption known as the Revolutionary War. Today, the Maryland State House (91 State Cir., 410/974-3400, www.msa.md.gov/msa/homepage/html/statehse.html, Mon.–Fri. 9 A.M.–5 P.M., Sat.–Sun. 10 A.M.–4 P.M., free admission) is the oldest state capitol building still in use by a state legislature (a lengthy renovation and upgrade was completed in January 2009). The original section, built of wood and plaster, was joined by a more modern (and upgraded) section in the early 20th century, and features Tiffany skylights and Italian marble columns. The Old Senate Chamber is where General George Washington resigned his commission to the Continental Congress; paintings of Maryland politicians line the walls (including portraits of all four Maryland signatories of the Declaration of Independence), along with period furniture, ship models, and other artifacts from the state's history. Maryland's legislature is the longest continuously meeting legislative body in the United States; the first session was in 1634. Guided tours, which last about an hour, begin at the State House Visitors Center, and are given daily at 11 A.M. and 3 P.M.

Sightseeing by Sailboat

When the weather is good and skies are clear but breezy, reserve a trip on one of the various watercraft that provide guided tours of Annapolis and the surrounding area. To keep things as authentic as possible, given Annapolis's Colonial-era history, climb aboard a sailing vessel. The *Woodwind* (Pusser's Landing at the Marriott Waterfront, 80 Compromise St., 410/263-7837, www.schooner woodwind.com, two-hour weekend sail admission $37 adult, $22 child, $35 senior)— and her identical sister, the *Woodwind II*—is a two-masted 74-footer that can take 48 guests. There's also a two-hour Sunday champagne brunch cruise.

Another Sunday brunch sail is offered by the *Liberté* (222 Severn Ave., Eastport, 410/263-8234, www.theliberte.com, $30 per person), a three-masted, 74-foot schooner that can accommodate about 49 people. These voyages last a couple of hours, and some offer food as well as a brilliant day on the water (literally, brilliant: don't forget sunglasses and sunscreen!).

St. John's College

In addition to the U.S. Naval Academy, the other unique bastion of higher education in Annapolis is this tiny school, founded in 1696, the curriculum of which is based solely on the so-called "Great Books" of history (and there's

no religious affiliation, despite the name). There are no textbooks here; instruction comes solely from the source material, no matter the subject. Freshmen start with the ancient Greeks; seniors study more contemporary works. It's not for everyone, obviously, but St. John's College (60 College Ave., 410/263-2371, www.stjohns college.edu, self-guided tours during daylight hours) has a reputation for turning out some very interesting young minds. The gorgeous campus doesn't hurt, either; lots of brick Georgian halls (McDowell Hall is the grandest) and dormitories, connected by tree-lined paths and grassy lawns. If you happen to be in Annapolis in April, see if you can catch the annual St. John's vs. the U.S. Naval Academy croquet tournament—this peculiar yearly match-up began in 1982 and is now a popular, quirky Annapolis tradition.

Thomas Point Shoal Lighthouse

If you're feeling frisky for a little summertime weekend adventure (and are relatively agile), you can take a boat ride out to a screwpile-type lighthouse like the one that now resides in Baltimore's Inner Harbor. The Thomas Point Shoal Lighthouse (tours meet at the Annapolis Maritime Museum's Barge House, 723 Second St., Eastport, 800/690-5080, www.thomas pointlighthouse.org) is about a half-hour boat ride from Eastport in the center of the Chesapeake Bay; once you arrive, you'll disembark, ascend a ladder, and climb into the lighthouse through a small hatch. A docent takes guests around the lighthouse, explaining the role of these screwpile structures, and how the U.S. Coast Guard is restoring this particular lighthouse. This tour (around $70) can be scratched if the weather or waves are foul; make reservations early, as only 18 passengers are allowed per boat trip.

Thurgood Marshall Memorial

The first African American to ascend to the Supreme Court of the United States, Baltimore native Thurgood Marshall was honored in 1994 (a year after his death) by the state of Maryland with this monument and statue, located outside the northwest side of the Maryland State

EXCURSIONS

House, on the Lawyers' Mall (College Ave. and Bladen St.). It's the spot where, in 1935, the Maryland Court of Appeals stood—and where Marshall (then a young lawyer) argued the *University v. Murray* case, which eventually helped end higher education segregation in Maryland state universities. Today, a life-size statue of Marshall stands before two pillars, one marked "Equal Justice," the other "Under Law." There are three other statues here: one is of Donald Murray, the plaintiff in that 1935 case; the other two are of children, symbolizing Marshall's work in 1954's *Brown v. Board of Education,* which desegregated America's public schools. There's also a timeline of important moments from Marshall's illustrious career.

(U.S. Naval Academy

As you stroll along Annapolis's 250-year-old brick sidewalks, you may notice hundreds of immaculately attired and groomed young men and women in blindingly white uniforms. These are some of the United States Naval Academy's 4,400-strong brigade of midshipmen, all of whom will become ensigns in the U.S. Navy (or second lieutenants in the Marine Corps) upon graduation. The Naval Academy is basically the U.S. Navy's university, much like West Point is the U.S. Army's, and it's a massive leviathan (some 340 acres) of imposing marble buildings and monuments that looms to the northwest of the tidy streets and yacht-filled piers of Annapolis. Security at the Academy is rigorous; armed military guards are a noticeable and constant presence, and getting in for a tour requires a valid photo I.D. Begin your exploration at the **Armel-Leftwich Visitor Center** (52 King George St., 410/293-8687, www.usna .edu/nafprodv/vc, Mon.–Sat. 9:30 A.M.–3 P.M., Sun. 12:30–3 P.M., reduced winter hours, admission $8.50 adult, $6.50 child, $7.50 senior) where you'll learn about the exploits of Academy graduates past (like the legendary John Paul Jones) and contemporary (like astronaut Alan Shepard). The walking tour, which takes an hour and 15 minutes, takes visitors through the Academy's well-kept grounds and buildings, including massive Bancroft Hall, the

the historic William Paca House and gardens in Annapolis

world's largest dormitory—which has its own Memorial Hall, where the names of all Academy graduates who have been killed in action are listed. Time your tour around noon to see the brigade march into formation and inspection; the precision and presence of the marchers is an amazing sight. And though it's not part of the main tour, stop by the **U.S. Naval Academy Museum** (118 Maryland Ave., 410/293-2108, www.nadn.navy.mil/Museum, Mon.–Sat. 9 A.M.–5 P.M., Sun. 11 A.M.–5 P.M., free admission), which has a great collection of artifacts, uniforms, fantastically detailed model ships, and maritime maps, prints, and paintings.

William Paca House

Of all the well-preserved 18th-century architecture in Annapolis, one of the most astounding buildings is the William Paca House (186 Prince George St., 410/267-7619, Mon.–Sat. 10 A.M.–5 P.M., Sun. noon–5 P.M., shorter winter hours, guided tours every hour, admission $8 adult, $5 child, $7 senior), even though it's not as untouched as it first appears. Paca (pronounced "Pay-ka") designed and supervised construction of this house himself; completed in 1765, the home has a couple of odd architectural features, owing to Paca's training as a lawyer, not an architect. A Maryland legislator during the Revolution, in 1776, he signed the Declaration of Independence; he later served as governor of Maryland. The abundance of Paca Blue (a sort of a dark robin's egg color) throughout the second floor of the house indicates the family's wealth. The rear gardens are impressive not only in their size and scale, but also because they have been returned to their Colonial-era splendor; for most of the 20th century, they were covered by a hotel that had been built on the site. That building (which included the Paca home) was to be leveled in 1965, but instead, Annapolis's preservationists acquired the property, removed the hotel only, and restored the gardens and Paca's house.

RESTAURANTS

Annapolis is Maryland's capital city; as such, a steady stream of politicians, lobbyists, and powerful citizens from across the state and the nation (not to mention visiting boaters) frequently stroll its charming streets in search of outstanding wining and dining options. There are plenty of more accessible options as well, and the quality of eateries here is generally superb; lifelong residents and VIP visitors just don't abide second-rate.

A new(ish) restaurant that secures a prime location on Main Street better be ready to impress, and **Aqua Terra** (164 Main St., 410/263-1985, www.aquaterraofannapolis.com, lunch Tues.–Fri. 11:30 A.M.–2:30 P.M., Sat.–Sun. 11:30 A.M.–5:30 P.M., dinner Sun.–Mon. 5:30–9 P.M., Tues.–Thurs. 5:30–10 P.M., Fri.–Sat. 5:30–11 P.M.) does just that. The intriguing American-Asian menu (like a mix of shrimp, filet medallions, and pheasant and cognac sausage) is generally inspired, and is served in a modern, open space. For waterfront options, head across the Sixth Street drawbridge to Eastport, and the creekside dining at █ **Carrol's Creek Café** (410 Severn Ave., 410/263-8102, www.carrolscreek.com, Mon.–Sat. 11:30 A.M.–4 P.M. and 5–10 P.M., Sun. 10:30 A.M.–1:30 P.M. and 3–9 P.M. and **O'Leary's Seafood** (310 3rd St., 410/263-0884, www.olearysseafood.com, Mon.–Sat. 5–11 P.M., Sun. 5–10 P.M.), where you'll be able to indulge your seafood cravings. (O'Leary's is the more upscale of the two).

Not in the mood for anything fancy? The venerable **Chick & Ruth's Delly** (165 Main St., 410/269-6737, www.chickandruths.com, Sun.–Thurs. 6:30 A.M.–11:30 P.M., Fri.–Sat. 6:30 A.M.–12:30 A.M.), is a city institution, where everyone from the governor to the groundskeepers eat. The interior is a riot of color and classic diner furniture, all reds and yellows, with a variety of deli sandwiches (it's a kosher-style restaurant) named for famous local and international figures, heroes, and characters. You'll see midshipmen, yacht owners, state senators, senior citizens, landscapers, and tourists all happily jostling through this Annapolis stalwart.

Another venerable establishment is the upscale **Middleton Tavern** (2 Market Space, 410/263-3323, www.middletontavern.com,

Mon.–Fri. 11:30 A.M.–1:30 A.M., Sat.–Sun. 10 A.M.–1:30 A.M.), located just off the City Dock. This bar and restaurant has hosted not only George Washington, but also Thomas Jefferson and Benjamin Franklin. The bar here is now best known for its oyster shooter: an oyster with cocktail sauce served in a shot glass, then chased with a beer. It's a tradition around these parts, but avoid it if you think you're not up to it—a reversal is not a pleasant experience.

SHOPS

Annapolis is a popular tourist destination, so the shopping here is geared toward the weekend visitor; arts, crafts, jewelry, and souvenirs are big staples here. If you want to just window-shop, take a slow stroll up Main Street. For those who need a large haul of souvenirs, there's no better store than **A.L. Goodies** (112 Main St., 410/269-0071, www.algoodies .com, Sun.–Thurs. 9 A.M.–10 P.M., Fri.–Sat. 9 A.M.–midnight), which has just about every Annapolis-, Maryland-, and Navy-themed item ever made. A variety of hand-blown and handcrafted glass artworks from modern artists delight shoppers at **Easy Street Gallery** (8 Francis St., 410/263-5556, www.easystreet gallery.com, open daily 10 A.M., closing hours vary seasonally). Old World crafts shine at **Plat du Jour** (220 Main St., 410/269-1499, www .platdujour.net, Mon.–Sat. 10 A.M.–6 P.M., Sun. 11 A.M.–6 P.M.), where French and Italian pottery and linens and other antiques make for tempting mementos. Large-format prints of Annapolis boating scenes, Maryland life, Baltimore, and other images from the 1940s, '50s, '60s, and '70s can be found at the **Marion Warren Gallery** (14 State Cir., 410/280-1414, www.marionwarren.com, Mon.–Wed. by appointment only, Thurs.–Fri. 2–6 P.M., Sat. 10 A.M.–6 P.M., Sun. 10 A.M.–5 P.M.). The largest art gallery in downtown Annapolis, featuring lots of nautically themed works by local artists, is the **McBride Gallery** (15 Main St., 410/267-7077, www.mcbridegallery.com, Mon.–Wed. and Fri.–Sat. 10 A.M.–5:30 P.M., Thurs. 10 A.M.–9 P.M., Sun. noon–5:30 P.M.).

HOTELS

The romantic character of Annapolis has long made it a favorite for Baltimoreans and Washingtonians looking for a nearby overnight getaway. There are many options for lodging, including many enticing bed-and-breakfasts and small hotels found in well-preserved old buildings. The only downside to Annapolis's charm and popularity is that prices are rather high; expect to spend anywhere from $160 for a weekday night to $280 and beyond for a weekend night. On the plus side, competition is hot, so expect to get a very nice weekend breakfast included in your room rate and hosts who are really working to earn your business.

It's hard to beat the location of the **(State House Inn** (25 State Cir., 410/990-0024, www .statehouseinn.com, $129–179), a large home built in 1786 that now has eight guest rooms furnished in period (or period-ish) furniture— several of which have whirlpool tubs. There's a nice big front porch on the State Circle side of this big yellow building, and while the hotel backs onto busy Main Street, inside it's quite quiet. Don't expect sparkling, immaculate conditions, but rather a lived-in, realistic inn that's more like a large B&B.

Just across the street from St. John's College is **Annapolis Royal Folly** (65 College Ave., 410/263-3999, www.royalfolly.com, $195–395). This large, slate blue 1870s-era home is adorned with extras like skylights, chandeliers, and a huge dining room. There are five guest rooms (out of 14 in the whole home), most of which offer serious extras (one has a private porch with outdoor hot tub; another occupies the entire third floor). The views of St. John's are so good that they should charge extra, though they don't; like most of the inns and B&Bs in Annapolis, you'll find your room is within a few blocks of the city's main attractions.

A few blocks east of State Circle, just outside the walls of the U.S. Naval Academy, rises the distinctive, cedar-shake **William Page Inn** (8 Martin St., 410/626-1506 or 800/364-4160, www.williampageinn.com, $190–295). This 1908 home has been restored with care and is now host to five guest rooms, ranging from the sprawling third-floor Marilyn Suite to the cozy Wilbur Room. Lots of period antiques fill the home and rooms, and the wrap-around porch makes for a great place to people-watch and relax.

If you'd like to get away from the (relative) bustle of downtown Annapolis, head across Spa Creek to Eastport and the picture-perfect **Inn at Horn Point** (100 Chesapeake Ave., Eastport, www.innathornpoint.com, $149–269). The Sequoia room offers the most amenities (like a gas fireplace and private balcony). The water taxi stops just three blocks from the inn, and conveys guests to Annapolis's City Dock; on foot, it's a 15-minute walk through the neighborhood and across the Spa Creek drawbridge.

INFORMATION
Visitors Center
The main Annapolis Visitors Center is located near a large public parking garage; take a parking spot here and walk down into the main part of town, as parking and traffic downtown is immensely difficult, especially during spring and summer. This main visitors center is at 26 West Street; it's open daily 9 A.M.–5 P.M. There's a smaller visitors information booth right at City Dock that's open 9 A.M.–5 P.M. daily from April to early October, with limited hours on weekends through November. The main center has lots of information, pamphlets, and brochures, as well as plenty of helpful guides and volunteers to assist you in planning your time in Annapolis. The

---

TERRIBLE TANKS AND DUCK DECOYS: TWO UNIQUE MUSEUMS

Head up I-95 from Baltimore about 45 minutes, and you'll find two very different but very intriguing museums.

The town of Aberdeen is the childhood home of Baltimore Oriole legend and Hall of Famer Cal Ripken, Jr. But even before Cal, Aberdeen made a name for itself for another reason: the Aberdeen Proving Ground (APG), one of the armed forces' playgrounds of weapons and explosives. APG was a place where the United States Army developed new technologies and firepower for use against America's foes. As the area around APG began to become more densely populated, some of the larger weapons testing was halted, though the sound of explosions is still common in the area. But APG also became a storehouse for the pistols, rifles, tanks, and other peculiar weaponry that the Army captured or confiscated during its history. Vast fields of famous and infamous tanks and artillery line the grounds of APG now, some of it rusting in place; thus was born the **U.S. Army Ordnance Museum** (2601 Aberdeen Blvd., Aberdeen Proving Ground, 410/278-3602, www.ordmusfound.org, daily 9 A.M.-4:45 P.M., free admission, donations re-

quested). You can check out gigantic Nazi railway cannon that could shoot across countries, fearsome Soviet tanks, and a wide assortment of small arms, as well as learn about how weapons are developed to maximize their destructive power. You'll need to enter APG to visit the museum and show the guards a valid ID.

A little farther up the road, in Havre de Grace, is a much less violent museum – though not a totally peaceful one. The **Havre de Grace Decoy Museum** (215 Giles St., Havre de Grace, 410/939-3739, www.decoymuseum.com, Mon.-Sat. 10:30 A.M.-4:30 P.M., Sun. noon-4 P.M., admission $6 adult, $2 child, $5 senior) is dedicated to the art and craftsmanship that goes into the creation of lifelike duck and other waterfowl decoys. Many of the decoys on display here are almost a century old, and the detail and attention that went into these figures is truly remarkable. More modern masters are also recognized here, and there are small displays that include boats and duck blinds. It's a wonderfully quirky museum that takes its celebration of the decoy – used to lure ducks and other waterfowl into the range of hunters' weapons – very seriously.

information booth has the same resources, just on a much smaller scale.

Media

The *Capital* is Annapolis's sole daily newspaper, and covers local issues and the various communities that surround the city. Annapolitans also read either the *Baltimore Sun* or the *Washington Post,* and sometimes both, depending on their needs and interests. The same split is true for television, as Annapolis can get stations from both Baltimore and D.C. On the radio, Annapolis has only a few indigenous stations, including **WNAV 1430 AM** (talk) and **WRNR 103.1 FM** (modern rock).

GETTING THERE AND AROUND
Getting There

Annapolis is 30 miles south of Baltimore. By car, the best route to take is to get to I-97, a relatively new road built expressly to connect Baltimore and Annapolis; from there, it's easy to reach Route 50/Route 301 (head east), and then turn right on Rowe Boulevard; go straight for a little over a mile, then bear right as you enter Annapolis. It takes about 35 minutes by car or bus—and **Greyhound**

(www.greyhound.com) does travel from downtown Baltimore (2110 Haines St., 410/752-7682) to Annapolis, though the Annapolis bus terminal is about two miles from the historic downtown, and you will need to secure a taxi to get there. There is no rail service.

Getting Around

Once you're in Annapolis, everything is reachable by foot, which is the best way to explore and enjoy this historic city. Most attractions are about a five-minute walk apart, though repeated trips up Main Street—which is a bit of a hill—could prove tiring to some people. The city operates a free (for downtown use) shuttle bus service; Annapolis Transit runs two lines (Navy Blue and State Shuttle, 410/263-7964, www.annapolis.gov/info.asp?page=7615) during daylight hours; the lines cover most of the historic area and also head up to the U.S. Navy-Marine Corps Memorial Stadium north of the city. There are sightseeing carriages for hire (rates run $20–80 for a 25-minute tour), and you can catch a taxi pretty easily around City Dock. The walk from downtown Annapolis across Spa Creek into Eastport takes about 10–15 minutes—longer if the drawbridge is up.

Frederick

Founded as a major trading outpost in Colonial America in 1745, Frederick was first settled by German immigrants, who were followed a century later by Irish men and women who'd come to make their fortunes in boom-time America. The town—which acts as a gateway to western Maryland and points beyond—was built at the intersection of trading and transport routes that headed to the fledgling nation's settlements and farms, and was a strategic town during both the Revolution (Francis Scott Key, who wrote "The Star-Spangled Banner" in Baltimore, called Frederick home) and the Civil War. Today, it's a popular small-town destination for residents of both Baltimore and nearby Washington,

D.C., to visit, eat, and shop (and, sometimes, even relocate). Frederick's charming downtown boutiques and abundance of antiques shops, as well as nearby historic attractions like the Civil War battlefield of Antietam, give visitors plenty of options. Though the surrounding countryside is being developed into suburban housing, downtown Frederick has maintained its great historic buildings and small-town culture.

SIGHTS
Adventure Park USA

On the way to Frederick, heading west on I-70, you might notice a modest roller coaster and a few wooden rooftops off to your left. This is

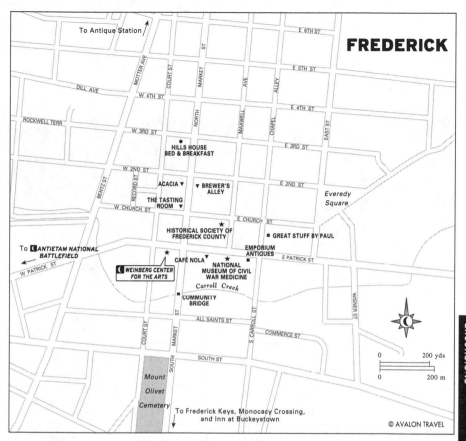

FREDERICK

To Antique Station

E 6TH ST

MOTTER AVE

COURT ST

MARKET ST

DILL AVE

W 4TH ST

E 5TH ST

AVE

ALLEY

E 4TH ST

ROCKWELL TERR

W 3RD ST

NORTH

MAXWELL

CHAPEL

EAST ST

HILLS HOUSE
BED & BREAKFAST

E 3RD ST

W 2ND ST

RECORD ST

BENTZ ST

ACACIA ▼

▼ BREWER'S
ALLEY

E 2ND ST

Everedy
Square

THE TASTING
ROOM ▼

W CHURCH ST

E CHURCH ST

HISTORICAL SOCIETY OF
FREDERICK COUNTY

★

■ GREAT STUFF BY PAUL

To ◖ANTIETAM NATIONAL
BATTLEFIELD

CAFÉ NOLA ▼

★

EMPORIUM
ANTIQUES

E PATRICK ST

W PATRICK ST

★

NATIONAL
MUSEUM OF CIVIL
WAR MEDICINE

◖WEINBERG CENTER
FOR THE ARTS

Carroll Creek

WISNER ST

■ COMMUNITY
BRIDGE

ALL SAINTS ST

COURT ST

MARKET ST

S CARROLL ST

COMMERCE ST

SOUTH ST

SOUTH ST

0   200 yds

Mount
Olivet
Cemetery

SOUTH

0   200 m

To Frederick Keys, Monocacy Crossing,
and Inn at Buckeystown

© AVALON TRAVEL

EXCURSIONS

Adventure Park USA (11113 W. Baldwin Rd, New Market, 301/865-6800, www.adventure parkusa.com, Sun.–Thurs. 10 A.M.–10 P.M., Fri.–Sat. 6:30 A.M.–12:30 A.M., reduced winter hours, admission $24.95 for a four-hour unlimited pass), a small but serviceable Wild West–themed amusement park that opened in 2005. Disneyland it's not, but it doesn't try to be—instead, it focuses on doing small well. There's the Wildcat Roller Coaster, the Horseless Carriage Go Karts, the West World Laser Tag…you get the idea. There's also miniature golf, paintball, an arcade, a rock wall for climbing, and the usual array of eats and souvenirs. Crowds aren't a huge concern at this park, so consider taking a nighttime roller-coaster ride and getting some ice cream to liven up the short trip back to Baltimore.

◖ Antietam National Battlefield

While most Americans have heard of Gettysburg—the Pennsylvania town that, in 1863, was the sight of the most costly battle of the U.S. Civil War, and the turning point of the conflict—not everyone has heard of Antietam National Battlefield (5831 Dunker Church Road, Sharpsburg, 301/432-5124, www.nps .gov/anti, Oct.–early May 8:30 A.M.–5 P.M., May 8:30 A.M.–6 P.M., Jun.–Sept. 8:00 A.M.–7 P.M., Sept.–Oct. 8:30 A.M.–6 P.M., admission $4 per person, $6 per family). Yet Antietam was just as important a battle, and one that changed the

EXCURSIONS

© GEOFF BROWN

Antietam National Battlefield, outside Frederick

character of the war. Just west of Frederick, near the town of Sharpsburg, the forces of Union General George McClellan and Confederate General Robert E. Lee collided as the Union troops attempted to keep Lee from further invading Union territory north of Washington, D.C. On the morning of September 17, 1862, nearly 100,000 troops engaged in battle across the rolling farmlands and woods of this part of the state. Twelve hours later, the carnage ended, and some 23,000 Americans were dead, wounded, or missing. It was the single bloodiest day of the Civil War; a day later, Lee's troops withdrew to Virginia. Many of the surrounding towns were turned into makeshift hospitals, aid stations, and morgues; recent improvements in medicine and surgical procedures probably saved countless lives (details on this aspect of the battle can be gleaned at the National Museum of Civil War Medicine in Frederick).

Begin your tour at the visitors center, located roughly in the center of the battlefield (which is spread out over some four miles of countryside). At the center you can watch two compelling films that set the scene for the brutal combat that took place here, and view

photos taken by some of the earliest war photographers—some of which show dead soldiers splayed across the same, now calm and green landscapes you'll be able to traverse. The tour is self-guided, and done via automobile, bicycle, or on foot, but you can get a park ranger to ride along with you for a more in-depth explanation of the battle and its repercussions. The tour is lined with picket fences of the types built by the battle's soldiers, as well as cannon and numerous monuments built to honor the soldiers of the various states who sent their young men here to fight for their respective countries.

Frederick Keys

As befits a small, picturesque American town like Frederick, the small, newly refurbished Harry Grove Stadium (capacity: 5,400) that rises near I-70 is home to the minor-league Frederick Keys (21 Stadium Dr., 301/662-0013, www.frederickkeys.com), a Class A affiliate of the major league Baltimore Orioles. This is the lowest level of professional baseball, so the action on the field can be a little less than stellar, but the atmosphere is very family-friendly, as are the prices (tickets top out at $11). There's a

Fun Zone for kids to run around and burn off steam, cheap hot dogs and beer, and post-game fireworks events throughout the year. Spending a night—and not a fortune—at a Keys game is a great way to cap off a day in historic Frederick.

Historical Society of Frederick County

A grand 1820 home built by a local physician is now home to the Historical Society of Frederick County (24 E. Church St., 301/663-1188, www.hsfcinfo.org, guided tours Mon.–Sat. 10 A.M.–4 P.M., Sun. 1–4 P.M., admission $3 adults, children free), which can provide a good backdrop for the history of the people and culture of the area after its settlement by German immigrants in the mid-1700s. A semi-permanent exhibit on those Teutonic settlers shows the customs and crafts they brought with them to the New World. The home is set up to reflect the various purposes it served over the past 180 years, from private home to orphanage, and there's a fine collection of tall case clocks (a specialty of Frederick's craftsmen). A back room is designed for kids to learn about the town and its history, and there's also a historical archives in the basement. There's a medium-sized garden out back that's worth a stroll, and the well-stocked gift and bookstore has a plethora of local history tomes and maps.

National Museum of Civil War Medicine

What started as one man's personal collection of Civil War–era medical ephemera and artifacts is now the National Museum of Civil War Medicine (48 E. Patrick St., 301/695-1864, www.civilwarmed.org, Mon.–Sat. 10 A.M.–5 P.M., Sun. 11 A.M.–5 P.M., admission $6.50 adults, $4.50 child, $6 senior). The museum demonstrates how, despite archaic medical techniques and education, dedicated physicians and surgeons managed to save thousands of soldiers' lives—but often at the cost of a limb. Disease was the biggest killer, causing nearly two-thirds of the war's deaths. Though most of the museum is fine for visitors of all ages, there are a few disturbing images

that could upset young kids. But the exhibits are often fascinating and provide an intriguing look into 19th-century medicine.

National Shrine of St. Elizabeth Ann Seton

Half an hour north of Frederick is the small town of Emmitsburg, which is the final resting place of Elizabeth Ann Seton, the first native-born American to be canonized as a saint. Born in New York City, this Episcopal woman of means converted to Catholicism in 1804 after a series of financial setbacks and the death of her husband. She moved to Emmitsburg in 1809, and spent the rest of her life guiding the Sisters of Charity of St. Joseph's sisterhood, which opened schools, operated orphanages, and worked with the sick and infirmed. She died in 1821; in 1975, Pope Paul VI canonized her, and today, a basilica at this shrine holds her tomb, as well as an altar of relics. The National Shrine of St. Elizabeth Ann Seton (333 S. Seton Ave., Emmitsburg, 301/447-6606, www.setonshrine.org, Tues.–Sun. 10 A.M.–4:30 P.M., Mon. basilica only 10 A.M.–4:30 P.M., free admission but donations requested) includes several buildings inhabited by or watched over by Mother Seton, as she was known during her life. At the visitors center, you'll be able to watch a short video about Mother Seton's life and work, as well as view some artifacts. She lived in two buildings on the site: the Stone House, in which she resided with some 15 other people; and the White House, where she held classes and sermons.

◖ Weinberg Center for the Arts

The Tivoli theater—complete with crystal chandeliers, marble, and silk wall coverings—opened in downtown Frederick in 1926 to host films, plays, musicals, and other artistic endeavors. Though the building fell into serious disrepair by the 1960s (and that was before the flood of 1976), local businesspeople and activists restored the theater and reopened it in 1978 as the area's finest performance venue. That year, the building was renamed for Frederick residents Dan and Alyce Weinberg, who bought the place in 1959 and helped spur its renovation. The theater's pride and joy is the original 1926 Wurlitzer organ, which is still played today. Shows at the Weinberg Center for the Arts (20 W. Patrick St., 301/600-2828, www.weinbergcenter .org) now include small symphonic works, classic old movies, dance, country artists, humorists, authors, and kids' stage shows. Check the Weinberg Center's schedule to see what's on stage during your visit.

RESTAURANTS

Downtown Frederick's popularity with urbanities from Baltimore and Washington, D.C., has helped it support a broad range of good restaurants, some of which use local produce from the surrounding farms of Frederick County whenever possible. At the luxury end of the culinary world, **The Tasting Room** (101 N. Market St., 240/379-7772, www.tastetr.com, Mon.–Sat. 11 A.M.–3 P.M.and 5 P.M.–close) is a modern, sleek restaurant and wine bar in a great people-watching location right in the heart of historic Frederick; offerings include foie gras, sushi-grade tuna, and lobster-whipped potatoes. Also in downtown Frederick is **Acacia** (129 N. Market St., 301/694-3015, www.acacia129.com, Tues.–Thurs. and Sun. 11:30 A.M.–10 P.M., Fri.–Sat. 11:30 A.M.–11:30 P.M.), a warm, un-fussy bistro that offers Asian-inspired dishes and plenty of fish and poultry options. **Brewer's Alley** (124 N. Market St., 301/631-0089, www.brewers-alley .com, Mon.–Thurs. 11:30 A.M.–9 P.M., Fri.–Sat. 11:30 A.M.–10:30 P.M., Sun. noon–9 P.M.) is a popular brewpub with an ambitious menu ideal for pairing with some of the establishment's year-round and seasonal beers. For a lighter meal, try **Café Nola** (4 E. Patrick St., 301/694-6652, www.cafe-nola.com, daily 7 A.M.–10 P.M.), where fresh-made salads and sandwiches can help sustain weary tourists (and antique hunters).

Just outside of town is **Monocacy Crossing** (4424 Urbana Pike A, 301/846-4204, www .monocacycrossing.com, Tues.–Thurs. 11:30 A.M.–9 P.M., Fri. 11:30 A.M.–10 P.M., Sat. 3–10 P.M., Sun. noon–8 P.M.), a hidden, homey local favorite with an emphasis on substantial dinners (such as beef medallions in bacon and lamb shank) and a small outdoor dining area.

ANTIQUE SHOPS

Frederick's history as a crossroads in early America means that the town was always awash in goods from across the region, so it's only natural that today, Frederick is one of the area's top stops for antique shoppers. Stores range in size from small shops along the main drags to huge multi-dealer warehouses on the outskirts. **Emporium Antiques** (112 E. Patrick St., 301/662-7099, www.emporiumantiques.com, Mon.–Sat. 10 A.M.–6 P.M., Sun. noon–6 P.M.) is the largest in downtown, and combines the lots of more than 100 dealers in a 55,000-square-foot complex of buildings offering everything from grand French furniture to pop culture bric-a-brac. North of downtown, **Antique Station** (194 Thomas Johnson Dr., 301/695-0888, www.pages.frederick.com/antiques/antique station.htm, Mon.–Fri. 10 A.M.–5 P.M., Sat. 10 A.M.–6 P.M., Sun. noon–6 P.M.) offers wares from some 200 dealers in a modern building. **Great Stuff by Paul** (www.greatstuff bypaul.com) has two locations, a sprawling old warehouse downtown (10 N. Carroll St., 301/631-0004, Mon.–Sat. 10 A.M.–6 P.M., Sun. 11 A.M.–5 P.M.) and a 52,000-square-foot behemoth store just north of historic area (257 E. 6th St., 301/631-5340, Mon.–Sat. 10 A.M.–6 P.M., Sun. 11 A.M.–5 P.M.). And if Frederick can't satiate your shopping needs, nearby New Market (east of Frederick) is known as the "Antiques Capital of Maryland."

HOTELS

The historic charms of Frederick can be pretty alluring, so if you decide to spend the night, there are two great options in town. If you want to pass the weekend strolling the streets, your best bet is **Hill House Bed & Breakfast** (12 W. Third St., 301/682-4111, www.hill housefrederick.com, $125–175), a three-story, four-room historic Victorian townhouse. It's the closest lodging to downtown's shopping and dining, but it's just far enough from the main strip to offer a little seclusion. Decorated with period furniture and antiques, two of Hill House's rooms have private balconies, and the Steeple Suite offers great views of the city's church spires (and even has its own kitchen).

Farther south, a short walk away from the relative bustle of downtown Frederick, is **Hollerstown Hill Bed & Breakfast** (4 Clarke Pl., 301/228-3630, www.hollerstownhill.com, $115–125), a large Victorian-era home in a residential neighborhood that offers a sweeping porch, garden and patio, and even a billiards table. The second-floor Cottage Garden Room has a great sleigh bed and a private porch that overlooks the gardens below, as well as the other historic homes of the neighborhood.

Outside of downtown Frederick, there's a wide range of chain motels available, as well as some other options; south of Frederick, in the charming little community of Buckeystown, is the **Inn at Buckeystown** (3521 Buckeystown Pike, Buckeystown, 301/874-5755, www.innatbuckeystown.com, $115–250). Housed in a converted 1897 Victorian-Italianate mansion, this seven-room inn has a good variety of rooms, some with shared baths. Popular rooms include the Serenity Suite, which has its own private porch, and the Victoriana Suite, with huge bay window views and a fireplace. If you're not a fan of Victorian decor, head west from Frederick to Middletown and the **Inn at Stone Manor** (5820 Carroll Boyer Rd., Middletown, 301/371-0099, www.stonemanorcountryclub.com/Bed_and_Breakfast.html, $200). A long, sturdy 18th-century home built of fieldstone, this inn is the most modernized of the region's lodging options, though antiques still abound. The views from all of the rooms of the estate's 100-acres of lawns, gardens, ponds, and trees are exceptional. Most of the rooms have whirlpool tubs, and amenities include fireplaces and private porches.

INFORMATION
Visitors Center
Head straight into historic downtown Frederick and the **Frederick Visitor Center** (19 E. Church St., 301/600-2888, www.fredericktourism.org, daily 9 A.M.–5 P.M.), which serves both the town and the county. There's generally at least two friendly staffers on the weekends to help you plan out your trip to the area, and there's a huge selection of brochures and pamphlets of the region's attractions. Pick up a copy of the *Destination Frederick County* magazine, produced by the tourism council, which has invaluable maps and guides to both the city and the outlying area. If you're not sure how to get your tour started, ask one of the staffers for recommendations.

Media
Frederick has one daily newspaper, the **Frederick News-Post,** that covers the city, county, and surrounding smaller municipalities. There's also the weekly **Frederick County Gazette,** one of a family of Maryland community newspapers. Frederick even has a monthly upscale lifestyle magazine, **Frederick,** which covers living in the area and offers information on events, dining, and shopping.

GETTING THERE AND AROUND
Getting There
Frederick lies nearly 50 miles west of Baltimore; the best means of travel is via car on I-70, a trip that should take about an hour. Be cautious about traveling this route during rush hour on Friday evenings, as traffic backups are common. **Greyhound** (www.greyhound.com) has a bus that runs from Baltimore (2110 Haines St., 410/752-7682) to Frederick's MARC train station (100 S. East St., 301/682-9716), about a half mile from the center of Frederick (note that the MARC train does not connect Baltimore and Frederick; it connects both cities to Washington, D.C., but not to one another).

Antietam National Battlefield is about 30 miles west of Frederick (45 minutes by car), and best reached via I-70; take exit 29 onto Maryland Route 65 and head south to the town of Sharpsburg.

Getting Around
It's possible to spend your entire trip to historic Frederick on foot, wandering through the

town's shops and sights, but brief car trips are necessary to see more of the area's attractions, particularly Antietam National Battlefield to the west. **TransIT** (301/600-2065, www .co.frederick.md.us/index.asp?NID=105), the local public transportation service, runs mostly during the week; service is curtailed on Saturdays, and does not operate on Sundays.

Easton and St. Michaels

Maryland's Eastern Shore is intriguing on many levels. First, it's (mostly) managed to retain its early American feel and character while the rest of the world has moved forward. This is still very agricultural land, occupied by fifth-generation farmers whose ancestors settled here in the 17th century. Even though several major cities are relatively nearby, the isolated geography of the Eastern Shore has kept out a lot of the modern world. Though millions of people pass through these parts on their way to the Atlantic Ocean resort towns of Ocean City, Maryland, and the Delaware beaches each year, very few people stop to do more than eat and fill up their gas tanks. After the construction of the Chesapeake Bay Bridge, some parts of the Eastern Shore gained residents and construction, but not too many people emigrated to this flat, undeveloped countryside.

These factors are probably why this area has become more popular in recent decades for wealthy professionals from Baltimore (and especially Washington, D.C.) looking for a tranquil second home. There's waterfront property everywhere, and numerous creeks and rivers cut gently through the lush, flat lands here. Some of the old mid-shore towns, like Easton and St. Michaels in Talbot County, have become thriving social hubs for life-long residents, tourists, and weekenders.

EASTON
Easton is the larger of the two towns, and lies about 90 minutes from Baltimore. Founded back in 1711, Easton grew around the site of the first Talbot County courthouse; today, it's a full-fledged small town, with plazas and historic homes, lanes, and alleys, and lots of bistros, restaurants, shopping, and taverns. It's also home to one of the Eastern Shore's gems, the restored Avalon Theatre, which really completes the small-town-America picture.

Sights
ACADEMY ART MUSEUM
You wouldn't expect to find a museum like the Academy Art Museum (106 South St., 410/822-2787, www.art-academy.org, Mon.–Sat. 10 A.M.–4 P.M., Wed. 10 A.M.–9 P.M.) in a small, off-the-highway town like Easton, but the collections here will impress any connoisseur. It's not the most regal building—it's an 1820s schoolhouse—but the artworks inside are exceptional. Sculptures, paintings, and photographs from the likes of Ansel Adams, Baltimore's Grace Hartigan, Roy Lichtenstein, and Robert Rauschenberg fill out the galleries. There's also a very solid collection of American and European works on paper (drawings, prints, and etchings, for example).

◖ AVALON THEATRE
A small-town America masterpiece that (thanks to preservationists) escaped demolition, this 1920 theater opened to rave reviews for its construction and design: glass doors, a soaring dome, a pipe organ, and other top-notch touches—which were subsequently removed and replaced with art deco designs and fixtures in the 1930s. After an expensive renovation in 1989, the Avalon Theatre (40 East Dover St., 410/822-7299, www .avalontheatre.com) eventually found its voice and role for the region, hosting performances from all sorts of artists. Rock bands, comedy troupes, duos and trios, classical music, country, soul, Broadway revivals and "hits" shows—all manner of performers take the proscenium stage at this mid-size theater (about 400 seats).

EXCURSIONS

HISTORICAL SOCIETY OF TALBOT COUNTY

Chronicling the changing ways of life of this part of the Eastern Shore, the Historical Society of Talbot County (25 S. Washington St., 410/822-0773, www.hstc.org, Mon.–Sat. 10 A.M.–4 P.M., Sun. 1–4 P.M., free admission) has a small collection of old photos, furniture, quilts, and artifacts from the people who lived here (both whites and African Americans), as well as items from the industries that helped the region prosper, like canneries and saw mills. Frederick Douglass was a Talbot County native, and artifacts from his time in Talbot, both before and after his escape, are on display here. There's a $5 guided tour of historic Easton homes that is offered Tuesday–Saturday and begins at 11 A.M.

PICKERING CREEK AUDUBON CENTER

The Pickering Creek Audubon Center (11450 Audubon Ln., 410/822-4903, www.pickering creek.org, trails open daily dawn–dusk) lies nine miles north of Easton (about 20 minutes by car). The 400-acre nature preserve is home to a wide variety of animals, from white-tailed deer to waterfowl, and covers marshes, fields, forests, and waterfront. Pickering Creek is part of the National Audubon Society, and membership in Audubon and/or Pickering Creek ($25 minimum, for one year) lets you use one of their canoes (available

Mon.–Fri. 9 A.M.–5 P.M., Sat. 10 A.M.–4 P.M.); the hiking trails are open and free to use for everyone. The two-mile Farm to Bay Trail winds through the deep woods to the water, and it's the best way to see some of the abundant fauna that calls this bucolic area home.

Restaurants

You'll find a wide array of dining options here, generally in a less-than-stuffy atmosphere (most people here are on vacation, after all). One of the town's most popular eateries morning, noon, and night is **Mason's** (22 S. Harrison St., 410/822-3204, www.masonsgourmet.com, coffee bar Mon.–Sat. 9 A.M.–5 P.M., lunch Mon.–Sat. 11:30 A.M.–2:30 P.M., dinner Tues.–Sat. 5:30–10 P.M.). It started out as a candy shop but has evolved substantially to include a coffee bar and to serve popular lunches (get soup and a sandwich and head for the porch) and casual, Continental dinners in the deep red dining room.

Opened in early 2008 by Andrew King, the former chef of the now-defunct-but-still-legendary Inn at Easton restaurant, **Thai Ki** (216 E. Dover St., 410/690-3641, www.thai-ki.com, lunch Mon.–Fri. 11:30 A.M.–3 P.M., dinner Mon.–Thurs. 5–9:30 P.M., Fri.–Sat. 5–11 P.M.) focuses on simple, freshly made Thai food like the kinds King ate during his travels through Asia. There's a placid golden Buddha watching over the space, and the simple, inexpensive food has many fans, though given the region's culinary tastes, no red-alert spiciness can be found on the menu.

THE CHESAPEAKE BAY BRIDGE

With the growth of Maryland in the 1930s, the need to move commerce from the agricultural Eastern Shore to the more populous parts of the state, and the desire to travel to Maryland and Delaware's beach resorts, the five-hour drive from Baltimore to the Eastern Shore — which wound around the bay — became too much to bear. Some residents and businessmen of the Eastern Shore and the rest of Maryland began to lobby for a bridge to connect this isolated section of the state with the mainland. Construction of a bridge crossing a narrow part of the Chesapeake Bay was approved in 1938, was interrupted by World War II, and resumed in 1947. When the Chesapeake Bay Bridge (www.baybridge.com) opened in 1952, it was — at a whopping 4.3 miles — the longest steel structure built over water in the world. It carries U.S. Routes 50 and 301 across the bay from Sandy Point, Anne Arundel County, into Kent Island, in Queen Anne's County; it was renamed the William Preston Lane Jr. Memorial Bridge in 1967 to honor the Maryland governor who had helped get approval for the bridge's construction.

Within about a decade, it was clear that the four-lane bridge was not big enough to handle increasing traffic. A second span of three lanes was approved, and completed in 1973; this is the northern bridge, which generally carries traffic westbound, though this can change during summer, when one of the lanes is turned into an eastbound lane. It can be a bit confusing to newcomers to the bridge, but just follow the hundreds of orange traffic cones and barrels and marker lights, and it will all make sense. The view of the bay from the top of the bridge (about 190 feet up) is epic, especially when the waters are teeming with sailboats and massive cargo ships.

Ironically, even though the bridge was designed (and expanded) to allow for smooth travel between the Eastern and Western Shores, it often serves as a congestion point for traffic. This is because the multiple lanes of traffic (three or four lanes) on either side of the bridge must narrow to two or three, and on summer holiday weekends the backups can go on for miles. Inclement weather can also affect bridge traffic, and the winds can be quite strong at the bridge's summit. There is one toll plaza, located on the eastbound lanes of Route 50 on the Western Shore; the toll is $2.50.

Some drivers cannot deal with the height and openness of the bridge; the Maryland Transportation Authority (www.baybridge.org) offers to connect these drivers with a private service to help them get across the span.

Those looking for a more relaxed dining experience should head to **Legal Spirits** (42 E. Dover St., 410/820-0765, www.shoreboys .com, Sun.–Thurs. 11:30 A.M.–10:30 P.M., Fri.–Sat. 11:30 A.M.–2 A.M.). The luxuriously thick cream of crab soup is a local favorite, and there are plenty of other options like sandwiches and salads that are best eaten in the bar, which is decorated with a variety of taxidermied animals. There's also a more formal dining room, and some serious dinner entrées (such as big steaks and crab-stuffed fish)—but the cream of crab soup is the star here.

At the Tidewater Inn, the modern **Restaurant Local** (101 E. Dover St., 410/822-1300 or 800/237-8775, www.tidewaterinn.com) features (not surprisingly) many dishes based on local seafood and produce; eating on their brick patio, near the outdoor fireplace, is strongly recommended.

Hotels
There are a variety of lodging options in Easton, but staying in the historic downtown area is ideal. In ascending order of size, here are three very different places to lay your head during your trip. First is the charming little **Bishop's House Bed & Breakfast** (214 Goldsborough St., 410/820-7290 or 800/223-7290, www.bishopshouse.com, $185–195), which is a well-restored and immaculate 1880s Victorian home just a couple of blocks from the center of town in a quiet residential neighborhood. There are five guest rooms, a full breakfast spread, and bicycles (and helmets) available for guests to borrow.

Just up the road is the much larger and more elegant **Inn at 202 Dover** (202 E. Dover St., 866/450-7600, www.innat202dover.com, $275–475), which also has five rooms, though four of these are suite-sized (and feature decor themes like Asia, England, and France). The inn is a former mansion, built in 1874, and has a sense of solidity and luxury, including a wonderful conservatory room. There's also a full gourmet restaurant in the home.

Last, and certainly not least, is the **Tidewater Inn** (101 E. Dover St., 410/822-1300 or 800/237-8775, www

.tidewaterinn.com, $140–279). This full-service (and recently redone) hotel has 84 guest rooms and suites in a variety of configurations, as well as meeting facilities, and even a women's outdoor apparel shop, in case you forgot your hip waders or hunting vest. The very good Restaurant Local, also newly remodeled, is here too.

Information
VISITORS CENTER
Stop in at the **Talbot County Visitors Center and Easton Welcome Center** (11 S. Harrison St., 410/770-8000, www.tourtalbot.org, daily 9 A.M.–5 P.M.) to get a map and some quick orientation to historic Easton. You can also find out about an array of other towns and attractions in Talbot County here.

MEDIA
Easton has one daily newspaper, the **Star-Democrat,** which covers much of the news of the mid-shore area, and publishes a pretty substantial Sunday edition. The **Tidewater Times** is a small-sized, Shore-themed monthly magazine featuring essays and news of the community. There are two radio stations here: **WCEI 96.7 FM** (adult contemporary) and **WEMD 1460 AM,** which plays old-time radio shows and artists and some local sports.

Getting There and Around
GETTING THERE
Traveling by car is your best bet to get to Easton, which located about 70 miles south and east of Baltimore (it's about an hour and a half drive). From Baltimore, leave town and drive south to I-97, toward Annapolis, and U.S. Routes 50 and 301. Cross the Chesapeake Bay Bridge, and continue on U.S. 50 south; turn right on Md. Route 331, which is Dover Road, and you'll soon end up right in the center of town (Easton has a good bit of sprawl around the highway; don't worry about the profusion of fast food restaurants and gas stations you see on the way in). **Greyhound** (www .greyhound.com) busses run from Baltimore (2110 Haines St., 410/752-7682) to Easton as well; the drop-off in Easton (9543 Ocean Gateway/ Rte. 50, 410/822-3333) is at a gas station and

EXCURSIONS

convenience store about two miles from historic downtown Easton. If you'd like to travel between Easton and St. Michaels, or all across this part of the Eastern Shore, there's the **MUST** (Maryland Upper Shore Transit, 866/330-MUST, www .mustbus.info) bus, but be aware that MUST has limited pick-up and drop-off points and runs only during daylight hours.

GETTING AROUND

Once you've made it to downtown Easton and parked your car, you can spend the day on foot exploring the historic buildings, shops, and eateries, and then maybe taking in a show that night at the Avalon. There are lots of other things to do outside of town (like the Pickering Creek Audubon Center) that will require a car, but it's easy to spend the whole trip just strolling through Easton.

ST. MICHAELS

Fifteen minutes west of Easton—and even farther from civilization—is St. Michaels, a much smaller town (it refers to itself as a village) located right on the Miles River. St. Michaels avoided a nocturnal bombardment by the British during the War of 1812 through an ingenious trick; residents hung lanterns in trees and ship rigging, which led the English gunners to aim away from the darkened town. Having escaped that peril, the town has gone on to become a major destination for weekend getaways and upscale travelers; the Inn at Perry Cabin is an Orient Express hotel, and the most exclusive resort hotel on the Eastern Shore. There are also lots of fine dining options, bed-and-breakfasts, and charming little shops and stores—leading St. Michaels to be dubbed "The Hamptons of the Chesapeake Bay," which has not thrilled all of the town's residents.

Sights
《 CHESAPEAKE BAY MARITIME MUSEUM

This sprawling campus and working boatyard is one of the few heritage museums to live up to its mission: you'll be able to walk past (and maybe sail aboard) working boats, learn about life as a waterman, and chart the history of modern-day (and pre-European settler) civilization on the fertile bay. There are year-round demonstrations, classes, and lectures, which let guests get a real feel (and, sometimes, smell) of the fishing life. The sound of saws, planes, and hammers means that sailors, carpenters, and shipwrights are at work in the boatyard restoring classic old vessels or improving newer ones. Think of the Chesapeake Bay Maritime Museum (213 N. Talbot St., 410/745-2916, www.cbmm.org, Jun. 1–Sept. 30, daily 10 A.M.–6 P.M., reduced winter hours, admission $13 adult, $6 child, $10 senior) as a real-life Colonial Williamsburg without the phony costumes or accents; these are real people who make themselves available to talk about their lives and tools and boats. At the Waterman's Wharf, a re-creation of a typical crabbing shanty, visitors can see (and try) the tools used to capture crabs, eels, and other edible aquatic life. This museum complex is a living tribute to the traditions of the bay and the people who have made their homes here for centuries, and well worth a lengthy visit. (Kids will love it, too.)

《 SKIPJACK TOURS

The lure of the water can be strong at places like St. Michaels, so if you want to experience firsthand what it's like to be a bay waterman, you're in luck. Skipjacks are sail-powered oyster-dredging boats, about 50 feet in length, that covered the waters of the bay in the 19th and 20th centuries. Today, with the state's ban on motorized boats near oyster beds, skipjacks and their descendents continue to harvest oysters from the bay. There are two working skipjacks that take out passengers: the **H.M. *Krentz*** (410/745-6080, www.oystercatcher.com, two-hour sails 11 A.M.–1 P.M., 2–4 P.M., $30 adult, $15 child) in St. Michaels, and the ***Rebecca T. Ruark*** (410/886-2176, www.skipjack.org, two-hour sails Mon.–Fri. 11 A.M.–1 P.M. and 6–8 P.M., Sat.–Sun. 11 A.M.–1 P.M., 2–4 P.M., and 6–8 P.M., $30 adult, $15 child), a brief drive south in Tilghman. Both are old vessels, but the *Ruark* is the most ancient mariner, as she was first built in 1886; the *Krentz* was launched in

the Chesapeake Bay Maritime Museum and the skipjack H.M. *Krentz* in St. Michaels

1955. Both ships offer two-hour sails, where the captains regale visitors with tales of life on the water and the difficulty of making a living as an oysterman, and even let passengers do some manual labor, including dredging up oysters. These are working oyster boats, so don't plan on donning your dress whites and navy blazers for these excursions. The *Krentz* departs from the Crab Claw Restaurant, located at 304 Mill Street in St. Michaels. In tiny Tilghman, the *Rebecca T. Ruark* is docked at Dogwood Harbor (look for the skipjack with the "29" sign on the rigging).

Restaurants

The dining options at St. Michaels run the gamut from no-frills crab houses to award-winning gourmet meals, all within an easy walk from one another. On the waterfront, there are several large restaurants that cater to both locals and tourists; if you're looking for a big pile of steamed crabs, try the outdoor deck at the **St. Michaels Crab and Steak House** (305 Mulberry St., 410/745-3737, www.stmichaels crabhouse.com, Tues.–Thurs. 11 A.M.–10 P.M., Fri.–Sat. 11 A.M.–11 P.M.). If you're not in the mood for cracking crabs, the seafood dishes at chef Michael Rork's waterfront **(Town Dock Restaurant** (125 Mulberry St., 410/745-5577 or 800/884-0103, www.town-dock.com, Mon.–Sat. 11:30 A.M.–9 P.M., Sun. 11 A.M.–8 P.M., Sun. brunch 11 A.M.–3 P.M., reduced winter hours) are a big hit; if you like salmon, the "Salmon Salmon" sandwich should be on your to-do list: it's pastrami-cured salmon, atop a grilled salmon filet, on focaccia. The town's perennially top-rated (by residents, visitors, and regional media) restaurant is the romantic and rustic yet modern **208 Talbot** (208 N. Talbot St., 410/745-3838, www.208talbot.com, Sun.–Thurs. 5:30–9 P.M., Fri.–Sat. 5:30–10 P.M., reduced winter hours), a very upscale gourmet restaurant that, while dedicated to superlative food (like fresh fish and steaks), is still a relatively laid-back operation.

Hotels

The gorgeous sunsets, the tranquil waters, the languid pace—all the things that make St. Michaels such a popular getaway mean that there are a number of lodging options here, from over a dozen bed-and-breakfasts to world-class resorts. And there's one place to stay here that makes everything else seem like an old cot in a leaky tent: the **(Inn at Perry Cabin** (308 Watkins Ln., 410/745-2200 or 866/278-9601, www.perrycabin.com, $330–770). This opulent retreat is centered around a sprawling, bright-white manor house right on the waters of the Miles River. There are more than 80 rooms, ranging from the merely wonderful to the unbelievably grand; there's also a brand-new Linden Spa here, along with free yoga and Pilates. Operated by the luxe Orient Express chain of exclusive hotels, the Inn at Perry Cabin is a lure for wealthy getaway couples, weddings, and anyone who wants to experience one of the best hotels in America.

Slightly smaller and less grand, but still wonderful, is the 20-room **Five Gables Inn & Spa** (209 N. Talbot St, 410/745-0100 or 877/466-0100, www.fivegables.com, $150–425). There are three kinds of standard rooms and two types of suites scattered throughout the four-house complex that makes up the Five Gables. There's also an Aveda spa on premises, plus a heated indoor pool.

There are lots of cozy little B&Bs throughout St. Michaels as well, usually in historic homes dating back to the late 18th century. One is **Dr. Dodson House** (200 Cherry St., 410/745-3691, www.drdodsonhouse.com, $165–270), a Federal-style brick house with wide two-story porches and only two rooms (both with wood-burning fireplaces) and a stellar reputation. Just a single house away from the waterfront, all of the shops and eateries of St. Michaels are an easy walk from here.

Information

VISITORS CENTER

St. Michaels doesn't have a major visitors center, so stop at the **Talbot County Visitors Center** (11 S. Harrison St., 410/770-8000, www .tourtalbot.org, daily 9 A.M.–5 P.M.) in Easton to pick up some brochures and get any information you may need—though St. Michaels is so small, getting lost or confused is rather difficult. You could also visit the tiny **St. Michaels Museum at St. Mary's Square** (St. Mary's Square, 410/745-9561, May.–Oct. Sat.–Sun. 10 A.M.–5 P.M.) for a walking map of the town and answers to any questions you may have.

MEDIA

St. Michaels gets most of its media from the surrounding larger cities; the Easton-published *Star-Democrat* covers the mid-shore area.

Getting There and Around

GETTING THERE

You'll need a car to get to St. Michaels—or a boat. By car, it's an 80-mile trip (which will take about one hour and 50 minutes); leave Baltimore and take I-97 toward Annapolis, then U.S. Routes 50 and 301. Cross the Chesapeake Bay Bridge, and continue on U.S. 50 south; turn right on Md. Route 331, which is Dover Road, and you'll soon drive through Easton. Stop here to get information at the Talbot County Visitors Center before heading to St. Michaels. Take Bay Street (Route 33) west; it will turn into St. Michaels Road.

It's possible to take a **Greyhound** (www .greyhound.com) bus from Baltimore (2110 Haines St., 410/752-7682) to Easton (9543 Ocean Gateway/Rte. 50, 410/822-3333) and then catch a **MUST** (Maryland Upper Shore Transit, 866/330-MUST, www.mustbus.info) bus to St. Michaels, but be aware that the MUST line has limited pick-up and drop-off points and runs only during daylight hours.

GETTING AROUND

You can pretty much abandon your car once you reach St. Michaels, as everything is a short walk from everything else. If you want to explore the region a bit more, you will need to drive or hire a boat. The skipjack *Rebecca T. Ruark* is southwest of St. Michaels in the even-smaller town of Tilghman, about a 12-mile, 25-minute drive west and south on Maryland Route 33.

BACKGROUND

The Setting

The waters that lap gently against the seawalls of Baltimore's Inner Harbor are those of the Patapsco River; the city rose on three small towns built here, where the Patapsco joins with the Jones Falls, grows larger, and travels some 12 miles to the legendary Chesapeake Bay. The land rises quickly to the north, heading away from the harbor. The bounty of the bay and ease of sea transport led to Baltimore's industrial boom, which defined the city's waterfront landscape until only recently. Much of the area outside Baltimore is still relatively underdeveloped, and north and northwest of the city are vast rolling hillsides and forests, as well as sprawling estates, horse and agriculture farms, and equestrian centers.

The neighborhoods of Baltimore are as varied as its citizens, ranging from 250-year-old waterfront communities to historic, European-inspired circles and parks to modern condos along the Harbor. Much of Baltimore has benefited from the resurgence that began in the mid-1980s and recently enjoyed a second burst of construction, renovation, and popularity. But right next to many of the neighborhoods you'll visit are areas that haven't benefited from

the city's good fortunes, and some of the city's greatest hidden treasures are located in areas best not visited after dark.

GEOGRAPHY AND CLIMATE

Baltimore is in roughly the north-central part of Maryland; it is some 130 miles from the eastern edge of the state (which lies on the Atlantic Ocean). The city curls around the broad Patapsco River, giving it the feel of being close to the ocean, rather than a riverfront metropolis. Much of downtown Baltimore is a mere 33 feet above sea level, yet despite being at the terminus of several small rivers, flooding is very rare here, unless a series of natural events manage to coincide (like, say, a hurricane arriving at high tide, which happened in 2003; it was the worst flooding in 70 years).

Baltimore covers about 91 square miles; 11 of those are water. (In contrast, Washington, D.C. takes up only 68 square miles.) In the western and northwestern part of the city, you'll notice a sudden increase in elevation; that's where the taller Piedmont Plateau meets the lower Atlantic Coastal Plain. Several small streams (called "runs" and "falls" here) wind through parts of the city, ultimately ending at the Inner Harbor. Most of these are hidden by modern construction or re-routed by channels, including the Jones Falls, which runs parallel to President Street on the east side of downtown.

Downtown Baltimore's terrain is relatively flat, but if you head north on foot, you'll really notice the rapid rise. It's generally a very walkable town (as ranked by some pedestrian advocacy groups), though the distances between attractions and destinations can be a bit daunting, and occasionally will involve heading through economically depressed neighborhoods.

There are four distinct seasons in Baltimore, with each offering the best (and worst) of its weather. Springs can be magnificent, as can autumns. Be aware that summers can be fantastically hot and humid (the average temperature is more than 88°F from June to August, with July's average reaching 91°F). Winters start mild, but can occasionally get very cold, and there's generally one major blizzard each year, usually in February. The city gets about 21 inches of snow a year, but it often comes in one single storm. Rainstorms are common—it rains about 43 inches a year in Baltimore—and sometimes spring up unexpectedly, along with lots of lightning and thunder, but generally do not last long.

ENVIRONMENTAL ISSUES

A visitor to 1930s Baltimore would have been treated to a pungent smorgasbord of smokes, smudges, acrid odors, and toxic substances, not to mention the danger of a pre-OSHA world in which industrial accidents were common and deadly. The very industries that built the city in scope, scale, and wealth were also contributing to the eventual health crises faced by its citizens, land, and water. Steel mills, chromium plants, and chemical facilities—all of which needed to be near the waters of the Inner Harbor, or needed the water itself—lined Baltimore's shores for miles. Many of those factories are closed now, and much of what industry still operates near the Harbor is much less environmentally damaging. But the echoes of those older days are still visible along the waterfront, and in the poor health patterns suffered by the city's older residents, many of whom spent decades working in those plants.

Ironically, the economic decline that hit the city starting in the 1960s did have one long-term benefit: It slowed down, and even ceased, production at a lot of these factories. As cheaper overseas facilities began to lure business away, Baltimore's once mighty factories shut down and laid off workers—terrible for the economic health of the citizens and city, but a relief to the people's bodies, and the surrounding water and air. Now, those industrial sites are being removed and replaced with high-end hotels, condominiums, and apartment towers, and the waterfront is being transformed once again by new construction. Even with the reduction in local sources of air and water pollution, summers in Baltimore can put a strain on people prone to respiratory issues with high heat, humidity, and ozone levels. Code Red Heat Alerts and Air Quality Action Days are declared by state environmental officials; information can be found at www.mde.state.md.us.

As far as the environmental impact of all the new construction, the best way to describe it would be "gradually improving." Many of the modern skyscrapers and projects around the city have a few environmental, energy-saving features, but there are only a handful of truly forward-thinking buildings in town. Construction projects by Johns Hopkins Hospital and the University of Maryland, Baltimore are meeting some LEED (Leadership in Energy and Environmental Design) standards, and a new hotel on President Street (Fairfield Inn & Suites) is the city's first LEED-certified hotel.

History

17TH AND 18TH CENTURIES

In 1608, when the English explorer Captain John Smith made his first voyage up the Chesapeake Bay to explore the largely unknown lands of what is now Maryland, he found that various Native American tribes had been living and working around the waters of the Patapsco River for tens of thousands of years, drawn by the area's fertile land and abundant animal and aquatic life. Smith met many Native Americans, sometimes with violent results as his party was attacked, but he also procured supplies and information from the more peaceful tribes he encountered. His reports back to England eventually led to European colonization and agricultural endeavors in the region, and helped lead to the founding of the Port of Baltimore, at Locust Point (which lies between Federal Hill and Fort McHenry) in 1706, in part to ship tobacco back to Europe.

Baltimore Town, the first proper European settlement in America to bear the name Baltimore (a tribute to Cecilius Calvert, the second Baron Baltimore), was established in 1729. Baltimore is the name of a town in County Cork, Ireland; it means "town of the big house." This outpost would eventually merge with two other small settlements, Jones Town and Fell's Point, to create a much larger Baltimore Town. During the American Revolution, Baltimore's crucial role as a provider of men, materiel, and ships made it a critical spoke in the burgeoning American industrial machine. On December 20, 1776, the second Continental Congress met in Baltimore, as Philadelphia was endangered by approaching British troops. This made Baltimore the nation's capital for a three-month period. Following independence, Baltimore City continued to grow, and was incorporated on December 31, 1796; the burgeoning city was the nation's third largest at that point.

19TH CENTURY

Though Baltimore escaped the Revolutionary War unscathed, the War of 1812 would prove far more perilous. Fresh from their successful destruction of the fledgling nation's capital in Washington, D.C., in 1814, a flotilla of warships and troop carriers had sailed up the Chesapeake Bay and up the Patapsco River, bound for Baltimore itself. The only thing that stood in their way was a series of sunken vessels, designed to block their entrance to the city's harbor, and a star-shaped defensive outpost called Fort McHenry. The fort's defenders held their ground despite a monstrous bombardment by the British, inspiring Francis Scott Key—held prisoner in a ship of that flotilla—to pen "The Star-Spangled Banner," which became the U.S. national anthem in 1931.

The Civil War affected the city's fortunes in different ways. The first shots fired of the war—even before the attack on Fort Sumter in South Carolina—were aimed by Baltimorean Confederate sympathizers at Union troops traveling by train through the city. Baltimore's anti-Union feelings ran deep, and slavery was

© GEOFF BROWN

Fort McHenry, where U.S. troops held off a British invasion during the War of 1812

still common in the city and outlying farms, estates, and plantations that made up much of rural Maryland. Those shots, fired by civilians, guaranteed the placement of a Union garrison in the city; the garrison's cannons still stand today atop Federal Hill, pointed at downtown just as they were in 1862. The war made many fortunes in the city, from railroad tycoons like John Work Garrett to merchants like Johns Hopkins, an abolitionist Quaker who would take the money he had made from supplying and supporting Union forces during the war and create a university and hospital that would bear his name and establish his legacy.

20TH CENTURY TO THE PRESENT

With the exception of the devastating February 1904 fire that destroyed 70 square blocks and more than 1,500 buildings, the first part of the 20th century was very good to Baltimore. Ships, steel, and goods that passed through the port—as well as other specialty products, from furniture to crops—brought jobs and wealth to

the city, which expanded into the surrounding countryside quickly, overtaking what had been country estates with blocks of row houses.

In 1948, Baltimore made a decision that would ultimately prove devastating, though at the time, it seemed shrewd. Baltimore City voted to stop annexing land from Baltimore County, which surrounds the city, and settle down to enjoy its growth, while the county remained rural and relatively less wealthy. When the new economy of the 1950s began to take hold, and people could move out to the suburbs with relative ease, that decision to remain separate from the county would result in the urban decay that is still present today. In 1950, during the peak of the city's health and wealth, Baltimore's population was about 950,000; today, there are 632,000 people who call Baltimore City home; and vast parts of the city contain unoccupied row houses and dilapidated commercial and retail buildings. Unlike in many other metropolitan areas, Baltimore City is an independent jurisdiction from Baltimore County; when residents (and their

THE GREAT BALTIMORE FIRE

On a cold February morning in 1904, a small fire broke out in a downtown Baltimore warehouse. When it was finally extinguished nearly 30 hours later, much of the center of the city was gone; some 70 blocks were reduced to rubble, and more than 1,500 buildings were destroyed. Only one life was lost, but the city was in shock – some 35,000 people had no workplace to go to, it was the dead of winter, and hope was in short supply. But under Mayor Robert McLane, Baltimore quickly rebounded and used the destruction of the city's downtown as an opportunity to remake the town into a modern metropolis. Streets were widened, a new sewer system was installed, and fire-prevention measures were instituted in the new construction to help ensure that the city would never again burn so easily. One of the few downtown buildings to survive still stands today: head to the old Alex. Brown building (it's now a Chevy Chase Bank) at 135 East Baltimore Street. Touted as being "fire-proof," the structure was completed in 1901; three years later, it lived up to the builder's claims.

This bank was one of the few survivors of the Great Baltimore Fire of 1904.

taxes) left, the county grew prosperous (2005 per capita income: $44,375), while the city withered (2005 per capita income: $31,607).

The latter part of the 20th century marked grim times for Baltimore. Long-simmering resentment held by the city's large African American population toward institutional and cultural discrimination and segregation in Baltimore was brought to a head following the April 1968 assassination of Dr. Martin Luther King, Jr. Rioting broke out and lasted for eight days; when it was finally over, some parts of the city were severely damaged (and remain so today), and the race relations were permanently altered. The steady stream of middle-class residents (both whites and African Americans) moving out to the county became a flood; parts of the city damaged by rioters were left in disrepair; and the power structure of Baltimore began to shift from whites to blacks. This shift, along with economic depression, led to a population and capital drain that nearly mortally wounded the city. But in 1980, the opening of the new Inner Harbor and Harborplace—built on the former site of underused piers, empty lots, and shacks—signaled the "Baltimore Renaissance," and showed America that the city wasn't going to abide an ignominious death. Baltimore elected its first African American mayor, Kurt Schmoke, in 1987, and its first female mayor, Sheila Dixon (also African American), in 2006. Despite a grim toll from drugs and poverty in many city neighborhoods, over the past two decades, the city has made constant, if not always large, gains economically. Baltimore is now a majority African American city; that group makes up about 65 percent of the population, though blacks also make up much of the ranks of the working poor and economically disadvantaged. That said, some prominent African Americans, both past and present—like late Supreme Court Justice Thurgood Marshall, and recent Presidential Medal of Freedom winner Dr. Ben Carson, the prominent Johns Hopkins pediatric neurosurgeon—have called Baltimore home.

Baltimore has been in the headlines in the

past decade for the achievements of hometown men and women, like Little Italy native and California congresswoman Nancy D'Alesandro Pelosi, who became the first female Speaker of the U.S. House of Representatives. In the world of sports, the Baltimore Ravens of the NFL won the 2000 Super Bowl, and local swimming phenom Michael Phelps grabbed an Olympic-record eight gold medals at the 2008 Summer Games in Beijing. Another locally born sports star, NBA player Carmelo Anthony, took home his own gold at the Beijing Games as part of the champion U.S. basketball team. The city has also gained a reputation as a popular, off-beat getaway destination.

Baltimore Today

The Baltimore you see today—abuzz with new office, hotel, and residential towers, and construction around the waterfront—is a concrete and steel monument to the work of the politicians and developers who managed to turn a wan, dirty, industrial harbor area into a place where exclusive developers like the Four Seasons and the Ritz-Carlton are now building. Some argue that the massive tax breaks given by the city to the firms behind these projects are too generous; others counter that getting wealthy residents to move to town and pay taxes here is worth the trade off. Built on the cornerstone formed by the wild success of Harborplace and the Inner Harbor, this second phase of Baltimore's rebirth spreads east, filling the land between the Inner Harbor and Fell's Point, and to the south, wrapping around the water from Federal Hill to Locust Point.

Baltimore has benefited from being close enough to other, larger, more expensive cities to be considered a real option for residence. During the real estate boom of the late 1990s and early 2000s, people priced out of nearby Washington, D.C., began to discover and move to Baltimore. This new blood and energy helped encourage and foster growth in the city, which had lost population every year from 1950 until 2007, when more people moved into Baltimore than left. The charm and relative affordability of historic, lively neighborhoods

New shops and residential towers now line parts of the waterfront.

© GEOFF BROWN

a vintage neon sign from The Block, Baltimore's small red-light district

brought young upscale residents into the city, sometimes pricing out the working-class folks who had helped maintain the neighborhood in sour economic times. New condominiums and luxury townhomes began to spring up all over town, a welcome sight after years of hemorrhaging population and boarded-up row houses. One peculiar aspect of old Baltimore that remains in action today is "The Block," a stretch of Baltimore Street east of downtown (and next to Baltimore City Police headquarters) that was once the scene of burlesque shows by legendary Baltimorean Blaze Starr. Today, most of the action is far seedier, and it's not a place to be at night. A few remnants of the old Block remain, but now it's mostly strip joints, adult bookstores, and a few greasy take-out restaurants.

Despite the questions with city leadership and the continuing issues with crime and drugs, the gains made by Baltimore in the past two decades have given residents a better and improved feeling about the future of this settlement on the shores of the Patapsco River.

Government and Economy

Even though the state capital lies a half-hour south in Annapolis, and much of the Washington, D.C.-area suburbs are home to the state's wealthiest areas, Baltimore City's government (as well as that of Baltimore County) still carries an awful lot of clout around the state. This is due to the region's population, industry, and voting power; the area is also the recipient of much of the state's financial aid, owing to the tough conditions that still exist throughout the city.

Baltimore's economic landscape has undergone a series of tough changes this century. The once-mighty industry that helped drive the city—the port, the railroads, and the steel mills—has waned substantially, and now Baltimore's main employment sector is health care. Still, the city's unemployment rate hovers around 6–7 percent, which is much higher than in the surrounding suburbs.

GOVERNMENT

Baltimore City's current governmental structure consists of a mayor, who exerts a great deal of power, and a City Council, which is somewhat less able to wield its might. There are 14 council members from districts across the city, and a council president. Both the mayor and the council members are elected for four-year terms, and the mayor has a three-term limit; council members have no term limits. Baltimore City's size means it also has plentiful representation in the state government's House of Delegates and state Senate. The state legislature meets for only 90 days each year in Annapolis, beginning in January.

Mayor William Donald Schaefer (1971–1987) was cited as a big, plain-spoken reason for Baltimore's renaissance during that time period. Much of the credit for the more recent resurgence in the city went to (and was claimed by) Mayor Martin O'Malley, who took office in 1999. Becoming the white mayor of a majority black city was no easy task; a confluence of political events, and the split of the black vote, put O'Malley into City Hall. Though a lot of the construction that began during his term was envisioned and approved during Mayor Kurt Schmoke's administration, the city gained a renewed sense of pride, possibility, and hope during the O'Malley years. The homicide rate went down for the first time in years, though it remains depressingly high.

O'Malley became governor of Maryland in 2004, leaving City Hall to his successor, City Council President Sheila Dixon. In 2006, she was elected as the city's first female mayor. A longtime political force in the city with a strong organization and the support of many groups, Dixon has gotten generally positive reviews during her first elected term, though she has a history of questionable dealings and favoritism toward companies that employ her relatives or close friends. A revelation of a secret romantic relationship with the head of one of the largest developers in the city (a firm that has gotten millions in city business) was one damaging scandal; her indictment by a state grand jury on 12 criminal counts, ranging from theft to perjury, was another.

ECONOMY

Baltimore's fortunes were first made on the waters of the Port of Baltimore, as tobacco and other goods from the New World were shipped back to Europe. Merchants and shipbuilders and suppliers began to set up shop as a young United States grew, and as industrial advances were made, Baltimore was seemingly always ready to take up the next big going concern. Bethlehem Steel and Bethlehem Shipyards were two enormous sibling factories just outside the city that employed some 35,000 people during their heyday in the mid-20th century; the Port of Baltimore was one of the busiest in the nation for more than a century. But with the economic downturns that began in the 1970s, being a solely industrial city was a death sentence. Baltimore's factories, mills, and eventually its neighborhoods began to empty, sag, and close.

What saved Baltimore? Health care—and the Inner Harbor. The growth of health care as an industry in America gave Baltimore hope that it wouldn't slide into further ruin, as it had watched so many other "rust belt" cities do. And the presence of Johns Hopkins Hospital (and what is now Johns Hopkins Health System)—perhaps the planet's most famous and renowned medical center, and 18-consecutive-time winner of *U.S. News & World Report*'s "Best Hospital" award—meant that Baltimore had an established, respected, and wealthy brand. Today, Johns Hopkins (through the health system, the university, and associated research and academic institutions) employs more than 45,500 people in Maryland; it's the largest private employer in the state, and claims to add more than $7 billion to Maryland's economy. There's another major hospital in the area, too: the University of Maryland Medical System (UMMS), which employs 13,000 people in Baltimore alone. And though many of the jobs Hopkins and UMMS provide are solid, high-salary positions, there hasn't been a direct replacement of the well-paying union jobs lost when the industrial sector collapsed.

In addition to Hopkins, Baltimore (and the surrounding area) has a few other major employers and well-capitalized companies, including tool manufacturer Black & Decker, mutual fund company T. Rowe Price, energy and power titan Constellation Energy, and spice-maker McCormick.

Health Care, Medical Research, and Biotechnology

Americans spend about $2.3 trillion on health care each year, and Baltimore's medical

Johns Hopkins Hospital, one of Baltimore's largest employers

institutions have gained a large share of that by earning a national reputation as some of the best in the country. Leading the way is the behemoth Johns Hopkins University and Johns Hopkins Hospital, which secures huge amounts of federal funding (more than $580 million in 2007, the most in the nation by $130 million), in addition to generating income on their own. Both Hopkins and UMMS have undergone large expansion and construction projects in the past five years— Hopkins on the east side of town, and UMMS on the west. These projects have helped spur off-shoot residential and commercial development, or encouraged renovation of nearby neighborhoods.

A number of specialized research centers call Baltimore home; most notable of these are the city's National Institutes of Health facilities, which include the AIDS research labs of famed Dr. Robert Gallo. There are a number of other major hospitals and health systems in the region as well, including MedStar and LifeBridge, which each operate several hospitals, as well as Mercy Hospital and the Greater Baltimore Medical Center.

Education

Baltimore City and the surrounding area are home to 16 colleges and universities of wildly different sizes, scopes, and missions. And just as in health care, Johns Hopkins is the big kahuna in town; the university (enrollment is about 4,500 undergraduates) is one of the nation's best, attracting students from across the nation and the globe. The university's reach extends beyond its Homewood campus to other schools and facilities across the region, as well as overseeing the School of Medicine, one of America's best and most prestigious medical schools.

There are a total of about 120,000 full- and part-time college students across the greater Baltimore region. They attend a wide variety of schools, from small, private liberal arts colleges like Goucher and Loyola to state schools like Towson University and University of Maryland, Baltimore County. In between these ends of the enrollment scale, there are two historically black colleges (Morgan State and Coppin State), the nationally ranked Maryland Institute College of Art and Peabody Institute, plus religious and other private colleges and universities.

Tourism

Baltimore wouldn't be the first place that would spring to mind if asked to name a city that depends on—and benefits greatly from—tourism. But ever since the opening of Harborplace, Baltimore has, for a variety of reasons, been a major draw to some of the more than two million people who live in the greater Baltimore metropolitan region. In 2005, Baltimore drew some 17.7 million visitors, counting both day-trippers and those who came to town for a longer stay; in comparison, Walt Disney World in Florida drew 17 million visitors to the Magic Kingdom in 2007. Those 17.7 million visitors to Baltimore dropped just under

The Inner Harbor's Baltimore Visitor Center is the best central location for tourist information.

$3 billion during their trips, making tourism one of the city's most profitable sectors, though the jobs created by tourism are somewhat seasonal and generally not high-paying. In fact, a lack of hotel rooms downtown had been an issue for years; with the completion of a new Hyatt and the renovations of several existing buildings, that has been largely addressed. It's a testament to smart urban rejuvenation, good planning, and canny marketing that a city like Baltimore can reap so many benefits from the tourist trade.

People and Culture

DEMOGRAPHICS

In 2007, for the first time since 1960, Baltimore managed to add more residents than it lost; this may not sound like the kind of stat that makes people jump for joy, but it's a moral and policy victory for the city's leaders—and often cited as a real indicator of Baltimore's resurgence.

There were 631,366 residents of Baltimore City in 2006 (the latest official federal stats); women made up 53.4 percent of the population. About 25 percent of the city is under 18 years of age, and 12 percent is over 65.

The city is majority African American and black (64.8 percent); whites (not Hispanic) make up 31.7 percent; and the rest is predominantly Latino and Asian. The ratio of African American and white citizens in Baltimore City is reversed in Baltimore County, a result of the "white flight" from Baltimore City that occurred in the 1960s and 1970s.

The majority of Baltimore's first colonial residents were of English or Irish origin; later, they were joined by Europeans from across the continent. Baltimore's port was second only to New York City's Ellis Island as an intake center for European immigrants in the 19th century; more than two million people may have first set foot in America by standing on the ground of Locust Point. Accordingly, Baltimore's neighborhoods took on the flavors and cultures of their residents' heritages; Little Italy, as well as Polish, German, Jewish, and Ukrainian enclaves formed around the harbor's neighborhoods.

Over the years, as Baltimore lost a huge chunk of population, the city took on a slightly underpopulated feel. Even today, it's not a very dense city; you'll never feel like you're in Manhattan, or London, or Beijing as you walk the city's sidewalks and waterfront promenade. Lines form only for the most popular clubs and

A statue of Christopher Columbus in Little Italy faces east, back across the Atlantic to Europe, home of many of Baltimore's first immigrant populations.

restaurants, and long-time residents will generally refuse to wait longer than five minutes for anything that doesn't involve a free meal, drink, or concert.

RELIGION

Maryland was founded in part to give persecuted Catholics from England and elsewhere a safe haven to practice their faith, and the nation's first Catholic cathedral and archdiocese was founded in Baltimore. The city's history as a point of immigration, transit, and commerce meant that people of all the major Christian faiths settled here and founded their respective houses of worship, from orthodox Ukrainians to German Lutherans to English Episcopalians. Jews also called Baltimore home, and grand old synagogues are scattered around town. Today, most of the city's residents are either Catholic or Protestant. Many of the city's best-attended churches are those serving the city's large (and majority) African American community, and most of these houses of worship are Baptist or African Methodist Episcopal (AME) churches.

ARTS AND CULTURE

Baltimore is best described as a bit of a cultural Madagascar. Because it was isolated from the truly innovative and exceptional arts scenes and pioneers, and it did not have the strong and well-endowed cultural institutions of major cities, Baltimore took what it could get and proceeded to evolve (or, in some cases, freeze) its own unique cultural scene, independent of much outside influence. That's proven to have been a good thing, in the long run, because with the "discovery" of Baltimore by artists and cultural mavens from New York City and Los Angeles in the past two decades, the city has gained credibility and respect for being a wonderland of offbeat, hidden talent.

But Baltimore also pays respect to venerated art traditions. The city is home to two nationally recognized arts colleges, the Maryland Institute College of Art (for visual artists) and the Peabody Institute (for musicians). There's also the Baltimore School for the Arts, a

DECIPHERING BAWLMERESE

Baltimorese (or "Bawlmerese," in Baltimorese) is the accent and manner of speech indigenous to white, working-class Baltimore City residents, who came to the city from places like Poland, Ireland, and, during World War II, America's Deep South. The accent is a unique mix of a southern drawl, an almost Cockney-like pronunciation of certain vowels and mangling of consonants, and a specific canter to speech. Terms like "hon" are frequently used as terms of endearment to family and strangers alike. The accent has become both a point of pride and of contention with Baltimoreans, as newcomers and others will adopt the accent to sometimes mock blue-collar white Baltimoreans. Yet there's an entire HonFest in Hampden each year that draws huge crowds and has a "Best Hon" contest.

This guide may help you understand some of the folks you meet in Baltimore, but be cautious about trying it yourself, because a lot of the people who speak with the Baltimore accent don't think they have an accent. So, here's a primer: chop off as many consonants as you can; speak with a tightness in your throat; toss some superfluous "r"s into words that don't have them; and pronounce all "o"s fatly and at the front of the mouth, so they sound like "ouh." Thus, "Maryland" phonetically becomes "Merlin," "wash" becomes "warsh," and "tourist" becomes "terst." Check out more examples at www.baltimorehon.com.

the Western musical and dance canons. But Baltimoreans like to rock out and dance and rap as well; Baltimore Club is a specific type of dance music with an insane number of beats per minute that will kick all the pretenders off the dance floor.

Culturally, Baltimoreans are an odd mix of North and South. You'll meet a lot of exceedingly polite and well-mannered people in Baltimore; you may also be told to do some things that are not physically possible by irate citizens.

Racial and economic divisions in the city are still prominent. African American Baltimore is a very different place from white Baltimore. Black Baltimore exists in its own parts of town and goes to its own churches and social clubs and events, an extension of the paths segregation forced African Americans to go down in order to maintain and grow their own communities. There are a few places in town where people of all races mingle together, including the Inner Harbor.

White Baltimore is the Baltimore most often portrayed in films and on TV: think of John Waters' movies, rife with large women in tent-like housedresses and beehive hairdos (in 2009, mind you). There's a celebration of Baltimore's "hon" culture (short for "honey," as in, "Hey hon, pass me the crab mallet!"), organized by Hampden's Café Hon restaurant, which hosts HonFest each summer. Some festival goers compete in a "Best Hon" contest dress up in cat's-eye glasses, big hair, and adopt the peculiar accent and dialect spoken by many white, working-class Baltimoreans of the mid-20th century. Many people who actually speak with a Baltimore accent (dubbed "Bawlmerese") aren't thrilled with their portrayal at these events, even though it is done out of adoration for a genuine city tradition and heritage.

Arts, Crafts, and Folk Traditions

The best place to start learning about Baltimore's cultural history is at the **Maryland Historical Society** (www.mdhs.org), which tracks the growth of the city and its traditions, particularly in crafts like furniture making, for which Baltimore became quite a hotspot

special public high school for creative and talented teens that has educated artists and actors like Tupac Shakur, Jada Pinkett Smith, and Traci Thoms.

Classical art and music has long been treasured by Baltimore's citizens, be they blue-bloods or blue-collar. The Baltimore Symphony Orchestra is well respected and well supported, and there are a variety of smaller companies and societies that perform classics from

in the early 19th century, exporting thousands of pieces of Baltimore Painted Furniture across the country.

Screen painting is a folk art peculiar to Baltimore; by painting pastoral or nautical scenes onto window screens or screen doors, locals realized they could both jazz up the fronts of their row houses and also keep folks outside from getting too clear a view of what was going on inside. With the proximity and density of row houses back in the early 20th century, these were both welcome discoveries. You can see some great examples at the **American Visionary Art Museum** (www. avam.org), which has a good display of the Baltimore Stoop, which is how Baltimoreans refer to the steps (often marble) that lead up to their brick row houses.

To see what some of the city's most intriguing artists are doing, head to the **School 33 Art Center** (www.school33.org), a city-run arts facility in an old school in Federal Hill that exhibits arts and provides studios. School 33 has lots of events, fundraisers, and tours throughout the year; the art here can vary from the very mainstream to the very experimental.

The Creative Alliance (www.creativealliance.org) is a popular organization that gets arts, artists, and citizens together to create and explore their respective worlds in new and interesting ways. The Creative Alliance works to preserve local traditions and arts and expose city kids to basic art principles, as well as teach them about Baltimore's art heritage. And it has the coolest reused building in town—the old Patterson movie theater in Highlandtown, just northeast of Canton.

Literature

The written word has long been a favorite way of Baltimoreans to express their desires, fears, appreciations, and opinions. The area seems to inspire people to write, perhaps because of the peculiarities of the town and its residents. Baltimore has played a central role in more than a few books; today, the city is the setting for the popular Tess Monaghan series of crime novels by former *Baltimore Sun* reporter Laura Lippman (who happens to be married to former *Baltimore Sun* reporter David Simon, creator of *The Wire*).

Baltimore is also a character in books, often woven into the novels of Pulitzer Prize–winner Anne Tyler, whose *The Accidental Tourist* was made into a film, some of which was shot in Baltimore. Johns Hopkins University's Writing Seminars are one of the nation's premier writers' programs and have seen such authors and poets as John Barth, Russell Baker (who was raised in Baltimore), J. M. Coetzee, Howard Nemerov, Robert Stone, Mark Strand, and other luminaries lecture or teach at Hopkins. Novelist Madison Smartt Bell teaches at Goucher, and Tom Clancy, whose bestselling novels centering on the derring-do of U.S. armed forces, is a Baltimore native.

As for non-fiction and criticism, there is no more studied or prolific scribe than the Sage of Baltimore, Henry Louis Mencken. During the early 20th century, H. L. Mencken—a writer for the *Sun*—authored innumerable essays and volumes of books opining on everything effecting the state, being, and mind of the American citizen. He enjoyed poking at commonly held "truths" and pointing out what he felt to be idiocy among his fellow Americans; Mencken played a large role in bringing about the 1925 Scopes Trial, which he dubbed the "Monkey Trial," as it made illegal (in Tennessee) the act of teaching evolution. Later examination of his works led to charges of bigotry, though many scholars have weighed his sometimes-cruel words against his always-honorable deeds. A large collection of Mencken's works and letters can be found in the **H. L. Mencken Room and Collection** at the Enoch Pratt Central Library; a new trove of Menckenia, numbering nearly 6,000 items, was recently acquired by Johns Hopkins University for its Sheridan Libraries.

Another famed chronicler is Pulitzer Prize–winner and historian Taylor Branch, who has called Baltimore home for decades. His three-part series, *America in the King Years,* examined Civil Rights–era U.S. history from 1954 to 1965. Branch has won several other prominent awards for his work, including a

MacArthur Foundation Fellowship (known as the "genius award").

Baltimore area poets are a small but impressive band. Ogden Nash was a native of Rye, New York, who spent 37 years in Baltimore. Former U.S. Poet Laureate Lucille Clifton lives just outside Baltimore in nearby Columbia. Fellow poet Elizabeth Spires (a Hopkins alum) teaches at Goucher College north of the city; her husband is Madison Smartt Bell.

Though he died and is buried here, Edgar Allan Poe did not write any of his classic tales of the macabre during the roughly three years he lived in Baltimore; still, the town claims him as one of its own, and the city's NFL team, the Baltimore Ravens, are even named in honor of his most famous work. The team's mascots? Three cartoonish ravens, named Edgar, Allan, and Poe. Yes, really.

Many other authors of note were either born here and moved elsewhere, or spent some formative years here. Pulitzer Prize–winner Upton Sinclair, whose *The Jungle* exposed the realities of the slaughterhouse, is a Baltimore native. Frederick Douglass, born a slave on Maryland's Eastern Shore, escaped from Baltimore to become a free man, abolitionist, and writer; his 1845 autobiography, *Narrative of the Life of Frederick Douglass, An American Slave* is now a classic of American letters. Hard-boiled detective novel scribe Dashiell Hammett was a Maryland native and grew up in Baltimore, where he later worked as a private dick. Gertrude Stein was a student at Johns Hopkins School of Medicine, but dropped out in 1901 to pursue other, more literary interests. And Leon Uris, best known for the novel *Exodus,* was born and raised in Baltimore.

Music

Perhaps the most famous song in America (after "Happy Birthday") was composed off the shores of Fort McHenry back in 1814, when Francis Scott Key penned "The Star-Spangled Banner." But many other great songs, songwriters, and musicians have gotten their start here or used Baltimore to springboard to bigger and brighter stages, most notably jazz legends Cab Calloway and Billie Holiday. A statue to Holiday was erected some years ago in the city, but because of construction at the installation site, the statue is currently difficult to find and even more difficult to enjoy.

African Americans with Baltimore roots or connections have made a lasting and meaningful impression on American music, beginning with legends like Calloway, Holiday, Eubie Blake (there's a small **Eubie Blake National Jazz Institute and Cultural Center** in midtown that hosts photo exhibitions and jazz performances), Cyrus Chestnut, Bill Frisell, The Orioles, and Chick Webb. Baltimore's Pennsylvania Avenue used to be home to several renowned clubs and venues for black performers, as segregation prevented them from taking the stage in white neighborhoods. The Royal Theater was the crown jewel of these venues and known nationwide, though today it's just an empty lot, and the rest of Pennsylvania Avenue's once-grand cultural sites are all gone or in massive disrepair. Some contemporary African American artists who've gone on to stardom from the small stage of Baltimore include Toni Braxton, Dru Hill and their former member SisQó, and Mario; local hip-hop artists and DJs who aren't household names but still pack houses around town (and in other parts of the world) include Rod Lee, Blaqstarr, and Ultra Naté. These artists provide a pretty good cross-section of what kind of music gets played here; the ubiquitous Baltimore House dance music, with its high-tempo beats, is also easy to find and hear (and feel, with a good bass system).

Baltimore's Southern, white tinges are revealed in the prevalence of country and bluegrass shows that are a regular occurrence around town. The city's large Irish American population means there are several traditional Irish pubs in town, many of which bring first-class musicians to Baltimore for regular weekend shows (unassuming **J. Patrick's** in Locust Point is a favorite). Baltimore has long been a steadfast, head-banging, hard rock town, but has appreciated quirkiness in its musicians as well. One look at the list of rock musicians who hail from Baltimore proves that fact: Tori Amos, David Byrne, John Doe (of the seminal L.A. band X), Greg Kihn, Gina Schock (drummer of The Go-Go's), and Frank Zappa were all born here, and a more diverse and inspired group would be hard to find. Counting Crows singer Adam Duritz is a Baltimore native, as are the members of the critically acclaimed band Animal Collective.

The city's current independent music scene has drawn a lot of national attention, including coverage from *Rolling Stone* and MTV. The biggest acts (relatively speaking) of this new indie world include the mellow duo Beach House, the group Celebration, rapper Cex, rapper Spank Rock, and Wham City, a musical

A CINEMATIC TOUR DE BALTIMORE

Since Barry Levinson's 1982 film *Diner* (or, if you were cooler, John Waters' 1972 *Pink Flamingos*) introduced movie audiences to the peculiarities of Baltimore, the city has been the setting for films and TV shows – both playing itself and standing in for a variety of other cities. HBO's popular show *The Wire* was filmed and set in Baltimore, though local politicians were not thrilled with the show's image of Charm City.

DOWNTOWN

The **Hollywood Diner** was the set for Barry Levinson's classic buddy movie *Diner;* it's also been in *Sleepless in Seattle, Tin Men,* and TV's *Homicide: Life on the Street.* Still an operating diner, the restaurant was moved from Fell's Point (where it was for *Diner*) to Saratoga Street, where it occupies a quiet corner near some parking lots north of City Hall.

FELL'S POINT

This is where you'll find the stately, if dilapidated, **City Pier** on Thames Street; this building played a police station in *Homicide: Life on the Street.* Doors on the east side of the building still have the words "Baltimore Police" painted on them, while on the right side is a plaque commemorating the show's cast and crew. *Sleepless in Seattle* was shot around the piers at the bottom of Broadway, where the Water Taxi docks, as was *Enemy of the State.* Near the corner of Fleet Street and South Broadway is the former **Copy Cat,** where *The Wire*'s Stringer Bell operated a real copy shop while helping to mastermind a drug cartel.

MOUNT VERNON

Much of Levinson's *Avalon* was filmed around Howard Street's **Antique Row,** a once-grand retail destination, and many of the antiques seen in *Guarding Tess* came from these shops.

Take a tour of the grand **Garrett-Jacobs Mansion,** a fantastic 19th-century urban palace; you might recognize its warm, rich interiors from a long list of films, including *Diner, 12 Monkeys,* and *He Said, She Said.*

If you're feeling particularly mondo, head to one of Baltimore's most storied gay bars, **The Drinkery.** It was just outside this venerable establishment that the actor Divine (Glenn Milstead) made cinematic history in *Pink Flamingos,* because this is where the fearless thespian did something far above and beyond the call of...um, "doody."

HAMPDEN

The neighborhood of Hampden has featured prominently in many John Waters films, and "The Avenue" (36th St.) has seen plenty of action in his films: The titular character in 1998's *Pecker* hails from this part of town and the 1988 film *Hairspray* (which begat the musical) was filmed primarily here (the 2007 film version of the musical was shot in Toronto).

Head to the corner of 30th Street and Remington Avenue, just south of Hampden, to find **Charm City Cakes,** baker Duff Goldman's cake shop, featured on the Food Network's *Ace of Cakes.* While you can take pictures outside the imposing stone building, no visitors are allowed and the windows are covered with thick black plastic.

collective fronted by a talented singer/song-writer/soundmaker named Dan Deacon.

Television and Film

Many Americans first got to know Baltimore through Barry Levinson's 1982 film *Diner,* which told the tale of a group of young men growing up in 1959 Baltimore. The film explored the city's dedication to friendships, class distinctions, football, and the culture of the diner, and is now considered a classic American movie. Then there were those who first learned about Baltimore from John Waters' 1972 *Pink Flamingos,* which chronicled the odd antics and exploits of a massive transvestite named Divine trying to keep her title as "The Filthiest Person Alive." That film showed another side of Baltimore, one that was much more strange, bizarre, and unrestrained by the mores of Baltimore society. Both films were honest chronicles of the experiences of Baltimore's residents, though the two couldn't be less alike in subject matter.

More recently, another realistic portrayal of Baltimore drew national and international praise and a devoted (if not vast) following: HBO's *The Wire,* which ran for five seasons and ended in 2008. Created by David Simon, a former *Baltimore Sun* reporter, the show took viewers into the bleak, desperate, and often hopeless world of Baltimore's drug economy, exposing the angels and devils on all sides. The show made local politicians a bit apoplectic, but critics called it the best show on television in the past decade, if not ever. Shot almost entirely in Baltimore, *The Wire* was a regular and beloved presence around town, and the stars of the series were embraced and adored

by both upstanding citizens and those whose lives too-closely mirrored those of the criminals on screen.

Though Baltimore was the site, in 1954, of the original *Romper Room,* one of the country's first television programs for children, the city's modern television career began with another David Simon project, *Homicide: Life on the Street.* Filmed frequently around Fell's Point, this show about Baltimore homicide detectives ran on NBC for seven years, from 1993 to 1999, and starred several notable actors, including Ned Beatty, Andre Braugher, and Yaphet Kotto. *Roc,* a Fox show set in Baltimore (though filmed in Los Angeles) and starring Baltimore native Charles S. "Roc" Dutton, aired from 1991 to 1994. More recently, Baltimore has been the set for the Food Network's *Ace of Cakes,* a reality show that tracks the trials, tribulations, and fondant disasters of baker Duff Goldman's Charm City Cakes, located near the Hampden neighborhood.

Baltimore has played itself in a long list of films; a brief list of the better movies includes three other "Baltimore" films by Barry Levinson: *Avalon, Liberty Heights,* and *Tin Men.* Also check out *The Accidental Tourist, Twelve Monkeys, Home for the Holidays, Ladder 49, Sleepless in Seattle,* and anything by John Waters. His most accessible films are *Hairspray, Cry Baby, Serial Mom* (starring Kathleen Turner, who studied drama at the nearby University of Maryland Baltimore County), and *Pecker.* Baltimore has also served as a celluloid stand-in for many towns, as its varied architecture can substitute for other, more expensive cities: check out *Enemy of the State, Live Free or Die Harder,* and *Washington Square.*

ESSENTIALS

Getting There

What's the best way to get to Baltimore, located about midway down the Eastern seaboard of the United States? It really depends on your point of origin. Baltimore is right on I-95, making it a cinch to reach from points north and south. If you live in a city like Philly, New York, or D.C., you might consider hopping on one of the many private buses that now run up and down the I-95 corridor, sometimes for ludicrously low fares. There's also rail travel, and Baltimore's Penn Station is right in the middle of the city (though not near any hotels).

Air travel is another option; Baltimore-Washington International Thurgood Marshall Airport is serviced by some low-cost carriers, and since it's not a hot destination city like Miami, airfares to Baltimore can dip if airlines want to entice folks to travel to Charm City.

You can even enter Baltimore by boat; from the Chesapeake Bay, just follow the Patapsco River up and into the docks and piers of Fell's Point.

BY AIR

Located 10 miles south, and just a 15-minute drive from downtown Baltimore, **Baltimore-Washington International Thurgood Marshall Airport** (410/859-7111, www.bwiairport.com) is one of the busier regional airports in the

nation. More than 21 million people moved through BWI in 2007, partly due to its recent expansions and its completion of an entire new gate for low-cost Southwest Airlines (www.southwest.com), which is responsible for more than half of the airport's passenger load. Unlike some modern airports, BWI's non-flying amenities—like full-scale malls and entertainment—are limited to a good variety of bars and restaurants, as well as some solid if uninspired shopping in the airport's Airmall, which is spread across the entire facility.

In addition to Southwest, seven major national carriers fly into and out of BWI, including the budget, Caribbean-centered USA3000 (www.usa3000.com). There are also a few international airlines, like Air Canada, Air Jamaica, and British Airways. One interesting note: because of BWI's proximity to Washington, D.C., not only do lots of Washingtonians come to BWI looking for cheaper fares than at Reagan National Airport, but the Transportation Security Administration road-tests new equipment and tactics at BWI quite often, so don't be startled to see some new gizmo or be asked some new questions during your screening here. For domestic flights, arrive at least one hour early; backups at the security checkpoints can be quite long during peak travel times. International flights require passengers to arrive at least two hours early.

BY TRAIN

Baltimore's central train station is **Pennsylvania Station** (1515 N. Charles St., 800/872-7245, www.amtrak.com), a massive old building that was renovated several years ago and is now a gleaming gem of a rail station. Amtrak service runs up and down the East Coast and to points west from this station seven days a week, making it a great option for those traveling from other Northeastern cities. (Alas, the vaunted and high-speed Amtrak Acela trains do not currently stop in Baltimore.) During the week, a commuter rail line called MARC (Maryland Area Regional Commuter) runs from Washington, D.C. to Baltimore and a few small stops north of the city; it's another reasonably priced option.

Amtrak times and rates run roughly as follows: from New York City, 2 hours 45 minutes, $64; from Philadelphia, 1 hour 15 minutes, $40; and from Richmond, Virginia, 4 hours, $40.

Pennsylvania Station—you'll know it by the large, modern, metal Male/Female statue out front—is located geographically very near the center of the city, and is within walking distance of Mount Vernon, but taking a cab or bus from the station to your final destination is recommended.

BY BUS

The city's main **Greyhound** station (2110 Haines St., 410/752-7682, www.greyhound .com) is located a few blocks south of downtown in a rough-and-tumble industrial section of South Baltimore. Service runs seven days a week, multiple times a day. Wandering around the neighborhood after dark is not a sound idea, but the station itself is generally secure and safe. Travel by taxi to downtown from the station; the walk is very long and not recommended for safety reasons, though it's possible to do during daylight. Note that there is also a Greyhound bus stop at the **Baltimore Travel Plaza** (5625 O'Donnell St., 410/633-6389), which is a mile or so east of Canton, and much less convenient to downtown.

A more cost-effective option may be to take one of the more home-spun bus operators that have sprung up in recent years. Running from New York City to Washington, D.C., with stops in Philadelphia and Baltimore, these small bus lines offer incredibly cheap rates (around $30 round-trip to New York City) and are a viable alternative to traditional bus transportation. One service with a relatively convenient midtown Baltimore location (though it's not near any lodging) is **MVP Bus** (1910 N. Charles St., 888/687-2871, www.mvpbus.com). Other private bus services, like those known as the "dragon bus" (named because of their ownership or operation by Asian American concerns), stop at Baltimore, but only at the Baltimore Travel Plaza, which is nowhere near downtown; a popular line is **Dragon Deluxe** (800/475-1160, www.dragondeluxe.com). There is also service by **MegaBus** (877/462-6342, www.megabus .com), but this line drops off and picks up far out in the suburbs (at the White Marsh Mall MTA Park & Ride), and travelers won't be able to secure a way to the city proper without taking a long MTA bus ride (Route 15), or making a phone call to a cab company.

BY CAR

Baltimore can be accessed by three Interstate highways: I-95, which runs north and south along the Eastern Seaboard; I-83, which begins in Baltimore and runs north up to Harrisburg, Pennsylvania; and I-70, which runs west to Frederick and into the heart of America.

Since Baltimore is right on I-95, it's easy to reach from points to the north (like Philadelphia, which is about two hours away by car, and New York City, just under three and a half hours) and south (Washington, D.C. is less than an hour away; Richmond, Virginia, is under three).

Getting Around

It's possible to traverse Baltimore by foot (and the occasional taxi or bus), depending on your itinerary, but having a car makes life a lot easier here. Either way, here's a handy guide to quickly figuring out where something is by its street address: If it's a street with a "north" designation (like North Highland Street), it's above Baltimore Street, which runs east to west; South Highland Street is below that. For east and west boundaries, the border is Charles Street, which runs one-way northbound right through the center of town (it is, however, a two-way street in Federal Hill and South Baltimore).

Though it's possible to get around via bus and light rail, Baltimore's public transportation is designed for weekday commuters and often doesn't run particularly close to attractions. Bicycles are not a bad option, though the long climb northward from downtown will test your fitness (and calves); new bike paths and lanes make this option less perilous than in years past.

AIRPORT

Getting to and from the airport is a breeze (if you're driving, it's located right off Md. 295, the Baltimore-Washington Parkway), and there are several easy ways to make the journey. First is the Light Rail (www.mtamaryland .com), which runs from Downtown Baltimore to a shuttle bus stop near the terminal. At $1.60, it's the unbeatable low-cost champ—but it doesn't run all the time (generally operates 6 A.M.–11 P.M. Mon.–Sat., with Sun. hours being severely reduced). When the trains aren't running, you'll need to take the 17 bus instead; the fare is still $1.60, but there are a lot more stops. The MARC commuter rail (www.mtamaryland.com), which runs between Baltimore's northern exurbs and Washington, D.C., also makes a stop at BWI; it's a cheap (around $6) alternative if it fits your arrangements.

The second option is to take one of the many shuttle vans, like the Super Shuttle (800/258-3826, www.supershuttle.com), that operate between Baltimore and either the major hotels or a pick-up point of your choosing. These can run about $25, but offer a good bargain compared to a private taxi.

Grabbing a cab to or from BWI can be a costly, if convenient, travel solution. If you're heading right downtown, it will cost about $35; heading farther into the city will increase the price. There are several cab services that serve BWI and Baltimore.

There is the usual armada of rental car agencies at BWI, offering varying rates depending on the type of vehicle you rent. Given Baltimore's often sparse parking space selection, a small, compact vehicle will suit you just fine around town. If you're planning on taking a day trip, a larger car might make the trip a little more enjoyable. The airport's new, centralized car rental facility is about a 10-minute drive from the airport itself.

PUBLIC TRANSPORTATION

Baltimore's public transportation system is operated by the **Maryland Transportation Authority** (410/539-5000, www.mtamaryland .com). Bus service runs throughout the city, though it is primarily used for weekday transportation to and from work; weekend schedules are less comprehensive and cover less of the city. There are a few central bus routes (like the 1, 3, 7, 11, and 17) that span the city well on the main north–south and east–west axes, but if you're trying to get somewhere away from the main attractions on a weekend, a bus is not the best option.

There are two public rail options as well, though both have only one line. The first is the Light Rail (www.mtamaryland.com), which runs from BWI Airport in the south all the way north to Hunt Valley Mall, in northern Baltimore County. This is a good option for traveling between certain areas, such as from Camden Yards to Mount Vernon, but the line does not provide any east–west coverage. The second rail option is the Metro Subway (www.mtamaryland .com); designed primarily for commuters from the northwestern suburbs heading into downtown and to Johns Hopkins Medicine's facilities on the east side of the city, this is an option for certain trips, but is not particularly useful for getting across town to sightsee. If you plan on heavy use of the system and want to purchase an MTA Transit Pass, you can do so at the **MTA Store** (6 St. Paul St., 410/454-7039) or online (www.mtamaryland.com/store).

DRIVING

While you can get around Baltimore by cab, bus, and foot, having a vehicle will make travel a lot faster and let you get out into the countryside and take a day trip or two. If you decide to rent a car after your arrival, there are numerous outlets for all the major rental agencies in town; your best bet is to check the companies' websites for specials and convenient locations.

Baltimore is laid out rather straightforwardly, but locals still like to carry around a map for some of the more obscure neighborhoods; try the Baltimore City and County map book from ADC (www.adcmap.com).

Parking can be tricky downtown during the week; the city has long suffered from a shortage of spaces, so if you're not at a major hotel (which will almost assuredly charge you extra to park in its garage), you'll probably be parking at a nearby surface lot, or you can take your chances with on-street parking.

Figuring out where and when you can and cannot park in certain places is a bit of a challenge if you're not used to city regulations. Many of the popular neighborhoods have time-based and resident-only parking restrictions, so read carefully any signs near where you've chosen to park; many major downtown thoroughfares prohibit parking on certain sides of the street during rush hours (southbound in the mornings, northbound in the afternoons). New electronic parking machines are common in Baltimore, but study the information on the machine nearest your parking space to determine the length of time you can stay, and hours of required pay parking (Sundays are free in most areas).

Driving while in Baltimore should be relatively painless if you have driven in a major city before; things move fast and with a purpose here, and lollygagging is not appreciated. If you're a cautious, slow driver who likes to sightsee through your windshield and stop in the middle of downtown to ask directions, be prepared for some colorful (and profane) suggestions on how to improve your driving.

If you're driving in Baltimore during an ice or snow event, be forewarned that the city's drivers are generally less than skilled when it comes to negotiating a vehicle through inclement weather.

TAXIS

There are several major (and several minor) cab companies in Baltimore: **Yellow-Checker** (410/685-1212) is the largest, but **Diamond** (410/947-3333) and **Royal** (410/327-0330) are other major providers. Even though the city has over 1,100 registered taxicabs, hailing (or finding) one in certain parts of town at certain times of night can be nigh on impossible, so either have a cab company's phone number with you and call from your cell phone, or have the restaurant or bar call you a cab (they're generally more than happy to do so, and getting a call from a business seems to improve response time). It costs $1.40 to get in a cab in the city, and $1 a mile after that. The limit to the number of passengers in a cab is four, more or less; a ride from Homewood to downtown should cost about $5. Taking a cab to or from BWI to a downtown hotel can cost about $35.

Somewhat surprisingly, the Yellow-Checker Cab Service in Baltimore has recently acquired several Toyota Prius hybrid cars, which you can call and try to request.

WATER TAXI

If you're planning on staying mostly around the Inner Harbor area, consider using the Water Taxi (410/563-3901, www.thewatertaxi .com) to get around. This regular shuttle service (look for the boats with blue awnings) makes 17 stops all across the harbor, going as far east as Fort McHenry (during the warm months), and covering all the major waterfront destinations from Locust Point clockwise to Fell's Point and Canton all year long. It's a beautiful way to see the city, and the captains are generally up for a chat, which can reveal some amazing salty tales of the city and the harbor.

BICYCLING

With the addition of many new bicycle lanes throughout the city, visitors to Baltimore will see more and more two-wheeled conveyances on city streets than in years past. A new Bicycle Master Plan for the city was created in 2006, and the results today are more (and more clearly marked) lanes, places to lock up bikes at popular destinations, and a more friendly environment. There are several local groups dedicated to riding in the city and getting people on bikes, like **Baltimore Spokes** (www .baltimorespokes.org) and **Velocipede** (www .velocipedebikeproject.org). That being said, riding a bike in Baltimore can still be a risky proposition, particularly on the busy

Baltimore's Inner Harbor

thoroughfares that barely have room for two lanes of cars. Baltimore has several very good bike trails that run through it, including the Gwynns Falls Trail and the Jones Falls Trail.

DISABLED ACCESS
Almost all of Baltimore has been modified to comply with the Americans with Disabilities Act, meaning that ramps or lifts are in place to allow all visitors to access businesses and sites. Note that in some parts of historic older neighborhoods, terrain may preclude travel by wheelchair. Both the MTA transit system (410/539-5000, www.mtamaryland.com) and private cab companies can provide specialized vehicles on request.

Tips for Travelers

TRAVELING WITH CHILDREN
For those heading to Baltimore with children, a few basic rules of common sense should apply. It's a real city, with real traffic, so kids need to be watched around downtown intersections, which can be confusing and often filled with cars and buses moving at very high speeds. There is also a light rail along Howard Street, which glides right along the sidewalks and can sneak up on unsuspecting pedestrians. Crowds at the Inner Harbor can be pretty thick during the warmer months, and lines to attractions can be long, so pack distractions and snacks accordingly. Public restrooms are generally unavailable in the city, and the few that exist are generally not recommended for use.

Parents looking for a good resource for things to do with the kids should check out *Baltimore's Child,* a monthly publication that covers mostly education and parenting but also has a good list of events and special happenings for kids (there's an online version at www.baltimoreschild.com).

WOMEN TRAVELERS
Baltimore is a great city for women traveling alone as long as they keep in mind the usual rules and avoid areas of potential issues, such as areas where overly intoxicated people congregate and cause mayhem. Most of the people you'll meet in Baltimore are friendly and willing to suggest great (and safe) places to visit on your own at various times of the evening. Bustling neighborhoods like Fell's Point and Federal Hill are safe at night because of the crowds, though deserted side streets (and much of downtown) can be more dicey for those traveling alone at night. Night is really the only time to be concerned about safety, as daytime incidents are very, very rare here, especially in busy areas. Police officers are not always easy to find in many areas, as they are off in the more high-crime areas of town, but the Inner Harbor area is very heavily patrolled at all times by officers on foot, on bicycle, and in small vehicles.

SENIOR TRAVELERS
Getting around the Inner Harbor area is a cinch, and there isn't much rowdiness there during the day to ruin your trip; the same is true with other neighborhoods, but those with lots of bars can be a bit much for those looking for a peaceful night out. Much of the waterfront area is very flat and good for walking, and while there are a good deal of stairs around, access ramps are plentiful. There's a good mix of both new and more traditional attractions, all of which are equipped to meet with any particular needs. Most of the big attractions and hotels will offer special rates for seniors, as well as additional discounts (and seniors can ride public transportation for about one-third of the normal cost); these aren't as popular at restaurants, so ask at individual eateries. Safety isn't an issue in the popular neighborhoods, though traveling alone at night in less-populated sections of town might court trouble. Baltimore's role as a healthcare hub for the region means there are a panoply of world-class hospitals in the downtown region, if needed.

GAY AND LESBIAN TRAVELERS

Baltimore is a popular city for gays and lesbians to both visit and live in; a generally well-informed and tolerant population makes for a refreshing lack of unpleasant experiences for gay residents and tourists. The grand homes and cultural sights that populate the Mount Vernon neighborhood have led many people to call the area home, and Mount Vernon is acknowledged to be the heart of the city's gay community, in terms of residents, events, and attractions.

Resources worth checking out include *Gay Life* (www.baltimoregaylife.com), the state's biggest gay, lesbian, bisexual, and transgendered bi-weekly newspaper, and the Gay, Lesbian, Bisexual, and Transgender Community Center of Baltimore and Central Maryland (www.glccb .org), which has some basic info and events listings. Baltimore Pride is the city's annual gay pride festival, held for more than 30 years; spanning a weekend in late June each year in the Mount Vernon neighborhood, the event draws thousands of attendees, performers, and vendors.

TRAVELERS WITH DISABILITIES

Almost all of Baltimore's most popular sights and attractions are easily accessible for all visitors, and city-wide compliance with the Americans with Disabilities Act (ADA) is relatively high, particularly in the downtown area. Neighborhoods like Fell's Point (lots of paving stones) and Mount Vernon (lots of hills and steps) might challenge visitors with disabilities, though even in those areas there are ways to get nearly everywhere. Most of the water-borne attractions in town can accommodate all tourist needs, given advance warning; the Water Taxi has ramps at all docks.

The Maryland Transit Administration (410/539-5000, www.mtamaryland.com/pwd) has expanded its ability to service customers with disabilities with more chair-lift local buses, while other transportation methods (like rail options, including light rail, the Baltimore subway, and MARC) can accommodate wheelchairs via elevators at the stations. The MTA offers reduced rates for people with disabilities that work out to be about one-third the regular cost of travel.

WEATHER

Baltimore's location near the coast, but not on it, and near the South, but not really in it, and near the Appalachian Mountains, but to the east of them, means that the city gets the best of, but not the worst of, the region's climates. The mountains fend off the brutal "lake effect" snowstorms that blanket cities to the west; the inland location means that tropical storms wear down by the time they hit the city; and while the heat and humidity can be dreadful, the scorching temperatures don't last as long as down south. Baltimore gets about 43 inches of precipitation each year, with 21 of that being from snow in January and February, mostly.

July is consistently the hottest month in Baltimore, with an average high of around 91°F. Note that temperatures in the center of Baltimore City will be significantly higher than in the less-dense regions of the city, as the swaths of concrete and blacktop serve as a heat sink, absorbing more of the summer's relentless sun. The coldest month is January, with an average high of 44°F, though an occasional arctic blast will sweep through, dropping temperatures into the teens at night.

Ozone and air quality are big problems during long, hot stretches of the summer, when the air stagnates and becomes unhealthy. Warnings are on the web (www.cleanairpartners.net), broadcast on radio and TV, and published in newspapers.

WHAT TO TAKE

The best guide for selecting clothing for Baltimore should be the weather forecast for your visit. If you're going to be walking around during the heat of summer, you should favor light clothes, as there is a lot of sun-exposed pavement to cover. Thunderstorms can spring up suddenly during spring and summer, so bringing an umbrella or raincoat for a multi-day visit is a wise idea. Nights can be cool in spring and autumn, and serious cold spells don't usually begin until January, which means you won't need your parka unless you're visiting during the few frigid months. A few of the city's large natural areas, like the Maryland Zoo, Fort

McHenry, and Patterson Park, can get pretty buggy during the warmer months, so if you're planning on spending a long afternoon at any of them, some insect repellent is a wise accoutrement. If you're a runner, the flat areas around the Inner Harbor are great for a medium waterfront circuit (Fell's Point to Fort McHenry and back is about 10 miles), so consider packing your running shoes and workout clothes.

Once a notoriously dress-down town, Baltimore has recently decided to spruce up its appearance a bit. Still, if your regular outfit is a golf shirt, loafers, and khakis, or a simple print dress or plain pants and flats, you'll fit in just fine. Note that most locations around the Inner Harbor are used to welcoming tourists in all manner of attire, and should have no issues with shorts and sneakers for dinner.

Some of the newer, more trendy restaurants and lounges do have (and enforce) dress codes, however, so you may want to do a little research before heading out for the evening. And a few of the city's more landmark restaurants require coats for men; venues like the symphony and the opera also preclude themselves to looking dapper. Consider bringing at least one more dressy outfit, like a coat and slacks or a nice dress, to make the most of your visit.

CONDUCT AND CUSTOMS
Smoking
In February 2008, smoking in bars and restaurants (along with almost all other public indoor spaces) was banned in Baltimore City and across the state. This has led to many notoriously smoke-filled places applying new coats of paint and changing their upholstery to get out the years of nicotine and smoke stench; thus, you'll never encounter so many Baltimore bars looking (or smelling) as good as they do now. A couple of cigar-centric bars and lounges have obtained permission to offer smoking areas, but they're not the kinds of places you would accidentally walk into and be surprised to smell smoke. One byproduct of the smoking ban is that the streets of Baltimore are now filled with people stepping outside of taverns and restaurants for a cigarette; sidewalks can be jammed with smokers and clouds of smoke, particularly in nightlife-rich areas like Fell's Point and Federal Hill.

Hours
Baltimore is a 2 A.M. town—except when it's a 1 A.M. town. Not every liquor license is created equal in Baltimore (there are both 1 A.M. and 2 A.M. licenses), so you may want to ask your barkeep when closing time is if you're about to order another round of martinis at 12:45 A.M. Two neighborhoods where getting caught in the late-night "drunk o'clock" rush hour can be a bit challenging are Fell's Point and Federal Hill; young males full of alcohol can be occasionally aggressive, though it's generally toward each other. Many taverns and clubs operate on "bar time," 10–20 minutes ahead of actual time. Restaurants begin closing their kitchens around 10 P.M., although on weekends you may be able to eat later. There are a multitude of great all-night dining options, if you enjoy basic meals that contain lots of grease and eggs. And downtown Baltimore can get pretty quiet after 6 P.M., especially on weeknights in the winter, though the Inner Harbor area is alive with activity well into the night throughout the year.

Tipping
Many service workers in Baltimore are thrilled to get a good tip because, frankly, some Baltimoreans can be lousy tippers. Maybe it's the city's thrifty, blue-collar past. At any rate, here's an opportunity to make an impression. Tip 15–20 percent on all food and beverage service, and you'll make a friend who could come in handy on a return visit. This tip range applies to other services like cabs and concierges, though it's on a sliding scale depending on the degree of difficulty of the job.

Tipping in hotels varies from place to place, but here's who should get something for their efforts, in order of appearance: the doorman who gets your bags, the concierge who maybe gets you some tickets to a ballgame or show, the person who brings room service, the housekeeping staff, and once again, the doorman who gets you a cab and gives you a tip on a restaurant. From $2–20 should cover all of these people, and will probably enhance the quality of your stay. If you stiff everyone, expect to get a similar level of assistance and information.

HEALTH AND SAFETY
Hospitals and Pharmacies
There are several major hospitals in the downtown area, with a few others located farther from the Inner Harbor. In the city's center are **Mercy Hospital** (www.mdmercy.com) and the huge **University of Maryland Medical Center** (www.umms.org); south of Federal Hill is **Harbor Hospital** (www.harborhospital.org); and east of Homewood is **Union Memorial Hospital** (www.unionmemorial.org). The legendary **Johns Hopkins Hospital** (www.hopkinshospital.org) and its various world-class specialty centers are located roughly a mile north of Fell's Point on North Wolfe Street, though Hopkins has other hospitals across the city and region.

Emergency Services
Call 911 if you have a serious medical or safety emergency (alternately, dial 311 if you have a non-critical emergency that may still require law enforcement, fire, or medical personnel). If the power goes out, call Baltimore Gas and Electric (BGE) at 877/778-2222. If you see a power line in a hazardous situation or smell natural gas, call BGE at 410/685-0123. Water and sewer problems are handled by the Baltimore City Department of Public Works; call 311. Baltimore City's Poison Control Center can be reached at 410/528-7701.

Safety
Much of the Baltimore discussed in this book is found within safe, healthy neighborhoods, where trouble is generally rare and crimes are minor. If a neighborhood is clean and you see people of all ages sitting out on their front steps, it's a safe place to be. Yet Baltimore has a serious reputation as a dangerous city, one it has earned through years of violence by young men against each other, generally as a result of the illegal drug trade. But much of this violence occurs in parts of town that 99 percent of tourists and visitors will never go (unless they are looking for locations used in the television show *The Wire*). In the words of a former Baltimore City Health Commissioner, "Baltimore is actually a very safe city if you are not involved in the drug trade. If you are involved, it is one of the most dangerous in the United States." This is a grim reality, but it is a true statement in all respects, and it should not preclude you from taking advantage of the chance to explore and experience this great American city.

It is only after dark that extra care should be used, and generally only in areas lying outside those discussed in this book—though even the safest neighborhoods may have unlit, secluded areas that are best left unexplored at night. The area north of Fell's Point and Little Italy can be unsafe at night, as can the area north of Canton, south of Federal Hill, and east and south of Homewood and Hampden. In Mount Vernon, there are generally lots of people and activity on certain blocks, surrounded by empty zones where crimes are more common.

Information and Services

MAPS AND TOURIST INFORMATION
The best central location for any maps, brochures, guides, and general information about sightseeing and exploring Baltimore can be found at the Inner Harbor's **Baltimore Visitor Center** (401 Light St., 877/225-8466, www.baltimore.org), the low glass building with the grey roof on the west side of the waterfront. Not only is this place filled with printed materials and helpful staffers, there are lots of kiosks and terminals where you can find out more info and even purchase tickets to events and attractions.

Fell's Point is the only neighborhood with its own full-time visitors center (1724 Thames

St., 410/675-6751, www.preservationsociety
.com); it's worth stopping by for information,
maps, and a look around at the artifacts, as
well as for recommendations from the staff.
Many of the major downtown hotels also offer
large selections of brochures and information,
and the concierges there should be able to help
with most basic inquiries, and can recommend
sights, restaurants, and other attractions.

MEDIA AND COMMUNICATION
Phones and Area Codes
There are two area codes in the Baltimore region: 410 and 443. The 410 area code has two
zones; in the north and west, it covers the central part of Maryland, including the city and
the counties of Baltimore, Carroll, and Howard,
among others; the southernmost area covers the
Annapolis area (Anne Arundel County) and
the Eastern Shore's many counties, and is considered a long-distance call. The 443 area code
was added in 1997, and often is used for cellular
telephones; it covers the same region as 410. You
must include the area code, whether it is 410 or
443, when dialing a phone number.

Internet Services
The **Enoch Pratt Free Library** (410/396-5430,
www.prattlibrary.org), Baltimore City's public
library system, offers Internet access to all library patrons; a library card is not required
for use. There are 22 branches of the library,
including the Central Library (400 Cathedral
St.), which is the only location to offer high-
speed wireless connectivity. Other free Wi-Fi
access spots include many of the city's coffee
shops, and even a couple of taverns. Many hotels and BWI Airport also Wi-Fi, though it's
not always free (BWI charges for it).

Mail and Messenger Services
There are many **United States Postal Service**
post offices in Baltimore; check www.usps
.gov or 800/275-8777 for locations. The central Baltimore post office is at 900 East Fayette
Street downtown, at the foot of I-83 and just
across the street from the Phoenix Shot Tower;
this sprawling building has extended hours and

services. There are also several **FedEx** (www
.fedex.com/us/officeprint/main) locations
in the city, as well as two **UPS** stores (www
.theupsstore.com) and other outlets like Mail
Boxes Etc. (www.mbe.com).

Messenger services are also available; best
bets include **Maryland Messenger** (www
.marylandmessenger.com) and **VMW Logistic**
(www.vmwlogistic.com).

Magazines and Newspapers
The *Baltimore Sun* is the city's major newspaper and only daily paper, and has won numerous
Pulitzer Prizes in its past. The *Sun's* parent company also publishes the free *b,* geared toward a
younger readership and published five days a
week. *City Paper* is the city's alternative weekly
free paper, and is a good resource for finding
bands, concerts, and other event listings.

Other publications include the *Baltimore
Business Journal,* which covers regional
business; the *Daily Record,* which covers law
and business; the *Catholic Review;* and the
Baltimore Jewish Times. The historic *Afro-
American Newspaper* (called "The Afro") is
one of the nation's oldest African American–
owned and –operated papers. *Gay Life* is the
state's primary weekly paper for the gay, lesbian,
bisexual, and transgendered communities.

Baltimore magazine is the city's glossy
lifestyle publication, and is the oldest city
magazine in the nation. Its regular "Best
Restaurants" and "Best of Baltimore" features
are handy guides to the city's top destinations.
Style is another lifestyle magazine that covers the region.

Radio and TV
There are six television stations in Baltimore,
covering all of the major networks and PBS,
seen locally on **Maryland Public Television**
(www.mpt.org, channel 22).

A good listing of Baltimore stations can
be found at www.ontheradio.net. The most
useful stations to know are **WERQ 92.3 FM**
(urban contemporary and hip-hop), **WPOC
93.1 FM** (country), **WEAA 88.9 FM** (jazz),
WBJC 91.5 FM (classical), **WTMD 89.7 AM**

RELOCATING TO BALTIMORE

Baltimore has done a surprisingly good job of marketing itself to out-of-towners, particularly from Washington, D.C., in the past decade – the city's relative affordability, great neighborhoods, and fun, quirky ethos and spirit are all selling points. The quasi-public agency that handles this is **Live Baltimore** (343 N. Charles St., 410/637-3750, www.livebaltimore.com), which has all sorts of materials and knowledgeable staffers to help those considering making Charm City their home. Their detailed neighborhood maps and information are second to none, and are frequently used by residents for research. They can also provide cost-of-living info, as well as information on taxes and fees and lots of other incredibly useful data.

FINDING A JOB

The city's Department of Human Resources lists jobs online at www.baltimorecity.gov/government/personnel/currlist.php. Johns Hopkins University and Hospital, as well as the University of Maryland Medical System (UMMS), are major employers in Baltimore, and are good places to look for work. Find their job postings online at www.hrnt.jhu.edu/jhujobs (for Johns Hopkins) and www.umms careers.com (for UMMS).

More online resources worth looking at include the usual career sites, more community-based operations like Craigslist (http://baltimore.craigslist.org), and those of the major city newspapers.

HOUSING

Live Baltimore is the preeminent source for information about finding a neighborhood that's right for you. It also has tips on finding a home or apartment to purchase (or rent) in Baltimore, though much of the information the agency provides is geared toward those purchasing a home. Homes for sale, and properties for rent, can also be found on community web listings, like Craigslist, or on the real estate pages (both printed and web) of the city's major local newspapers, particularly the *Baltimore Sun* and the *City Paper*. Unlike some major cities, if you're looking to rent, you don't need to acquire the services of a realtor. If you are looking to buy, however, there are several major real estate companies that will be happy to help you find a place to purchase (Long and Foster and Coldwell Banker are the region's largest). There are also an increasing number of web options for direct buyer and seller transactions.

(alternative), and **WBAL 1090 AM** (news and talk). Baltimore's public radio station is **WYPR 88.1 FM,** which plays NPR shows and local interest broadcasts.

PUBLIC LIBRARIES

Baltimore's public library system, the **Enoch Pratt Free Library** (www.prattlibrary.org), is one of the first in the nation, and remains one of the better city libraries in America today. First begun in 1882, with a gift of more than $1 million from Enoch Pratt, the library he envisioned "shall be for all, rich and poor without distinction of race or color, who, when properly accredited, can take out the books if they will handle them carefully and return them." That was a big deal back in 1882, as Baltimore was still a very segregated city. The central library first opened in 1886 (then on Mulberry Street) followed by several branches soon thereafter; a large donation from Andrew Carnegie in the early 20th century allowed for even more branches to open. Despite some budget cuts and branch closures in the 1990s, the library has recently begun to add new branches and update buildings and services to better serve Baltimore's citizens.

The current **central library** at 400 Cathedral Street (410/396-5430) was built in 1931, and today houses more than 3,500,000 books, periodicals, tapes, and other publications. An addition was added a few years ago, which included a new and expanded African American collection and a new home for the Maryland

© GEOFF BROWN

one of the first public libraries in America, the Enoch Pratt Free Library

Room—a collection of Baltimore- and Maryland-specific publications and tomes, and an intriguing place to browse.

PLACES OF WORSHIP

Baltimore (and Maryland) was founded in part by Catholics who were unwelcome in England; fittingly, Baltimore is home to the nation's first cathedral and first archdiocese. But many other religions found a home in Baltimore, and their houses of worship can be found all across the city. Protestant and Catholic churches abound throughout Baltimore; some are grand and historic, while others are more humble places to commune with a higher power. Jewish communities also flourished here, though many city Jews moved to the county in the mid- and late 20th century and set up new synagogues there.

The *Catholic Review* newspaper provides lots of good information on Catholic services and community events; the **Archdiocese of Baltimore** has a useful website at www.archbalt.org. The **Basilica of the Assumption** (409 Cathedral St., 410/727-3565, www.baltimorebasilica.org) is the city's grandest Catholic cathedral and the first in the United States.

The *Baltimore Jewish Times* is a good resource for finding out about the variety of Jewish congregations in Baltimore City and the surrounding suburbs; **The Associated: Jewish Community Federation of Baltimore** has a comprehensive list as well at www.associated.org.

Baltimore's traditionally African American churches are some of the most popular in the region, and serve as both anchors of the community's spiritual health and advocates for the community's physical needs and concerns. The largest and most established congregations include **Bethel AME Church** (1300 Druid Hill Ave., 410/523-4273, www.bethel1.org) and **Leadenhall Baptist Church** (1021 Leadenhall St., 410/539-9334).

Buddhists should explore the website of the **Buddhist Network of Greater Baltimore** (www.bngb.org) to find a nearby group or center; Muslims can contact the **Islamic Society of Baltimore** (www.isb.org) for a list of places to attend prayers.

MAJOR BANKS

Once home to several major local banking concerns, Baltimore is now just another branch city, albeit one served by a wide variety of national financial corporations. **Bank of America, M&T Bank,** and **PNC** have many branches and ATMs across the city. A few local banks remain, including **First Mariner Bank, Harbor Bank,** and **Provident Bank.** Expect to pay from $2–3 per ATM transaction if the machine is not operated by your bank.

RESOURCES

Suggested Reading

HISTORY, NONFICTION, AND GENERAL INFORMATION

Bell, Madison Smartt. *Charm City: A Walk Through Baltimore.* Crown Publishing Group, 2007. Bell, an award-winning novelist, took a variety of strolls through some of Baltimore's best-known and least-traveled neighborhoods, using the slow pace of a walk to unfurl the history and character of each area. This is a great book to familiarize yourself with the city, its past, and its residents.

Hayward, Mary Ellen and Shivers, Frank R., Jr. *The Architecture of Baltimore.* Johns Hopkins University Press, 2004. A beautiful book that's an update of a classic tome that chronicled the creation of the city. This new version, a hefty 416 pages, uses photos, maps, and narrative to tell the tale of Baltimore's buildings.

Hirschland, Ellen B. and Ramage, Nancy Hirschland. *The Cone Sisters of Baltimore: Collecting at Full Tilt.* Northwestern University Press, 2008. A fascinating look at the lives and pursuits of the modern-art-collecting Cone sisters (Claribel and Etta), written by the great-niece and great-great-niece of the Cones. A great companion book to a tour of the Cone Collection at the Baltimore Museum of Art.

Sandler, Gilbert. *Jewish Baltimore: A Family Album.* Johns Hopkins University Press, 2000. Sandler is the city's most prominent social historian, first as a journalist, and then as a civic resource, hired on by foundations and museums for his knowledge. This book traces the growth of, and life within, the Jewish communities of Baltimore, and their gradual migration to the suburbs.

Shopes, Linda. *The Baltimore Book: New Views of Local History.* Temple University Press, 1993. This book provides a more scholarly and critical look at the history of Baltimore, focusing on populations that were often not beneficiaries of boom times, including women and African Americans.

Simon, David and Burns, Edward. *The Corner.* Broadway Books, 1998. Few books manage to explain the nation's (and Baltimore's) ruin due to illegal drugs, as well as show the immediate and long-term human toll, as this book, by the creator of *The Wire.*

LITERATURE AND FICTION

Lippman, Laura. *Baltimore Blues.* Avon, 2007. The first of the former *Sun* reporter's Tess Monaghan crime novel series, this quick read has Tess tailing a loathed defense attorney through Baltimore's streets—and then investigating his murder.

Lippman, Laura. *Baltimore Noir.* Akashic Books, 2006. Lippman serves as editor of this collection of crime fiction featuring Charm

City and its less-savory inhabitants: 16 tales of malfeasance and murder, set all over town, rich in local lore and color.

Mencken, H. L. *Happy Days: Mencken's Autobiography: 1880–1892*. Vintage Books, 1982. The first of Mencken's three-volume "Days" autobiography, this book tracks the days and thoughts of a young Mencken in the bustling Baltimore of the late 19th century.

Tyler, Anne. *The Accidental Tourist.* Ballantine Books, 2002. Almost all of Tyler's rich, character-driven books are set in Baltimore, but this tale of a heartbroken couple is the one with the most fans. Tyler's 1989 novel *Breathing Lessons* won the Pulitzer Prize.

Suggested Viewing

All of the features listed here are available on DVD from a variety of sources.

Diner. Directed by Baltimore native Barry Levinson, this 1982 film re-creates his experiences growing up in Charm City during 1959. A great film, and a great primer on Baltimore life.

Global Harbors: A Waterfront Renaissance. This revealing 2008 documentary traces the development of Baltimore's revolutionary Inner Harbor, interviews the main players in the project and its creation, and reveals how its success drew international attention and copycats.

Hairspray. John Waters' 1988 breakthrough (to a wider audience, that is) film traces the trials and tribulations of Tracy Turnblad in 1962 Baltimore, confronting prejudices and bigotry while also learning to dance—and love. This film, which is filled with music but not a true musical, begat the hit Broadway production, which begat a 2007 film version of that musical. Stick with this, the original, which was shot in Baltimore.

The Wire. No other television show has so defined or revealed a city as former newspaper writer David Simon's unrelenting look at the effect of the war on drugs on the citizens of Baltimore—from regular people, to addicts, to cops, to crime kingpins, to school kids, to the media. The series first aired on HBO in 2002, and lasted for five seasons.

Internet Resources

GENERAL INFORMATION

Baltimore Area Convention and Visitors Association
www.baltimore.org
Operated by BACVA, this is a very comprehensive and user-friendly site, offering listings and information on the city, attractions, and events. A great single-site resource to answer many basic (and even some obscure) questions about Baltimore. Visitors can also find special deals and bargain packages for tourists here.

Baltimore Collegetown Network
www.baltimorecollegetown.org
This collaboration between 16 Baltimore-area colleges and universities provides tips on how to navigate the city; places to eat, drink, and hang out; and cultural suggestions. Useful for college kids, and people traveling with teens

looking for something to do that won't bore them to death.

Bawlmerese
www.baltimorehon.com
This good-natured listing of examples of the local dialect ("Baltimorese," which in that dialect is said as "Bawlmerese") is a pretty thorough listing of the ways some white working-class Baltimoreans speak; the dialect itself is beginning to vanish due to urban gentrification.

City of Baltimore
www.ci.baltimore.md.us
The city's official website provides links to the mayor's office, city council, and the numerous city agencies that keep Baltimore moving and working. There's a surprising amount of info here, as well as great ways to contact city officials or answer civic questions.

Enoch Pratt Free Library
www.prattlibrary.org
In addition to providing the library catalog online, this site has plenty of historic and cultural information and suggestions. There are also links to the numerous ways to contact a librarian to ask a question, from getting an important date in Baltimore history to more scholarly queries.

Live Baltimore
www.livebaltimore.com
Created as part of Baltimore's efforts to lure residents and show off the city's charms, this website is also a great place to learn about the town's varied neighborhoods, and there are dozens of useful links and informative pages to be found here.

EVENT LISTINGS

Baltimore Fun Guide
www.baltimorefunguide.com
A colorful, easy-to-use collection of events, exhibits, and more, searchable by lots of different criteria, and there are special offers and package deals to be found here, too.

City Paper
www.citypaper.com
The city's independent, alternative weekly's website has the best guide to the less-traditional events, activities, and happenings that are going on in Baltimore.

Metromix Baltimore
www.baltimore.metromix.com
Operated by the *Baltimore Sun*'s parent company, this website offers information on an enormous amount of events, restaurants, clubs, and more of Baltimore's social goings-on, though the details can be a little scant.

BALTIMORE'S BEST BLOGS

Baltimore Grows
www.baltimoregrows.com
The city of Baltimore has undergone a tremendous amount of construction, renewal, and change in the past decade, and though this blog hasn't been around the whole time, it does a very good job covering the latest projects and upgrades to the city, as well as offering a little commentary about Baltimore's transformation.

Bmore Art
www.bmoreart.blogspot.com
Dedicated to the city's growing and vibrant independent arts scene, Bmore Art is a broad and comprehensive guide to what's happening at galleries, worthwhile upcoming shows, crafts, and general news about Baltimore arts and artists.

The Mobtown Shank
www.sugarfreak.typepad.com
A mix of politics, music, art, and Baltimore events, all presented with a vociferously liberal bent and (generally) a knowing wink. Run by the co-owner of Hampden's Atomic Books.

Index

A

Aberdeen: 197
Academy Art Museum: 204
Adventure Park USA: 198
adventure sports: 146
African American Heritage Festival: 128
air travel: 227, 229
Amaranthine Museum: 50
American Visionary Art Museum, The: 41
Annapolis: 191-198
Antietam National Battlefield: 199
antique shops, Frederick: 202
antique shops, Howard Street: 173
Antreasian Gallery, The: 115
aquatic center: 144
arts: 114-123
arts and leisure: 112-149
Artscape: 128
arts, crafts, and folk traditions: 222
Avalon Theatre: 204

B

Babe Ruth Birthplace and Museum: 27
background: 211-226
Baltimore-Annapolis Trail: 133
Baltimore Blast: 139
Baltimore Book Festival: 129
Baltimore Burn: 138
Baltimore Maritime Museum: 27
Baltimore Museum of Art: 50
Baltimore Museum of Industry: 42
Baltimore Orioles: 135
Baltimore Public Works Museum: 35
Baltimore Ravens: 138
Baltimore Rowing Club: 141
Baltimore Running Festival & Marathon, The: 130
Baltimore Streetcar Museum: 44
B&O Railroad Museum: 53
banks: 238
baseball: 135
Basilica of the Assumption: 44
bicycling: 133, 231
Bikram Yoga: 149

Billie Holiday & Cab Calloway Vocal Competition: 129
biotechnology: 218
Brown Memorial Presbyterian Church: 46
bus travel: 228

C

Canton: 20; map 3 8-9
Canton Kayak Club: 141
Capt. Don's Fishing Charter: 142
Carroll Park: 147
Carroll Park Skateboarding and Bike Facility: 149
car travel: 229, 230
Center Stage: 117
C. Grimaldis Gallery: 115
Charles Carroll House: 191
Charles Theatre, The: 121
Charm City Bowl: 146
Charm City Roller Girls: 140
Charm City Skate Park: 149
Charm City Yoga: 149
Chesapeake Bay Bridge: 206
Chesapeake Bay Maritime Museum: 208
children, traveling with: 232
cinema: 121, 225, 226
Clifton Park: 148
climate: 212
concert venues: 119
Contemporary Museum, The: 46
crab: 62, 82
Creative Alliance at the Patterson: 117
Current Gallery: 115
Cylburn Arboretum: 132

D

demographics: 220
disabilities, travelers with: 233
disabled access: 232
Dominic "Mimi" DiPietro Family Ice Skating Center: 148
Domino Sugars Sign, The: 43
Downtown and Inner Harbor: 20; map 1 4-5

Downtown Sailing Center: 141
Dr. Samuel D. Harris National Museum of Dentistry: 29
Druid Hill Park: 132
duckpin bowling: 146

E
Easton: 204-208
economy: 218-220
Edgar Allan Poe House & Museum: 54
Edgar Allan Poe's Grave: 34
education: 219
emergency services: 235
environmental issues: 212
essentials: 227-238
events: 124-130
Evergreen: 55
Everyman Theatre: 117
excursions: 188-210

F
farmers markets: 92
Federal Hill: 21; map 4 10-11
Federal Hill Park: 43
Fell's Point: 20; map 2 6-7
Fell's Point Visitor Center: 36
festivals: 124-130
film: 225, 226
1st Mariner Bank Arena: 119
fishing: 142
Flower Mart: 126
football: 138
Forest Park: 148
Fort McHenry National Monument and Historic Shrine: 55, 132
14Karat Cabaret, The: 118
Fourth of July: 129
Frederick Douglass-Isaac Myers Maritime Park: 36
Frederick Douglass "Path to Freedom" Walking Tour: 144
Frederick: 198-204
Frederick Keys: 200
Free Fall Baltimore: 130

G
galleries: 115

Gallery Imperato: 116
Garrett-Jacobs Mansion: 46
gay and lesbian travelers: 233
geography: 212
George Peabody Library: 47
Geppi's Entertainment Museum: 29
golf: 147
government: 217-218
Goya Contemporary: 116
Great Baltimore Fire: 215
Greater Baltimore: map 7 16-17
Great Halloween Lantern Parade, The: 130
G Spot, The: 116
Gwynns Falls Trail: 133
gyms: 142

H
Hampden and Homewood: 21; map 6 14-15
Harborplace: 29
Havre de Grace Decoy Museum: 197
health: 235
health care industry: 218
health clubs: 142
Heritage Walk: 144
High Zero Festival: 126
Hippodrome Theatre, The: 119
Historical Society of Frederick County: 201
Historical Society of Talbot County: 205
history: 213-217
Homewood: see Hampden and Homewood
Homewood House: 51
HonFest: 126
horse racing: 139
hospitals: 235
hotels: 175-187; see also Hotels Index
hours: 234
Howard P. Rawlings Conservatory and Botanic Gardens of Baltimore: 52

IJK
ice skating: 148
IMAX Theater at Maryland Science Center: 121
information: 235-238
Inner Harbor: see Downtown and Inner Harbor

Internet resources: 240
Internet services: 236
itineraries: 22-24
Jewish Museum of Maryland: 37
Johns Hopkins University Spring Fair: 126
Joseph Meyerhoff Symphony Hall,
    The: 120
kayaking: 141
Kinetic Sculpture Race: 127
Kunta Kinte-Alex Haley Memorial, The: 191

L
lacrosse: 139
Lacrosse Museum & National Hall of
    Fame: 52
Lake Montebello: 134
Landmark Theatres: 121
language: 222
LatinoFest: 127
Light Street Cycles: 134
literature: 223
Little Italy: 20; map 2 6-7
Lyric Opera House, The: 120

M
MAC Harbor East: 142
magazines: 236
mail: 236
maps, tourist: 235
Maryland Art Place: 30
Maryland Film Festival: 127
Maryland Historical Society: 47
Maryland Hunt Cup: 127
Maryland Science Center: 30
Maryland State House: 192
Maryland Zoo in Baltimore: 52
Mayor's Christmas Parade, The: 124
Meadowbrook Aquatic Center: 144
media: 236
medical research: 218
Meredith Gallery: 116
Merritt Athletic Clubs Canton: 142
Merritt Fort Avenue: 143
Merritt's Downtown Athletic Club: 143
MICA Brown Center: 122
Miracle on 34th Street: 124
Mount Clare Mansion: 56
Mount Pleasant: 148

Mount Vernon: 21; map 5 12-13
Mount Vernon Walking Tours: 144
movie theaters: 121
music: 224

NOP
National Aquarium in Baltimore: 31
National Great Blacks in Wax Museum: 57
National Museum of
    Civil War Medicine: 201
National Shrine of St. Elizabeth Ann
    Seton: 201
neighborhoods: 20-21
newspapers: 236
nightlife: 96-111; *see also* Nightlife Index
Night of 100 Elvises, The: 125
North Central Railroad Trail: 134
Otakon: 129
outdoor movies: 123
packing tips: 233
parks: 131
Patterson Bowling Center: 147
Patterson Park: 40
people and culture: 220-226
pharmacies: 235
Phoenix (Old Baltimore) Shot Tower: 37
phones: 236
Pickering Creek Audubon Center: 205
Pier 6 Concert Pavilion: 121
Pimlico Race Course: 139
planning tips: 20-21
Port Discovery Children's Museum: 33
Preakness Stakes, The: 127
Princeton Sports: 135
public libraries: 237
public transportation: 230

QR
radio: 236
reading, suggested: 239
recreation: 131-149
Reginald F. Lewis Museum of Maryland
    African American History & Culture: 38
religion: 45, 221, 238
relocating to Baltimore: 237
resources: 239-241
restaurants: 58-95; *see also* Restaurants
    Index

Ride the Ducks Baltimore: 145
Riverside Park: 132
Robert E. Lee Park: 133
Robert Long House: 37
roller derby: 140
Rotunda Cinematheque, The: 122
rowing: 141

S
safety: 235
sailboat, Annapolis sightseeing by: 193
sailing: 141
Schaumburg, Wayne: 146
School 33 Art Center: 116
Secrets of a Seaport Walking Tour: 145
Segs in the City: 146
Senator Theatre, The: 123
senior travelers: 232
services: 235-238
shops: 150-174; see also Shops Index
sights: 25-57
skateboarding: 149
skipjack tours: 208
smoking: 234
soccer, indoor: 139
Sports Legends Museum at Camden
    Yards: 33
S.S. John Brown: 40
St. Anthony Italian Festival: 128
Star-Spangled Banner Flag House: 38
steeplechase: 127
St. John's College: 193
St. Michaels: 208-210
Stoneleigh Lanes Duckpin Bowling
    Center: 147
St. Patrick's Day Parade: 125
streetball: 143
Sub-Basement Artist Studios: 116

T
taxis: 230
television: 225, 226, 236

tennis: 148
Thanksgiving Parade: 130
theater: 117
Theatre Hopkins: 118
Theatre Project: 118
Thomas Point Shoal Lighthouse: 193
Thurgood Marshall Memorial: 193
Tidewater Yacht Service: 142
tipping: 234
tips for travelers: 232-235
Top of the World Observation Deck: 34
Tour du Port: 130
tourism: 219
tourist information: 235
tours, guided and walking: 144
train travel: 228
transportation: 227-232
Trapeze School of Baltimore: 146

UVWXYZ
U.S. Army Ordnance Museum: 197
U.S. Naval Academy: 194
U.S.S. Constellation: 34
Vagabond Theater: 118
Velocipede Bike Project: 135
viewing, suggested: 240
Walters Art Museum: 48
Washington Monument, The: 49
Washington Monument Lighting: 126
water taxi: 231
Wayne Schaumburg: 146
weather: 233
Weinberg Center for the Arts: 201
West Marine: 142
Westminster Hall and Edgar Allan Poe's
    Grave: 34
Whartscape: 129
William Paca House: 195
women travelers: 232
yoga: 149
Zippy Tours with Zippy Larson: 146

Restaurants Index

Abacrombie: 85
Akbar: 89
Aldo's: 73
Ambassador Dining Room, The: 94
Amicci's: 71
Angelo's Pizza: 90
Annabel Lee Tavern: 74
Attman's: 73
b: 86
Baltimore Cupcake Company: 83
Ban Thai: 60
Bertha's: 69
Bicycle, The: 79
Birches: 74
Black Olive, The: 69
Blue Agave: 83
Blue Moon Café: 64
Blue Sea Grill: 62
Bo Brooks: 76
Brass Elephant: 88
Brewer's Art, The: 86
Brick Oven Pizza: 69
Burke's Café: 60
Caesar's Den: 71
Café Hon: 90
Cakelove: 76
Captain James Landing: 64
Cazbar: 63
Chameleon Café, The: 95
Charleston: 65
Cinghiale: 67
City Café: 86
Claddagh Pub: 75
Common Ground, A: 91
Corks: 80
Da Mimmo: 71
Della Notte: 73
Ding How: 65
Dogwood: 92
Donna's (Homewood): 91
Donna's (Mount Vernon): 86
Du Claw Brewing Co.: 64

Dukem: 88
Faidley Seafood: 62
Gecko's: 77
Germano's Trattoria: 71
Gertrude's: 92
Golden West Café: 94
Harvest Table: 78
Helen's Garden: 75
Helmand, The: 84
Henninger's Tavern: 65
Hollywood Diner: 61
Hull Street Blues: 78
Iggie's: 88
India Rasoi: 74
Indigma: 89
Ixia: 86
Jimmy's Restaurant: 68
Joe Squared: 87
Junior's Wine Bar: 80
Kali's Court: 69
Kumari: 89
La Cazuela: 68
La Scala: 73
La Tavola: 73
Lebanese Taverna: 69
Louisiana: 68
L. P. Steamer's: 81
Mama's on the Half Shell: 77
Matsuri: 79
Matthew's Pizzeria: 76
McCormick & Schmick's: 74
Minato: 84
Nacho Mama's: 77
Neo Viccino: 89
Nick's Fish House: 95
Nick's Oyster Bar: 83
Obrycki's Crab House: 67
Papermoon Diner: 93
Pazo: 70
Pazza Luna: 83
Peter's Inn: 66
Petit Louis Bistro: 95

Phillips Harborplace: 61
Pierpoint: 66
Prime Rib, The: 84
Py: 76
Regi's: 81
Rocket to Venus: 93
Rusty Scupper: 83
Ryleigh's Oyster: 84
Sabatino's: 71
Salt: 67
Sascha's 527 Café: 87
Shucker's: 65
Sip & Bite Restaurant: 68
SoBo Café: 81
Sotto Sopra: 88
Sushi Hana: 95
Suzie's Soba: 91

Tapas Teatro: 90
Ten-O-Six: 79
Thai Landing: 84
Thairish: 85
Three: 75
Tio Pepe: 90
Tutti Gusti: 77
Vaccaro's: 74
Watertable: 63
Werner's Restaurant: 60
Wharf Rat, The: 61
Wine Market, The: 81
Woodberry Kitchen: 93
XS: 88
Yabba Pot, The: 94
Ze Mean Bean Café: 68

Nightlife Index

An die Musik Live: 98
Bartender's: 100
Brewer's Art, The: 100
Captain Larry's: 101
Cat's Eye Pub, The: 101
Charm City Art Space: 98
Chesapeake Wine Company, The: 107
Club 1722: 110
Club Bunns: 110
Club Charles: 101
Club One: 100
Club Orpheus: 100
Coconuts Cafe: 110
Depot, The: 100
Drinkery, The: 110
Duda's Tavern: 102
Eden's Lounge: 108
8x10: 99
Explorer's Lounge: 102
Friends: 102
Grand Central: 111
Grand Cru: 107
Havana Club: 108

Hippo, The: 111
John Steven: 102
J. Patrick's Irish Pub: 103
Little Havana: 103
Mahaffey's: 103
Max's on Broadway: 103
Metro Gallery: 99
Mosaic: 108
Mount Royal Tavern: 104
Mum's: 104
One Eyed Mike's: 105
Ottobar, The: 99
Paradox: 110
Power Plant Live!: 105
Pub Dog, The: 105
Ram's Head Live: 99
Red Maple: 108
Sonar: 99
13th Floor, The: 106
Tusk Lounge, The: 106
V-NO: 107
Wharf Rat, The: 106
Zeeba Lounge: 109

Shops Index

About Faces: 166
American Visionary Art Museum Eye
   Shop: 165
An die Musik: 156
Another Period in Time: 172
Antique Center at Federal Hill: 172
Antique Row Stalls: 172
Arundel Mills Mall: 171
Atomic Books: 156
Avenue Antiques: 172
Babe: 160
Baltimore Chop, The: 156
Baltimore Clayworks: 155
Bediboo: 168
Belvedere Square: 171
Benjamin Lovell: 169
Blu Vintage: 160
Bratt Decor: 168
Cloud 9: 160
Coradetti Glassworks: 155
Corduroy Button: 168
Craig Flinner Gallery: 173
Crosskeys Antiques: 173
Cupcake: 160
Daedalus Books and Music: 157
Dimensions in Music: 157
Dogma: 168
Doubledutch Boutique: 161
Drusilla's Books: 173
Dubey's Art and Antiques: 174
El Suprimo: 158
Form: 161
Gallery, The: 171
Glarus Chocolatier: 165
Good Yarn, A: 156
Handbags in the City: 161
Holly G.: 162
Housewerks: 154
Howl: 168
Imperial Half Bushel, The: 174
In Watermelon Sugar: 165

Joanna Gray of London: 169
Jos. A. Bank: 159
Kashmir Imports: 162
Kelmscott Bookshop, The: 158
Kiss N Make Up: 166
Le Petit Cochon: 166
Lovelyarns: 156
Maja: 166
Ma Petite Shoe: 169
Matava Too: 169
Milagro: 162
M Salon: 167
Normal's Books and Records: 158
Nouveau: 164
Pad: 164
Patrick Sutton Home: 164
People United, A: 162
Poppy and Stella: 170
Pretentious Pooch: 169
Read Street Books: 158
Red Tree: 164
Reptilian Records: 158
Samuel Parker Clothier: 159
Sassanova: 170
Second Chance: 154
Seeds: 167
Shine Collective: 162
Shofer's: 165
Shop Gentei: 160
SoBotanical: 167
Sound Garden, The: 159
South Moon Under: 163
Sprout: 167
Studio 921 Salon & Day Spa: 167
Su Casa: 165
Towson Town Center: 171
Trixie's Palace: 163
True Vine, The: 159
2910 on the Square: 166
Urban Chic: 163
Village of Cross Keys: 172

Hotels Index

Admiral Fell Inn, The: 181
Baltimore Hostel: 178
Baltimore Marriott Waterfront: 182
Blue Door on Baltimore: 182
Brookshire Suites: 178
Celie's Waterfront Inn: 182
Courtyard by Marriott: 183
Days Inn Inner Harbor: 178
1840s Carrollton Inn: 184
Fairfield Inn & Suites: 184
4 East Madison Inn: 186
Four Points by Sheraton BWI Airport: 187
Hampton Inn and Suites Inner Harbor: 178
Hilton Baltimore: 179
Homewood Suites by Hilton Baltimore: 183

Hopkins Inn: 186
Hotel Monaco Baltimore: 179
Hyatt Regency Baltimore: 180
Inn at Henderson's Wharf, The: 183
Inn at the Colonnade: 187
Inn at 2920: 185
InterContinental Baltimore: 180
Peabody Court by Clarion: 186
Pier 5 Hotel: 184
Radisson Hotel at Cross Keys: 187
Renaissance Harborplace Hotel: 180
Scarborough Fair B&B: 185
Sheraton Baltimore North: 187
Springhill Suites by Marriott: 180
Tremont Plaza: 181

Acknowledgments

Even though this book has only one name on the cover, there is a long list of people whose advice, aid, confidence, and work made this guide possible.

First, I want to dedicate this book to my father, Peter Brown, and my mother, Terri Jo Brown, who died while I was working on the first round of edits. She was a genealogist, researcher, and writer herself, and I know that writing this book—my first—made her proud; so, here's to Ma. My parents—and particularly my mom—encouraged me to read and develop a love of the written word, and they helped me to be a writer.

My first thanks go to two old Baltimore friends. First is the fantastic Jim Duffy, from whom I have learned how to be both a better writer and a less-ornery person. And thanks also go to Christine Spangler, who always has my back.

I also want to thank all of my colleagues at *Baltimore* magazine over the years, with two people in particular getting special thanks. Katie Swartz did a great job helping me get my proposal materials together; and the wonderful Marge Shaw, who still keeps me on the straight-and-narrow.

At Avalon, most importantly, comes acquisitions director Grace Fujimoto, who signed me up for *Moon Baltimore*—I thank her for her confidence and her patience. I want to thank production coordinator Elizabeth Jang, whose enthusiasm and curiosity helped me to take the best photos I've ever taken in my life. Editor Kathryn Ettinger brought order and guidance to a project that, very occasion-ally, seemed a bit too much for one person (that would be me) to keep in coherent order. Kevin Anglin and Albert Angulo turned my roughly marked, multi-colored, microscopi-cally detailed notes into great maps; as a big cartography nerd, you have my thanks.

There is a long list of people here in Baltimore who went out of their way to help me research and write this book, and I cannot thank you all individually, but you know who you are, and you have my sin-cere thanks, and I probably owe you some drinks. In particular, I want to thank ev-eryone at Baltimore's great historic sites, museums, and attractions for all of their help. In particular, Phyllis Feldmann at Evergreen, Catherine Arthur at Home-wood House, and the staff at Mount Clare Mansion were incredibly helpful. The Bal-timore Area Convention and Visitors Asso-ciation (BACVA) and the Maryland Office of Tourism also provided great informa-tion and photos. Also, I want to thank the amazing Carole Carroll and Craig Cur-ley for their kindness, and for revealing so many of Baltimore's secret and magnificent stories and events.

Finally, I want to give the greatest thanks my wife, Stacey Mink, for being so resolute in her support, criticism, suggestions, and enthusiasm. From the words to the photos to countless road trips and research jaunts, Stacey made this book better by pushing me to always do my best job, and I cannot thank her enough for her help. You are the best thing ever. Now, let's go eat.

www.moon.com

DESTINATIONS | ACTIVITIES | BLOGS | MAPS | BOOKS

MOON.COM is all new, and ready to help plan your next trip! Filled with fresh trip ideas and strategies, author interviews, informative blogs, a detailed map library, and descriptions of all the Moon guidebooks, Moon.com is all you need to get out and explore the world—or even places in your own backyard. As always, when you travel with Moon, expect an experience that is uncommon and truly unique.

MAP SYMBOLS

Expressway	Highlight	Airfield	Golf Course
Primary Road	City/Town	Airport	Parking Area
Secondary Road	State Capital	Mountain	Archaeological Site
Unpaved Road	National Capital	Unique Natural Feature	Church
Trail	Point of Interest		Gas Station
Ferry	Accommodation	Waterfall	Glacier
Railroad	Restaurant/Bar	Park	Mangrove
Pedestrian Walkway	Other Location	Trailhead	Reef
Stairs	Campground	Skiing Area	Swamp

CONVERSION TABLES

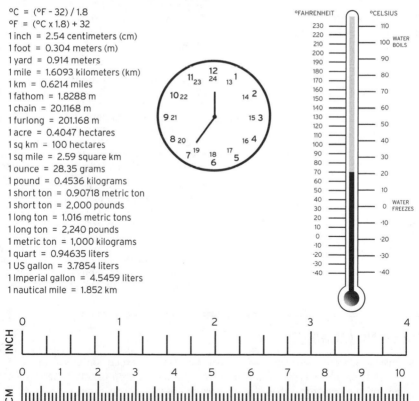

°C = (°F - 32) / 1.8
°F = (°C x 1.8) + 32
1 inch = 2.54 centimeters (cm)
1 foot = 0.304 meters (m)
1 yard = 0.914 meters
1 mile = 1.6093 kilometers (km)
1 km = 0.6214 miles
1 fathom = 1.8288 m
1 chain = 20.1168 m
1 furlong = 201.168 m
1 acre = 0.4047 hectares
1 sq km = 100 hectares
1 sq mile = 2.59 square km
1 ounce = 28.35 grams
1 pound = 0.4536 kilograms
1 short ton = 0.90718 metric ton
1 short ton = 2,000 pounds
1 long ton = 1.016 metric tons
1 long ton = 2,240 pounds
1 metric ton = 1,000 kilograms
1 quart = 0.94635 liters
1 US gallon = 3.7854 liters
1 Imperial gallon = 4.5459 liters
1 nautical mile = 1.852 km

MOON BALTIMORE
Avalon Travel
a member of the Perseus Books Group
1700 Fourth Street
Berkeley, CA 94710, USA
www.moon.com

Editor: Kathryn Ettinger
Series Manager: Erin Raber
Copy Editor: Ellie Behrstock
Graphics Coordinator: Elizabeth Jang
Production Coordinator: Elizabeth Jang
Cover Designer: Elizabeth Jang
Map Editors: Albert Angulo, Kevin Anglin
Cartographers: Kat Bennett,
    Chris Markiewicz, Lohnes & Wright

ISBN-10: 1-56691-984-3
ISBN-13: 978-1-56691-984-5
ISSN: 1947-8801

Printing History
1st Edition – June 2009
5 4 3 2 1

Front cover photo: American Visionary Art Museum © Geoff Brown

Title page photo: Baltimore row houses © Geoff Brown

Interior color photos: page 2 (left) Howard P. Rawlings Conservatory; (middle) ornate architecture; (right) American Visionary Art Museum, all © Geoff Brown; page 18 (thumbnail) Maryland Historical Society © Geoff Brown; (bottom) playful dolphins at the National Aquarium Courtesy The National Aquarium in Baltimore; page 19 (top left) Poe original gravesite © Geoff Brown; (top right) view from Federal Hill © Geoff Brown; (bottom left) Preakness Courtesy Baltimore Area Convention and Visitors Association; (bottom right) Mount Vernon Place United Methodist Church © Geoff Brown; page 20 (bottom left) © Geoff Brown; (bottom right) Courtesy Baltimore Area Convention and Visitors Association; pages 21–24 all © Geoff Brown

Printed in the United States by RR Donnelley

KEEPING CURRENT

If you have a favorite gem you'd like to see included in the next edition, or see anything that needs updating, clarification, or correction, please drop us a line. Send your comments via email to feedback@moon.com, or use the address above.